Violence on Television
Distribution, Form,
Context, and Themes

www.erlbaum.com

Violence on Television
Distribution, Form,
Context, and Themes

Barrie Gunter
Jackie Harrison
Maggie Wykes
University of Sheffield

LAWRENCE ERLBAUM ASSOCIATES, PUBLISHERS
2003   Mahwah, New Jersey   London

Lawrence Erlbaum Associates, Inc., Publishers
10 Industrial Avenue
Mahwah, NJ 07430

Cover design by Kathryn Houghtaling Lacey

Library of Congress Cataloging-in-Publication Data

Gunter, Barrie
    Violence on television : distribution, form, context, and
    themes / Barrie Gunter, Jackie Harrison, Maggie Wykes.
        p. cm.
    Includes bibliographical references and index.
    ISBN 0-8058-3719-1 (cloth : alk. paper)
    ISBN 0-8058-4464-1 (pbk. : alk. paper)
    1. Violence on telvision. I. Harrison, Jackie, 1961-
    II. Wykes, Maggie, 1951-   III. Title
    PN1992.8.V55 G87   2002
    303.6—dc21   2002069255
                                                    CIP

Books published by Lawrence Erlbaum Associates are printed on acid-free paper, and their bindings are chosen for strength and durability.

Printed in the United States of America
10 9 8 7 6 5 4 3 2 1

Contents

Preface

Concern about violence on television has its roots in a familiar societal response to the appearance of any new form of public entertainment that appeals to the masses. But, once firmly established, an initial welcome is replaced by suspicion of its power to influence the public. Such anxiety usually emanates from the ruling establishment, which suspects a ubiquitous mass medium of possessing the capacity to exert significant social and political influence. Rather than attending to the positive social functions that a communications medium might serve, focus instead primarily rests on its capacity for promulgating social ills. This attitude has certainly been true with regard to the usual establishment stance toward television. Governments worry about the role such a mass medium plays in promoting antisocial conduct, religious bodies worry about its role in undermining the moral fiber of society, and advertisers, who provide much of the financial support for the medium, worry that the public images of their brands will suffer if they are advertised within violent programs.

The critics of television accuse the medium of presenting too much violence and of cynically using violence instead of quality scripts to attract audiences to its entertainment programing. It can also be observed that television appears to have developed a predilection for reality-based programs with violent themes. Fictional violence is being supplanted by real-life violence. Thus, television no longer provides pure escapism from everyday life, but all too frequently reflects it back at the public, and in doing so magnifies the presence of the negative elements in society.

The ultimate concern about television violence, however, is founded on the view that it contributes toward social violence. This process operates through a number of psychological mechanisms. The alleged preoccupation of television with violence, both in its entertainment and factual programing, may exaggerate the extent to which violence really occurs in society, leading regular television viewers to become more fearful about their own safety. Repeated exposure to this diet of violence may also cause viewers to become habituated to it. This means that any initial emotional reactions to violence become reduced and cease to have an impact. This may, in turn, lead to a less caring or more callous disposition toward violence in reality, because violence becomes regarded as an acceptable mode of conduct. At a more individual level, research evidence has accumulated, largely through laboratory experimentation, indicating an enhanced likelihood of violent behavior among those who watch specific violent portrayals. Thus, in addition to longer term dispositional changes in viewers as a function of continued exposure to television violence over time, there may be short-term aggressive response triggered by exposure to violent incidents on screen.

The important question for those who regulate the medium and who are the appointed guardians of the public interest is whether these concerns about television are warranted. Furthermore, does the observation that television is permeated by violence ring true when the medium's output is objectively and systematically examined? This book is concerned with shedding some light on these questions. The research on which it reports did not investigate the alleged effects of television violence. It did, however, systematically examine the extent to which violence occurred on television within a specified time frame. In doing so, it took into consideration the evidence from the media effects literature where that evidence had indicated that specific attributes of violence could enhance or reduce the degree to which harmful audience responses might occur upon viewing that violence. The research itself took place within a wholly British context, but many of the principles that it demonstrated about the distribution of violence on television probably apply to television systems elsewhere. To lend weight to this argument, a comparison was made between these British findings and data provided by a similar American study conducted at the same time. The comparisons indicated considerable degrees of similarity in the nature of television violence in the two countries on measures that were common to both studies.

Public opinion about potentially problematic television content carries considerable weight in Britain in addition to any supposed harms that may be contingent on watching screen violence. Indeed, in Britain, broadcasters are required by law to ensure that whatever they transmit does not cause offence to the audience. The evidence for psychological harms of televised violence, although not totally dismissed, is not accepted with the same conviction as it is in the United States. The evidence for harmful effects is regarded as inconclusive in Britain, although codes of practice for program makers embrace a number of harmful effects notions in the cautionary notes they sound for broadcasters. In the United States, the case for harmful effects has been largely accepted. The debate has moved on to consider what can or should be done about violence on television.

The debate about television violence in the United States is complicated by the fact that freedom of speech is protected by statute and therefore censorship is technically unconstitutional. At the same time, if it can be proven that a television broadcast contains material that people find deeply offensive, is unsuitable for children, or some individuals might react to in an antisocial manner, then there is a clear case for action of some sort to be taken. Whereas shying away from the idea of selective censorship, the alternative approach, which is more consistent with the First Amendment, is to devise a system in which media consumers are protected from exposure to content that might cause them offence or might be deemed unsuitable for young viewers. This early warning system would allow viewers to know in advance if programs contain problematic material so that they could filter it out from their own viewing diet or that of their children. The system would entail providing programs with ratings and advisories about their contents, specifically indicating whether they contained material of a violent, sexual, or profane nature. The system could be activated in an individual's (i.e., parent's) absence through a device inside the television set (V-chip) that could be set to scramble the signal for any unsuitable program the viewer wished to block out. Hence, in theory, parents could control their children's viewing even when not physically present in the home.

Although this system circumvents the conflict between censorship and freedom of speech legislation, it does not directly address the issue of harm that has been accepted within the United States in the case of televised violence. This is because the classification system for programs is not grounded in empirical evidence about adverse audience reactions to screen violence. To establish such a system would require a comprehensive taxonomy of factors known to exacerbate antisocial or undesirable audience responses to violent portrayals. The American television industry has so far opted not to devise such an early warning system for its viewers. The British television industry, likewise, lacks such a system. In addition to determining what have been called 'risk factors" in television violence (i.e., those attributes that appear to mediate adverse audience reactions), however, one would also need to monitor television to determine the extent to which potentially worrying violent portrayals occur and how they are distributed across the television schedules. In particular, it would be important to know how often portrayals occur that combine a number of these problematic attributes. Such portrayals might be especially likely to give rise to adverse audience reactions.

The research in this book was mindful of all these issues. For British television in the mid-1990s, it revealed that it would be misleading to assume that the schedules were permeated with violence. Whereas a large number of violent incidents were registered across the output that was monitored, significant proportions of this violent material were concentrated in a relatively small part of the total broadcast output analyzed. Furthermore, violent incidents characterized by high risk factors were relatively rare. This is not to say that no problematic portrayals of violence were found. There were indeed instances of violence that were horrific, gory, graphic, painful, and bloody. However, these portrayals tended to occur in broadcasts where they might have been expected and at times of the day that were chosen because of the relative scarcity of children in the audience. This research indicates that television violence needs to be examined from a number of different measurement perspectives to achieve a balanced impression of its prevalence, amount, and distribution.

ACKNOWLEDGMENTS

The research reported in this book derived from two projects that took place between 1994 and 1996. The research was carried out by a team based at the Department of Journalism Studies, University of Sheffield. Thanks are due to John Arundel, Rhiannon Osborn, Vincent Campbell, and Malcolm Crawford, who helped at various stages on the second project. The projects could not have been carried out without the financial support of the British Broadcasting Corporation (BBC) and Independent Television Commission (ITC), who funded the first project, and the Broadcasting Standards Council (now Commission), British Sky Broadcasting (BSkyB), Channel Four, and Independent Television (ITV), who joined the BBC and ITC in funding the second project.

—*BG, JH, and MW*
May 2001

Chapter 1

Violence on Television: The Parameters of Concern

Concern about television violence has centered on its capacity to cause both harm and offence. These consequences of violent portrayals are not the same, yet they are often conflated in debates about the responsibilities of broadcasters toward their audiences and the need for tighter regulation of programs. The alleged harms of television violence have numbered among the most publicly debated and scientifically investigated social issues (Cumberbatch, 1989; Gunter, 1994; Paik & Comstock, 1994; Potter, 1999). Offence is a matter of personal taste. The notion of harm is distinct from taste. A violent portrayal may be regarded as distasteful, but may not result in any harmful side effects. Elsewhere, audiences may enjoy a screen portrayal of violence. But, the same portrayal can also be scientifically demonstrated to give rise to potentially or actually harmful consequences if one viewer decides to copy it or if certain sections of the audience become either more accepting of such behavior or more afraid of becoming victims of such violence themselves.

The fact that some viewers may dislike televised violence may be insufficient testimony to back calls for its abolition or for stronger regulation and control of its appearance. For one thing, those critics of television violence may comprise an unrepresentative minority of the viewing population as a whole. For another, the content they wish to bring under tighter control may have no immediate or lasting adverse effects on audiences. In contrast, certain forms of televised violence may pass without comment and comprise important ingredients defining the entertainment value of a program. Yet, a case could be made for such content to be restricted or banned should convincing scientific evidence emerge that exposure to it can cause serious harms for viewers. Maintaining this balance between the need to allow broadcasters to satisfy audience tastes and needs, and avoidance of offence or harm is an ongoing problem for media regulators.

Other issues also have an important bearing on whether televised violence represents a problem in need of serious action by social policymakers and the regulatory agencies charged with implementing rules and codes of practice. Discussion about violence has been at the heart of a wider debate about the principle of media censorship and regulation. Whereas many broadcasters have developed their own codes on the presentation of violence in programs to which producers of news, drama, and other forms of entertainment are expected to adhere, in some countries more fundamental questions have been asked about whether censorship is appropriate at all.

In the United States, for example, there is an uneasy tension between the enactment of legislation that curtails the content of broadcasts and the fundamental value of free speech, especially as it applies to the press (and other media) as outlined in the First Amendment to the Constitution. Here, it is regarded as fundamental to the principle of a democratic society for the media to be able to publish anything without political hindrance. At the same time, there is public recognition of a need for some flexibility in the interpretation of free speech rights, where some published speech might act against the best interests of the public and society at large. There may be cases when the restriction of speech is the safer social option, especially when there is a suspicion that it reduces the chances of occurrence of adverse or potentially harmful consequences. This type of argument has been used to endorse U.S. government attempts to limit the negative social effects of televised violence (Roberts, 1998).

The need to tighten legislation and accompanying regulatory controls over televised violence has resulted in part from a growing public concern about this issue. This allegedly growing concern has been fueled, in part, by evidence that has emerged from the significant body of published scientific research concluding that violent television content can harm viewers. Children, teenagers, and adults are all regarded as potentially susceptible to a range of undesirable psychological side effects following exposure to such material. It has been contended that violent portrayals provide imitable problem-solving actions, often enacted by attractive role models, that may be copied by members of the audience. Televised violence may lend justification to the use of violence by viewers themselves. Routine exposure to such content may also cause viewers to become used to witnessing violence and to adopt a less caring attitude about victims of violence. Equally, regular viewing of violence on television could create an impression among viewers that it reflects on the status of society, which as a result may be viewed as a more violent, dangerous and frightening place to live (Donnerstein, Slaby, & Eron, 1994; Gerbner, Gross, Morgan, & Signorielli, 1994; Paik & Comstock, 1994; Potter, 1999).

One solution to this conflict between a fundamental democratic principle and an increasingly urgent need to curtail the alleged antisocial effects of media violence has been to move away from the notion of regulatory restrictions on transmitted content and toward the idea of empowering media consumers. In practice, this solution requires the provision of more and better quality information about programs in advance of transmission so that viewers can decide whether or not they want to watch. This information should have special value for parents who wish to decide on the suitability of particular programs for their children.

In the United States, new legislation was introduced in 1996 encouraging the television industry to create a voluntary code for rating programs or to have one imposed by the broadcast industry regulator, the Federal Communications Commission (Spitzer, 1996). This proposed ratings system was also to be linked with the so-called V-chip (viewer chip) technology installed in TV sets. Under the 1996 US Telecommunications Act, all new TV sets from 2000 on must include this technology. V-chips enable viewers to block out reception of programs rated as unsuitable for children.

Much debate surrounding the V-chip, the rating system for program content, and other possible solutions reflected the conflicting concerns about protecting the public from adverse effects of media violence while preserving the integrity of the First Amendment. The press in the United States provided widespread coverage of this subject and frequently represented tighter broadcasting legislation as a threat to free speech (Hoffner, 1998). This concern was not hard to understand. The acceptance of tighter regulation of broadcast content might represent the thin end of a wedge that might eventually lead to closer examination of practices followed by the press themselves.

In the pursuant political debate about this issue, political opinion was sensitive to the allegedly prevailing public opinion on the matter. This sensitivity is understandable given the potential political ramifications of unpopular public policy decisions. Indeed, even the courts exhibited sensitivity to contemporary trends in public opinion when asked to rule on the debate, acting therefore as a barometer of social mores (Marshall, 1988).

This book examines the nature of violence on television in the United Kingdom. The research on which this investigation is based consisted of a large content analysis of terrestrial and satellite broadcast television output in the mid-1990s. As such, it comprises a descriptive study of the representation of violence on television. Although such data cannot demonstrate anything about the impact of televised violence or about public opinion toward it, there are important reasons why links should be made between purely descriptive analyses of programs and the potential of their content to give rise to certain types of audience reaction. First, a descriptive analysis of the nature of television violence establishes how serious a problem it represents. Whereas a critical press may accuse broadcasters of loose controls over content and cite findings from public opinion surveys in support of such accusations, the only way to arrive at a comprehensive definition of the nature of what programs present to viewers is to conduct a direct analysis of programs themselves. Second, research into media violence effects and audience reactions to programs has identified specific features of violent portrayals and of the programs in which they might appear that mediate audience responses. This means that not all forms of violence give rise to the same audience reactions. Further, the same violence shown in different program settings and contexts may give rise to varying effects or reactions among viewers. Hence, the measurements taken by a content analysis can be designed to take account of these factors and to indicate the extent to which certain types of violence—which exhibit attributes rendering them likely to give rise to particular types of audience response—occur.

The need to include this kind of measurement sensitivity in content analysis studies of televised violence was increasingly emphasized by scholars working in this field during the last decade of the 20th century. Following earlier studies of audience perceptions of television violence, which indicated a need to go beyond a single definition of violence in the analysis of its on-screen representation (e.g., Gunter, 1985; Hodge & Tripp, 1986; Van der Voort, 1986), a number of studies in the 1990s embraced different levels of content measurement (Mustonen & Pulkkinen, 1993; *National Television Violence Study*, 1997, 1998; Potter et al., 1995, 1997). Some researchers have also referred to the need to employ a system that does not simply quantify violence in its totality, but also classifies the nature of its occurrence in terms of "risk factors" (*National Television Violence Study*, 1997). The latter represent attributes of violent portrayals identified in the media effects literature as playing important mediating roles in relation to the intensity or nature of viewers' responses to violence.

IMPORTANCE OF POTENTIAL HARM

The notion of risk factors in relation to the classification of television violence is important because it represents a conceptual link between the purely descriptive methodology of content analysis and the findings on harmful media violence effects. Although content analysis does not measure media effects, it can meaningfully embrace knowledge of such effects, especially where there is evidence that specific types of psychological impact are enhanced or reduced by the presence of mediating variables in association with violent portrayals.

The key risk factor attributes identified by the *National Television Violence Study* (1997) were nature of perpetrator of violence, nature of target of violence, reason for violence, presence of weapons, extent and graphicness of violence, realism of violence, rewards and punishments associated with violence, consequences of violence for victims, and the presence of humor. These attributes have been identified in media effects research as having a mediator role in relation to learning of aggression from media, desensitization to violence consequent on exposure to media violence, and enhanced fear of personal victimization following regular exposure to media violence (*National Television Violence Study*, 1997, 1998).

In addition to the risk factors, it is also important to be aware of developmental differences in the way viewers react to television content. Children may respond to televised violence differently from adults. Hence, some attributes are especially significant in relation to the way children might react. The rewards and punishments associated with violent portrayals are especially important in this context. Children may learn aggressive behavior patterns from watching television. The likelihood with which such learned behaviors may be reenacted by children can depend on whether on-screen perpetrators of these behaviors are rewarded or punished for their actions. Rewarded on-screen violence is more likely to be copied, whereas punished on-screen violence inhibits the learning of aggression among young viewers (Bandura, 1986; Paik & Comstock, 1994). However, for young children to grasp the consequences of on-screen portrayals of violence, it was usually necessary for associated rewards or punishments to occur immediately after these behaviors. Children younger than age 10 have been found to be less able to grasp the links between motives and events and events and their consequences when these elements are widely separated in the narrative of the program (Collins, 1983).

Relating their catalog of on-screen violent portrayals to the known mediators of screen violence effects, the *National Television Violence Study* (1998) reported for mainstream U.S. network and cable television that the perpetrators of violence were mostly human, adult, White, and male, and they were more often bad guys than good guys. The targets of violence exhibited a similar character profile to perpetrators. Most violence was committed for reasons of personal gain, anger, or self-protection. Around one in three violent interactions were portrayed as justified. Guns were used in about one in four violent interactions. In addition, most televised violence was fictional but nevertheless appeared to be fairly realistic and feasible in real life. Most violence was not punished immediately; punishments were usually meted out at the end of the program. Good guys tended not to be punished for their use of violence, however. More than one half of all violence produced no observable harmful or painful consequences to victims, and very little violence was shown in graphic detail. Four in ten violent scenes were presented in a humorous context. Such an analysis, therefore, went beyond earlier numerical quantifications of violent acts on screen, to elaborate the extent to which potentially harmful portrayals of violence occurred. To go beyond this level of analysis, it will be important to discover more about the prevalence and position (in terms of program and time and day) of violent depictions that combine a number of high risk attributes. These will be the portrayals to which closest regulatory or consumer advisory attention should be given.

IMPORTANCE OF PERCEPTION AND OPINION

The importance of public opinion about television violence stems, in part, from its political and legal significance. Public support for censorship, for example, provides important ammunition for those political lobby groups who would wish to see more restrictive legislation introduced to curb the alleged harms of media violence. Such ammunition may be especially significant in countries like the United States, where calls for increased censorship conflict with the fundamental democratic value of protected free speech. A number of studies have indicated, however, that public support does exist for censorship of certain forms of media under appropriate circumstances. Such restrictions have received public support where they relate to violent media (Fisher, Cook, & Shirkey, 1994; Rojas, Shah, & Faber, 1996), pornography, and especially sexual violence (Fisher et al., 1994; Gunther, 1995; Thompson, Chaffee, & Oshagen, 1990).

In the United Kingdom, public opinion about violence on television is significant because broadcasting legislation requires television producers to take necessary steps to ensure that their programs do not cause offence to viewers. Supplementary codes of practice flesh out this legal requirement, and codes on the depiction of violence are published to provide guidelines to producers both in the public and commercial sectors of television broadcasting.

The significance of public opinion data to the classification of television program content represents a tricky question in its own right. In order to determine whether such data have any value at all in this context, it is essential to examine carefully the nature of the questioning used in surveys and whether the opinions measured provide any real clues concerning how people think or feel about particular types of violence.

There is a prevailing understanding, regularly fed by newspaper-sponsored opinion polls, that the public generally believes there is too much violence on television. Such polls also reputedly reveal a significant degree of concern among the public about the possible harms caused by televised violence, especially where children are concerned. Unfortunately, few polls yield data about use of policy or editorial decisions. Frequently, these polls oversimplify public attitudes and lack the focus to pinpoint whether there are specific types of content about which citizens are mostly concerned (Gunter & Stipp, 1992). There are three other factors that should be underlined about public attitudes concerning television violence. First, viewers may at the same time voice concern about violence on television in general while exhibiting little concern about violence in specified programs that contain violence, provided the presentation of the violence is judged to be appropriate to the story line and not gratuitous (Gunter & Wober, 1988). Second, viewers may find verbal descriptions of specific types of television violence potentially offensive, but are still willing to concede the right of others to watch such material should they wish to do so (Gunter & Stipp, 1992). Third, survey respondents may be more willing to perceive potential harm in media violence for others than for themselves, a pattern of response known as the "third-person effect" (Hoffner et al., 1999; Innes & Zeitz, 1988; Rojas et al., 1996).

The third-person effect has emerged as a particularly sensitive predictor of support for strict censorship of media. Whereas most people believe themselves to be relatively immune to adverse or harmful effects of media, they do not believe the same thing about others. The greater the perceived likelihood of adverse media effects on society or on people other than themselves, the greater the support for stricter censorship of sex and violence in the media (Fisher et al., 1994; Gunther, 1995; Hoffner et al., 1999). Greater exposure to sexual or violent media content, however, was associated with less willingness to censor such content (Fisher et al., 1994; Gunther, 1995). Those who apparently view television violence regularly wish to retain unrestricted access to their preferred entertainment. Some researchers have interpreted this finding as evidence for a desensitization effect, with heavier viewers of violence being less personally worried about it and less inclined to see it as harmful (Donnerstein et al., 1994; Hoffner et al., 1999).

These results do not indicate if particular kinds of violence are regarded as being especially problematic as potential sources of offence or harm to viewers. To find out more about this point, researchers need to use methodologies that measure viewers' perceptions of violence more directly. Such research has identified a variety of factors that influence individuals' judgments about the seriousness of violent actions and interactions.

In a study not directly connected with media, Forgas, L. B. Brown, and Menyhart (1980) examined the way people classified real-life aggressive scenarios. This investigation was concerned with the attributes individuals take into account when determining whether or not a particular act is defined as aggressive. Four principal characteristics emerged in this respect: (a) the perceived likelihood that the act would happen in everyday life, (b) the degree to which the sympathy lies with the aggressor or victim, (c) the degree to which the aggressor was provoked or performed a premeditated first strike, and (d) the degree to which the act was officially sanctioned or likely to evoke punishment.

In ascertaining the way viewers respond to specific content features, one approach has been to obtain opinions about extracts of media content in which those features have been isolated. In this context, for instance, media researchers have explored viewers' perceptions of televised violence or the emotional reactions of children to frightening media content.

The immediate reactions of viewers to program excerpts have been measured in the context of identifying the attributes taken into account by individuals when judging the seriousness of televised violence. Greenberg and Gordon (1972c) presented young boys with a series of violent scenes, taken from movies and programs, which differed in terms of various attributes such as the use of weapons and degree of harm caused to victims. After each scene, respondents provided a series of evaluative ratings. Scenes in which weapons were featured or in which actors harmed themselves or another person were rated as more violent and less acceptable than scenes in which weapons were not featured or where harm, although intended, did not occur. Scenes depicting damage to another person were rated in more serious terms than scenes depicting property damage.

In another series of experiments in Britain, a similar approach was used to assess viewers' evaluative ratings of violence-containing clips from British and American crime dramas, westerns, science series, and cartoons. After each clip, which lasted for up to 2 minutes, viewers gave their ratings along a series of 7-point adjective scales. Scenes were shown singly or in pairs for comparative judgments. The program clips were selected to isolate specific features such as genre, dramatic context, physical setting, use of weapons, degree of harm to victims, and gender or perpetrators and victims. Results showed that the perceived seriousness of violence was strongly associated with the realism of the setting, the degree of observable harm caused to victims, the use of certain types of weapon (sharp instruments), and the gender of the attacker and victim (Gunter, 1985).

Research with children, using laboratory-based experimental methodologies, has explored their emotional reactions to different types of television content. Many studies used a combination of continuous physiological measures and immediate postviewing psychological reactions. Physiological measures have included facial expressions, heart rate, and electrical conductivity of the skin (galvanic skin response, GSR). The latter measures are all known to provide reliable indicators of emotional responses. Psychological measures generally comprised verbal responses, describing their feelings or how much they liked the material shown to them.

Some studies have investigated the mediating effect of the realism of television portrayals on children's emotional responding and enjoyment. Osborn and Endsley (1971) obtained continuous measures of GSR from 4- and 5-year-old children while they watched either a cartoon or noncartoon program excerpt that was either violent or nonviolent. A postviewing interview was then conducted with the children to find out which clip(s) they found to be "scariest." The program featuring human characters with violence was selected as the scariest of the four clips and also produced the highest GSRs.

A Swedish study used the analysis of children's facial reactions while viewing to measure how emotionally aroused they were by different scenes of violence (Lagerspetz, Wahlroos, & Wendelin, 1978). Preteenage children were shown 5-minute extracts from television programs that depicted physical violence, verbal violence, cartoon violence, and nonviolent behavior. The children's facial expressions were videotaped while they were watching and then subsequently judged by coders trained to identify the emotional meaning of such expressions. The children viewed in pairs and were unaware of being observed for their reactions. Facial expressions were classified according to nine evaluative scales: joyful–serious, afraid–not afraid, worried–not worried, angry–indifferent, understands–incomprehension, concentrated–distracted, tense–calm, active–immobile, and withdrawal–no withdrawal. The children were interviewed afterward to nominate their most liked film clip. The strongest emotional reactions occurred to the clips depicting the most realistic violence. Such scenes invoked the greatest expressions of fear and worry, tenseness and anger. Cartoon violence elicited joy and understanding and along with more formulaic physical violence, generated the greatest concentration.

Heart rate was used to measure degree of emotional response to televised violence in a study with preteenage children, age 8 to 11 (Surbeck & Endsley, 1979). In this investigation, the children were each shown two 3-minute video clips depicting exactly the same series of violent acts. However, one clip involved human actors and the other involved puppets. The children were tested in an experimental room designed to resemble a living room in someone's home. They were wired up to heart-beat apparatus for pretesting several days before the actual experimental session and then again while being shown the two television clips. After viewing had finished, they were taken to a separate room for further testing. Here they were shown some photographs from each clip and asked to say "how scary it was" and which clip they liked best. Neither version was overwhelmingly preferred, but the more realistic version was seen as more scary. Heart rates were observed to drop during the violent incidents in each clip, reflecting greater attentiveness at those points.

Other laboratory investigations have shown that children display higher emotional arousal when viewing television scenes in which a character displays expressions of fear than for scenes that focus on the frightening stimulus that causes those fear expressions, as evidenced through immediate postviewing verbal response of young viewers and continuous physiological measures such as galvanic skin response and skin temperature change (Wilson & Cantor, 1985).

Watching a scary film or program with someone else present can sometimes moderate children's emotional responses. In one experiment, preschool children watched one of two versions of a suspenseful movie clip, either alone or with an older brother or sister. One version portrayed the scene as a dream sequence with a prolog and epilog to provide cues to the fact that the depicted events were part of a dream (Wilson & Weiss, 1993). This scene, taken from a television movie called *Invaders from Mars*, shows a boy following a woman into a cave. He proceeds down a long dark tunnel until he reaches a cavern in which a spaceship occupied by a number of giant creatures is found. The boy hides behind a wall and watches the women and the creatures. At this point, a commercial break occurs. The scene continues after the break. The woman notices the boy and threatens to get him. He runs out of the tunnel and escapes into the forest outside.

After watching the scene, the children were asked how scared they felt while watching it and how much they liked it. The children's facial expressions were also continuously monitored and videotaped while they were viewing and were later categorized by coders. The preschoolers who viewed with an older sibling were no better than those who watched alone in identifying the dream sequence version, but were generally less emotionally aroused by this suspenseful scene when watching with someone else. As a result, they also liked the film better. Many of the very young children in this experiment were unable to understand and identify the cues that indicated when the sequence was portrayed as a dream.

Research has been conducted among children whose reactions to full-length programs were gauged under controlled viewing conditions. In one case, pre-children's involvement in a program, as indicated by their degree of visual attention to the screen, was related to the degree of action, but not significantly to the amount of violence it contained (Potts, Huston & Wright, 1986).

Van der Voort (1986) measured children's perceptions of televised violence at three schools in Holland. In all, 314 children, ages 9 to 11, were shown full-length episodes from eight television series. These series included realistic crime drama (*Starksy and Hutch, Charlie's Angels*), adventure series (*Dick Turpin, The Incredible Hulk*), and fantasy cartoons (*Scooby Doo, Tom and Jerry, Popeye, Pink Panther*).

Immediately after showing each program, a postexposure questionnaire was filled in by children measuring 10 perception variables: readiness to see violence, approval of violent actions seen in the program, enjoyment of the violence seen, evaluation of the program, emotional responsiveness, absorption in the program, detachment while watching, identification with the program's chief characters, perceived reality of the program, and comprehension and retention of program content. Van der Voort investigated whether programs perceived to be realistic were also more absorbing for children who would thereby respond to them with more emotion and less detachment than they showed toward programs perceived to be more fantastic.

Results showed that law enforcement programs were rated as the most realistic of those programs presented to the children in this study. Thus, *Starsky and Hutch* and *Charlie's Angels* were perceived to be realistic, whereas *The Incredible Hulk, Dick Turpin*, and cartoons were seen as fantastic. Realistic programs were watched with more involvement, more emotion, and less detachment. The two crime drama series were also regarded as containing the most violence.

It is clear from this body of research that viewers' reactions to screen violence are often mediated to a significant degree by the nature and form of the portrayed violence and by the setting or context in which it occurs. Both children and adults are sensitive to these features and display different perceptual and emotional reactions to what they are viewing as a function of the attributes associated with a violent portrayal. The perceived realism of violence has repeatedly emerged as a crucial variable that influences the perceived seriousness of a range of violent portrayals. The acceptability of violent depictions for audiences can vary with the program in which they occur. In addition, the degree of harm caused to victims of violence on screen is a key factor, especially when emotional reactions are measured. When the full horror of violence or graphic images of the pain and suffering of victims are shown, viewers' responses to televised violence are much more severe.

Yet, there are many portrayals of violence on television that do not cause viewers to react. Scenes that occur in fantasy contexts, scenes that involve animated characters, and scenes in which events occur in a humorous context may be subjectively rated as essentially nonviolent even though they contain behavior that would objectively be defined as violent in nature. On this evidence, it is important for content analysis studies to embrace, to some degree at the point of analysis or subsequent data interpretation, the known or expected reactions of viewers to specific types of violent portrayal. These reactions could represent weighting factors that enable a simple violent counting exercise to have more meaning in terms of the prevalence of violent incidents that might be problematic for audiences.

IMPORTANCE OF ATTRACTION TO VIOLENCE

Turning the violence debate around, questions have been asked about the attractiveness of violence to audiences and the role that it might play in drawing viewers to programs. Attraction to violence in entertainment has a history that predates the modern mass media and can be traced back to the popularity of violent sporting spectacles in Greek and Roman times (Guttmann, 1998). In the present context, interest in the attractiveness of observers to screen violence centers on whether it offers any further clues about the classification of violence, in this case, in terms of what individuals enjoy watching. Within the context of contemporary broadcast entertainment, there is a conventional wisdom that violence sells—that is, it enhances audience enjoyment of programs (C. H. Hansen & R. D. Hansen, 1990).

Evidence for the attractiveness of violence on television has derived from a number of sources. Cantor (1998) identified three senses in which the notion of the attractiveness of televised violence can be demonstrated. The first sense is the manifestation by viewers of *enjoyment* while viewing programs with violence. Often this is measured by observing viewers' facial reactions or degree of visual attentiveness in front of the screen. A second indicator is *selective exposure*, which is demonstrated when a viewer's knowledge that a program contains violence increases the likelihood of choosing to view it compared with other programs believed to contain no violence. A third indicator is *genre popularity*, as evidenced by the power of a genre characterized by its violence to attract large numbers of viewers as compared with other types of program. Television industry measures of audience size are indicative of the last type of attraction.

So, is violence important or even essential to entertainment value in television programs? U.S. studies have directly examined whether the presence or absence of violence makes any difference to the audience size of programs or how much viewers enjoy programs. The level of violence in programs, as measured through content analysis, was found to be unrelated to their audience sizes (Diener & DeFour, 1978). In a more direct comparison, experiments were conducted in which groups of viewers evaluated violent and nonviolent versions of the same programs. Higher violence content did not result in viewers liking the programs more (Diener & DeFour, 1978; Diener & Woody, 1981). Unfortunately, violence was treated in generalized terms throughout this research. No attempt was made in any study to find out if program enjoyment was differentially linked to the presence or absence of specific types of violence.

In a subsequent experimental study with children, Potts, Huston, and Wright (1986) compared reactions to programs that systematically varied in the amount of violence and action they contained. Program enjoyment, as measured by visual attention to the screen, was not significantly related to whether or not violence was present.

Research conducted with a national television audience panel in Britain revealed that viewers' perceptions of violence were linked to their enjoyment of programs they had watched. In fact, perceiving a program to contain violence was associated with lower appreciation of it, especially among women viewers. This finding was found to occur across a number of drama series on British television. In the case of one crime drama series, however, viewers' perception that it contained justified violence used by good guys in measured response to provocation enhanced their appreciation of the program. Men's and women's viewing enjoyment, however, indicated that a program should have many twists and turns of plot (Wober, 1997).

Advance knowledge that a program might contain violence may attract viewers who enjoy viewing violence. Herman and Leyens (1977) examined adult viewing patterns for televised movies on Belgian television over a 4–year period. Participants were members of a viewing panel who, every 15 minutes, noted which program they were watching and how much they liked each program. Belgian television regularly broadcasts advisories about films in order to alert the public to programs containing violent or sexual material. Results showed that panel members liked films with and without advisories equally well. However, films that carried advisories attracted larger audiences. Unfortunately, no controls were employed for other content or thematic factors that may have influenced movie preferences.

Hamilton (1998) examined the impact of viewer discretion warnings on viewing levels for prime-time movies broadcast between September 1987 and September 1993. Hamilton found that descriptions in *TV Guide* that involved murder or family crime themes were significant positive predictors of a movie's overall audience size. In contrast, *TV Guide* descriptions involving the theme of murder were a significant negative predictor of audience levels among children from age 2 to 11 and teens from age 12 to 17. However, such audience ratings data do not make it clear if children or their parents were responsible for limiting viewing by children.

Other research with television ratings data has indicated that genres vary in their popularity and certain types of programs regularly attract bigger audiences than others. In the United States, many programs most watched by children, which are intended for younger audiences, contain fast-paced action and violence, often in cartoon form. Of programs targeted at the general family audience, situation comedies tend to attract the largest numbers of child viewers (Stipp, 1995). Once again, it is difficult to ascertain from television ratings data alone whether the large child audiences reflect selectiveness on the part of children themselves or whether program choices are being made for them by parents.

INDIVIDUAL DIFFERENCES IN ATTRACTION TO TV VIOLENCE

Viewers have long been known to exhibit varying reactions to violence, whether presented within drama and entertainment or in the news (Gunter, 1985; Gunter & Wober, 1988). Some viewers are attracted by violence, others are repelled by it. Women are turned off by violence, and men enjoy watching programs with tense moments (Wober, 1997). Is violence an essential ingredient of good drama and entertainment? Can its use be justified on this basis? Are correlational relations between people's reported exposure to media violence and measures of their personal aggressiveness merely indicative of a preference for violent entertainment that is motivated by an assertive, dominant personality?

The appeal of violent entertainment is more pronounced among certain personality types (Atkin, Greenberg, Korzenny, & McDermott, 1979; Friedman & R. L. Johnson, 1972; Krcmar & Greene, 1999; Robinson & Bachman, 1972; Weaver, 1991). It can also have greater temporary appeal among individuals who might not otherwise exhibit a preference for it, for example, as a means of coping with environmental threat (Boyanowsky, 1977; Boyanowsky, Newtson, & Walster, 1974).

Elsewhere evidence has emerged that violence is enjoyed and sought after by some sections of the audience. Research with sibling pairs has indicated that although they may exhibit similar viewing patterns, despite differing in their individual aggressiveness, the more aggressive siblings generally enjoyed violent entertainment more (Lynn, Hampson, & Agahi, 1989). Research from Spain indicated that enjoyment of cartoon violence among teenagers is most pronounced among those with sensation seeking, impulsive, and more aggressive personalities. Such individuals were also more likely to have reported viewing violent movies (e.g., *Rambo, Robocop, Lethal Weapon, Universal Soldier*) and to perceive them as less violent (Aluja-Fabregat & Torrubia-Beltri, 1998). There may be various reasons for these individual differences in viewing preferences.

One explanation for the enjoyment of screen violence is that it is exciting and therefore arousing. Such arousal can be pleasurable in its own right (Zillmann, 1978). Extending this arousal notion, the excitement may be wrapped up with fear. Although a fear response itself is unpleasant, relief from that fear is pleasant. Thus, evoking fear under controlled circumstances can give rise to pleasure once the fear has been overcome. Hence, viewers may choose to watch frightening movies to test themselves and because the sense of achievement from facing up to a fear or the sense of relief once the cause of the fear has gone away represent an intrinsic part of the entertainment experience (Blumer, 1933; Himmelweit, Oppenheim, & Vince, 1958; Wilson, Hoffner, & Cantor, 1987; Zillmann, Weaver, Mundorf, & Aust, 1986).

The entertainment value of violent drama on television may also stem from its role in reinforcing viewers' values, beliefs, and attitudes. For example, reality-based crime programs have been found to hold especially strong appeal for young people who hold punitive attitudes and display authoritarian personality profiles. Such programs frequently presented criminals being caught and punished and as coming off worse in violent altercations with the police. Such themes were enjoyed by individuals who believed in severe punishment for offenders (Oliver & Armstrong, 1995). This belief reinforcement effect was also supported by findings that showed people with strong just world beliefs were among the most regular viewers of crime-drama programs. Such programs were dominated by themes whereby justice prevailed and the bad guy was caught and punished in the end. This story line confirmed the belief that the world is a just place (Gunter & Wober, 1983).

In summary, there is mixed evidence concerning whether or not violence in programs is a critical feature that enhances their overall popularity among audiences. Basic ratings data have revealed that programs with violence often are among the most watched programs on television. What these data do not reveal, however, is whether it is the violence per se that is the key driving factor behind program popularity or

whether there are other factors at play, within the programs themselves, in relation to when they are scheduled, or in the social context
that viewing takes place. Attempts tp experimentally manipulate the violence in programs have provided little evidence that greater violence
leads to higher ratings. Yet, there is evidence indicating a preference
for violent entertainment among certain sections of the audience, defined by their personality type or current mood state. Viewers may enjoy being aroused by screen violence as an experience in itself. In
addition, for some viewers, scenes of violence in which bad guys must
face the consequences for their misdeed may offer some reassurance
that the world is really a just and safe place. Unfortunately, research
into the appreciation of screen violence has provided few insights that
would fit nicely into a taxonomy of violence that has meaning or significance for viewers.

CONCLUSIONS

The debate about television violence has a long history spanning as
many years as the medium itself. The portrayal of violence in drama is
widely established as a natural element of storytelling, and the reporting of violence in the news is recognized as a fact of life. Yet, public concern about violence on television has been persistently raised by critics
and lobbyists who regard it as undesirable and a contributing cause of
social ills. In response to this public pressure and in recognition of the
power of the medium for which they are responsible, broadcasters have
embraced these concerns in codes of practice and guidelines for program
makers that draw attention to the need for care when depicting or reporting on violence. These codes are sensitive to types of effect on viewers that have been associated with violent portrayals and to public
opinion about whether specific types of portrayal are regarded as acceptable or unacceptable.

A common accusation is that television contains too much violence.
This is a matter of opinion rather than of fact. Nevertheless, it begs the
question of how much violence television does indeed transmit and
about the extent to which it permeates the television schedules. Systematic studies of television output have been mounted over the past 50
years in an attempt to provide hard evidence on this subject (e.g.,
Gerbner & Gross, 1976; McCann & Sheehan, 1985; *National Television
Violence Study*, 1997, 1998; Remmers, 1954; Schramm, Lyle, & Parker,
1961; Shaw & Newell, 1972; Smythe, 1954; Williams, Zabrack, & Joy,
1982). Such research has indicated that television is permeated by violence, significant proportions of programs contain violence, and some
violence-containing programs present substantial numbers of violent
incidents.

What this all means in terms of the way audiences might respond and
for broadcast policymakers and regulators is less clear. Much of the

early content analysis research focused on the production of objective counts of violent incidents. Such data were descriptive in nature and indicated how much violence occurred with selected program samples within a fairly narrow definition of violence. It was unclear whether such counts of violent acts were meaningful in that they represented a barometer of the levels of program attributes that were significant in relation to viewers' evaluations of programs or other psychological reactions to them. This problem has been increasingly recognized by researchers who have begun to adopt more sophisticated methods of violence definition and program coding that take into account what is known about audience response to different types of televised violence (*National Television Violence Study*, 1997, 1998; Potter, 1999; Potter & Smith, 1999).

The next chapter turns to methodological issues in more detail. In addition to providing details about the methodology used in the study discussed herein, wider issues related to the investigation of violent content on television are examined.

Chapter 2

Issues of Measurement and Analysis

A fundamental question about violence on television concerns how much of it is shown. To answer, the usual approach has been to employ a counting procedure through which specified on-screen incidents and events, and the characters involved in them, are enumerated. This methodology yields a *content analysis* of programs producing a primarily quantitative assessment of violence. Content analysis is a descriptive methodology and, as such, does not measure audience reactions or program effects. Nevertheless, some content analysis research is used as a basis for media effects research in areas of inquiry such as agenda-setting or cultivation analysis (Rogers & Dearing, 1988; Signorielli, 1990). Furthermore, content analysis research can itself be informed by audience research concerned with public reactions to programs or the psychological effects of viewing certain types of portrayal. Such research may offer insights into the classification of content, thus providing an enhanced form of content analysis sensitive to the way viewers respond to television (Gunter, 1985; Kunkel et al., 1995).

The quantitative nature of content analysis means that much emphasis has been placed on what it reveals about the amount of violence on television. Over the years, however, estimates of how much violence is shown on television have varied widely from one study to another. In some cases, these variations result from the studies being conducted in different countries where the overall amount and range of television programs and the compositions of television schedules differ in marked degrees. In other instances, inconsistent research findings have arisen because of methodological differences between studies. Thus, studies within the same country have produced different results because they have used different definitions of violence, different program samples, and different ways of quantifying violence.

When conducting content analysis research on television violence, therefore, there are several issues of measurement and analysis that need to be considered. Researchers have to make decisions about the definition of violence on which all coding will be based, the units of analysis that will be applied, the sampling of content to be analyzed, the analysis of the attributes of violence, and the assessment of reliability of the analysis.

DEFINING VIOLENCE

The definition of violence is a key factor in any research on media violence. This is especially true in relation to the analysis of the representation of violence on screen. There are many different definitions of violence. Thus, the amount of violence that might be present in a television program may depend on what the viewer regards as violent in the first place. More restrictive definitions of violence will produce lower counts of violent incidents, whereas broader definitions will produce higher counts for the same media output.

Psychological Perspectives on Aggression

Various definitions of violence have derived from scholarly investigations of the subject. Early psychological definitions of aggression defined it as a behavior designed to cause injury to another organism. The intention to cause injury was regarded as a key factor (Dollard, Doob, Miller, Mowrer, & Sears, 1939). Later developments in the theory of aggression encompassed behavior that not only caused injury to another person or living creature, but also resulted in the destruction of property (Bandura, 1973). Furthermore, whether an act that caused harm to another person could be construed as being "aggressive" depended on the nature, context, and purpose of the action. Thus, a dentist carrying out repairs on a patient's teeth might cause that individual pain and may, indeed, need to inflict "injury" as part of the treatment. Such socially sanctioned activity would not normally be defined as "aggression" or "violence". However, should the same dentist use a drill as an instrument of torture to inflict pain on a victim for purely selfish, sadistic purposes or to coerce the victim into a course of action against their will, such behavior would be construed as "violent."

The intention to cause injury has repeatedly been a central feature of psychological definitions of aggression. Some definitions have focused on purely physical harm, but some writers have also included psychological or symbolic harm as a defining aspect of aggression (Berkowitz, 1993). Indeed, some theoreticians have produced taxonomies of actions in broadening the overall concept of aggression. In some cases, attention has centered on the perpetrator of the violence. For example, Berkowitz (1994) proposed four dimensions for categorizing aggression: (a) instrumental versus emotional acts (acts done for purposes of coercion or the establishment of power are instrumental, whereas those intended primarily to inflict harm are emotional), (b) physical versus verbal acts, (c) indirect versus direct attacks on a target, and (d) controlled or premeditated versus impulsive acts. Other researchers have examined violence from the perspective of the target or victim. Muncer, Gorman, and A. Campbell (1986) asked groups of prison inmates and college students to group together violent acts into types. Three principal dimensions appeared to dominate the groupings: physical versus verbal forms of aggression, violence between strangers versus violence between acquaintances, and provoked versus unprovoked violence.

Galtung (1975) offered a broad definition of violence as a phenomenon that is "present when human beings are being influenced so that their actual somatic and mental realisations are below their potential realisations" (p. 111). Galtung distinguished five dimensions of violence. The most significant was structural (or indirect) as compared to personal (or direct) violence. Structural violence was defined in terms of states of injustice in the social system, where no concrete actor is discernible. Acts of personal violence were those in which the cause of the violence could be directly attributed to a concrete human being. Other distinctions were then made between physical and psychological violence; violence with or without an object (that suffers); the manifest or latent aspect of violence (i.e., is the violence directly observable?); and the degree of intention with which the violent act is committed (intended or unintended). According to Galtung, these dichotomised dimensions could be used in any combination leading to a typology with 32 different categories of violence.

Content Analysis Perspectives on Aggression

A variety of definitions of violence have been drawn up by media researchers in studying violence on television. Perhaps the most utilized definition of violence was developed by Gerbner and was used in research spanning more than 20 years (Gerbner, 1972; Gerbner & Gross, 1976; Gerbner et al., 1994). This single, normative definition envisaged violence as: "the overt expression of physical force (with or without a weapon) against self or other, compelling action against one's will on pain of being hurt or killed, or actually hurting or killing" (Gerbner, 1972, p. 31). This definition was also used by researchers who analyzed violence on television in Australia (McCann & Sheehan, 1985), Britain (Halloran & Croll, 1972), Japan (Iwao, de Sola Pool, & Hagiwara, 1981), and New Zealand (Haines, 1983). Accidental violence is included and the definition of violence is applied in the same way regardless of context. For Gerbner, this normative approach was appropriate because it was the *prevalence* of violence that was regarded as the main source of harmful effects.

Other research used Gerbner's definition as a basis, but then added further features. A Canadian study reported by Williams, Zabrack, and Joy (1982) enhanced it with the specifications that it "must be plausible and credible; no idle threats, verbal abuse, or comic gestures with no credible violent consequences. May be intentional or accidental; violent accidents, catastrophes, acts of nature are included" (p. 366).

Alternative definitions of violence for content analysis purposes broadened out the definition of violence and tried to specify in more detail the kinds of incidents to be counted. In another U.S.-based study of television violence, violence was defined as "that which is psychologically or physically injurious to another person or persons whether intended or not, and whether successful or not" (Greenberg, Edison, Korzenny, Fernandez-Collado, & Atkin, 1980, p. 102). These researchers started with Gerbner's definition, but expanded their focus because they wanted "to examine a fuller range of negative social behaviors available from television. A variety of noxious behaviors other than violence is available on television" (p. 102). In their definition, they delineated four major components: physical aggression, verbal aggression, theft, and deceit. They chose these negative behaviors because they were "considered as modelable by social learning theorists and child psychologists" (p. 102). This broader perspective influenced a number of later studies (J. D. Brown & K. Campbell, 1986; S. L. Kaplan & Baxter, 1982; Oliver, 1994; Potter & Vaughan, 1997; Potter et al., 1995; Potter & Ware, 1987).

Within the physical aggression category, Greenberg and his colleagues began with Gerbner's definition but expanded it beyond attacks (with and without weapons) and included physical control or restraint of others, physical invasion of privacy, and elaborated fighting (e.g., fistfights among multiple people in which individual acts are indistinguishable). They added verbal aggression (verbal hostility, verbal rejection, and verbal threats) along with deceit and theft because these behaviors were also considered disruptive of society, and they provided models of behavior for viewers.

Potter and his colleagues (1995) defined violence as "any action that serves to diminish in some physical, social, or emotional manner" (p. 497). This definition included "a wide range of portrayals as suggested by Berkowitz's conception. We include verbal forms of aggression, not just physical forms. We include psychological and emotional harm to the victim, not just physical harm. We include indirect as well as direct attacks.. And we include impulsive or non-premeditated acts of aggression" (p. 497). The receiver of the aggression could be another person, the perpetrators, or a nonhuman entity such as an animal, an inanimate object, or society in general.

Potter and Vaughan (1997) replicated the study of Greenberg and his colleagues (1980) to find out if rates of different types of violence had changed from the mid-1970s to mid-1990s. They found that overall rates of physical violence stayed the same (12.7 vs. 12.3 acts per of violence per hour), but rates of verbal violence had climbed (from 22.3 to 27.0 acts per hour). This change was even more clear within two genres. With situation comedies, physical violence stayed the same (7.2 acts per hour), but verbal violence went up from 33.5 to 41.9 acts per hour. With action-adventure programs, physical violence was about the same (18.2 vs. 21.5 acts per hour), but verbal violence went up (from 22.0 to 28,6 acts per hour).

Oliver (1994) developed a coding scheme for four types of aggressive behaviors: verbal aggression, threat of physical aggression, unarmed physical aggression, and armed physical aggression. Basing her definitions on the work of Greenberg, she defined verbal aggression or noxious symbolic messages containing criticism, insults, cursing, or a negative affective reaction. Threats of physical aggression were overt verbal and nonverbal warnings of intentions to cause physical harm to a person. Unarmed physical aggression was the attacking of one human being by another that involves contact with any body part but does not involve weapons or other objects. When weapons or objects were used in an assault, it was regarded as armed physical aggression. Only aggressive behaviors visible on screen were coded.

In a Finnish study, television violence was defined as "actions causing or designed to cause harm to oneself, or to another person, either physically or psychologically, including implicit threats, non-verbal behavior, and outbursts of anger directed towards animals and inanimate objects" (Mustonen & Pulkkinnen, 1997, p. 173). This definition of violence had been influenced more by Williams et al. (1982), than by Gerbner's definition. These researchers included portrayals of the mere victims of violence, if the connection between violent behavior and a victim's injuries was clearly established. Antisocial activities with no aggressive connotations, such as deceit and theft, or mere negative affective or hostile reactions unaccompanied by physical injury or damage, were excluded from the analysis as well as verbal reports of violence. Psychological harm was understood from actions in which one person assaulted another through verbal insults, threatening or scornful gestures, or forcing someone to do something against their will.

THE IMPORTANCE OF CONTEXT

The analytical scheme represented by many content analysis studies concerned primarily with establishing the prevalence of violence on screen has been challenged because such summative quantitative measures are poor indicators of audience reactions (Gunter, 1981, 1985; Van der Voort, 1986). Viewers do not perceive violence in a unitary fashion, but differentiate between portrayals on the basis of their form, their perpetrators, and their context (Gunter, 1985). It has already been acknowledged that content analysis does not represent audience research. Nevertheless, content coding frames need to be sensitive to how audiences may respond to screen violence in the definitions of violence they use as their foundation.

The National Television Violence Study (NTVS) attempted to devise a framework for analysis to address this issue more directly. This study was funded over a 3-year period (1994–1997) by the National Cable Television Association in the United States. It developed an elaborate methodology to assess not just the quantity of violence depicted on American television, but also the nature of violent portrayals and contexts within which violence occurred (Kunkel et al., 1995; Potter et al., 1996; Wilson et al., 1996).

The NTVS developed a definition of violence that embodied three concepts: the notion of credible threat of violence, the overt occurrence of violent behavior, and the harmful consequences of unseen violence. The idea of credible threat covered situations where an individual threatened another in such a way that there was a realistic likelihood that violence would follow, with the perpetrator having the clear means to carry out such action. The harmful consequences of unseen violence covered scenes where people are depicted suffering from some kind of pain or discomfort and indeed actual physical damage may be shown, and where other clues from the story line establish that they were a victim of violence.

Much emphasis was also placed on the context in which violence occurred and an elaborate framework of analysis was created to enable a comprehensive classification of violence in terms of a range of attributes: its dramatic setting, motivational context, graphicness, rewards and punishments, severity of consequences for victims, physical form, and the nature of the perpetrators and victims. All these factors were rationalized in terms of their significance as possible mediators of audience response to media depictions of violence as signaled by published research literature on media effects (Kunkel et al., 1995).

In a parallel project sponsored by the American broadcast television networks, the UCLA Television Monitoring Project conducted a study of the representation of violence on television that avoided using a precise definition of violence (Cole, 1995, 1996). Instead, the emphasis was placed on "distinguishing between violence that raises issues of concern and that which does not" (Cole, 1995, p. 22). Coders were given 14 criteria to use when considering the violence issue: the time of the broadcast, presence of an advisory for viewers, whether the violence was integral to the story, graphicness, length of violence, number of scenes in a show, glorification of violence, who commits violence, realism, consequences, the manner in which violence is used to attract viewers, the alternatives to violence presented, weapons, and intentionality. Significantly, coders were not mandated to use all these criteria and they could ignore them and mark down their personal impressions instead if they so wished. The only programs labeled as violent were those that raised a concern with a coder.

The definitions of violence used in media research have exhibited some degree of variation. All contain a core element of intentionality on the part of a perpetrator to commit a behavioral act that could cause injury or harm to a target, but the range of behaviors subsumed under this broad concept has varied from study to study. Another fundamental consideration when conducting a content analysis of television violence is how the definition of violence should be applied to quantify violence on screen. To facilitate this exercise, the researcher must go beyond the initial violence definition to specify the basic units of measurement that derive from it.

UNITS OF ANALYSIS

The *unit of analysis* is the quantity that is counted in a content analysis. It is the smallest element of such an analysis. In written content, the unit of analysis might be a single word or symbol, a theme, or an entire article or story. In television and film analyses, units of analysis can be characters, behavioral actions, or entire programs. Specific rules and definitions are required for determining these units and to ensure agreement between coders in their identification and cataloging of on-screen action.

The analysis of violence in television programs requires a multilevel approach because programs have complex narrative structures. Potter (1999) advised that researchers, in analyzing program content, must recognise that violence can be measured at different levels. At the base level, individual violent incidents, such as a single punch or gunshot, can be separately counted. In all probability, however, a violent interaction may involve more than one character engaged in an altercation that may last long enough for several punches to be thrown or a number of shots to be fired. Indeed, in some instances, more than one type of violence could be featured, with each violent act being met by a violent response. Such incidents could be analyzed at the "scene" level. This would be less concerned with counting individual violent behaviors and place more emphasis on the overall violent nature of a sequence of activity on screen. At a higher level still, it may be possible to assess the violent nature of an entire program in terms of the extent to which it is permeated by violence or the degree to which the violence dominates the narrative at key points.

The analysis of program violence can also take into account different attributes of violence. These are discussed later. But the researcher might ask a number of questions of portrayed violence. Is the violence realistic? Is it graphically portrayed? Are lots of people involved? Was anyone hurt or killed? Why did the violence occur? Who were the aggressors and victims? Was the violence rewarded or punished? Was the violence justified? The important point to make is that it is not only the overall amount of violence in the program that is crucial. The nature of the violence and the nature of the overall theme of the program are important too, especially in the context of how viewers may react to what they see (Gunter, 1985; Van der Voort, 1986).

In analyzing television programs for the occurrence of violence, researchers have often focused on the microlevel, looking at brief incidents of violence. Each incident may last for a matter of seconds and display a short-lived violent interaction between characters on screen (Gerbner, Gross, Morgan, & Signorielli, 1980a; McCann & Sheehan, 1985; Potter & Ware, 1987; Potter et al., 1997).

Researchers have also used larger narrative units (e.g., the scene), which typically last a minute or two as characters engage in a sequence of violent behaviors and where the consequences of these actions are also displayed (Center for Media and Public Affairs, 1994; Mustonnen & Pulkkinen, 1993; Wiliams et al., 1982).

At the macrolevel, researchers have used the entire program as the unit of analysis and have examined all the contextual information throughout the program narrative to draw conclusions about the meaning of violence in television shows (Gerbner et al., 1980a; McCann & Sheehan, 1985; Williams et al., 1982). At this level, if violence occurs at all, the program is classified as being violent.

Some thematic analyses have characterized studies that have analyzed film and television violence over time using program and movie synopses. D. G. Clark and Blankenberg (1972) analyzed program synopses from the American listings magazine, *TV Guide*, from 1953 to 1969. They coded all prime-time programs that appeared from their listings descriptions to contain violence. Although some agreement was found between this method of coding and analysis of programs themselves, synopsis coding led to a general underestimate of violent programs. Another study of synopses examined the presence of crime themes featured in cinema films released in Britain between 1945 and 1991. In the case of crime films, allocation to this category meant that the "primary form of the narrative is on the cause or consequences of illegal activities, central characters included criminals, victims and those who work in the criminal justice system (e.g., private eyes, amateurs, police, courts, gangsters)" (J. Allen, Livingstone, & Reiner, 1997, p. 92).

These different approaches can yield a number of different types of quantitative statistics about media violence. The amount of violence on television can be expressed in terms of its totality (i.e., total number of violent acts coded, total amount of program running time occupied by violence), its prevalence in the schedules (e.g., percentage of programs on television that contain any violence), its rate of occurrence (i.e., average number of violent acts per program, average number of violent acts per hour), and its prominence (e.g., proportion of program running time occupied by violence).

Most research has focused on the basic unit of the violent act or interaction. Some have used combinations of different units, such as acts, aggressors, and victims of violence. Others have coded at more than one level. Head (1954), for example, looked at the specific actions of characters, the numbers of program scenes that contained violence, and broader dynamics of violent interactions. William et al. (1982) coded the general tone of the program and segments of programs that contained violence. McCann and Sheehan (1985) used three levels of measurement: the program as a whole, each specific violent action in the program, and the presence of specific classes of characters in violent programs.

Some analysts have combined a number of "micro" elements (e.g., individual violent behaviors, counts of perpetrators and victims) and other features (e.g., where the violence occurred, the extent to which the violence resulted in injury or death). Gerbner produced a "violence profile," which supposedly presented an objective and meaningful indicator of the amount of violence contained in programs. This profile comprised two sets of indicators: the *violence index* and the *risk ratios*. The violence index represented the percentage of programs containing any violence at all, the frequency and rate of violent episodes per program and per hour, and the number of leading characters involved in violence either as aggressors or as victims. The risk ratios signified a character's chances of involvement in violence and, once involved, the likelihood of positive or negative consequences for them. The risk ratios was actually a composite of two measures: the violent-victim ratio, which denoted the chances of being an aggressor or a victim, and the killer-killed ratio, which estimated the risk of being a killer or being killed (Gerbner & Gross, 1976).

The definition of violence and accompanying units of analysis utilized by Gerbner and his colleagues were challenged by Coffin and Tuchman (1972). In particular, they noted that other analyses with which they compared Gerbner's work had tended not to include violence that occurred in humorous or comic settings, accidental violence, and acts of nature (e.g., earthquakes and volcanic explosions) within their frameworks of analysis. An argument was ventured that any definition of violence that was applied in a unitary fashion to all programs and contexts would not fully represent the public's view of violence. It might be better and more ecologically valid to include a weighting system that would take into account the probable variations in audience response that would occur to violence in serious and humorous settings.

In following through this point, Gunter and J. Harrison (1998) noted:

> The measurement of violence on television is a difficult problem because violence definitions must be developed as a starting point, and then those definitions must be consistently applied to television content. The more complex the definitions that are deployed, the more difficult it becomes to ensure that they are applied in a similar and consistent fashion by different coders. The significance of such qualitative input to the definition of violence, in which potentially harmful or upsetting violence is distinguished from innocuous content, is that it precludes the adoption of a system which represents little more than a mechanical catalog with little meaning or utility. (p. 45)

Gerbner and his colleagues countered that their work had been misunderstood. Input from media effects or audience reactions research had no relevance to their definition of violence or their analytical framework. Their aim had been to examine overall structural patterns of content, not all of which would be consciously apprehended by viewers (Eleey, Gerbner, & Tedesco, 1972a). Nevertheless, stereotyped patterns of portrayals were conceived to represent "messages" about social reality that would gradually be absorbed by viewers over time into their mental maps of the world. A later challenge called into question the validity of Gerbner's violence index as a true measure of violence on television because it combined nonviolent and violent factors, shifts in either of which could alter the overall index score (Blank, 1977a, 1977b).

In the *National Television Violence Study* (1997, 1998, 1999), units of analysis were defined at more than one level. Whereas previous television violence content analysis studies had largely focused on counting violent acts, this study went beyond that level to include more global measures of violence that better represented the context features of violence. Three levels of measurement were devised: the PAT, the scene, and the program. A PAT represented an interaction between a perpetrator (P), an act (A), and a target (T). A sequence of PATs, either continuous and uninterrupted or separated by brief cutaways or scene changes, might comprise a violent scene and afford an opportunity to examine relations between discrete acts. The researchers then argued that larger meanings could be conveyed by the pattern of violence considered as a whole within a program, which could only be effectively interpreted when analyzed in the wider context in which it occurred.

Potter and S. L. Smith (1999) used data from the NTVS and examined whether the contextual information presented at one narrative level was consistent with the contextual information presented at another. According to these researchers, "In the meaning cues across narrative strata, viewers are presented with uniform information that can be used to construct interpretations of the meaning of the violence in that program" (p. 122). However, the meaning cues may be inconsistent across different levels of measurement. This could then provide confusing messages about violence. Potter and Smith provided an example of a program in which a perpetrator wreaks havoc, shooting and injuring or killing victims throughout much of the duration of the story, without adverse consequences to herself. Then, at the end of the program, she is finally caught and prevented from committing further offences. At the microlevel, most individual violent acts in this program would be coded as unpunished. At the macrolevel, however, the program would be coded as containing violence that is ultimately punished.

Potter and Smith constructed a fourfold typology for the analysis of program violence that combined microlevel and macrolevel analyses and depictions that present violence as bad and should be punished (pro-social theme) as opposed to presentations of violence as acceptable conduct (antisocial theme). Under this typology, a pro-social theme could be present at micro- and macrolevels, an antisocial theme could be present at both levels, a pro-social theme could be present at microlevel, with an antisocial theme present at the macrolevel, or an antisocial theme could dominate the microlevel, but an overriding pro-social theme emerges at the macrolevel.

SAMPLING OF CONTENT

Once the body of media content to be examined has been specified, the researcher has to determine how much of that content to analyze and devise a sampling frame to guide its selection. With a medium such as television that broadcasts without interruption every day, the potential universe of content is very large. It is therefore not feasible to analyze all output over extended periods of time, especially in television markets characterized by multiple television channel reception. Nevertheless, it is necessary that the researcher samples sufficient programming to yield an analysis that can be deemed to be reasonably representative of television output in general. In research to date, sampling variations have occurred as a function of the number of days selected, the number of hours per day, the number of channels and the program genres on which the researchers have chosen to focus.

Within the research literature, the program samples used in television content analyses have varied widely in size. Studies of television violence have been based on samples ranging from a few hours to thousands of hours of broadcast output. Lichter and Amundsen (1992) analyzed a single day of programing. Poulos, Harvey, and Liebert (1976) looked at two Saturday mornings.

The most typical program sample comprises one week of output. However, even then, there may be variations in the way that that amount of content was selected. Some studies have focused on prime-time programs (Center for Media and Policy Affairs, 1994; Potter & Ware, 1987; Potter et al., 1995). Others have combined prime-time programs with weekend daytime programs (Gerbner & Gross, 1976; Gerbner, Gross, Morgan, & Signorielli, 1980a; Greenberg et al., 1980). Such samples were justified in that they comprised the programs broadcast when audiences for television are largest.

Other researchers have compiled program samples from the most-watched programs on television, but without restricting their selections to industry-designated prime-time hours. Williams et al. (1982) selected the top-rated 100 programs for adults, the top 100 programs among teenagers, and the top 100 among children. There was considerable overlap among these three groups, with the result that the final sample comprised 109 distinct programs. Oliver (1994) focused on the selection of specified television series and looked at every episode of five series broadcast over a 3-month period. Other studies have analyzed 2 or more weeks of output in total (Broadcasting Standards Council, 1993; Gunter & J. Harrison, 1998; Potter & Ware, 1987).

Most content studies have analyzed programs from three or four channels (Gerbner et al., 1980a; Greenberg et al., 1980; Mustonen & Pulkkinen, 1993; Potter et al., 1995; Potter & Ware, 1987; Sherman & Dominick, 1986). Other studies have exceeded this norm: Schramm et al. (1961) with 5 channels, Smythe (1954) with 7 channels, Gunter and J. Harrison (1998) with 8 channels, Lichter and Amundsen (1992) with 10 channels, and the *National Television Violence Study* (1997, 1998, 1999) with 23 channels.

Studies of television violence have also varied in terms of the program genres that have been sampled. Some studies have focused on one specific genre, such as crime drama (Dominick, 1973; Estep & Macdonald, 1983), reality-based programs (Oliver, 1994), prime-time drama (Gerbner & Gross, 1976, Gerbner et al., 1980), and music videos (Baxter, Piemer, Landini, Leslie, & Singletary, 1985; J. D. Brown & K. Campbell, 1986; Sherman & Dominick, 1986). Other studies have analyzed different fictional genres, but avoided factual programs (Greenberg et al., 1980; Potter & Ware, 1987). A few studies have used an all inclusive approach and analyzed all major genres on television covering drama, news, and entertainment (Gunter & J. Harrison, 1998; Mustonen & Pulkkinen, 1993).

Another important aspect of content sampling, in addition to the types of content selected is the way in which sampling is conducted. Studies of television violence have, for the most part, sampled *program output*. Some researchers have sampled program and film *synopses* (J. Allen et al., 1997; D. G. Clark & Blankenberg, 1972). Sampling has been conducted by time as well as by series. In some studies, researchers have sampled episodes from designated television series (Center for Media and Public Affairs, 1994), or on the basis of the most watched programs on air (Williams et al., 1982). The usual approach has been to sample by time. This might entail taking one or more weeks intact and analyzing all programs within that period (Dominick, 1973; Gunter & J. Harrison, 1998). Alternatively, selected days can be sampled and programing taken intact from those days or from specific day-parts (e.g., evening programs) (Potter et al., 1995).

Simplistic sampling frames based on taking one real week of television output intact, particularly when the selected programs were restricted in terms of genre (e.g., drama only) and day-part (e.g., prime time only), have been challenged for failing to represent sufficiently the nature of television output in general (Kunkel et al., 1995). Gerbner (1972; Gerbner & Gross, 1976) was criticized for failing to include many important program genres, some of which could have been expected to contribute toward television's overall violence profile (Coffin & Tuchman, 1972). Elsewhere, it was noted that the variation of programing throughout the television season was such that it is was unlikely that one intact week of output would represent the nature of program output throughout the year (Blank, 1977a).

The question of content sampling was examined very closely by the *National Television Violence Study* (1997). This project analyzed a far larger sample of program output than most previous studies. The study sampled all programs broadcast on 23 channels from 6.00 a.m. to 11.00 p.m. over a 20-week period. The programs were chosen with a modified version of the equal probability of selection method. Two half-hour time slots (defined by hour of day and day of week) were randomly selected for each channel during each week that sampling occurred. Once a time slot was selected, the *TV Guide* was consulted and the program corresponding to that time slot was entered into a scheduling grid. This procedure was run until a full composite week of programs for each channel had been compiled.

ANALYSIS OF VIOLENCE ATTRIBUTES

The significance of assessing attributes of violence stems from the findings of research on media violence effects and audience reactions to programs that have shown that audience responses to television violence vary with the form it takes and context in which it appears. Violence is not treated as a homogeneous entity by ordinary people. Crucial distinctions are made between different types of violence. The objective judgments of researchers about violence on screen may yield analytical frameworks that deliver reliable measures, but may not reflect the views and reactions of the audience (Buckingham, 1993a; Gunter, 1985). Even children's perceptions of violence in programs differ from the estimates provided by content analysis (Van der Voort, 1986).

In a series of experimental studies of audience perceptions of televised violence, Gunter (1985; Gunter & Furnham, 1983, 1984) found that viewers distinguished between violent portrayals according to the realism of their surrounding context, the motives of perpetrators, the nature of targets or victims, the form of the violence, and the consequences of violence for victims. In a later study of audience perceptions of television violence, Sander (1997) found that the core element of a viewer-based definition of violence focused on the dimension of "physical violence," thus corroborating the predominant feature of most a priori violence definitions used content analysis research. However, this element explained just 23% of the variance in public definitions of violence. Other factors, such as the realism of the setting, use of humor, psychological and legal justification, intention, and psychological and physical harm were also central aspects of defining behavior as violent.

In a German study of violence on television, Groebel and Gleich (1993) used a comprehensive typology for describing different aspects of aggressive acts on television. In this scheme, the aggression was: (a) either physical or verbal (psychological); (b) against human beings, animals, or things; (c) against self or others; (d) direct or indirect; (e) instrumental or destructive; (f) reactive or goal oriented; (g) intentional or unintentional; (h) done with harm intended or not intended; (i) with or without physiological arousal; (j) inside or outside an aggression-supporting environment; (k) socially legitimized or not legitimized; (l) punished or unpunished; (m) spontaneous or planned; (n) harm causing or nonharm causing; (o) associated with short- or long-term effects; and (p) produced effects that were noticeable or not noticeable to the actor.

On reviewing the media violence effects evidence, the *National Television Violence Study* (1997) identified a number of "risk factors" that could be used to classify violence on screen. These included elements such as the nature of perpetrators and victims, graphic nature and consequences of violence, rewards and punishments associated with violence, presence of humor, use of weapons, and overall realism of setting. One member of the research group behind this project subsequently recommended that all acts of violence should be coded on eight criteria:

1. Level of act (from serious to minor)
2. Type of act (physical or verbal)
3. Intentionality (premeditated to accidental)
4. Degree of harm to victims
5. Type of harm (physical, emotional, psychological)
6. Level of openness (covert to overt)
7. Level of reality (fantasy to full reality)
8. Level of humor (farce to serious)

According to Potter (1999)

> Recording violence on all these dimensions would result in a more complete picture of the nature of violence on television. Effects researchers could then use this richer information to design their stimulus materials more precisely instead of regarding violence as a monolithic concept. There are many different kinds of violence, and these different kinds are likely to influence viewers in different ways. (p. 80)

RELIABILITY

Content analysis is a methodology that sets out to provide systematic and verifiable measures of the character of media output. The essence of this approach is that it is grounded in a framework concerned with minimizing the influence of personal opinion or subjective judgment on the part of researchers or the individuals employed to undertake the detailed monitoring work. A key concept in content analysis is reliability. To check that two or more coders have followed the same instructional set in the same way when analyzing programs, the researcher must compare their independent analyses to ensure that they are the same. In other words, coders must apply the coding frame—that is, the measuring instrument applied to the content—in a consistent fashion.

The extent to which high levels of consistency or reliability are achieved can vary with the nature of the exercise. It may depend on whether judgments are being made about manifest content or latent content, how many coders are used, the amount of content on which reliabilty checks are made, and the method used for computing reliability.

Making judgments about latent content such as the gender of perpetrators and victims, whether violence involved a weapon, or whether a victim was hurt can often be fairly straightforward because these features are visible on screen. More complex coding is required to assess the motives of aggressors because this relates to a more abstract concept that can only be determined by making a close study of the story line and relationships among characters. Achieving high levels of reliability across coders may prove more difficult with these less manifest aspects of programs because coders must use their own judgments to a greater extent.

Consistency among coders can also be more difficult to achieve as the number of coders used increases. Maintaining consistency across coders requires careful quality control checks on the part of the researcher. This can become more problematic as the number of individuals with different perspectives on violence increases. In most content analysis studies with modest content samples, pairs of coders are used (e.g., Mustonen & Pulkkinen, 1993; Potter & Ware, 1987). Other studies of larger content samples have used greater numbers of coders, numbering from 5 to more than 40 (Gerbner & Gross, 1976; *National Television Violence Study*, 1997, 1998, 1999; Oliver, 1994).

With small content samples, all content may be double coded (S. L. Kaplan & Baxter, 1982). With larger samples, this is not usually feasible and so subsets of content are selected to be coded twice. It is typical to run a reliability check as such on about 10% of the original program sample (e.g., Potter et al., 1995; Potter & Ware, 1987), although some researchers have used larger percentages of the main content sample (Dominick, 1973—23%; Williams et al., 1982—15%).

MEASUREMENT OF TELEVISION VIOLENCE IN BRITAIN

The research presented in this book is based on a large-scale content analysis study of British television. The study ran for a total of two television seasons, starting in October 1994 and ending in July 1996. The analysis of each television season comprised distinct projects. The first of these projects was reported in detail elsewhere (Gunter & J. Harrison, 1998). This book focuses on results from the second project, although comparisons between the two are made throughout. The content analysis was concerned with producing a quantitative assessment of the prevalence, amount, and distribution of violence on British television, together with an examination of the attributes of violence and the context in which violence occurred.

Definition of Violence

Any content analysis of television violence begins with a definition of violence that represents the core ingredient of the frame of reference that drives the analysis. In the current study, violence was defined as "any overt depiction of a credible threat of physical force or actual use of physical force, with or without a weapon, which is intended to harm or intimidate an animate being or a group of animate beings. The violence may be carried out or merely attempted, and may or may not cause injury. Violence also includes any depiction of physically harmful consequences against an animate being (or group of animate beings) that occur as a result of unseen violent means." (Gunter & J. Harrison, 1998).

Table 2.1 shows how this definition was displayed on the coding schedule as an *aide memoir* to coders. It was divided into a number of separate components, with key points emboldened to draw attention to them. In addition, coders were provided with a separate information sheet that presented further stipulations and considerations to be borne in mind while coding. There were seven such stipulations or considerations:

1. An *overt depiction* means that the violence is occurring on the screen. The threat, the act, or the harmful consequences are shown or heard in the action of the plot. Verbal recounting of previous threats/acts of physical force or talking about violence does not in itself count as violence.

2. *Physical force* refers to action intended to cause physical pain or injury to an animate being, or to the use of physical tactics (e.g.,

TABLE 2.1
Definition of Violence

- Any overt depiction of a credible threat of physical force or the actual use of physical force
- With or without a weapon
- Which is intended to harm or intimidate an animate being or a group of animate beings or inanimate objects (i.e., property)
- Whether carried out or merely attempted
- Whether or not the action causes injury
- The acts of violence may be intentional or accidental (in the context of an intentional violent event—e.g., a car crash during a car chase)
- Violent accidents and catastrophes (if caused by human agents—e.g., a terrorist bomb explodes on a plane causing the plane to crash)

strong-arming) that are intended to coerce the action of another in a way that threatens harm. Physical force must be enacted by an animate being; physical force or harm that occurs as a result of an act of nature (e.g., earthquake) is not counted as violence. Physical force can be perpetrated against the self or against another.

3. A *credible threat* means that within the context of the plot the perpetrator must display an intent to harm. Joking threats that have no believable intent to harm are not included (e.g., A character who is embarrassed and says "I could kill you for saying that").

4. An *animate being* refers to any human, animal, or anthropomorphized creature (nonhuman that possesses human attributes such as the ability to move, talk, think, act against something). A group of animate beings can involve several creatures or more abstract collections of creatures such as institutions or governments.

5. Violence must be involve *at least one human or anthropomorphized being*, either as perpetrator or as victim. An act of nature involving two or more animals that threaten or harm each other is not considered violence so long as the animals are not anthropomorphized (i.e., possess human-like characteristics like talking, thinking).

6. *Accidents* that involve physical harm are considered violence only when they occur in the context of an ongoing violent event (e.g., police chase a robber who accidentally falls off a building during the pursuit) or when they involve the use of weapons (e.g., two children are playing with a gun that goes off and hits one of them).

7. Physical force against *property* (e.g., breaking a window, setting fire to a building) will be considered violence only when it is directed at intimidating, punishing, vandalism, or seeking revenge against an animate being. Property damage due to accidents, even in the context of an ongoing violent event, will not be considered as violence.

In addition to these stipulations, a further set of guidelines was provided in respect to defining a violent act. These provided guidance to coders in determining when a violent act, as a unit of measurement, began and ended. There were three specific features that were taken into account in determining a violent act as a unit of analysis. If a perpetrator performed the same behavior, such as punching a target repeatedly without a break, then this would be counted as a single violent act. It began at the point at which the first punch was thrown and ended once the last punch had been delivered. If a perpetrator performed an act of violence against a target and then the target retaliated, then this would count as two acts of violence. If the same perpetrator, in attacking a target, changed the form of violent behavior, then this would again signal two violent acts. Thus, if the perpetrator in question punched the target and then shot at that same target, this would be classified as two distinct violent acts.

Coding Schedule

The coding schedule presented the definition of violence that coders were instructed to use. It also contained a series of questions about each program and about the nature of any violent acts depicted in the program.

The schedule was broadly divided into two parts. The first part was completed for every program and obtained general information about the program itself, such as the channel on which it appeared, its transmission date, start time, length, genre code (31 different program types were used), and country of origin. General questions were then posed about whether it contained any violence at all, and if so, how much violence it contained in terms of number of violent acts, violent sequences, and amount of violence in seconds. A further question asked if there was a warning about violent content before or during the program. Finally, coders were given the opportunity to add any further comments at the foot of the page concerning difficulties they experienced with coding the program in question.

The second part of the coding schedule was completed for those programs that contained any violence. A coding framework was provided to enable coders to supply details about the nature of the violence. Thus, information was provided about the historical setting, environment, and country or location where the violence took place. A list of 52 codes for types of violent acts was used to indicate the nature of the violence. A separate list of 47 codes for types of weapons of aggression was also included. Further contextual details included whether the act was "first strike" or "retaliatory," the dramatic setting, dramatic outcome (blood, pain, and horror), and the types of injuries caused.

The coding schedule for each violent act also probed for details about the status and type of aggressor and victim(s) and, in each case, the aggressor's and victim's gender, ethnic origin, age, and (for the aggressor only) their apparent goals or objectives.

Program Samples

The periods recorded were selected at the discretion of the researchers and were not disclosed to the project's sponsors in advance of when videotaping took place. There were four periods comprising composite weeks made up by selecting Monday from one week, Tuesday from the following week, and so on to Sunday from the seventh week. Thus, a total of 28 days were videotaped from 28 separate weeks over a period spanning from July 1995 to June 1996. Tapes ran from 6 a.m. to 6 a.m. each day. The videotapes covered 10 channels, including the 4 terrestrially transmitted channels, BBC1, BBC2, ITV, and Channel 4. In addition, six channels were selected for analysis that were available via satellite transmissions, Sky One, UK Gold, Sky Movies, The Movie Channel, Sky

Sports, and TNT/Cartoon Network. The first eight of these channels had also been analyzed in the previous year's study. Thus, year-on-year comparisons in terms of amount, distribution, and character of violence could be made for these eight channels. Although not representing a random sample, the start date for each phase of videotaping was randomly selected from within a 4-week window.

All programs were recorded on Panasonic Nicam video recorders using 4-hour VHS tapes played at normal speed, except for overnight taping, when they were played at half speed, enabling 8 hours of programing to be captured on a single tape. A bank of 10 machines was used to carry out the taping, with one machine being dedicated to each channel. In addition, further machines were used to capture those short periods that might have been lost during tape changeovers.

Table 2.2 shows the number and distribution of coded programs across the 10 channels aggregated over the 28 days of the program sample. A total of 6,254.1 hours of programing was recorded in the 1995–1996 study. This figure is significantly greater than the 4,715.34 hours of programing taped and analyzed in the 1994–1995 study. There were 3,473 programs coded on terrestrial channels and 3,764 coded on the six satellite channels.

Coded programs were classified into 32 different genres, which could be clustered into six superordinate genres: drama, entertainment, factual, sport, children's programs, and music/arts/religion. Table 2.3 presents a summary of the distribution of genres across the four terrestrial and two nonthematic satellite entertainment channels. It should be noted that the movie channels, being thematic, comprised mostly cinema films. The latter represented some 90% of these channels' programing, with the remainder being occupied by animated cartoons,

TABLE 2.2
Distribution of Coded Programs by Channel

	1994–1995	*1995–1996*
BBC1	855	876
BBC2	815	800
ITV	989	1,030
Channel 4	735	767
Terrestrial	3,394	3,473
Sky One	730	863
UK Gold	754	788
Sky Movies	334	345
Movie Channel	395	392
TNT/Cartoon Network	–	941
Sky Sports	–	435
Satellite	2,212	3,764
Total	5,606	7,237

TABLE 2.3
Number of Coded Programs per Channel by Genre

	All N	BBC1 N	BBC2 N	ITV N	Ch.4 N	Sky 1 N	UK Gold N
Drama							
Cinema films	1,059	41	40	57	76	5	27
Non–U.K. long run series	379	43	11	80	19	88	138
U.K. long run serials	360	20	5	62	21	–	252
Other non–U.K. series/ials	291	12	18	22	32	178	29
Other U.K. series/ials	131	24	14	22	22	6	43
Made–for–TV films	40	6	7	9	8	–	1
Single plays	6	1	1	2	2	–	–
Total	2,266	147	96	232	180	277	490
Children's Programs							
General children's programs	430	79	80	82	63	95	14
Children's cartoons	1,351	75	71	100	98	164	6
Total	1,781	154	151	182	162	259	20
Sport	630	50	50	22	54	13	12
Factual							
News–national	451	195	71	157	28	–	–
Documentaries	228	34	70	26	74	23	–
Hobbies/leisure	156	45	53	24	24	7	3
Current affairs (PSE)	207	35	91	45	36	–	–
News–regional	138	48	3	87	–	–	–
Current affairs (CA)	9	3	2	4	–	–	–
Current affairs (SE)	3	–	3	–	–	–	–
Total	1,192	360	293	343	162	30	3
Entertainment							
Situation comedy	231	20	19	9	49	31	103
Other comedy	120	15	22	16	12	15	40
Variety	18	–	–	7	7	–	4
Family/people shows	20	9	–	9	–	1	1
Cartoon/animation	32	1	2	3	16	9	–
Chat shows	272	47	18	58	55	92	2
Quiz/games shows	270	45	17	43	42	75	46
Special events	13	6	3	3	–	1	–
Total	976	143	81	148	181	224	196
Music/arts/religion							
Arts programs	8	1	3	–	4	–	–
Music–contemporary	51	6	12	29	4	–	–
Pop video	70	–	2	12	1	54	1
Music–classical	7	1	4	1	1	–	–
Religious programs	21	9	5	6	1	–	–
Total	157	17	26	48	11	54	1
Other	213	5	102	33	16	1	52

a small amount of documentary material usually about movies, and program-length previews. Sky Sports comprised sports programs and TNT/Cartoon Network showed children's programs during the day and films and some drama at night.

Across all channels, over 31% of coded programs were various forms of drama, including cinema films, made-for-TV films, drama series and serials, and single plays. This represented the single biggest genre in terms of numbers of programs analyzed. More than one in six programs (17%) coded was a factual programs. These programs included national and regional news, current affairs (political, social and economic issues; consumer affairs, and special events), documentaries, and programs about hobbies or leisure activities. Sport was treated as a separate category and accounted for nearly 9% of programs coded.

The third biggest program category in this sample was children's programs (nearly 26% of all programs analyzed). Children's programs comprised children's cartoons and other programs made especially for children. Entertainment programs represented nearly 14% of coded programs and included situation comedy, quiz and game shows, chat shows, family/people shows, other comedy shows, and small numbers of variety shows, cartoons for the general audience, and special events. A small proportion of the coded output (1%) comprised music, arts, and religious programs.

The program composition of terrestrial and satellite entertainment channels exhibited some degree of variation. Even though drama was the most represented genre in terms of numbers of coded programs over all eight channels, it is clear that it was not the most represented genre on the terrestrial channels. Here, the greatest single proportion of programs coded were factual programs. There were, however, relatively few factual programs on the satellite channels. Nearly 6 out of 10 programs on Sky One (58%) and 9 out of 10 (90%) on UK Gold were in the drama and entertainment categories. One in 3 coded programs on Sky One were children's programs (see Tables 2.3 and 2.4)

On the thematic channels (Sky Movies, The Movie Channel, Sky Sports, and TNT/Cartoon Network), most coded programs belonged to the dominant thematic category for that channel. However, in each case, that category did not account exclusively for all the programs coded on that channel. On The Movie Channel, 87% of coded programs were cinema films, with another 12% falling into the category of children's programs. There was also a small number of made-for-TV films (4) on this channel. On Sky Movies, 97% of coded programs were cinema films, with a small proportion (just over 2%) classified as children's programs. On TNT/Cartoon Network, 84% of coded programs were children's programs (mostly cartoons) and a further 15% were cinema films. On Sky Sports, 97% of coded programs were classified as sport. Two programs were categorized as quiz shows, and a further four programs were unclassified.

TABLE 2.4

Distribution of Coded Programs per Channel by Genre

	All %	BBC1 %	BBC2 %	ITV %	Ch.4 %	Sky 1 %	UK Gold %
Drama							
Cinema films	14.7	4.7	5.0	5.6	9.9	0.6	3.5
Non-U.K. long run series	5.3	4.9	1.4	7.9	2.5	10.3	17.8
U.K. long run serials	5.0	2.3	0.6	6.2	2.7	–	32.6
Other non-U.K. series/ials	4.0	1.4	2.3	2.2	4.2	20.7	3.7
Other U.K. series/ials	1.8	2.7	1.8	2.2	2.9	0.7	5.6
Made-for-TV films	0.6	0.7	0.9	0.9	1.0	–	1.4
Single plays	0.1	0.1	0.1	0.2	0.3	–	–
Total	31.4	16.8	12.0	23.0	23.5	32.3	63.3
Children's Programs							
General children's Programs	6.0	9.0	10.0	8.1	8.2	11.1	1.8
Children's cartoons	18.7	8.6	8.9	9.9	12.8	19.1	0.8
Total	24.7	17.6	18.8	18.0	21.1	30.2	2.6
Sport	8.7	5.7	6.3	2.2	7.1	1.5	1.6
Factual							
News-national	6.3	22.2	8.9	15.6	3.7	–	–
Documentaries	3.2	3.9	8.8	2.6	9.7	2.7	–
Hobbies/leisure	2.2	5.1	6.6	2.4	3.1	0.8	0.4
Current affairs (PSE)	2.9	4.0	11.4	4.5	4.7	–	–
News-regional	1.9	5.5	0.4	8.6	–	–	–
Current affairs (CA)	0.1	0.3	0.4	0.4	–	–	–
Current affairs (SE)	*	–	0.4	–	–	–	–
Total	16.5	41.1	36.7	34.0	21.2	3.5	0.4
Entertainment							
Situation comedy	3.2	2.3	2.4	0.9	6.4	3.6	13.3
Other comedy	1.7	1.7	2.8	1.6	1.6	1.7	5.2
Variety	0.2	–	–	0.7	0.9	–	0.5
Family/people shows	0.3	1.0	–	0.9	–	0.1	0.1
Cartoon/animation	0.4	0.1	0.4	0.3	2.1	1.0	–
Chat shows	3.8	5.4	2.3	5.6	7.2	10.7	0.2
Quiz/games shows	3.7	5.1	2.2	4.3	5.5	8.7	5.9
Special events	0.2	0.7	0.4	0.3	–	0.1	–
Total	13.5	16.3	10.1	14.7	23.7	26.1	25.3
Music/arts/religion							
Arts programs	0.1	0.1	0.4	–	0.5	–	–
Music-contemporary	0.7	0.6	1.5	2.9	0.5	–	–
Pop videos	1.0	–	0.3	1.2	0.1	6.3	0.1
Music-classical	0.1	0.1	0.5	0.1	0.1	–	–
Religious programs	0.3	1.0	0.6	0.6	0.1	–	–
Total	2.2	1.9	3.3	4.8	1.4	6.3	0.1
Other	3.0	0.6	12.8	3.3	2.1	0.1	6.7

* Less than 0.05%

Coding and Reliability

The coding of data in this research was performed by a sample of individuals who were resident in the Sheffield area, England. A pool of 25 coders were recruited (13 males and 12 females), between ages 18 and 60. The coders were drawn from a range of occupational backgrounds, although all had carried on their education to university level or equivalent.

The coders were required to master all aspects of the coding frame and the supplementary instructions that accompanied it. Key concepts and terms were described in full and illustrations were provided where necessary to ensure that definitions and their mode of application were understood.

The content analysis focused on pre-defined occurrences of acts of violence. In addition to this basic-level quantification of televised violence, coders were trained to identify and catalog various attributes of violence that provided some detail about the nature of the violence being depicted. The coders participated in a series of training sessions before the coding exercise began. These sessions were designed to familiarize coders with the details of the coding schedule and to ensure they understood the definition of violence, the instructions for distinguishing individual violent acts, and the general procedures under which the content analysis was to be conducted. Feedback was provided about performance in these pilot exercises and any ambiguities that arose concerning any aspects of the coding frame and procedure were discussed in full in settings where all coders were present. There were opportunities provided for coders to express any concerns they had and to obtain clarification on any points of apparent ambiguity. In total, coders were engaged in around 20 hours of instruction and practice before the study proper began.

It is important in any content analysis research that coders utilize the coding frame in a consistent manner. Coders must be prepared to adopt key definitional terms in the same way. The coding procedure and training of coders should be designed to minimize, as far as possible, the application of subjective judgments by coders. Although coders may, subjectively, hold widely varying opinions about particular portrayals of violence, they must not allow their personal views to contaminate the objective assessments of on-screen activity they are required to describe.

Intercoder consistency was checked both qualitatively and quantitatively. Qualitative checks comprised continuous monitoring of the judgments made by coders at key decision points in the application of the coding frame. The coding procedure involved the compilation of two datasets. The first dataset contained general information about each separate program, such as its time of transmission, length (in minutes), channel, country of origin, and aggregate measures of violent content (total number of violent acts and sequences, and length of time occupied by violence). The second dataset concerned violent acts and contained codes relating to 23 different attributes, such as setting (historical, geographical, environmental), form (type of violence, weapons used), motives for violence, consequences of violence, demography, and role-type of aggressors and victims. Each violent act also had codes for channel program, program genre, and program length.

Returned coding sheets were checked to make sure that correct codes had been applied for programs and violent acts. Coders' aggregate violence scores in the program dataset were checked against the separate violent act coding sheets they had returned for that program to make sure they matched. Consistent errors, either of arithmetic or the application of codes, on the part of coders triggered further one-on-one training and instructional sessions with the researchers.

Quantitative checks on reliability of coding focused on two aspects of the coding process: level of agreement between coders in general violence counts for programs and level of consistency in the application of attribute codes and assignment of code values to violent acts.

Reliability checks at the program level involved double coding of selections of monitored programs from across the 4 weeks for which videotapes were made. There were 254 cases of double coding in total, covering all the major program genres. Checks were run for violent acts, violent sequences, and violence minutage.

Across the 254 double-coded programs, percentages of paired codings that achieved perfect agreement and varying degrees of disagreement were calculated. In respect to violent acts and violent sequences, separate percentages were calculated for pairings for which there was disagreement on one act/sequence, as well as for those with differences in two, three, and four or more acts/sequences. For the measure of violence in terms of amount of time occupied by violence, agreement and disagreement percentages were calculated once again, with separate disagreement percentages computed for difference margins of 1–2 seconds, 3–5 seconds, 6–10 seconds, and 11+ seconds. The results are summarized in Table 2.5.

TABLE 2.5

Reliability of Program Coding for Violence

	Violent Acts		Violent Sequences			Violence Minutage	
	N	%	N	%		N	%
Perfect match	190	74	201	79	Perfect match	154	61
Disagreement							
One act/sequence	33	13	30	12	1–2 seconds	47	19
Two acts/sequence	13	6	10	4	3–5 seconds	26	10
Three acts/sequence	8	3	3	1	6–10 seconds	16	6
Four+ acts/sequence	10	4	10	4	11+ seconds	11	5

Note: Total number of paired codings = 254.

These results indicate that the highest levels of reliability occurred for coding of violent sequences, with nearly 8 out of 10 pairings (79%) achieving perfect agreement in measuring the numbers of violent sequences contained within a program. Reliability was somewhat lower for counts of violent acts, with nearly 3 of 4 pairings (74%) achieving perfect agreement. In the case of a further 1 in 8 pairings, there was only a slight disagreement of one act or sequence difference. Thus, over 9 in 10 pairings (91%) achieved perfect or near perfect agreement in counts of violent sequences, and well over 8 in 10 achieved these levels of performance in respect to violent acts counts.

Reliability levels were lower for the assessment of violence minutage. In this case, however, given the intricate nature of the process of timing violence, it may be appropriate to allow more latitude in extent of disagreement. Over 6 of 10 pairings (61%) achieved perfect agreement, whereas a further 1 in 5 (19%) disagreed by just 1 or 2 seconds, and a further 1 in 10 (10%) disagreed by between 3 and 5 seconds. Thus, 9 of 10 pairings (90%) achieved either perfectly matching or very close estimates of amount of violence in terms of seconds of program running time occupied by violence.

Attribute coding reliability for individual violent acts was checked for each attribute on the violent act coding frame. A sample of 12 violent acts, taken from a number of different program genres and depicting a variety of forms of violence, were coded by 23 coders. Consistency across coders was assessed across 23 separate attribute measures for each violent act: length (in seconds), historical setting, environmental setting, geographical location, type of action, form of violence, type of weapon, motivational context, injury consequences, dramatic detail (blood, pain horror), aggressor status, aggressor role-type, aggressor demography (gender, age, and ethnicity), aggressor goal, victim status, victim role-type, and victim demography (gender, age, and ethnicity).

Each attribute could be judged in terms of a designated number of values. For example, for historical setting there were six values: distant past, recent past, present, near future, distant future, uncodable. In the reliability analysis a 12 (acts) by 23 (coders) matrix was constructed for each attribute. The attribute values allocated by each coder to each of the 12 violent acts were entered into this matrix. The modal value was then identified for each attribute, and occurrences of this value were then aggregated to produce a single score. This score was divided by the total number of cells (276) in the matrix and multiplied by 100 to produce a percentage agreement score. The target score of acceptability was 70% agreement. Across all 23 violent act attributes, the average agreement score among coders was 70% (with a range of from 51% to 89%). Although agreement percentage levels for some attributes were below 60%, these relatively low levels of consistency stemmed very often from understandable ambiguities between values that were semantically fairly similar.

The lowest scoring attributes, in terms of reliability of coding, were environmental setting (51%), victim role-type (52%), aggressor role-type (55%), aggressor goal (56%), and injury type (58%). With environmental setting, the major difficulty seemed to occur in distinguishing effectively between suburban and small town locations and between "rural" and "uninhabited" codes. With victim role-type, value attribution consistency level was reduced by confusion over armed forces versus inanimate objects codes. Coders were sometimes uncertain about whether heavy armored vehicles qualified strictly as inanimate objects, and the code "armed forces" was taken to refer more specifically to armed forces personnel.

With aggressor role-type, some confusion existed between the allocation of codes for legitimate and nonlegitimate law enforcers, and petty versus serious criminal types. In the latter case, "serious" generally meant crimes of a serious nature, such as armed robbery, assault and battery, and other incidents where the stakes were high. With law enforcers, in the absence of cues that clearly identified law enforcers as legitimate upholders of the law (i.e., police officers), even though characters might be acting on behalf of the legal system, there were occasions when insufficient additional information was present to enable coders to allocate values more accurately.

With aggressor goals, the key problem concerned distinctions between violence in the service of evil or ambition, and between ambition, evil, and desire for money. There were portrayals in which these motives were not mutually exclusive. Finally, confusion over injury values stemmed predominantly from the allocation of codes for various forms of minor injury, such as "minor injury," "stunned," and "bruised."

The remainder of the book is devoted to reporting the results from this research. This account begins in the next chapter with an overview of the main quantitative results concerning the amount of violence on British television and its distribution across various television channels and program genres. Comparisons are made between the 1995–1996 results and those obtained in the 1994–1995 analysis. Chapter 4 examines the form of violence on television in terms of the nature of the violent behavior portrayed and the use of weapons. Chapter 5 explores the motives and consequences of televised violence. Violent acts were classified in terms of the broad motivational context in which they occurred and the specific goals evidenced by perpetrators of violence. The outcomes of violence were classified in terms of their seriousness and violent acts were also classified according to the graphic nature of depictions of blood, pain, and suffering experienced by victims of violence. All of these specific attributes have previously been linked to audience reactions to televised violence.

The analysis then shifts to a close-up examination of a number of other themes. Chapter 7 deals with the subject of violence in programs aimed at children in the audience. There has long been concern about the effects of television violence on children, but to what extent are programs targeted at younger viewers guilty of regular displays of violent conduct? What forms are taken on by violence in children's programs? Should these programs be regarded as a cause for concern?

Chapter 8 turns to soap operas, perhaps the most popular program genre on television. These long-running serialized dramas give viewers an opportunity to get to know characters, their relationships, and the settings in which story lines are usually played out better than any other program type. The realism that characterizes soap operas also renders them potentially influential forms of entertainment. But how violent are soaps? What kinds of violence do they show? Given the greater than average degree of involvement of viewers in these dramas, can the violence they show been regarded as likely to have a significantly greater impact than that occurring in most other genres?

Chapter 9 moves from fiction to fact on television. This chapter examines violence that occurs in news programs. In addition to presenting results on the amount of violence and types of violence shown in the news, it will consider the results in the wider context of editorial decision making and news values. Does violence make a story newsworthy? Is there any evidence that news editors include violence gratuitously, possibly to attract viewers? Does the presentation of violence in the news meet the requirements of broadcasters' own policies about news violence?

Chapter 10 draws comparisons between the amount and nature of violence on television in Britain and the United States. These comparisons draw on data from the National Cable Television Association's *National Television Violence Study*. This study was conducted between 1994 and 1997. The British findings are compared with those from the NTVS data gathered between 1994 and 1996—the two studies that ran in parallel with those conducted in Britain. This analysis focuses on those measures the two investigations had in common.

Chapter 11 considers the relevance of research into the representation of violence on television to wider social policy debates about program ratings, advance warnings to parents, the provision of information about programs in electronic program guides, and the regulation of television in the future. It draws on debates that have been conducted in the United States and Europe. It considers issues concerned with control over not only the type of violence, but also its distribution across programs.

Chapter 3

Amount and Distribution of Violence on Television

Concern about television violence has frequently centered on the amount of violence shown. Critics accuse television of showing too much violence, which some portray as a virtually unavoidable ingredient of programs. Regular exposure to such a viewing diet has been invoked as an explanation for increased fear of personal victimization among viewers (Gerbner & Gross, 1976; Gerbner et al., 1994), and is also seen as cause of densensitization to violence (Cline, Croft, & Courier, 1973; Drabman & Thomas, 1974). The argument that there is widespread concern about the amount of violence on television has received further support from public opinion surveys in which a majority of respondents has agreed that television is too violent (see Gunter & Wober, 1988).

Many of these findings have little value to broadcast regulators or policymakers charged with making television a safe and socially responsible medium. Research into the alleged longer term harms of exposure to television has failed to pinpoint whether it is violence in general that is the problem or whether certain kinds of violence are more problematic than others. Meanwhile, public opinion data that focus on very broad impressions of television are equally uninformative in this context. Moreover, there is ample evidence that public opinion can be contradictory and that general views about television are frequently inconsistent with the attitudes individuals hold about specific programs (Gunter & Stipp, 1992; Gunter & Wober, 1988).

The starting point must be an objective analysis of what appears on screen, followed by further classification of that material, taking into account evidence from relevant audience research. Before examining the different forms of violence and the contexts in which it can occur (all of which is important to audience reactions), consider what is known about the general amount and distribution of screen violence.

Long-term effects on audiences frequently make reference to the overall quantity of violence on television, but is there as much television violence as some critics claim? Furthermore, does violence permeate the schedules, or is it concentrated predominantly on certain channels, at certain times of day, or in specific programs? A quantitative content analysis can shed light on these questions.

In addition to examining the overall distribution of violence on British television, this study investigated the occurrence of violence at different times of the day and in different program genres. The relation between the appearance of violence and transmission time is important because of concerns about the exposure of children to violence on television. In Britain, for example, the broadcast regulators employ a Family Viewing Policy that requires broadcasters to avoid presenting material before 9:00 p.m. that might be unsuitable for children. After 9:00 p.m., there is a gradual relaxation of that restriction. But the regulators do recognize that there is no time in the evening when no children are watching. Indeed, in providing a diverse program service designed to cater to a wide array of tastes and interests, it is inevitable that some material unsuitable for younger viewers may be broadcast. The Family Viewing Policy represents a shared contract between broadcasters and parents, whereby broadcasters undertake to be primarily responsible for safeguarding the interests of children during the first part of the evening, and then gradually hand over that responsibility to parents in the later part. The policy is mindful of the fact that two thirds of television viewing households in Britain have no resident children.

There is further flexibility in the guidelines where encrypted television channels are concerned. These channels are made available via satellite or cable transmission and consumers must pay a subscription charge to have the signal decoded. Under these circumstances, it is assumed that parents exert a greater degree of control over reception. Hence, more adult material may be shown on such channels and at an earlier time than would be permitted on open-access channels. Channels providing movies are among the most popular subscription channels. In Britain, the movie channels provide advance classifications and advisories about the suitability of movies for young audiences. Broadcasters use a system based on the cinema film classifications used by the British Board of Film Classification.

The current analysis examines the presence and distribution of violence across program genres. Genre is an important basis for the classification of programs. Viewers develop expectations about programs when they know in advance the genre to which a program belongs (Neale, 1983). Such expectations play an important part in determining how audiences will respond to programs (Morley, 1981). Gunter and J. Harrison (1998) observed:

> There is ... a close connection between the concept of "genre" and the assumptions that are made about the potential popularity of programs. This

notion is in turn tied to an assumption that genre attributes play a central role in assisting audiences with their interpretation and understanding of programs, a factor that is envisaged as being linked to audience appreciation. (p. 161)

With information about its genre, audiences can not only begin to formulate in advance their ideas about what to expect, but can also judge the degree to which a given program is faithful to its type. The genre of a program is closely tied to judgments about its realism and this element is a key mediating variable in connection with audience responses to screen violence (Berkowitz & Alioto, 1973; Feshbach, 1972; Noble, 1975; Reeves, 1978). Furthermore, in more realistic program contexts, viewers become more attuned to other factors, such as the form or nature of violence, the types of perpetrators and victims, and the consequences of violence (Gunter, 1985).

QUANTITATIVE MEASURES

The amount of violence on television was expressed in a number of different ways. There were three principal measures of the quantity or amount of violence on television: the total number of violent acts, the total number of violent sequences, and the total amount of transmission time occupied by violent material. In addition, there were five principal measures of prevalence of violence: the proportion of programs that contained any violence at all, the average number of violent acts per violence-containing program, the average number of violent acts per hour, the average number of violent sequences per violence-containing program, and the proportion of program running time occupied by violence. These measures were used to indicate levels and distribution of violence on different television channels and, in subsequent chapters, for different time bands and different program genres.

Programs Containing Violence

Across the 28 days analyzed, a total of 3,248 programs (45% of coded programs) were found to contain some violence. This is the total for the 10 channels monitored during 1995–1996. Taking the 8 channels that were monitored over 2 years, the total containing any violence in Year 2 was 2,385 (47% of programs monitored on these channels) compared with 2,084 (37% of total monitored) in Year 1. Year-on-year, therefore, a marked increase was noted in the numbers of programs that contained any violence (see Table 3.1). This increase was nonsignificant for the four terrestrial channels (BBC1, BBC2, ITV, and Channel 4, $\chi^2 = 1.9$), but significant for the four satellite channels (Sky One, UK Gold, Sky Movies, and The Movie Channel, $\chi^2 = 112.9$, $df = 3$, $p < .001$).

TABLE 3.1
Number of Programs Containing Violence

Channel	No. of Programs 1994–1995	No. of Programs 1995–1996	% Programs 1994–1995	% Programs 1995–1996
BBC1	234	250	27	29
BBC2	189	196	23	25
ITV	299	352	29	34
Channel 4	223	268	30	35
Terrestrial	944	1,066	28	31
Sky One	273	418	37	48
UK Gold	285	290	38	37
Sky Movies	263	272	79	79
Movie Channel	319	339	81	86
Satellite	1,140	1,319	52	63
All Channels	2,084	2,385	37	47
TNT/Cartoon Network	–	720	–	77
Sky Sports	–	143	–	33
Satellite	1,140	2,182	52	60
All Channels	2,084	3,248	37	45

Note: Aggregated data over 28 days

On the terrestrial channels alone, trends can be taken back to 1986, when 29% of programs monitored in a BBC-funded study were found to contain violence (across BBC1, BBC2, ITV, and Channel 4), as compared with 28% found to contain violence in programs monitored on these channels in 1994–1995 and 31% on programs monitored in 1995–1996. The findings for individual terrestrial channels also showed a pattern of consistency over time on this measure of the prevalence of television violence, with a 1986 analysis showing violence in 28% of programs on BBC1, 26% on BBC2, and 32% each on ITV and Channel 4 (Cumberbatch, Lee, Hardy, & Jones, 1987).

There were variations across television channels in the proportion of programs monitored that contained any violence. Programs on the satellite television channels were twice as likely, proportionately, to contain any violence, as were programs on the four terrestrial channels. Indeed, the satellite channels monitored in this research made a more substantial contribution toward the overall increase in violence-containing programs than did the terrestrial channels. On the terrestrial channels, there was a relatively slight increase in numbers of violence-containing programs year-on-year. The greatest actual number of such programs occurred on ITV, which along with Channel 4 also contained the greatest percentage of such programs out of those monitored. The six satellite channels exhibited far higher percentages (although not necessarily higher actual numbers) of violent programs than did the terrestrial channels. A clear majority of films broadcast on the two movie channels, Sky Movies and The Move Channel, contained any violence. The same pattern was true for the TNT/Cartoon Network.

Violent Acts and Violent Sequences

Overall, a grand total of 33,161 violent acts were cataloged across the 28 days of broadcast output monitored in 1995–1996. Of these violent acts, 24,068 occurred on the eight channels also monitored in 1994–1995, representing an increase, year-on-year, of 2898 violent acts. In all, in 1995–1996, 7,921 violent acts were found on the four terrestrial channels compared with 25,240 violent acts on the six satellite channels (see Table 3.2).

The channel displaying the single greatest number of violent acts was TNT/Cartoon Network, with a total of 7,220 acts of violence. The other major contributors, once again, were the movie channels, Sky Movies and The Movie Channel. Among the terrestrial channels, the greatest number of violent acts occurred on ITV, with a total of 3,186.

Year-on-year every channel monitored in 1994–1995, except UK Gold, showed an increase in the total number of violent acts cataloged. Significant increases occurred on the four terrestrial channels, which together showed a 27% rise in violent acts in 1995–1996 compared with the year before ($\chi^2 = 9.8$, $df = 3$, $p < .02$). On the four satellite channels for which year-on-year comparisons are possible, violent acts increased in number by around 8%, but given the overall number of violent acts

TABLE 3.2

Number and Frequency of Violent Acts

Channel	Total Number 1994–1995	Total Number 1995–1996	No. Per Program 1994–1995	No. Per Program 1995–1996
BBC1	1,406	1,652	5.9	6.6
BBC2	1,115	1,352	5.9	6.9
ITV	2,385	3,186	8.0	9.1
Channel 4	1,333	1,731	6.0	6.7
Terrestrial	6,239	7,921	6.3	7.5
Sky One	3,714	4,095	13.5	9.8
UK Gold	1,706	1,652	6.0	5.7
Sky Movies	4,758	4,523	18.1	16.6
Movie Channel	4,753	5,877	15.0	17.3
Satellite	14,931	16,147	13.1	12.2
All Channels	21,170	24,068	9.7	10.1
TNT/Cartoon Network	–	7,220	–	10.0
Sky Sports	–	1,873	–	13.1
Satellite	14,931	25,240	13.1	11.6
All Channels	21,170	33,161	9.7	10.2

on these channels, this represented a significant change ($\chi^2 = 96.8$, $df = 3$, $p < .001$).

The trends for violent sequences are very similar to those for violent acts. A total of 19,106 violent sequences were cataloged across the 10 channels monitored in 1995–1996. Over 13,000 of these occurred on the 8 channels analyzed across 2 years, which revealed a year-on-year increase of just over 22%. A significantly bigger increase in violent sequences occurred on the terrestrial channels (up by 35%) than on the satellite channels (up by just over 16%), which were monitored in 1994–1995 and 1995–1996.

Rates of Violence in Programs

The distribution of violence on television was examined in terms of the average number of violent acts appearing in violence-containing programs. These results are also shown in Table 3.2. Of all the programs monitored, violence-containing programs contained an average of just over 10 acts of violence per program. This figure was almost exactly the same for the eight channels monitored over 2 years, indicating a small increase in the average occurrence frequency of violent acts in violent programs.

Violence-containing programs on the satellite channels generally contained more violent acts (11.6) than did violent programs on the four terrestrial channels (7.5). There were marked variations between channels, however. The greatest average number of violent acts per violence-containing program occurred for the two movie channels, Sky Movies and The Movie Channel. This finding is not surprising given the fact that programs on these two channels comprise mostly feature films with a longer average running time than programs found on other nonmovie channels.

To remove this confounding factor of program length, average rates of occurrence of violent acts per hour were calculated for violence-containing programs on each channel. This revealed that average rates of occurrence of violent acts in violence-containing programs on Sky Movies (9.7 per hour) and The Movie Channel (10.6 per hour) were actually lower than the average for all satellite channels monitored (12.2 per hour). Furthermore, they were lower than the average for the four terrestrial channels (11.2 per hour). The highest rates of violence per hour in violence-containing programs occurred on TNT/Cartoon network (17.6 per hour) and Sky One (17.1 per hour). A comparison of violent act rates per hour in 1996 with those found in 1986 showed increases for BBC1 (2.4 to 2.9), BBC2 (2.1 to 2.6), and ITV (3.6 to 4.7).

Duration of Violence

The overall amount of time occupied by violence in all programs monitored was 5,227.2 minutes (87.1 hours), of which 1,045.6 minutes

(17.4 hours) occurred on the four terrestrial channels and 4,181.7 minutes (69.7 hours) on the six satellite channels. There were 2,232.7 minutes (37.2 hours) of violence on the four satellite channels monitored in 1994–1995 and 1995–1996. Year-on-year, therefore, there was an increase in minutes of violence for those 8 channels monitored across two consecutive years of just under 7% (6.6%). The terrestrial channels contributed more to this increase (up by 16.9%) than did the satellite channels (up by 2.4%). The overall increase in minutes of violence, year-on-year, was significant for both the four terrestrial channels ($\chi^2 = 57.2, df = 3, p < .001$) and for the four satellite channels ($\chi^2 = 33.6, df = 3, p < .001$).

In absolute terms, the greatest amount of violence in terms of minutes of program running time occurred on Sky Movies, followed by The Movie Channel and Sky One. Among the terrestrial channels, ITV contained the greatest amount of violence in terms of this measure (see Table 3.3).

Over all 10 channels, minutes of violence occupied 1.39% of all program running time (see Table 3.4). This figure dropped to 1.09% of program running time in respect to violence on the 8 channels also analyzed in 1994–1995. This represented a marginal (.02) year-on-year increase. The proportion of program running time occupied by violence increased year-on-year for the terrestrial channels, but decreased on the four satellite channels analyzed across 2 years. Even so, the proportion of program running time occupied by violence on these satellite channels (1.42%) was nearly double the figure for terrestrial channels (0.72%). Terrestrial channels exhibited an increase in the proportion of

TABLE 3.3

Duration of Violence

Channel	Duration of Violence in Minutes 1994–1995	Duration of Violence in Minutes 1995–1996	Year-on-Year Difference
BBC1	167.7	237.6	+41.7%
BBC2	142.4	188.1	+32.3%
ITV	442.8	413.8	–2.0%
Channel 4	141.5	205.8	+45.4%
Terrestrial	894.4	1,045.6	+16.9%
Sky One	618.9	680.3	+9/9%
UK Gold	243.4	148.4	–39.0%
Sky Movies	728.4	712.2	–2.2%
Movie Channel	590.0	691.8	+17.2%
Satellite	2,180.7	2,232.7	+2.4%
All Channels	3,075.0	3,278.3	+6.6%
TNT	–	643.2	
Sky Sports	–	1,305.8	
Satellite	2,180.7	4,181.7	
All Channels	3,075.1	5,227.2	

TABLE 3.4

Duration of Violence as a Percentage of Total Program Running Time

Channel	Duration of Violence in Minutes 1994–1995	Duration of Violence in Minutes 1995–1996	Year-on-Year Difference
BB	0.51	0.74	+.23
BBC2	0.46	0.52	+.06
ITV	1.11	1.03	−.08
Channel 4	0.37	0.57	+.20
Terrestrial	0.61	0.72	+.11
Sky One	1.74	1.70	−.04
UK Gold	0.75	0.37	−.38
Sky Movies	1.99	1.91	−.08
Movie Channel	1.62	1.73	+.11
Satellite	1.53	1.42	−.09
All Channels	1.07	1.09	+.02
TNT	–	1.60	
Sky Sports	–	3.84	
Satellite	1.53	1.81	
All Channels	1.07	1.39	

program running time occupied by violence across the 2 years, from 0.61% in 1994–1995 to 0.72% in 1995–1996, but both figures were lower than that reported in 1986 (1.1%). The channel with the single greatest proportion of program running time occupied by violence was Sky Sports (3.84%). As is revealed later in this chapter, nearly all the violence on this channel comprised boxing or wrestling matches.

Contribution of Programs Containing High Quantities of Violence

The aforementioned general measures of violence on television reported above provide a variety of different indications about the amount of violence in programs broadcast on different television channels. Between 4 and 5 in 10 programs (45%) were found to contain some violence, although this violence accounted for only around 1% of program running time. The numbers of distinct violent acts and the frequencies with which they occurred varied markedly from one channel to the next. These general measures of violence need to be treated with some caution because they may give misleading impressions about the distribution of violence across the television schedules. In the first study conducted in 1994–1995, it was found that a few programs contained considerable amounts of violence and contributed disproportionately to the overall violence levels registered for particular channels. This analysis was repeated again in the second study.

Analyses were computed to identify those programs containing 50 or more violent acts and 5 minutes or more of violence in terms of program running time. In addition to this, the top ten most violent programs, according to each of these measures, were calculated for each channel. Further analyses indicated the extent to which 50+ violent acts and 5 minutes plus programs, and the top tens in terms of violent acts and violence minutage, contributed to the overall violence scores of each television channel.

A total of 81 programs was identified across all 10 television channels containing 50 or more violent acts. These programs represented 1.1% of all programs monitored. These programs contained a total of 5,936 violent acts, or 22.8% of all the violent acts coded in this study. Table 3.5 summarizes the findings of this analysis for each of the 10 channels. Here it can be seen that in the case of three channels—BBC2, Channel 4, and Sky One—there were no programs that crossed the 50 violent acts threshold. For the remaining channels, a small proportion of programs on each channel accounted for a considerable percentage of the total violent acts cataloged for that channel.

On BBC1 and ITV, for instance, 0.3% of programs accounted for nearly 13% of the violent acts on those channels. On five out of the six satellite channels for which programs with 50+ violent acts were found, 1.8% of programs monitored on those channels accounted for nearly one quarter (24.2%) of their violent acts.

The top 10 violent programs in terms of violent acts were computed (see Table 3.6). This listing is dominated by films broadcast on the two movies channels, Sky Movies and The Movie Channel, but with the lowest placed entries being cartoons. The most violent program coded in

TABLE 3.5
Numbers of Violent Acts in Most Violent Programs (50+ Violent Acts)

Channel	No. Of Programs	Programs with 50+ Acts as % of All Programs	Violent Acts in 50+ Programs	Violent Acts in 50+ Programs as % of Total Violent Acts
BBC1	3	0.3%	208	12.6%
BBC2	–	–	–	–
ITV	9	0.9%	605	19.0%
Channel 4	–	–	–	–
Terrestrial	12	0.3%	813	16.8%
Sky Movies	20	5.8%	1,475	32.6%
Movie Channel	23	5.9%	1,773	30.2%
Sky One	–	–	–	–
UK Gold	1	0.1%	153	9.3%
TNT	15	1.6%	974	13.5%
Sky Sports	10	2.3%	748	39.9%
Satellite	69	1.8%	5,123	24.2%
All Channels	81	1.1%	5,936	22.8%

TABLE 3.6
Top Ten Violent Programs (Violent Acts)

Program Title	Channel	Acts
1. Demolition Man (Sept. 3, 1995, 10:00 p.m.)	Movie Channel	167
2. The Hidden 2 (July 18, 1995, 1:40 a.m.)	Movie Channel	118
3. The Killer (May 9, 1996, 1:10 a.m.)	Sky Movies	117
4. Little Ninjas and the Lost Treasure (Sept. 3, 1995, 8:00 a.m.)	Movie Channel	107
5. Guyver—Dark Hero (May 9, 1996, 2:50 a.m.)	Sky Movies	104
6. Showdown in Little Tokyo (April 2, 1996, 11:30 p.m.)	Sky Movies	103
7. Blood In, Blood Out (Aug. 10, 1995, 11:35 p.m.)	Sky Movies	100
8.= TC 2000 (Oct 24, 1995, 3:00 a.m.)	Sky Movies	98
8.= Super Chunk: The Impossibles (June 9, 1996, 1:00 p.m.)	TNT/Cartoon Network	98
10. Tom and Jerry (Dec. 2, 1995, 5:00 p.m.)	TNT/Cartoon Network	97

this study in terms of violent acts was the Sylvester Stallone movie, *Demolition Man*, with 167 violent acts.

The contribution of the top 10 programs on each channel to that channel's overall violent act count was calculated. The results are summarized in Table 3.7, which includes the equivalent results for the previous year as well. As this table shows, the 10 most violent programs account for a substantial proportion of the overall violence for most channels. These programs made the smallest contribution to overall violent act counts on Sky One and TNT/Cartoon Network.

For the terrestrial channels, the top 10 programs contributed more than one fifth of the total violent acts found on those channels. On Sky

TABLE 3.7
Proportion of all Violence on Each Channel Contributed by Top 10 Violent Programs (Violent Acts)

Channel	1994–1995 Number of Violent Acts	1994–1995 % of Violent Acts	1995–1996 Number of Violent Acts	1995–1996 % of Violent Acts
BBC1	395	28.1	460	27.9
BBC2	269	24.1	310	22.9
ITV	508	21.3	697	21.9
Channel 4	292	21.9	322	18.6
Sky One	795	21.4	383	9.4
UK Gold	333	19.5	463	28.0
Sky Movies	1,007	21.2	919	20.3
Movie Channel	803	16.9	988	16.8
TNT	–	–	713	9.9
Sky Sports	–	–	748	39.9

Sports, they contributed a remarkable 40% of violent acts. Even on the movie channels, where a substantial majority of broadcasts were found to contain violence, it is clear that a substantial proportion of that violence actually occurred in a relatively small part of the total output.

An analysis of the frequency of violent acts per hour in the most violent programs, violence-containing programs in general, and averaged across all channel output revealed the extent to which the most violent programs were more violent than violent programs as a whole (see Table 3.8). Across all channels, the 10 most violent programs per channel scored an average of more than 36 acts of violence per hour. This can be compared with an average of over 11 acts per hour for violence-containing programs in general.

Violent programs on the satellite (subscription) channels contained, on average, more violent acts per hour than did violent programs on terrestrial channels. The gap between the terrestrials and satellite channels for violent programs as a whole, however, was small, whereas the difference in average rates of occurrence of violent acts per hour in the most violent programs was much more significant. This finding reflects the fact that the most violent programs on channels such as Sky Movies, The Movie Channel, Sky One, and Sky Sports were heavily laden with violent acts.

Violent Act Strata

Another way of illustrating the distribution of violence across the television schedules is to show how violent acts are spread across programs containing large, moderate, and small numbers of violent acts. To pro-

TABLE 3.8

Frequency of Violent Acts in 10 Most Violent Programs

Channel	Most Violent Program	All Violent Programs	All Channel Output
BBC1	31.9	10.1	2.9
BBC2	19.3	10.4	2.6
ITV	37.7	13.8	4.7
Channel 4	24.6	10.4	3.5
Terrestrial	28.8	11.2	3.4
Sky Movies	49.7	9.7	7.7
Movie Channel	50.2	10.6	9.2
Sky One	58.9	17.1	8.3
UK Gold	27.6	7.4	2.7
TNT	45.3	17.6	13.5
Sky Sports		10.6	3.5
Satellite	41.3	12.2	7.5
All Channels	36.6	11.7	5.8

Note: 1995–1996 data only

duce this type of analysis, violence-containing programs were divided up in terms of how many violent acts they contained, according to the following five strata: 1–5 violent acts, 6–9 violent acts, 10–19 violent acts, 20–49 violent acts, and 50+ violent acts. The latter category has already been examined. For each of these stratum, figures were computed showing the number of violence-containing programs it represented and total number of violent acts contributed by the programs in that stratum.

Table 3.9 shows that more than one half the programs containing violence across all channels monitored contained five or fewer acts of violence. Around 14% of violence-containing programs contained 20+ acts of violence, but in total these programs contributed over one half of all the violent acts cataloged. This finding further confirms earlier observations that a relatively small number of programs contribute most of the violence found on television during the periods monitored in this study.

Programs containing 5 minutes or more of violence comprised nearly 3% of all programs monitored. These 194 programs contained over 55% of the total violence minutage recorded across all programs monitored. Programs that passed this threshold represented just over 4% of programs monitored on the 6 satellite channels and around 1% of programs monitored on the 4 terrestrial channels. These programs represented nearly 70% of the violence minutage on the satellite channels and nearly 39% of the violence minutage on the terrestrial channels (see Table 3.10). These findings indicate the extent to which a small proportion of very violent programs contributed to the overall amount of violence cataloged on these 10 television channels.

The 10 most violent programs were computed over all channels in terms of violence minutage and entirely consisted of boxing and wrestling matches televised on Sky Sports. Together they contained an aggregated total of 10.8 hours of violence, averaging 65.1 minutes of violence per program. These 10 programs represented just 0.1% (1 in 100) of all programs monitored, but contributed 12.5% of all violence minutage (see Table 3.11).

TABLE 3.9

Distribution of Violence Across Violence-Containing Programs Stratified by Numbers of Violent Acts—All Channels

No. of Acts	No. Of Programs with Violence	% Distribution of Programs with Violence	No. Of Violent Acts	% of Violent Acts
1–5	1,637	50.6	4,043	12.2
6–9	509	15.7	3,708	11.2
10–19	627	19.4	8,562	25.8
20–49	384	11.6	10,912	32.9
50+	81	2.5	5,936	17.9
Total	3,238	100.0	33,161	100.0

TABLE 3.10

Contribution of Program with 5 Minutes or More of Violence to
Total Violence Minutage

	Total Number Programs	Programs with 5+ Min Violence	Programs with Min Violence as % of All Programs	Total Violence Minutage in 5+ Min Programs	% of All Channel Violence in 5+ Min Programs
BBC1	876	10	1.1%	120.4	50.7%
BBC2	800	8	1.0%	60.2	32.0%
ITV	1,030	12	1.2%	175.9	42.5%
Channel 4	767	7	0.9%	60.6	29.4%
Terrestrial	3,473	37	1.1%	417.1	38.7%
Sky One	863	22	2.5%	283.9	41.7%
UK Gold	788	3	0.4%	25.3	17.0%
Sky Movies	345	40	11.6%	426.1	60.0%
Movie Channel	392	39	10.0%	349.3	50.5%
TNT/Cartoon Network	941	13	1.4%	124.4	19.3%
Sky Sports	435	40	9.2%	1,277.9	97.9
Satellite	3,764	157	4.2%	2,486.9	69.5%
All Channels	7,237	194	2.7%	2,905.4	55.6%

A further analysis was computed to identify the top 10, most violent programs outside sport. With sports broadcasts excluded, an alternative top 10 emerged consisting of a mixture of movies and British and overseas television dramas, with both the satellite and terrestrial channels having entries in the top 10 listing (see Table 3.12). The most violent program in this listing was a film called *Shootfighter*, which was transmitted on Sky Movies. This contained nearly 28 minutes of violence. In all, there were four film entries from Sky Movies and The Movie Chan-

TABLE 3.11

Top 10 Violent Programs (Min of Violence)

Program Title	Channel	Minutes
1. WWF Royal Rumble (Jan. 22, 1996, 3:00 p.m.)	Sky Sports	119.0
2. WWF XII (April 1, 1996, 1:00 a.m.)	Sky Sports	113.9
3. Live Boxing (Nov. 24, 1995, 9:00 p.m.)	Sky Sports	59.1
4. Big Time Boxing (Nov. 24, 1995, 2:00 a.m.)	Sky Sports	57.0
5. Ringside Boxing (Sept. 3, 1995, 10:00 a.m.)	Sky Sports	56.0
6. Ringside Boxing (Feb. 6, 1996, 12:30 p.m.)	Sky Sports	55.7
7. Boxing (Nov. 8, 1995, 7:30 p.m.)	Sky Sports	53.6
8. Boxing (Dec. 10, 1995, 9:00 a.m.)	Sky Sports	50.8
9. Boxing (April 22, 1996, 8:00 p.m.)	Sky Sports	43.0
10. Big Time Boxing Live (April 23, 1996, 12:30 a.m.)	Sky Sports	42.7

TABLE 3.12

Top 10 Violent (Nonsports) Programs (Min of Violence)

Program Title	Channel	Minutes
1. ShootFighter (Aug. 18, 1995, 11:55 p.m.)	Sy Movies	27.9
2. Bad Bascombe (Aug. 2, 1995, 11:00 p.m.)	TNT/Cartoon Network	27.4
3. TC 2000 (Oct. 24, 1995, 3:00 a.m.)	Sky Movies	26.8
4. Soldier, Soldier (Oct. 31, 1995, 9:00 p.m.)	ITV	21.8
5. Wings of the Apache (Dec. 10, 1995, 2:55 p.m.)	BBC1	21.6
6. Inhumanoids: The Movies (Feb. 14, 1996, 8:15 a.m.)	Movie Channel	21.5
7. The Killer (March 2, 1996, Midnight)	Sky Movies	21.3
8. Billy Two Hats (Dec. 3, 1995, 12:25 a.m.)	BBC1	18.1
9. Medics (Nov. 24, 1995, 9:00 p.m.)	ITV	17.4
10. Star Trek (April 22, 1996, 5:00 p.m.)	Sky One	17.3

nel, one entry from TNT/Cartoon Network, one entry from Sky One, and two each from BBC1 and ITV. The two ITV entries were the highest scoring British productions, namely episodes from *Soldier, Soldier* and *Medics*.

The contributions made by the top 10 programs to overall violence minutage levels per channel in 1995-1996 were compared with figures for 1994–1995 (see Table 3.13). These results indicated negligible year-on-year variations for ITV, UK Gold, and The Movie Channel, small changes for BBC2 and Sky Movies, and more substantial shifts for BBC1, Channel 4, and Sky One. In the case of BBC1 and Channel 4, the top ten programs in terms of violence minutage accounted for a larger proportion of overall violence minutage in 1995–1996 than in 1994–1995. For Sky One, the year-on-year trend was in the opposite di-

TABLE 3.13

Proportion of All Violence on Each Channel Contributed by Top 10 Violent Programs (Violence Minutage)

Channel	1994–1995 Amount	1994–1995 %	1995–96 Amount	1995–1996 %
BBC1	1.1 hours	37.9	2.0 hours	50.7
BBC2	1.0 hours	41.8	1.1 hours	36.3
ITV	3.0 hours	40.8	2.7 hours	39.8
Channel 4	0.7 hours	29.5	1.2 hours	35.7
Sky One	3.6 hours	35.2	2.0 hours	26.0
UK Gold	1.2 hours	29.6	0.8 hours	32.3
Sky Movies	2.4 hours	20.2	2.9 hours	24.8
Movie Channel	2.0 hours	20.4	2.4 hours	20.8
TNT	–	–	1.8 hours	16.8
Sky Sports	–	–	11.3 hours	51.7

rection, with the top 10 programs accounting from a substantially smaller proportion of overall violence minutage this year compared with last.

Violence Minutage Strata

As with the earlier violent acts analysis, violence-containing programs were stratified according to the amount of violence they contained, in terms of minutes or seconds of program running time. Seven such strata were created: 1–9 seconds of violence, 10–19 seconds, 20–49 seconds, 50–99 seconds, 100–199 seconds, 200–299 seconds, and 300+ seconds of violence.

Table 3.14 shows the distribution of violence-containing programs and violence minutage across these seven strata for all channels considered together. Just under one in five violence-containing programs were found to contain at least 100 seconds of violence each. Together these programs accounted for more than three quarters of all violence minutage found on the 10 channels monitored in this study.

TIME OF TRANSMISSION

Violence on television was assessed in relation to the time of transmission. This analysis was carried out to ascertain if levels of violence in violence-containing programs varied across the day. The significance of this analysis stemmed from the attempts by British broadcasters to ensure that the interests of children and their families are served in respect to transmission of programs whose content may be deemed unsuitable for very young viewers. There is, of course, a need to balance the need to protect children against the need to cater to the mature tastes of the wider adult audience. To this end, broadcasters employ a Family

TABLE 3.14

Distribution of Violence Across Violence-Containing Programs Stratified by Amount of Violence (All Channels)

No. of Seconds	No. Of Programs Violence	% Distribution of Programs with Violence	Amount of Violence (Min)	% of Violence Minutage
1–9	927	28.6	67.3	1.3
10–19	503	15.5	117.3	2.2
20–49	706	21.9	379.3	7.3
50–99	476	14.7	563.5	10.7
100–199	321	9.9	751.9	14.4
200–299	111	3.4	444.1	8.5
300+	194	6.0	2,903.9	55.6
Total	3,238	100.0	5,227.2	100.0

Viewing Policy that aims to create a balance between these two sets of needs. The balance is struck by ensuring that programs with violent content unsuitable for children to watch are restricted to those times when younger members of the audience are less likely to be viewing television. Thus, up to 9:00 p.m. in the evening on the mainstream terrestrial channels and certain satellite channels, no material may be shown that is unsuitable for children. After 9:00 p.m., there is a gradual relaxation of this rule (ITC, 1991).

On encrypted television channels, for which viewers have to pay an additional fee over the basic subscription, there may be a further relaxation of these requirements. On these channels, which are generally available via satellite or cable reception, the point at which more adult material may be shown is brought forward from 9:00 p.m. to 8:00 p.m. Further, such channels may be permitted to show material after 10:00 p.m. that would not normally be allowed on nonencrypted (i.e., terrestrially transmitted) channels or basic subscription (encrypted) channels.

For the purposes of the time of transmission analysis, the day was divided into a number of time bands to represent peak-time, non-peak-time, and pre- and post-watershed periods. Common time bands were used to compare the four terrestrial channels and four of the six satellite channels (Sky One, UK Gold, TNT/Cartoon Network and Sky Sports). In each case, here, the day was divided into five time bands: 6:01 a.m. to 6:00 p.m., 6:01 p.m. to 9:00 p.m., 9:01 p.m. to 10:30 p.m., 10:31 p.m. to midnight, and 12:01 a.m. to 6:00 a.m. For the two satellite movie channels, the day was broken into four time bands: 6:01 a.m. to 8:00 p.m., 8:01 p.m. to 10:00 p.m., 10:01 p.m. to midnight, 12:01 a.m. to 6:00a.m.

Data are presented for numbers of violent programs, violent acts, violent sequences, and amount of violence measured in minutes for violence-containing programs. As well as presenting data for the total amounts of violence coded on different television channels within particular time bands, data are also shown for the average amounts of violence occurring in violence-containing programs and amounts occurring per hour in violent programs. The measures of rates of occurrence of violence have more meaning here than do measures of total amounts of violence because the time bands vary in length. Therefore, longer time bands might be expected to contain larger amounts of violence because they cover greater amounts of broadcast time. What is more significant is whether programs containing any violence are generally more violent when they are broadcast after a particular watershed (e.g., 9:00 p.m.) than when they are shown at an earlier time.

In examining differences in levels of violence as a function of time of transmission, two distinct sets of time bands were deployed. In the case of 8 out of the 10 channels monitored, the day was divided into five time bands (as indicated in Table 3.15, which shows the numbers of programs per time band for each channel containing violence). On these

TABLE 3.15

Number of Programs Containing Violence by Time of Day

	6 a.m. 6 p.m.	6 p.m. 9 p.m.	9 p.m. 10:30 p.m.	10:30 p.m. Midnight	Midnight 6 a.m.
BBC1	137	41	41	19	12
BBC2	94	38	27	22	15
ITV	192	34	28	34	64
Channel 4	139	34	27	17	41
Terrestrial	562	147	123	92	132
Sky One	244	55	46	21	52
UK Gold	153	49	27	30	31
TNT/Cartoon Network	513	75	22	20	90
Sky Sports	71	24	13	11	24
Satellite	981	203	108	82	197
All Channels	1,543	350	231	174	329

Note: 1995–1996 data only

eight channels, violence-containing programs were recorded through-out the day. There were marked differences between channels, however, in the numbers of violent programs associated with particular day-parts.

During the daytime (between 6 a.m. and 6 p.m.) significantly more violence-containing programs appeared on the four satellite channels (Sky One, UK Gold, TNT/Cartoon Network, and Sky Sports) than on the four terrestrial channels. TNT/Cartoon Network contained the greatest number of violence-containing programs of any channel during the daytime hours. Most of this material comprised cartoons. Sky One was the second biggest contributor of violent programs during this day-part, and most of this material comprised cartoons, children's ad-venture series imported from overseas, and sport (e.g., wrestling).

Among the terrestrial channels, the greatest number of violence-con-taining programs during the day occurred on ITV, with the smallest number appearing on BBC2. During the early evening (6 p.m. to 9 p.m.), in what is generally regarded as family viewing time on the ter-restrial channels, the four satellite channels once again exceeded the terrestrials in terms of numbers of violent programs. Among the terres-trial channels, the channels were far more evenly matched in terms of violence-containing programs in the early part of the evening. The BBC channels, however, were found to have slightly more violent programs during this period than ITV and Channel 4.

During the later part of the evening, between 9 p.m. and 10.30 p.m. and between 10.30 p.m. and midnight, violence-containing programs were generally found to be more prevalent during the earlier of those two time bands across seven of the eight channels during the period for which monitoring was carried out. The exception to this rule was ITV.

BBC1 and Sky One exhibited a dramatic drop in violence-containing programs after 10.30 p.m. Both channels scored easily the highest number of programs with any violence during the immediate post-9 p.m. period. During the overnight hours, postmidnight, numbers of violence-containing programs were highest of all on TNT/Cartoon Network, and ITV was recorded as showing the largest number of violence-containing programs among the terrestrial channels at this time.

On the two satellite movie channels, Sky Movies and The Movie Channel, the distribution of television violence was examined across four time bands: 6 a.m. to 8 p.m., 8 p.m. to 10 p.m., 10 p.m. to midnight, and midnight to 6 a.m. During the daytime and early evening period, The Movie Channel showed more violence-containing programs (mostly cinema films) than did Sky Movies (204 vs. 137). The Movie Channel also showed more programs with violence than Sky Movies during the midevening (8 p.m. to 10 p.m.) period (26 vs. 21) and the postmidnight period (72 vs. 67). Sky Movies presented more violence-containing programs than The Movie Channel, however, during the late evening (10 p.m. to midnight) period (47 vs. 37).

Violent Acts

Table 3.16 shows the total numbers of violent acts coded by time band for the four terrestrial channels and four nonmovie satellite channels. Data are shown for 1994–1995 and 1995–1996. For the reason already given, there is little meaning to any comparisons between time bands because of their length variations, but a useful comparison can be made between the year-on-year differences in violent act totals for time bands on different channels.

Over the six terrestrial and satellite channels analyzed in 1994–1995, the results for 1995–1996 showed that the total numbers of violent acts had increased in four out of the five day-parts: 6 a.m. to 6 p.m. (up by 19%), 6 p.m. to 9 p.m. (up by 17%), 10:30 p.m. to midnight (up by 26%), and midnight to 6 a.m. (up by 88%). There was a reduction in violence, year on year, for the 9 p.m. to 10.30 p.m. period (down 13%). On the terrestrial channels taken together, total violent act levels increased significantly for every time band. Numbers of violent acts increased by 40% for the daytime and afternoon period (6 a.m. to 6 p.m.; $\chi^2 = 22.5$, $df = 3$, $p < .001$), by 18% for the early evening period (6 p.m. to 9 p.m.; $\chi^2 = 22.5$, $df = 3$, $p < .001$), by 9% for the immediate post-9 p.m. period (9 p.m. to 10:30 p.m.; $\chi^2 = 29.6$, $df = 3$, $p < .001$.), by 34% for the late night period (10:30 p.m. to midnight; $\chi^2 = 8.3$, $df = 3$, $p < .05$), and by 11% for the overnight period (midnight to 6 am; $\chi^2 = 8.5$, $df = 3$, p < .05).

On the two satellite channels that were analyzed in 1994–1995 and in 1995–1996 (Sky One and UK Gold), total numbers of violent acts in-

TABLE 3.16
Total Number of Violent Acts in Violence-Containing Programs on Terrestrial and Satellite Entertainment Channels as a Function of Time of Transmission

	1994–1995					1995–1996				
	6 a.m. 6 p.m.	6 p.m. 9 p.m.	9 p.m. 10:30 p.m.	10:30 p.m. Midnight	Midnight 6 a.m.	6 a.m. 6 p.m.	6 p.m. 9 p.m.	9 p.m. 10:30 p.m.	10:30 p.m. Midnight	Midnight 6 a.m.
BBC1	605	172	259	158	212	791	134	257	178	292
BBC2	473	272	172	80	118	635	355	135	88	139
ITV	931	223	227	244	760	1,535	244	244	354	809
Channel 4	735	122	103	64	307	923	195	193	113	307
Terrestrial	2,744	789	761	546	1,397	3,884	928	829	733	1,547
Sky One	2,656	421	383	173	81	2,781	464	369	101	380
UK Gold	757	138	353	135	326	691	191	107	242	421
Satellite	3,413	559	736	308	407	3,472	655	476	343	801
TNT/Cartoon Network	–	–	–	–	–	5,149	697	222	374	778
Sky Sports	–	–	–	–	–	1,187	221	132	1,514	3,395
Satellite	–	–	–	–	–	9,808	1,573	830	2,231	4,974
(All Channels)	6,157	1,348	1,497	854	1,804	7,356	1,583	1,305	1,076	2,348
All Channels	–	–	–	–	–	13,692	2,501	1,659	2,964	6,521

creased significantly during the daytime and afternoon period ($\chi^2 = 5.4$, $df = 1, p < .02$). During the early evening, there was a nonsignificant increase in violent acts on these channels ($\chi^2 = 3.1$, n.s.). During the post-9 p.m. period, in contrast, there was a significant decrease in total numbers of violent acts (down by 35%; $\chi^2 = 79.8, df = 1, p < .001$). The late night (up 11%; $\chi^2 = 47.6, df = 1, p < .001$) and overnight (up 97%; $\chi^2 = 86.7, df = 1, p < .001$) periods, however, exhibited significant increases in total numbers of violent acts.

Average rates of occurrence of violent acts were calculated to indicate more about the density of violence on television at different times of the day. Rates of occurrence were computed in two ways: first, the average frequency of occurrence of violent acts per violence-containing program, and second, the average rate of occurrence of violent acts per hour. Table 3.17 shows the average number of violent acts per violence-containing program on the four terrestrial channels and four nonmovie satellite channels. In the case of the terrestrial channels and two of the satellite channels, data are presented for 2 years of analysis.

In 1995–1996, the highest rates of occurrence of violence in violent programs generally occurred in programs broadcast after midnight. Violent programs shown during the early hours of the morning on these eight channels, during the periods monitored, contained on average nearly 12 acts of violence. The highest average rate of all occurred on BBC1, where overnight violence-containing programs averaged over 24 acts of violence. Other channels exhibited high average violent act rates for programs shown after midnight were UK Gold, ITV, and Sky Sports.

In the case of BBC1, UK Gold, and ITV, however, significant contributions toward overall numbers of violent acts occurring in postmidnight transmission were made by handful of programs. On BBC1, for example, more than one half (53.1%) of the violent acts occurring in programs shown after midnight occurred in just two movies—*Gymkata*, which contained 88 violent acts, and *Remo—Unarmed and Dangerous*, which contained 153 violent acts—equivalent to 36.3% of all postmidnight violent acts on that channel. On ITV, three foreign films—*Sartana* (91 violent acts), *Anaam* (76 violent acts), and *Jeena Marna Tere Song* (61 violent acts)—contributed more than one in four (28.2%) of violent acts occurring on that channel after midnight.

The second most violent time band, in terms of average frequency of violent acts in violence-containing programs, was the daytime/afternoon period. The overall channel average was boosted particularly by high scoring programs shown during this day-part on Sky Sports, Sky One, and TNT/Cartoon Network. The major contributing programs here were wrestling on Sky Sports and Sky One, and cartoons on The Cartoon Network and Sky One.

In 1994–1995, a notable finding was the increase in average rates of violent act occurrence in violence-containing programs broadcast in the immediate post-9 p.m. period compared with the early evening period before 9 p.m. In the 1995–1996 analysis, although the average fre-

TABLE 3.17

Average Number of Violent Acts per Violence-Containing Program on Terrestrial and Satellite Entertainment Channels as a Function of Time of Transmission

	1994–1995					1995–1996				
	6 a.m. 6 p.m.	6 p.m. 9 p.m.	9 p.m. 10:30 p.m.	10:30 p.m. Midnight	Midnight 6 a.m.	6 a.m. 6 p.m.	6 p.m. 9 p.m.	9 p.m. 10:30 p.m.	10:30 p.m. Midnight	Midnight 6 a.m.
BBC1	5.0	4.4	7.3	6.9	11.4	5.8	3.3	6.3	9.4	24.3
BBC2	5.4	8.2	5.1	5.6	7.0	6.8	9.3	5.0	4.0	9.3
ITV	6.8	6.4	8.4	9.0	11.1	8.0	7.2	8.7	10.4	12.6
Channel 4	6.0	4.8	5.6	6.5	7.0	6.6	5.7	7.2	6.7	7.5
Terrestrial	5.8	6.0	6.6	7.0	9.1	6.8	6.4	6.8	7.6	13.4
Sky One	16.8	9.9	12.9	8.1	4.1	11.4	8.4	8.0	4.8	7.3
UK Gold	5.0	4.8	9.2	5.2	8.2	4.5	3.9	4.0	8.1	13.6
Satellite	10.9	7.4	11.1	6.7	6.2	8.0	6.2	6.0	6.5	10.5
TNT/Cartoon Network	–	–	–	–	–	10.0	9.3	10.1	18.7	8.6
Sky Sports	–	–	–	–	–	16.7	9.2	10.2	5.8	11.2
Satellite	–	–	–	–	–	10.7	7.7	8.1	9.4	10.2
(All Channels)	7.5	6.4	8.1	6.9	8.1	7.2	6.3	6.5	7.2	12.4
All Channels	–	–	–	–	–	8.7	7.0	7.4	8.5	11.8

quency of violent acts again showed an increase post-9 p.m. compared with pre-9 p.m., this increase was modest, with the post-9 p.m. average falling from the level of the year before. The most marked increases in violent act rates did not occur until much later at night in 1995–1996.

The second violent act frequency analysis examined average rates of occurrence of violent acts per hour during each day-part. Table 3.18 shows the results of this analysis for the four terrestrial channels and four nonmovie satellite channels. This table shows a different pattern of results from the analysis of average rates of violence per violence-containing program. The most significant difference between these two measures can be found in the postmidnight period. This period delivered the highest rates of violent acts, when the basis of analysis was the occurrence of violence in violent programs. When examining rates of violence per hour, however, the postmidnight period was to be the least violent period. The explanation lies in the fact that the postmidnight period actually contained relatively few really violent programs, but a number of these programs contained very high numbers of violent acts. They pushed up the average violent act frequency score for postmidnight violence-containing programs. On an average rate per hour basis, however, the violent act frequency was significantly reduced because much of the postmidnight time contained none or very little violence.

The average rate of violent acts per hour measure also revealed a more pronounced increase in violence during the immediate post-9 p.m. period, although not as pronounced as that which occurred in 1994–1995. Indeed, the average rate of violence per hour in 1995–1996 showed a marked decrease on the figure for 1994–1995. The average hourly rate of violent acts exhibited a significant increase for the daytime/afternoon period. This increase was contributed toward most of all by the daytime hourly violent act rate for TNT/Cartoon Network. As noted earlier, the violence in this case was nearly all animated and found in cartoons. When removing the two new channels (TNT/Cartoon Network and Sky Sports), the average rates of violent acts per hour across all day-parts, except one, were reduced. The exception was the hourly rate for the period immediately after 9 p.m., which was higher when these two channels were removed from the analysis.

The other main quantitative indicator of the amount of violence used in this research was the amount of program running time occupied by violence. Using this measure, the total amount of violence in minutes was computed for each of five day-parts in the case of the four terrestrial channels and four nonmovie satellite channels. The results are summarized in Table 3.19.

Year-on-year, minutes of violence increased on the four terrestrial channels in the case of three day-parts, but only one of these results, for late peak-time, was significant: 6 a.m. to 6 p.m. (up 39%; $\chi^2 = 2.8$, n.s.), 9 p.m. to 10:30p.m. (up 26%; $\chi^2 = 14.0$, $df = 3$, $p < .01$), and midnight to 6 a.m. (up 16%; $\chi^2 = 3.7$, n.s.). In the case of the other two day-parts,

TABLE 3.18

Average Number of Violent Acts per Hour on Terrestrial and Satellite Entertainment Channels as a Function of Time of Transmission

	1994–1995					1995–1996				
	6 a.m. 6 p.m.	6 p.m. 9 p.m.	9 p.m. 10:30 p.m.	10:30 p.m. Midnight	Midnight 6 a.m.	6 a.m. 6 p.m.	6 p.m. 9 p.m.	9 p.m. 10:30 p.m.	10:30 p.m. Midnight	Midnight 6 a.m.
BBC1	1.8	2.0	6.2	3.8	1.3	2.4	1.6	6.1	4.2	1.7
BBC2	1.4	3.2	4.1	1.9	0.7	1.9	4.2	3.2	2.1	0.8
ITV	2.8	2.7	5.4	5.8	4.5	4.6	2.9	5.8	8.4	4.8
Channel 4	2.2	1.5	2.5	1.5	1.8	2.7	2.3	4.6	2.7	1.8
Terrestrial	2.1	2.4	4.6	3.3	2.1	2.9	2.8	4.9	4.4	2.3
Sky One	7.9	5.0	9.1	4.1	0.5	8.3	5.5	8.8	2.4	2.3
UK Gold	2.3	1.6	8.4	3.2	1.9	2.1	2.3	2.5	5.8	2.5
Satellite	5.1	3.3	8.8	3.7	1.2	5.2	3.9	5.7	4.1	2.4
TNT/Cartoon Network	–	–	–	–	–	15.3	8.3	5.3	8.9	4.6
Sky Sports	–	–	–	–	–	3.5	2.6	3.1	1.5	1.6
Satellite	–	–	–	–	–	7.3	4.7	4.9	4.7	2.8
(All Channels)	3.1	2.7	6.0	3.4	1.8	3.7	3.1	5.2	4.3	2.3
All Channels	–	–	–	–	–	5.1	3.7	4.9	4.5	2.5

TABLE 3.19

Total Amount of Violence (in Minutes) on Terrestrial and Satellite Entertainment Channels as a Function of Time of Transmission

	1994–1995					1995–1996				
	6 a.m. 6 p.m.	6 p.m. 9 p.m.	9 p.m. 10:30 p.m.	10:30 p.m. Midnight	Midnight 6 a.m.	6 a.m. 6 p.m.	6 p.m. 9 p.m.	9 p.m. 10:30 p.m.	10:30 p.m. Midnight	Midnight 6 a.m.
BBC1	74.7	19.3	33.1	13.3	27.4	111.5	10.5	28.3	39.7	47.6
BBC2	55.7	44.3	21.4	8.4	12.9	95.5	46.4	15.0	15.1	16.2
ITV	110.2	33.6	41.8	113.9	142.0	137.0	16.1	56.7	56.0	148.1
Channel 4	71.4	11.8	10.1	5.4	42.9	91.0	20.1	34.5	10.4	49.8
Terrestrial	312.0	109.0	106.4	141.0	225.2	435.0	93.1	134.5	121.2	261.7
Sky One	481.1	80.4	25.7	15.6	16.2	429.6	122.4	79.5	15.1	33.7
UK Gold	103.6	16.9	55.2	17.6	50.3	61.2	15.7	9.9	18.7	43.0
Satellite	584.7	97.3	80.9	33.2	66.5	490.8	138.1	89.4	33.8	76.7
TNT/Cartoon Network	—	—	—	—	—	375.1	70.4	30.1	56.3	111.3
Sky Sports	—	—	—	—	—	775.0	110.6	105.2	40.1	273.9
Satellite (All Channels)	—	—	—	—	—	1,640.9	319.1	224.7	130.2	461.9
(All Channels)	896.7	206.3	187.3	174.2	291.7	925.8	231.2	233.9	155.0	338.4
All Channels	—	—	—	—	—	2,075.9	412.2	448.6	285.2	723.6

minutes of violence levels decreased significantly, by 15% for the 6 p.m. to 9 p.m. period ($\chi^2 = 9.6$, $df = 3$, $p < .05$) and by 14% for the 10:30 p.m. to midnight period ($\chi^2 = 38.4$, $df = 3$, $p < .001$). Early evening decreases on terrestrial channels were, in fact, restricted to just two of these channels, BBC1 and ITV. On BBC2 and Channel 4, levels of violence increase for this day-part. In the case of the late evening (10:30 p.m. to midnight) period, the overall decrease for terrestrial channels taken together disguises the fact that a year-on-year decrease in minutes of violence for this day-part occurred only in the case of one of these channels—ITV. On ITV, there was a substantial decrease in minutes of violence in the late evening that outweighed the increases occurring on the other three terrestrial channels.

On the two satellite channels for which 2 years of data are available (Sky One and UK Gold), minutes of violence increased significantly in the case of two out of the five day-parts: 9 p.m. to 10:30p.m. (up 11%; $\chi^2 = 58.9$, $df = 1$, $p < .001$) and midnight to 6 a.m. (up 15%; $\chi^2 = 6.0$, $df = 1$, $p < .02$). For the daytime/afternoon period, between 6 a.m. and 6 p.m., total minutes of violence decreased significantly, year-on-year (down 16%; $\chi^2 = 5.7$, $df = 1$, $p < .02$). Whereas the minutes of violence on these two channels increased, year-on-year, for the 6 p.m. to 9 p.m. period, this change was nonsignificant ($\chi^2 = 1.5$, n.s.). There was virtually no change at all for the late evening (10:30 p.m. to midnight) period. The largest amount of violence, in terms of minutes of violence, occurred on Sky Sports, especially during the 6 a.m. to 6 p.m. and midnight to 6 a.m. periods, when much of the wrestling and boxing transmissions occurred.

Comparisons between day-parts were made in terms of the average amounts of violence (in minutes) that occurred in violence-containing programs as a function of time of transmission. For those channels monitored over 2 years, average minutes of violence per violent program decreased during the 6 a.m. to 6 p.m. period (1.3 min to 0.9 min), the 6 p.m. to 9 p.m. period (1.0 min to 0.9 min), and the 10:30 p.m. to midnight period (1.4 min to 1.1 min), but increased year-on-year for the 9 p.m. to 10:30 p.m. period (1.0 min to 1.1 min) and for the postmidnight period (1.3 min to 1.8 min).

Violence levels of the two satellite move channels, Sky Movies and The Movie Channel, were examined for four day-parts: 6 a.m. to 8 p.m., 8 p.m. to 10 p.m., 10 p.m. to midnight, and midnight to 6 a.m. Year-on-year comparisons revealed that violent act levels increased most noticeably during the mid to late evening periods, with an increase of 27% in total violent acts during to 8 p.m. to 10 p.m. period (643 to 818) and of 28% in the 10 p.m. to midnight period (1,653 to 2,117). Daytime, afternoon, and early evening, or pre-peak-time (6 a.m. to 8 p.m.) violent act levels increased by 9% over both movie channels taken together (4,576 to 4,978), whereas the overnight violent act count decreased by 6%, year-on-year (2,639 to 2,487).

The total minutes of violence results indicated year-on-year increases in amount of violence across the two satellite movie channels for the pre-peak-time (6 a.m. to 8 p.m.) period (up by 9%, 612 to 666) and for the late night (10 p.m. to midnight) period (up by 40%, 230 to 321). The peak-time, 8 p.m. to 10 p.m. period showed a marginal decrease in minutes of violence (96 to 94), year-on-year, whereas the postmidnight period exhibited a more significant decrease (down by 15%, 379 to 324).

On the minutes of violence measure, taking the two channels together, average amounts of violence per violence-containing program showed no difference between daytime/early evening (2.0 min for both years) and midevening periods (1.8 min in 1994–1995 and 2.0 min in 1995–1996). After 10 p.m., however, average minutes of violence exhibited an increase (3.3 min to 3.8 min), signifying that programs during this later period tended to contain more violence. After midnight, average minutes of violence fell away again to become much closer to pre-10 p.m. levels.

PROGRAM GENRES

The distribution of violence on television was examined in terms of the types of programs in which it occurred. The key measures used here included the numbers of programs in each genre in which violence occurred, the distribution of violent acts and violent sequences by genre, and the amount of violence in minutes per genre. For a number of these measures, year-on-year comparisons are made with the results from the 1994–1995 analysis.

Over all programs monitored, the genre contributing the greatest number of violence-containing programs was children's programs, of which 1,134 contained some violence (35% of all violence-containing programs) across the 10 channels covered by this analysis. The genre next most likely to contain violence-containing programs was cinema films, of which 865 contained violence (27% of violence-containing programs). A further 586 violence-containing programs (18%) occurred within the drama category comprising various British-produced and overseas drama series and serials, made-for-TV movies and single plays; 211 violence-containing programs (7%) occurred in factual output; 205 violence-containing programs (6%) in sports output; 167 violence-containing programs (5%) in entertainment output; and finally 40 violence-containing programs among music, arts, and religious programs. In the latter group of program types, much of the violence detected was found in music videos.

The basic unit of measurement of violence on television in this study was the violent act. Across the seven major genres of programing, cinema films emerged as the most significant contributor by a large margin. Table 3.20 shows the actual numbers of violent acts found in each major genre for the 1994–1995 and 1995–1996 analyses. In the case of 1995–1996, two sets of figures are presented. The left-hand column shows the distribution of violent acts across genres aggregated over

TABLE 3.20

Distribution of Violent Acts by Program Genre

Program Genre	1994–1995 N	1994–1995 %	1995–1996 Year-on-Year N	1995–1996 Year-on-Year %	1995–1996 Overall N	1995–1996 Overall %
Cinema films	11,263	53	12,797	54	14,035	43
Drama	3,420	16	3,614	15	3,651	11
Children's programs	4,008	19	5,288	22	11,233	34
Sport	728	3	599	3	2,470	7
Factual	1,013	5	666	3	666	2
Entertainment	510	2	578	2	580	2
Music/arts/religion	150	1	273	1	273	1

those channels that were also monitored in 1994–1995. Thus, these fig-ures provide a year-on-year comparison of rates of violent acts. The right-hand column presents the figures for all channels monitored in 1995–1996.

The second major contributor of violent acts after cinema films were children's programs, providing over one in three violent acts coded for these genres in 1995–1996. Other genres were, relatively speaking, much smaller contributors of violent acts.

Year-on-year, the contribution of cinema films to violent acts re-mained largely unchanged in percentage terms, and the same was true for most other genres. In 1995–96, children's programs made a some-what larger contribution to violent acts than they had in 1994–1995, and factual programs made a smaller contribution, year-on-year. Over-all, however, the total number of violent acts increased. Violence in fac-tual programs exhibited a trend in the opposite direction, showing a marked year-on-year fall in actual violent act numbers.

The other key measure of violence was the amount of program run-ning time occupied. Table 3.21 shows the distribution of minutes of vio-lence across the major program genres. The year-on-year figures show minutes of violence aggregated over those channels monitored both in 1994–1995 and 1995–1996, whereas the "overall" column shows the total amount of minutes of violence over the 10 channels monitored in 1995–1996.

Cinema films were again revealed to be a major contributor, espe-cially in the year-on-year analysis. Overall, however, sport figures prominently, largely due to the inclusion of Sky Sports in this year's analysis. The third biggest contributor overall was children's programs, for which minutes of violence also exhibited a year-on-year increase. These results also reveal the very modest overall contribution made to violence levels by factual programs and entertainment.

CONCLUSIONS

The findings reported here illustrate the varying impressions about how much violence is shown on television that can be given by different quantitative indicators of on-screen violence. Measures, such as num-bers of violent acts per hour or per program and the proportion of pro-grams that contain violence, often give the impression that there are large amounts of violence on television. These types of measures have typified earlier content analysis research in which emphasis was placed on rates of occurrence of violent incidents (Cumberbatch et al., 1987; Gerbner, Gross, Jackson-Beeck, Jeffries-Foz, & Signorielli, 1977, Gerbner, Gross, Signorielli, Morgan, & Jackson-Beeck, 1979). One im-plication of the average hourly rate is that viewers can expect to find the reported number of violent acts every hour they view. The fact that there may be wide discrepancies between channels, day-parts, pro-

TABLE 3.21

Distribution of Amount of Violence (Minutage) Across Program Genres

Program Genre	1994–1995 N	1994–1995 %	1995–1996 Year-on-Year N	1995–1996 Year-on-Year %	1995–1996 Overall N	1995–1996 Overall %
Cinema films	1,614	53	1,713	51	1,918	36
Drama	446	12	495	15	495	9
Children's programs	435	14	561	17	990	19
Sport	400	13	318	10	1,623	31
Factual	87	3	78	3	78	2
Entertainment	51	2	53	2	53	1
Music/arts/religion	12	*	110	3	110	2

Note: Year-on-year figures are for eight channels monitored in 1994–1995.
Overall figures for 1995–1996 are for all 10 channels monitored.
* Less than 0.5%

grams from different genres, and even programs from the same genre is overlooked.

The current study reported more than 33,000 violent acts in 3,248 programs, which represented 45% of all programs coded on 10 television channels over 28 days of broadcast output. A total of 6,254 hours of programing was monitored. On this evidence there was an average of 10+ violent acts per program and more than 5 violent acts per hour. This would appear to support critics who claim that television is permeated with violence. But these are also misleading statistics. Although a little under one half of all programs analyzed contained at least some violence, other quantitative indicators showed that these violent programs varied markedly in the amount of violence they contained.

A few very violent programs made a disproportionate contribution to overall levels of violence. A total of 81 programs was identified across all 10 channels in 1995–1996 that contained 50 or more violent acts. These programs represented 1.1% of all programs monitored. Together, these programs contained a total of 5,936 violent acts, or 22.8% of all the violent acts coded in this study. Some channels were found to contain more violent acts than others. But even on specific channels, a substantial proportion of all violence occurred in a relatively small number of programs. On Sky Sports, the top 10 programs in terms of violent acts contributed nearly 40% of all violent acts on that channel. On the terrestrial channels, the top 10 programs contributed, on average, at least one fifth of all the violent acts on each channel. Thus, a great deal of television violence is concentrated in small parts of the total broadcast output. It is not the case that televised violence is distributed evenly across the television schedules.

A more robust measure of the amount of violence on television may be found in the amount of program running time occupied by violence. Two violent acts may differ in length and thus, in a quantitative sense alone, they may not represent "equal" amounts of violence. Of course, even if their lengths were equal, they might still not represent equal "degrees" of violence in the eyes of viewers (see Gunter, 1985; Van der Voort, 1986). The significance of the amount of time filled by violence lies primarily in its indication of the opportunity viewers may have to be exposed to it. The smaller the portion of a program in which violence occurs, regardless of its nature, the greater the likelihood that it could be missed by viewers. Given the propensity of viewers to pay less than continuous attention to the screen or to exhibit less than continuous physical presence in the viewing room while the set is switched on, this finding is quite poignant (see Bechtel, Achelpohl, & Akers, 1972; Gunter, Furnham, & Lineton, 1995).

The overall amount of time occupied by violence over the period coded in the current study was 5,227.2 minutes (87.1 hours), of which 1,045.6 minutes (17.4 hours) occurred on the four terrestrial channels and 4,181.7 minutes (69.7 hours) on the six satellite channels. Thus, eight tenths (80%) of all violence occurred on the encrypted channels.

Over all channels, violence occupied 1.39% of all program running time. These findings underline the point that violence is not evenly distributed across television output and, in any case, represents only a tiny proportion of all broadcast airtime.

Around 3% of all programs monitored were found to contain at least 5 minutes of violence. Together, these programs contained over 55% of total minutes of violence recorded. Around 4% of the programs coded on the six satellite channels and 1% of those analyzed on the terrestrial channels passed this 5-minute threshold and accounted, respectively, for 70% and 39% of violence-occupied airtime on these channels.

The 10 most violent programs in terms of minutes of airtime occupied by violence on each channel were found, in every case, to have contributed significantly to overall violence levels. On the terrestrial channels, at least one third of all violence-occupied airtime was contributed by the 10 most violent programs. In the case of BBC1, the top 10 programs contributed more than one half the total violence-occupied airtime (50.7%) for the channel. On the satellite channels, the top 10 programs in terms of violence-occupied airtime accounted for at least one fifth of all violence-occupied airtime.

The general level of violence was disproportionately inflated by a small number of programs containing exceptionally large quantities of violence. The most violent programs tended to be either sports broadcasts, usually wrestling or boxing, or films originally made for the cinema. If these programs were discounted, then the overall levels of violence on television would drop by a considerable margin.

Contact sports could significantly inflate the overall amount of violence-occupied airtime on a channel. For example, on Sky Sports, the percentage of program running time occupied by violence when wrestling and boxing were included was 3.84%. The figure fell to 0.56% upon removal of wrestling and boxing. On BBC1, three boxing or wrestling broadcasts occurred during the 28 monitored days. These broadcasts accounted for 15% of all violence-occupied time on the channel.

The most violent channels in terms of violent act counts and percentage of programs that contain any violence were the two premium movie channels, Sky Movies and The Movie Channel. On these two channels, 79% and 86% of programs, respectively, contained violence, and together they contributed one third (34%) of all violent acts across the 10 channels. Yet, on Sky Movies, less than 6% of all movies contributed one third (33%) of violent acts on the channel. On The Movie Channel, less than 6% of movies contributed 3 in 10 violent acts (30%) found on the channel. The top 10 movies in terms of violence-occupied time account for between one quarter and one fifth of all violence-occupied airtime on Sky Movies and The Movie Channel (24.8% and 20.8%, respectively).

The amount of violence broadcasts on television varied with the time of day. Average violent act rates in violence-containing programs provided some indication about whether the density of violence varied greatly as a function of day-part. Across nonexclusively movie channels (i.e., excluding Sky Movies and The Movie Channel), violent act rates were highest in programs broadcast after midnight (11.8). Programs broadcast immediately after 9 p.m. (7.4) contained higher average violent act rates than did programs broadcast during the immediately preceding day-part (7.0). Daytime violent act rates (8.7) were higher than those registered in the evening, however. This was largely a function of the relatively high rates of violence found in cartoons.

In keeping with the expectations of Family Viewing Policy, violent act rates were markedly higher post-9 p.m. than pre-9 p.m. on the terrestrial channels. In general, average hourly violent act rates were higher during the 9p.m. to midnight period than during the early evening. These rates dropped dramatically among programs shown after midnight. The latter finding indicated that even though there may have been relatively average rates of violence per program after midnight, this violence generally occurred in long programs (i.e., movies), which brought down the average hourly rate.

Violence-occupied airtime also varied with day-part. In general, the average amount of violence in minutes per violence-containing program was greater immediately after 9 p.m. than immediately before it. This finding was true of all channels, except BBC2, which exhibited a drop in average violence-occupied airtime in violent programs shown after 9 p.m. compared with those shown before 9 p.m. On the two satellite movie channels, Sky Movies and The Movie Channel, the day was divided into four day-parts. The key boundaries were 8 p.m. and 10 p.m. Programs shown after 10 p.m. and before midnight contained the highest rates of violent acts (25.2) and greatest average amount of violence-occupied airtime (3.8 minutes).

A number of important variations in levels of violence were associated with program genre. Once again, however, the genres judged to be the worst offenders depended on which quantitative measures were examined. The genre contributing the greatest number of violence-containing programs was children's programs (43% of all violent programs). The biggest genre contributor to the overall violent act count, however, was cinema films (43%), with children's programs in second place (34%). The average hourly rate of violent acts was generally highest in cinema films and children's programs. The greatest contributor of violence in terms of program running time was cinema films (36% of total violence-occupied airtime), followed by sport (31%) and children's programs (19%).

The current analysis has indicated that there are various ways in which the quantity of violence on television can be expressed. Different measures of television violence can give different impressions about how much violence is contained in television programs. Although a substantial minority of programs over the channels and days monitored were found to contain at least some violence, in terms of overall program running time, violence represented a small part of television output. What also emerged was the fact that, in addition to violence on television occurring at a low level in terms of program running time, much of the television output monitored contained little or no violence at all. Less than 3% of the programs monitored contributed well over one half (56%) of all violence-occupied airtime. This indicates that the great proportion of programs either contained no violence at all or relatively small amounts of it. These findings suggest a need to rethink the notion that television is permeated by violence. Whereas violent acts are distributed across a substantial minority of programs, much of this violence is contained in just a handful of broadcasts.

Chapter 4

Forms of Violence on Television

Violence on television can take many different forms. This chapter examines the different kinds of violent behavior that were found on British television, with special reference to the kinds of weapons used by perpetrators. For example, violent actors may use their body as a weapon (e.g., punching or kicking a victim) or they may use handheld weapons (e.g., guns, knives, or some other object). Some violence on screen that takes place in military contexts may involve more sophisticated forms of aggression, including bombs or explosives, missiles, tanks, aircraft, and ships. In other cases, more subtle forms of violence, such as poisoning or psychological torture, may be used. This aspect of screen violence is important because viewers are known to be sensitive to the form of violence in their emotional reactions to and their perceptual judgments of television portrayals. There has also been some indication that the presence of weapons can serve as a trigger to aggressive behavior among viewers.

It was observed in the early 1960s that viewers who watched a knife fight scene from a movie displayed increased punitiveness toward others in a laboratory setting as compared with similar viewers who were shown a nonviolent scene (Walters & Thomas, 1963; Walters, Thomas, & Acker, 1962). Some years later, research conducted among 5- to 9-year-old children found that they behaved in a more hurtful than helpful way toward their peers after watching a crime drama sequence containing a chase, two fistfights, two shootings, and a knife scene than after watching an exciting sports sequence (Liebert & R. A. Baron, 1972). Although these experiments suggest that scenes depicting the use of weapons may trigger antisocial conduct in viewers, they do not differentiate between forms of violence in terms of their individual capacity to produce specific types of audience response.

WEAPONS EFFECT

The significance of images of weapons may have the power to trigger aggression in observers because they serve as reminders of violence that has been learned in the past (Berkowitz, 1970; Berkowitz & LePage, 1967). Behavioral research on the so-called weapons effect has produced mixed evidence for this effect. Studies have reported that the presence of actual weapons or pictures of weapons in the laboratory was sufficient to make an already angered person more likely to behave aggressively toward the source of his anger under controlled conditions (Berkowitz, 1971; Berkowitz & LePage, 1967; Leyens, Cisneros, & Hossay, 1976; Leyens & Parke, 1975; Tannenbaum, 1971). Other laboratory studies failed to produce this effect (Cahoon & Edmonds, 1984, 1985; Halderman & Jackson, 1979; Page & Scheidt, 1971). Some studies even produced the opposite effect, finding that the presence of weapons reduced aggression (A. Buss, Booker, & E. Buss, 1972; Ellis, Wienir, & Miller, 1971). A meta-analysis of 56 published experiments found that the presence of weapons or images of weapons in the same environment as the tested individuals could enhance their aggressive responding whether or not they had previously been angered (Carlson, Marcus-Newhall, & Miller, 1990).

The different results may be linked to the type of dependent measure used by different researchers. Studies that used real behavior as the dependent variable showed a weapons effect (e.g., Berkowitz & LePage, 1967; Caprara, Rentz, Amolini, D'Imperio, & Travaglia, 1984; Leyens & Parke, 1975; Page & O'Neal, 1977). When the dependent variable is a self-report of probable behavioral control or response in a given situation, there is less support for the weapons effect. Participants who see weapons and are given a chance to physically harm another person afterward, will display enhanced aggressiveness as compared to others who have not been shown weapons. In contrast, when participants are asked to report their own hostility in hypothetical situations, they do not show this effect.

The weapons effect is also sensitive to the type of participant. Page and Scheidt (1971) ran three experiments on college students and were able to find the weapons effect in only one study in which the participants were slightly sophisticated and aware of the purpose of guns. This finding was reflected in a meta-analysis of research into situational aggression cues by Carlson et al. (1990), who reasoned that the weapons effect is limited to participants who are low in sophistication and evaluation apprehension.

DIFFERENTIATING FORMS OF VIOLENCE

Throughout most of this research, however, the emphasis was placed on whether the presence of a weapon caused different observer reactions than the absence of a weapon. Only one study made an attempt to vary the levels of violent content to find out if the degree of aggressiveness associated with an image could be significant to the strength of participants' reactions. Leyens and Parke (1975) compared viewers' behavioral aggressive reactions under a mood of anger and frustration, following exposure to photographic slides that had been defined as high, moderate, or low in aggressive content. These slides depicted, respectively, a revolver, a whistle, and a box of chocolates. Exposure to the revolver slide elicited the most aggression. However, the validity of the whistle slide as an image of moderate aggression must be questioned.

According to Berkowitz (1990), weapons such as guns and knives are more likely than unconventional means to instigate or prime aggression in viewers because they are commonly associated with previous violent events stored in memory. Thus, "a television portrayal that features traditional weapons poses the greatest risk for the so-called 'weapons effect' on audiences" (Kunkel et al., 1996, p. I-21)

Research into viewers' perceptual distinctions between different kinds of violence has provided clearer insights into the significance of this attribute of on-screen violence. An American study of boys' perceptions of scenes from programs that involved different types and degrees of violence indicated that viewers learn from an early age to differentiate between scenes of violence on the basis of their form. In this case, scenes of violence that involved weapons such as hand guns or rifles were rated as more violent and less acceptable than scenes depicting hand-to-hand combat (Greenberg & Gordon, 1972c).

British research among adult viewers also found that ratings of the seriousness of television violence were influenced by the means of violence being used. Scenes featuring shootings and stabbings were perceived as far more violent than fight scenes in which antagonists used their fists. Within the same research program, violent scenes from a western film were rated in a series of pair-wise comparisons to produce an overall rank order from most to least violent: (1) a fight with sword, (2) a knife throwing incident, (3) cannons being fired at a fortress, (4) a gun fight in a street, (5) a perpetrator clubbing a victim from behind with a gun butt, and (6) a fistfight between two protagonists. The same research found that program context could mediate audience perceptions of different physical forms of violence. Viewers were much more sensitive to the means of violence in a contemporary and more realistic dramatic setting than in one removed from everyday reality (Gunter, 1985).

PREVALENCE OF VIOLENT FORMS

Some previous content analysis studies have differentiated violent scenes or violent actions in terms of the form of violence depicted. American research conducted over many years reported that over one half the incidents of violence coded in mainstream network, prime-time television involved the use of weapons (other than the aggressor's own body) (Gerbner, 1972; Gerbner et al, 1979, 1980a). The nature, levels, and distributions of weapons on screen over time were observed to remain fairly stable (Gerbner et al, 1979, 1980). In a study of music videos, more than one in three violent acts (35%) were committed with a weapon (Sherman & Dominick, 1986).

By the mid-1990s, on American television, the most commonly occurring means of violence was that using *natural means*, which meant violence in which perpetrators used their body as a weapon (i.e., punching, pushing, kicking, tripping, etc.). The second most commonly occurring form of violence involved the use of a handheld firearm. In reality-based programs, guns were used in more than 4 in 10 (44%) of visually depicted violent interactions (*National Television Violence Study*, 1997, 1998).

Further research on the data collected by the National Television Violence Study in the United States explored the issue of "graphicness." This included an assessment of the role of weapons in scenes of televised violence (Potter & Smith, 1999). In this context, graphicness was operationally defined in terms of how much blood and gore was shown and the degree to which the actions of perpetrators and the suffering of victims were shown in close-up (occupying 65% or more of the screen), in long shot, or not at all. These authors found that graphicness in television violence was more likely when conventional weapons (e.g., guns and knives) were used, and more so when heavy weaponry was depicted. When perpetrators used heavy weaponry—such as missiles, bombs, torpedoes, bazookas, and hand grenades—the portrayals were less graphic than when perpetrators fired a gun or stabbed their victims.

Previous content analysis studies of violence on television in Britain distinguished between forms of violence. Researchers at the British Broadcasting Corporation found that shootings featuring hand guns and rifles (39% of violence) and fistfights (37%) were the most commonly occurring forms of violence on British television in the early 1970s. These were followed in decreasing order of prevalence by stabbing instruments (12%), domestic items such as chairs or vases (8%), specialized instruments such as traps or poisons (8%), hitting or lashing instruments (7%), and finally military equipment and explosives (6%) (Shaw & Newell, 1972).

By the mid-1980s in Britain, television violence was found frequently to involve shootings, fistfights, and other kinds of physical assault such as tripping or shoving, and the deployment of a wide range of more specialized forms of violence (Cumberbatch et al., 1987). The body was used in more than one in three (35%) incidents of televised violence observed in this study, and objects such as knives and clubbing instruments added a further one in eight violent forms (12%). One third of violent incidents on British screens involved some form of shooting instruments (e.g., guns, bows, and arrows).

FORMS OF VIOLENCE ON BRITISH TV IN THE 1990S

The results reported up to this point focused on purely quantitative measures of amounts of violence and where they occurred in the broadcast output that was monitored. It is important, however, to go beyond simple counts of violence to examine the shape and form it takes on. Violence, as defined for the purposes of this study, covers a variety of behaviors, styles, and instruments of aggression. As already pointed out, the nature of portrayed violence has significant implications for how viewers are likely to respond to it.

This research examined the nature of violent forms on television in three ways. First, each violent act was classified according to whether it represented a first strike or retaliatory acts by a perpetrator, or self-inflicted action of characters or persons against themselves. Second, violent acts were categorized into 53 different types of behavioral activity. Third, all violent acts were classified in terms of the kinds of weapons or instruments of aggression that were used. Here, 48 different coding categories were used. The data obtained were able to show which types of violence were most commonly occurring and, in the case of violence known through audience research, to represent potentially problematic content for viewers and how often such incidents occurred.

PROACTIVE VERSUS REACTIVE VIOLENCE

Adopting a pattern that will be followed throughout this chapter, the results obtained in the 1995–1996 analysis of British television will be compared with those found in 1994–1995. The great majority of violent acts coded in 1995–1996 represented "first strikes" by a perpetrator. Nearly 7 in 10 (69.1%) fell into this category, shifting hardly at all from the year before (69.5%). More than 1 in 4 violent acts in 1995–1996 (27.8%) represented retaliatory acts (1994–1995, 26.7%). A tiny number took the form of self-inflicted violence (0.8%). Year-on-year, there was little overall change in the occurrence of these types of violence. Both years showed an increase in first strike aggression compared with findings from 1986, when 60% of violent acts were coded as falling into this category of violence (Cumberbatch et al., 1987).

The aforementioned patterns of violence were repeated fairly closely in respect to each of the terrestrial channels in the 1995–1996 analysis (see Table 4.1). The major departure occurred in the case of BBC2, where there was a substantially higher than average number of acts that remained uncoded on this dimension.

A similar pattern of results largely prevailed for the six satellite television channels included in the current study. There was, however, a somewhat larger than average proportion of violent acts classified as retaliatory on The Movie Channel and Sky Sports, and especially on the latter. In the case of Sky Sports, this is probably a function of most of the

TABLE 4.1

Proactive and Reactive Violence on Terrestrial Channels

	% of Violent Acts	
	1994–1995	*1995–1996*
BBC1		
First strike	72.1	70.7
Retaliatory	25.1	24.7
Self-inflicted	0.5	0.6
Cannot code	2.3	4.1
BBC2		
First strike	71.8	69.3
Retaliatory	15.9	24.3
Self-inflicted	0.2	0.5
Cannot code	12.2	5.8
ITV		
First strike	69.7	68.3
Retaliatory	26.7	28.3
Self-inflicted	0.6	0.5
Cannot code	3.0	5.8
Channel 4		
First strike	72.1	71.5
Retaliatory	22.4	26.2
Self-inflicted	0.7	0.3
Cannot code	4.9	2.0

violence occurring in contact sports, such as boxing and wrestling, where both protagonists in a bout readily inflict violence (see Table 4.2).

FORMS OF VIOLENT BEHAVIOR

Violent acts were differentiated in terms of the nature of the displayed behavior. Types of violence were coded under 53 different categories. These categories were then grouped together under nine broad headings: use of body, handheld weapons, execution, injury outcomes, torture/cruelty, threat of violence, property, military/explosions, and miscellaneous.

The most commonly occurring types of violence involved use of the body (12,724 or 38% of acts), followed by incidents involving handheld weapons (9,519, or 29% of acts), and incidents involving the threat of violence (4,621, or 14% of acts). These three broad categories of violence were also the most prevalent forms of violence recorded in the 1994–1995 analysis. Less frequently occurring categories were violence involving military weapons or explosions (1,056 acts, or 3%), violence classified according to various types of injury outcome (747 acts, or 2%), violence involving property (675 acts, or 2%), with various forms

TABLE 4.2
Proactive and Reactive Violence on Satellite Channels

	% of Violent Acts	
	1994–1995	1995–1996
Sky One		
First strike	64.6	68.3
Retaliatory	34.0	27.8
Self-inflicted	0.2	0.3
Cannot code	1.2	3.6
UK Gold		
First strike	74.7	72.2
Retaliatory	22.8	25.2
Self-inflicted	0.7	0.6
Cannot code	1.7	2.0
Sky Movies		
First strike	70.0	68.9
Retaliatory	25.5	28.7
Self-inflicted	0.7	1.0
Cannot code	4.1	1.4
Movie Channel		
First strike	69.0	65.9
Retaliatory	27.6	31.7
Self-inflicted	0.4	0.4
Cannot code	3.1	2.0
Sky Sports		
First strike	–	60.5
Retaliatory	–	37.2
Self-inflicted	–	–
Cannot code	–	2.2
TNT/Cartoon Network		
First strike	–	73.0
Retaliatory	–	23.8
Self-inflicted	–	1.7
Cannot code	–	1.4

of torture (322 acts) and executions (168 acts) being relatively rare (see Table 4.3)

The 10 most commonly occurring types of violence found in the 1995–1996 analysis are listed in Table 4.3, and comparisons are made with results from 1994–1995. The composition of the two lists is exactly the same, although certain forms of violence have changed their rank. The overall numbers for 1995–1996 are larger, of course, because two additional channels were monitored. The ranks and percentages of total acts represented by each type provide interesting points of comparison, year-on-year.

Violence involving a perpetrator pushing or tripping a victim and violence involving a shooting were the two most common forms in both

TABLE 4.3

Top 10 Types of Violence

		1994–1995				1995–1996	
		No. Acts	% Acts			No. Acts	% Acts
1.	Shoot at	4,183	19.8	1.	Push/trip	6,148	18.5
2.	Push/trip	3,707	17.5	2.	Shoot at	5,950	17.9
3.	Punch	2,314	10.9	3.	Attempted violence	3,719	11.2
4.	Hit/object	1,868	8.8	4.	Hit/object	3,053	9.2
5.	Verbal threat	1,653	7.8	5.	Punch	3,006	9.1
6.	Kick	1,141	5.4	6.	Sport aggression	1,921	5.8
7.	Attempted violence	754	3.6	7.	Kick	1,338	4.0
8.	Throwing	717	3.4	8.	Verbal threat	902	2.7
9.	Explosion	499	2.4	9.	Throwing	744	2.2
10.	Sport aggression	486	2.4	10.	Explosion	646	1.9

years, although they swapped first and second positions. "Attempted violence" moved up from seventh place to third place in 1994–1995, exhibiting a marked increase in its rate of occurrence. Violence in which a perpetrator hit a victim with an object was in fourth position both years running, and violence involving one actor punching another slipped from third to fifth position. The increased prevalence of sport aggression is primarily a function of the inclusion of Sky Sports in the 1995–1996 analysis, and pushed violence involving an aggressor kicking a victim down one place. Verbal threat also fell away to some extent in 1995–1996, and neither the rank nor the frequency of occurrence of violence involving a perpetrator throwing something at a victim or explosions changed significantly (see Table 4.4).

Channel Differences

Aggregating over the different types of violent behavior, the percentages of violent acts represented by different major categories of violence were calculated. These are summarized, for the terrestrial channels, in Table 4.5. These data show that violence on television, for the channels and periods monitored, was dominated by various forms of unarmed aggression, using various parts of the body (e.g., hand or fist, foot, head, etc.) and, second, by handheld firearms and involved perpetrators shooting at their intended target. Use of the body as a weapon characterized more than one third of all violence on the terrestrial channels. The use of handheld weapons accounted for nearly another third of violent acts. In addition, around 1 in 10 violent incidents on screen comprised the threat of violence, rather than the actual carrying through of

TABLE 4.4
Types of Violent Act

	% of Violent Acts	
	1994–1995	*1995–1996*
Use of Body		
Push/trip	17.5	18.5
Punch	10.9	9.1
Kick	5.4	4.0
Throwing	3.4	2.2
Slap	2.1	1.7
Fall/throw	1.0	1.0
Strangle	0.9	0.9
Bite	0.7	0.8
Scratch	0.1	0.1
Total	42.3	38.3
Handheld		
Shoot at	19.8	17.9
Hit with Object	8.8	9.2
Stab	2.0	1.0
Fire	0.3	0.2
Poison	0.2	0.2
Spray	0.1	0.1
Total	31.2	28.6
Execution		
Electrocution	0.2	0.3
Decapitation	0.1	0.1
Lethal Injection	0.1	*
Gassing	0.1	0.1
Hanging	*	*
Total	0.5	0.5
Injury Outcomes		
Crushed	0.8	0.5
Wounding	0.5	0.2
Cut	0.5	0.3
Burn	0.4	0.6
Self Wounding	0.2	0.3
Trample	0.2	0.2
Fracture of Bones	0.1	0.1
Blinding	0.1	*
Total	2.8	2.2
Torture/cruelty		
Torture	0.2	0.2
Bullying	0.2	0.4
Cruelty	0.2	0.1
Psychological Torture	0.2	0.2
Rape	0.1	0.1
Total	0.9	1.0

(continued)

TABLE 4.4 (continued)

	% of Violent Acts	
	1994–1995	1995–1996
Threat of Violence		
Verbal Threat	7.8	2.7
Attempted Violence	3.6	11.2
Total	11.4	13.9
Property		
Damage to Property	1.1	1.6
Damage to Car	0.4	0.3
Car Explosion	0.1	0.1
Total	1.6	2.0
Military/explosions		
Explosion	2.4	1.9
Bombardment	1.5	0.8
Other Disaster	0.1	0.3
Sink/scuttle	0.1	0.1
Chemical Explosion	0.1	*
Nuclear Explosion	0.0	*
Total	4.2	3.1
Miscellaneous		
Sport Aggression	2.4	5.8
Trap	0.9	1.8
Abduction	0.7	0.8
Supernatural	0.5	0.6
Sabotage	0.1	0.2
Suffocation	0.1	*
Drown	0.1	0.1
Cannibalism	0.1	*
Disease	0.0	*
Total	5.7	9.3

* less than 0.05%

an aggressive response. On these occasions, an aggressor made an overt threat toward an intended victim and indicated a clear intention to do the victim some harm.

Thus, although a variety of different forms of violent behavior can be observed on mainstream television channels, this behavior tends to be dominated by relatively few categories of behavior. In the case of the terrestrial channels, the pattern of violent behavior forms observed in 1995–1996 exhibited a similar character and distribution to the pattern seen in 1994–1995.

A similar analysis was conducted for the satellite television channels monitored in this study. Generally, the observations made about violent forms on the terrestrial channels held true also for the satellite channels. Violence involving the use of the body as a weapon, or involving the use

TABLE 4.5

Distribution of Major Types of Violence on Terrestrial Channels

	% of Violent Acts			
	BBC1	BBC2	ITV	Channel 4
1994–1995				
Use of body	45.4	35.5	42.0	41.9
Handheld weapon	29.9	34.2	28.7	29.2
Threat of violence	7.9	6.8	12.2	10.0
Military/explosions	2.8	10.2	5.2	4.1
Injurious outcomes	2.7	3.1	2.8	2.3
Property related	1.8	3.1	1.1	1.0
Torture/cruelty	0.5	2.0	0.8	1.3
Execution	0.6	0.7	0.3	0.8
Miscellaneous	5.6	4.7	5.7	8.1
Uncoded	2.8	0.8	0.8	1.5
1995–96				
Use of body	40.7	35.7	36.7	39.6
Handheld weapon	27.1	31.7	32.5	32.1
Threat of violence	10.5	15.4	12.0	11.9
Military/explosions	4.4	6.0	3.0	3.9
Injurious outcomes	2.2	2.0	1.7	1.4
Property-related	3.3	1.7	2.7	2.4
Torture/cruelty	1.9	1.3	0.5	0.7
Execution	0.5	0.4	0.6	0.2
Miscellaneous	8.8	4.9	9.5	6.9
Uncoded	0.5	0.8	0.8	1.0

of handheld firearms, was predominant across all satellite channels, with the exception that handheld weapons hardly featured at all on Sky Sports. In the latter case, most violent acts were categorized under "miscellaneous," a general heading that subsumed the category of "sport aggression" (see Table 4.6).

The threat of violence was, with the exception again of Sky Sports, solidly in third place among the most frequently occurring forms of violence. Indeed, this category represented a larger percentage of violent acts on satellite channels than on terrestrial channels.

Across the 2 years for which this analysis of television violence has run, the distribution of different forms of violence in 1995–1996 resembled that from 1994–1995. There were no signs of any radical change in the dominant forms of violence occurring on these channels. Interestingly, even on TNT/Cartoon Network (a new channel included for the first time in the current study), where most violence occurred in cartoons, the distribution of violent forms took on a similar pattern to that observed on other channels where cartoons made a much less significant contribution to overall violence.

TABLE 4.6

Distribution of Major Types of Violence on Satellite Channels

	Sky One	UK Gold	Sky Movies	Movie Channel	Sky Sports	TNT/Cartoon Network
				% of Violent Acts		
1994–1995						
Use of body	43.6	46.0	42.3	36.6		
Handheld weapon	28.0	24.0	33.3	34.7		
Threat of violence	9.6	15.0	11.6	13.0		
Military/explosions	3.3	5.0	3.3	3.5		
Injurious outcomes	1.5	1.6	3.2	3.8		
Property-related	1.9	2.5	1.3	1.2		
Torture/cruelty	0.5	0.7	1.0	0.7		
Execution	0.6	0.7	1.0	0.7		
Miscellaneous	9.4	3.3	2.3	3.2		
Uncoded	1.3	1.2	1.2	1.2		
1995–1996						
Use of body	39.9	43.8	39.3	39.7	38.1	35.1
Handheld weapon	26.2	29.2	30.8	31.4	1.2	31.0
Threat of violence	13.5	14.0	17.2	17.5	0.2	14.7
Military/explosions	3.8	3.5	1.9	2.9	0.1	3.7
Injurious outcomes	1.4	2.0	2.9	2.0	0.1	3.6
Property-related	1.5	2.3	2.1	2.3	0.2	1.9
Torture/cruelty	1.1	0.6	1.2	1.1	–	1.3
Execution	0.6	0.3	0.4	0.5	0.1	0.8
Miscellaneous	11.3	3.7	3.8	3.0	60.0	6.5
Uncoded	0.6	0.6	0.5	0.3	0.2	1.4

The most commonly occurring forms of violence were also examined for each channel. For the two BBC channels, there was little variation from the overall top 10 membership. The top 10 composition exhibited little if any change, year-on-year. Violence involving shootings and someone pushing or tripping someone else represented the most common forms of violence on these two channels. Attempted violence improved its rank and frequency of occurrence in 1995–1996 as compared with 1994–1995 for both channels (see Table 4.7).

The most frequently occurring forms of violence on the commercial terrestrial channels were similar to those observed on the BBC channels. In the case of both ITV and Channel 4, the most popular forms of depicted violent behavior involved perpetrators shooting at, pushing or tripping, or punching victims. In confirming earlier results, threatened or attempted violence also featured among the most frequent types of violent act on both channels.

Comparing the results from 2 years of analysis revealed that the top 10 listings for both channels remained largely unchanged. In fact, with ITV, there were no changes in the composition of the top 10, only in the positions of individual categories of violence within that listing. On

TABLE 4.7

Top 10 Types of Violence on BBC Channels

	1994–1995	% Acts		1995–1996	% Acts
BBC1					
1.	Push/trip	20.2	1.	Push/trip	23.5
2.	Shoot at	19.3	2.	Shoot at	17.2
3.	Punch	12.5	3.	Punch	8.9
4.	Hit with object	8.9	4.	Attempt. viol.	8.5
5.	Verbal threat	5.7	5.	Hit with object	7.5
6.	Throwing	4.5	6.	Sport aggression	4.6
7.	Sport aggression	3.8	7.	Property damage	3.1
8.	Kick	3.0	8.	Explosion	2.5
9.	Slap	2.8	9.	Throwing	2.5
10.	Attempted violence	2.2	10.	Kick	2.4
BBC2					
1.	Shoot at	22.1	1.	Shoot at	22.9
2.	Push/trip	16.8	2.	Push/trip	18.9
3.	Hit with object	9.4	3.	Attempted violence	12.0
4.	Verbal threat	4.9	4.	Punch	8.4
5.	Bombardment	4.5	5.	Hit with object	7.9
6.	Explosion	4.4	6.	Verbal threat	3.4
7.	Kick	3.3	7.=	Explosion	2.7
8.	Throwing	2.7	7.=	Kick	2.7
9.	Slap	2.1	9.	Use of trap	2.4
10.	Attempted violence	2.0	10.	Slap	2.1

Channel 4, there was one change, with property damage coming into the top 10 and violence involving an aggressor hitting a victim with an object falling away (see Table 4.8).

Turning to the satellite channels, the two nonthematic channels, Sky One and UK Gold, produced top 10 listings for forms of violence in which, once again, shootings, pushing or tripping, and punching occupied the top slots. Attempted or threatened violence also figured prominently in each top 10 listing. Year-on-year, there were few changes in the nature of the behaviors that represented the most frequently occurring forms of violence shown on screen on these channels. There was just one change in the composition of the top 10 on Sky One, with damage to property disappearing and kicking coming in. On UK Gold, there were two changes to the top 10 violent forms listing. Violence involving a perpetrator throwing something at a victim and violence involving damage to property fell outside the top 10 in 1995–1996, with sports aggression and incidents in which aggressors slapped their victim entering the listing (see Table 4.9).

On the two satellite movie channels, Sky Movies and The Movie Channel, the most frequently occurring forms of violence were largely the same as those seen on other channels (e.g., shootings, pushing/tripping, punching, and threatened or attempted violence). As elsewhere, year-on-year, there were more similarities than differences between the

TABLE 4.8

Top 10 Types of Violence on Independent Television Channels

	1994–1995	% Acts		1995–1996	% Acts
ITV					
1.	Push/trip	21.2	1.	Shoot at	22.9
2.	Shoot at	20.2	2.	Push/trip	17.3
3.	Punch	11.1	3.	Attempted violence	9.0
4.	Verbal threat	8.6	4.	Hit with object	8.3
5.	Hit with object	6.9	5.	Punch	7.9
6.	Kick	3.8	6.	Sport aggression	5.9
7.	Attempted violence	3.6	7.	Kick	4.9
8.	Sport aggression	3.4	8.	Verbal threat	3.0
9.	Explosion	3.3	9.	Property damage	2.2
10.	Throwing	2.2	10.	Explosion	2.1
Channel 4					
1.	Shoot at	18.7	1.	Shoot at	22.6
2.	Push/trip	15.5	2.	Push/trip	17.7
3.	Punch	12.2	3.	Punch	10.7
4.	Hit with object	9.2	4.	Attempted violence	10.7
5.	Verbal threat	7.1	5.	Hit with object	8.7
6.	Sport aggression	6.3	6.	Kick	4.3
7.	Kick	4.3	7.	Sport aggression	4.2
8.	Throwing	3.9	8.	Slap	2.4
9.	Slap	3.5	9.	Property damage	1.7
10.	Explosion	2.4	10.	Explosion	1.7

top 10 listings. On Sky Movies, violence involving stabbings and explosions fell outside the top 10, and were replaced by sports aggression and violence in which an aggressor threw something at an intended victim. On The Movie Channel, stabbings again, together with violence in which a victim was crushed, fell away from the top 10, and were replaced by violence involving property damage and kicking (see Table 4.10).

On TNT/Cartoon Network, the most frequently occurring forms of violence were push/trip (18.5%), hitting with an object (14.9%), shooting (14.7%), attempted violence (12.4%), punching (7.6%), use of a trap (3.7%), throwing an object or projectile at an intended victim (3.1%), explosions (2.6%), kicking (2.6%), and verbal threat (2.4%). Despite the fact that most of the violence on this channel occurred in cartoons, the most frequent forms of violence identified were similar to those found on other channels. On Sky Sports, 60% of violent acts were categorized as sports aggression, with a further 14% involving pushing or tripping and 7% punching behavior.

TYPES OF WEAPONS

Violence was classified not only in terms of types of behavior, but also according to the different types of weapons used. There were 48 ba-

TABLE 4.9

Top 10 Types of Violence on Satellite Entertainment Channels

1994–1995	% Acts		1995–1996	% Acts
Sky One				
1. Shoot at	19.4	1.	Push/trip	19.8
2. Push/trip	15.6	2.	Shoot at	18.8
3. Punch	11.6	3.	Attempted violence	11.2
4. Hit with object	7.4	4.	Punch	8.8
5. Sport aggression	6.1	5=	Kick	6.1
6. Throwing	6.0	5=	Hit with object	6.1
7. Verbal threat	5.1	7.	Sport aggression	6.0
8. Attempted violence	4.5	8.	Throwing	3.0
9. Explosion	2.4	9.	Verbal threat	2.3
10. Property damage	1.3	10.	Explosion	2.3
UK Gold				
1. Push/trip	25.8	1.	Push/trip	26.1
2. Shoot at	16.3	2.	Shoot at	16.3
3. Verbal threat	12.8	3.	Attempted violence	10.9
4. Punch	9.3	4.	Hit with object	10.7
5. Hit with object	5.5	5.	Punch	10.0
6. Kick	4.1	6.	Verbal threat	3.1
7. Explosion	2.9	7.	Sport aggression	2.4
8. Throwing	2.7	8.	Slap	2.3
9. Attempted violence	2.2	9.	Kick	2.2
10. Property damage	2.0	10.	Explosion	2.2

sic-level weapon types applied in this classification. These were further reduced to 11 broad categories: body, gun (military), gun (criminal), other shooting instrument, knife/stabbing instrument, throwing instruments, clubbing instruments, vehicle, animal, other instruments (including chemicals, electricity, gas), and other varied instruments.

Considering first the pattern of usage of different instruments of aggression across all channels for the total period of analysis, the most commonly used weapons comprised various parts of the body. In all, nearly one half of the acts of violence cataloged (16,125, or 48.6% of acts) involved the use of the assailant's body as a weapon. Nearly 3 in 10 violent acts (29.5%) involved the use of the fist or hand alone. Other subcategories of this general category comprised karate/martial arts moves, kicking, headbutting, throwing/pushing, use of some other body part (e.g., elbow or knee), or in a very few instances, the use of a false hand (see Table 4.11).

The next most prevalent types of weaponry comprised some form of military hardware (machine gun, pistol, rifle, explosives, other military hardware), which comprised nearly 13% of violent acts overall. The category was followed by the use of guns in criminal contexts (7% of violent acts). As in 1994–1995, the most common single type of weapon was the use of a hand gun, usually in a criminal context.

TABLE 4.10
Top 10 Types of Violence on Satellite Movie Channels

1994–1995	% Acts		1995–1996	% Acts
Sky Movies				
1. Shoot at	20.7	1.	Shoot at	21.1
2. Push/trip	16.9	2.	Push/trip	16.9
3. Punch	10.5	3.	Attempted Violence	13.2
4. Hit with object	9.1	4.	Punch	9.2
5. Verbal threat	8.5	5.	Hit with object	7.6
6. Kick	6.9	6.	Kick	5.6
7. Attempted violence	3.1	7.	Verbal threat	4.1
8. Slap	3.0	8.	Slap	2.5
9. Stab	2.9	9.	Sport aggression	2.3
10. Explosion	2.2	10.	Throwing	1.9
Movie Channel				
1. Shoot at	19.5	1.	Push/trip ·	20.6
2. Push/trip	12.8	2.	Shoot at	20.0
3. Hit with object	11.6	3.	Attempted violence	13.9
4. Punch	10.6	4.	Hit with object	9.2
5. Verbal threat	7.9	5.	Punch	8.9
6. Attempted violence	5.1	6.	Kick	4.3
7. Throwing	3.1	7.	Verbal threat	3.6
8. Stab	2.9	8.	Slap	2.1
9. Slap	2.1	9.	Property damage	1.8
10. Crushed	1.8	10.	Throwing	1.6

Other categories of weapons, in order of frequency of occurrence, were the use of other shooting instruments (e.g., laser weapons, bow and arrow, cross-bow, flame thrower, water cannons, etc.), use of a knife or stabbing instrument (including a sword, dagger, domestic knife, hunting knife, hook, etc.), clubbing instrument (e.g., a stick, truncheon/bat, whip/cane, axe, or hammer), a throwing instrument (e.g., a spear or lance), use of a variety of means of poisoning or destroying a victim (e.g., chemicals/drugs, electricity, gas, boiling liquid, etc.), use of a vehicle, and use of a trained animal.

Over all channels, the single most frequently occurring instrument of violence was the fist or hand. This occurred almost four times as often as the second most frequently occurring type of weapon, which was another part of the body. In 1995–1996, the top 10 types of weapons were dominated by the use of various parts of the body as a weapon and by the use of handheld firearms (e.g., hand gun, laser weapon, pistol, and rifle). If violence did not involve an assailant hitting, pushing, or kicking a victim, then it involved a victim being shot at. Year-on-year, the composition of this top 10 listing was largely unchanged. There was one new entrant: use of a pistol replaced use of a machine gun (see Table 4.12).

TABLE 4.11
Types of Weapons Used in Acts of Violence

	% Violent Acts	
	1994–1995	*1995–1996*
Body		
Fist/hand	28.3	29.5
Kick	4.4	4.6
Karate/martial arts	3.9	2.7
Throw/push	2.9	4.0
Headbutt	0.4	0.4
False hand	0.1	0.1
Other part of body	4.7	7.3
Total	44.7	48.6
Gun (Military)		
Machine gun	3.2	2.2
Rifle	3.1	2.7
Pistol	2.9	3.8
Explosives	1.9	2.0
Military hardware	1.8	2.1
Total	12.9	12.8
Gun (Criminal)		
Handgun	7.5	5.5
Shotgun	2.2	1.2
Sawn-off shotgun	0.3	0.1
Total	10.0	6.8
Knife/Stabbing Instrument		
Sword	4.1	2.8
Dagger	1.3	0.7
Domestic knife	0.4	0.3
Hunting knife	0.4	0.2
Hook	0.1	0.1
Other stabbing instrument	1.0	0.8
Total	7.3	4.9
Other Shooting Instrument		
Laser weapon	3.7	4.2
Bow and arrow	0.8	0.6
Cross-bow	0.2	0.1
Flame thrower	0.1	0.2
Tear gas	0.1	*
Water cannons	0.0	0.1
Total	4.9	5.2
Clubbing Instrument		
Stick (various)	2.6	2.3
Truncheon/baseball bat	0.7	0.8
Whip/cane	0.4	0.6
Pickaxe/axe	0.4	0.3
Hammer	0.3	0.5
Stone	0.1	0.2
Total	4.5	4.7

(continued)

TABLE 4.11 *(continued)*

	% Violent Acts	
	1994–1995	*1995–1996*
Throwing Instrument		
Spear or lance	0.6	0.4
Other projectiles	1.6	1.2
Total	2.2	1.6
Vehicle		
Car	0.8	0.5
Lorry	0.1	0.1
Bulldozer	*	0.1
Chariot	0.0	*
Other vehicle	0.6	0.5
Total	1.5	1.2
Animal		
Trained animal	0.3	0.3
Other Instruments		
Chemical/drugs	0.4	0.4
Electricity	0.3	0.4
Liquid	0.2	0.3
Gas	0.1	0.2
Boiling liquid	0.1	0.1
Total	1.1	1.4
Other	10.3	12.6
Multiple	0.7	–

* less than 0.05%

TABLE 4.12
Top 10 Weapon Types

		1994–1995				*1995–1996*	
		No. Acts	*% Acts*			*No. Acts*	*% Acts*
1.	Fist or hand	5,972	28.3	1.	Fist or hand	9,801	29.5
2.	Handgun	1,559	7.5	2.	Other body part	2,428	7.3
3.	Other body part	1,004	4.7	3.	Hand gun	1,839	5.5
4.	Boot/kick	933	4.4	4.	Boot/kick	1,523	4.6
5.	Sword	861	4.1	5.	Laser weapon	1,388	4.2
6.	Karate	831	3.9	6.	Throw/push	1,315	4.0
7.	Laser weapon	788	3.7	7.	Pistol	1,253	3.8
8.	Machine gun	675	3.2	8.	Sword	939	2.8
9.	Rifle	667	3.1	9.	Karate	907	2.7
10.	Throw/push	625	2.9	10.	Rifle	882	2.7

Channel Differences

On the four terrestrial channels, violence was dominated by the use of the body as a weapon or by the use of guns either in military or criminal contexts. Together these weapon types accounted for well over one half of all violent acts on each channel. There were a few modest degrees of variation between channels. Use of the body as weapon accounted for a smaller proportion of violent acts on BBC2 than on the other terrestrial channels. The depiction of military weaponry, meanwhile, accounted for a smaller proportion of violent acts on BBC1 than other terrestrial channels (see Table 4.13).

The presence of stabbing instruments was more pronounced among violent acts on the two BBC channels than on the two commercial terrestrial channels. The use of shooting instruments other than military weaponry or firearms in criminal contexts, however, comprised a smaller proportion of violent acts on BBC1 than on the other three channels.

Turning to the satellite channels, violence was found to exhibit a similar pattern in terms of the distribution of different types of weaponry. In

TABLE 4.13

Distribution of Different Types of Weapons on Terrestrial Channels

	% of Violent Acts			
	BBC1	*BBC2*	*ITV*	*Ch.4*
1994–1995				
Body	45.7	36.0	42.9	46.8
Gun (military)	15.3	21.3	14.5	14.0
Gun (criminal)	9.9	6.2	13.8	7.0
Knife/stabbing instrument	3.4	7.2	4.6	4.8
Clubbing instrument	3.6	6.0	3.8	3.9
Throwing instrument	6.9	2.4	2.6	4.0
Other shooting instrument	3.5	4.9	1.6	4.7
Vehicle	1.0	1.1	2.0	0.6
Animal	0.1	0.3	0.3	0.3
Other instrument	12.9	13.7	13.2	14.2
1995–1996				
Body	47.9	40.2	47.0	45.0
Gun (military)	9.9	15.1	16.0	15.1
Gun (criminal)	10.7	9.6	9.8	9.7
Knife/stabbing instrument	5.6	6.5	3.0	3.0
Clubbing instrument	4.1	4.7	3.7	3.5
Throwing instrument	2.2	1.6	1.0	1.8
Other shooting instrument	3.7	7.0	4.5	5.9
Vehicle	1.7	0.6	1.9	0.8
Animal	0.7	0.1	0.5	0.1
Other instrument	13.4	14.5	12.4	15.1

general, violent portrayals were again dominated by the use of the body as a weapon, and the use of guns either in military or criminal contexts. Year-on-year comparisons across the two nonthematic channels (Sky One and UK Gold) and the two movie channels (Sky Movies and The Movie Channel) indicated similar weapon type profiles in 1994–1995 and 1995–1996. Once again, Sky One exhibited an especially pronounced other shooting instrument profile, which largely reflects the use of futuristic shooting weapons in science fiction settings on this channel.

In the 1995–1996 study, two new satellite channels were added—Sky Sports and TNT/Cartoon Network. In the latter, violence occurred mainly in cartoon settings. In the case of the former, most violence occurred in the context of contact sports like boxing and wrestling. It is not surprising, then, to find that most of the violence on Sky Sports involved the use of the body as weapon. This category was also prominent on TNT/Cartoon Network, although no more so than on other channels (see Table 4.14).

TABLE 4.14
Distribution of Different Types of Weapons on Satellite Channels

	% of Violent Acts					
	Sky One	UK Gold	Sky Movies	Movie Channel	Sky Sports	TNT/Cartoon Network
1994–1995						
Body	53.9	48.9	43.5	39.1		
Gun (military)	5.0	11.4	13.5	15.0		
Gun (criminal)	4.5	9.7	14.7	8.7		
Knife/stabbing instrument	3.9	4.3	8.2	12.7		
Clubbing instrument	3.4	3.3	4.6	5.4		
Throwing instrument	1.4	1.5	1.7	2.7		
Other shooting instrument	13.2	6.8	1.4	2.6		
Vehicle	2.7	1.9	1.1	1.1		
Animal	0.4	0.1	0.3	0.3		
Other instrument	0.9	1.6	0.9	1.1		
Other/multiple weapons	10.2	10.2	9.6	10.9		
1995–1996						
Body	50.4	52.2	47.3	45.6	96.4	40.9
Gun (military)	4.6	9.2	17.8	13.4	0.1	6.8
Gun (criminal)	8.4	11.3	12.0	12.8	0.2	7.2
Knife/stabbing instrument	5.0	5.7	6.4	7.7	0.2	3.8
Clubbing instrument	2.8	4.4	4.5	5.4	0.9	7.0
Throwing instrument	1.2	1.2	0.9	1.9	0.2	2.2
Other shooting instrument	12.4	2.9	0.6	2.4	0.2	5.3
Vehicle	1.2	0.8	1.4	0.9	0.1	1.6
Animal	0.3	0.2	0.3	0.2	–	1.6
Other instrument	13.6	12.1	8.8	9.8	2.0	24.8

The 10 most popularly used weapons were listed for each channel in turn to provide further insights into the profile of weaponry on different terrestrial and satellite television channels. On the two BBC channels, the use of the hand or fist was the more frequently occurring type of weapon. In addition, other uses of the body as a weapon, together with the use of handheld firearms, were the most commonly occurring instruments of violence.

There were more similarities than differences in top 10 weapons listings for these two channels, year-on-year. Two types of weapon, "other" projectiles and use of a pistol, fell out of the BBC1 top 10 in 1995–1996 to be replaced by military hardware and use of a sword. On BBC2, there were three changes. Falling out of the top 10 from 1994–1995 were use of rifles, explosives, and stick, which were replaced by use of a laser weapon, pistol, and throw or push (see Table 4.15).

On the two commercial terrestrial channels, a similar profile was found in the top 10 listings of most commonly occurring weapon types. Once again, use of the body as a weapon and use of handheld firearms dominated the listings for ITV and Channel 4. Year-on-year, the top 10 listings maintained a slightly lower level of consistency than that ob-

TABLE 4.15
Top 10 Weapon Types on BBC Channels

	1994–1995	% Acts		1995–1996	% Acts
BBC1					
1.	Fist/hand	32.9	1.	Fist/hand	26.4
2.	Handgun	5.9	2.	Throw/push	8.3
3.	Throw/push	4.6	3.	Other body part	6.3
4.	Rifle	4.2	4.	Hand gun	5.8
5.	Machine gun	4.1	5.	Boot/kick	3.9
6.	Other body part	3.8	6.	Laser weapon	3.4
7.	Shotgun	3.7	7.	Military	3.2
8.	Kick	3.6	8.	Machine gun	2.8
9.	Other projectiles	3.2	9.=	Shot gun	2.4
10.=	Laser weapon	2.9	9.=	Sword	2.4
10.=	Pistol	2.9			
BBC2					
1.	Fist/hand	25.4	1.	Fist/hand	25.7
2.	Military hardware	8.7	2.	Laser weapon	6.6
3.	Hand gun	5.4	3.	Military	5.7
4.=	Sword	5.1	4.	Other body part	5.6
4.=	Rifle	5.1	5.	Hand gun	4.9
6.	Other body part	4.3	6.=	Sword	4.0
7.	Boot/kick	3.6	6.=	Throw/push	4.0
8.	Explosives	3.5	8.	Machine gun	3.6
9.=	Machine gun	2.5	9.	Pistol	3.3
9.=	Stick	2.5	10.	Boot/kick	2.6

served with the two BBC channels. There were four changes to the top 10 for ITV and three in the case of Channel 4. On ITV, use of a shotgun, sword, explosives, and karate fell out of the listing, and in came use of a laser weapon, military hardware, pistol, and throw or push. On Channel 4, use of a sword, various projectiles, and explosives fell out of the top 10 and, in 1995–1996 were replaced by use of military hardware and machine guns (see Table 4.16).

On the two nonthematic satellite channels, Sky One and UK Gold, use of the body as a weapon and use of handheld firearms again dominated the top 10 listing. On Sky One, however, use of such instruments as a laser weapon and the use of karate were more prominent than in other top 10 listings, reflecting the program sources of much of the violence on this channel, namely, futuristic science fiction series and children's action series featuring martial arts heroes. There were two changes to the listings of each channel. On Sky One, use of a stick and vehicle as weapons fell out of the top 10 and were replaced in 1995–1996 by use of explosives and a pistol. On UK Gold, use of a machine gun and military hardware did not make the 1995–1996 list. There was one new entrant, use of a sword (Table 4.17).

TABLE 4.16

Top 10 Weapon Types on Independent Television Channels

	1994–1995	% Acts		1995–1996	% Acts
ITV					
1.	Fist/hand	28.9	1.	Fist/hand	29.3
2.	Handgun	9.7	2.	Hand gun	6.6
3.	Other body part	6.1	3.	Rifle	5.8
4.	Machine gun	4.9	4.	Other body part	5.8
5.	Shotgun	4.1	5.	Boot/kick	5.4
6.	Boot/kick	3.3	6.	Laser weapon	3.9
7.	Karate	3.2	7.	Military	3.4
8.	Rifle	3.0	8.	Machine gun	3.4
9.	Explosives	2.9	9.	Throw/push	3.3
10.	Sword	2.4	10.	Pistol	3.1
Channel 4					
1.	Fist/hand	34.5	1.	Fist/hand	29.9
2.	Handgun	5.4	2.	Hand gun	7.0
3.	Rifle	4.2	3.	Pistol	6.9
4.	Boot/kick	4.1	4.	Laser weapon	5.6
5.	Pistol	3.9	5.	Throw/push	4.7
6.	Laser weapon	3.5	6.	Other body part	4.7
7.	Sword	3.3	7.	Boot/kick	4.5
8.	Other projectiles	3.1	8.	Rifle	
9.	Other body part	2.9	9.	Military	3.8
10.=	Explosives	2.7	10.	Machine gun	2.5
10.=	Throw/push	2.7			2.0

TABLE 4.17
Top 10 Weapon Types on Satellite Entertainment Channels

1994–1995		% Acts	1995–1996		% Acts
Sky One					
1.	Fist/hand	27.7	1.	Fist/hand	31.1
2.	Laser Weapon	12.4	2.	Laser weapon	11.8
3.	Other body part	7.5	3.	Karate	6.9
4.	Boot/kick	6.8	4.	Other body part	6.3
5.	Karate	6.3	5.	Boot/kick	4.3
6.	Throw/push	5.0	6.	Hand gun	4.0
7.	Handgun	3.6	7.	Sword	3.6
8.	Stick	2.4	8.	Explosives	2.7
9.	Sword	2.1	9.	Throw/push	1.8
10.	Other vehicle	1.9	10.	Pistol	1.7
UK Gold					
1.	Fist/hand	37.1	1.	Fist/hand	37.0
2.	Handgun	6.2	2.	Handgun	6.9
3.	Laser weapon	5.6	3.	Other body part	5.9
4.	Boot/kick	4.3	4.	Throw/push	5.1
5.	Other body part	4.0	5.	Boot/kick	3.9
6.=	Rifle	2.6	6.	Rifle	3.2
6.=	Machine gun	2.6	7.	Laser weapon	2.8
8.	Throw/push	2.3	8.	Sword	2.7
9.=	Pistol	2.2	9.	Pistol	2.7
9.=	Shotgun	2.2	10.	Shot gun	2.2
9.=	Military hardware	2.2			

On the two satellite movie channels, Sky Movies and The Movie Channel, there was very little difference in the top 10 listings from those witnessed for other channels. Use of the hand or fist was once again the most frequently occurring instrument of aggression, situated considerably ahead of the next most frequently occurring type of weapon, which in 1995–1996 (on these channels) was the use of a pistol. For both channels, top 10 listings were dominated by various uses of the body as a weapon and use of handheld firearms.

On Sky Movies, there were three changes to the top 10 listing from 1994–1995 to 1995–1996. Use of a part of the body other than the foot or hand, use of a shotgun, and use of a stick as instruments of aggression were replaced by use of a pistol, use of military hardware, and use of a throw or push. On The Movie Channel, there was just one change in weapon types. Use of a throw or push replaced use of a stick in 1995–1996 (see Table 4.18).

On TNT/Cartoon Network, the top 10 weapon types were use of hand/fist (23.3%), other body part (10.2%), laser weapon (4.9%), boot/kick (3.6%), throw/push (3.1%), stick (3.0%), hand gun (2.6%), pistol (2.6%), explosives (2.5%), and a sword (2.2%). As noted before,

TABLE 4.18
Top 10 Weapon Types on Satellite Movie Channels

1994–1995		% Acts	1995–1996		% Acts
Sky Movies					
1.	Fist/hand	25.7	1.	Fist/hand	27.9
2.	Hand gun	11.4	2.	Pistol	9.3
3.	Karate	6.7	3.	Hand gun	8.8
4.	Machine gun	5.1	4.	Karate	6.7
5.	Boot/kick	4.5	5.	Oth. body part	5.2
6.	Other body part	4.1	6.	Boot/kick	4.6
7.	Sword	3.4	7.	Machine gun	3.7
8.	Shotgun	3.0	8.	Sword	3.3
9.=	Rifle	2.8	9.	Rifle	3.0
9.=	Stick	2.8	10.	Throw/push	2.5
9.=	Military hardware	2.2			
Movie Channel					
1.	Fist/hand	25.3	1.	Fist/hand	27.9
2.	Sword	8.9	2.	Pistol	9.3
3.	Handgun	6.9	3.	Hand gun	8.8
4.	Pistol	5.3	4.	Karate	6.7
5.	Rifle	4.2	5.	Oth. body part	5.2
6.	Other body part	3.8	6.	Boot/kick	4.6
7.	Kick	3.5	7.	Machine gun	3.7
8.	Stick	3.3	8.	Sword	3.3
9.	Karate	3.2	9.	Rifle	3.0
10.	Machine gun	3.1	10.	Throw/push	2.5

much violence on this channel occurred in cartoons. Nevertheless, the top 10 weapons listing exhibited a remarkable degree of similarity to the listings for other channels. On Sky Sports, the majority of violent acts involved the use of the hand or fist (64.4%), boot or kick (10.5%), throw or push (8.8%), or headbutt (1.2%). This reflected the fact that nearly all the violence on this channel occurred in contact sports such as boxing or wrestling.

CONCLUSIONS

This chapter examined the varying forms in which violence on British television occurred. The nature of violent scenes, in terms of the kinds of behaviors displayed and the different types of aggressive instruments that were deployed, holds more than simple intrinsic interest. The form that violence takes on screen is important in the context of audience reactions. Viewers differentiate between violent scenes, in part, in terms of the type of violence featured. Certain forms of violence are rated as more violent and more disturbing than others (Gunter, 1985). Unarmed combat is usually regarded as less problematic than violence involving the use of weapons such as firearms or knives.

Behavioral psychologists have also found that the mere presence of weapons can serve as a cue to aggression among observers (Berkowitz & LePage, 1967; Carlson et al., 1990). In the current study, violent portrayals were classified under 53 different categories of behavior and according to 48 different types of weapon. Much violence on television, however, was dominated by a relatively small number of forms of violence. The top 10 violent forms accounted for around 82% of all violent acts across 1994–1996. The top 10 weapon types accounted for around two in three violent acts (66%–67%) across the 2 years of program monitoring. The most commonly occurring types of violence overall were those involving the use of the body (12,724 or 38% of violent acts), incidents involving handheld weapons (9,519, or 29% of acts), or incidents involving the threat of violence (4,621, or 14% of acts). The 10 most commonly occurring types of violence included incidents in which an assailant pushed or tripped another person (18.5% of acts), shot at a target (17.9%), or attempted to attack a target but did not complete or carry out that action (11.2%). The 10 most frequently occurring types of violence in 1995–1996 were very similar to those found in 1994–1995. Hence, the presence of violence involving the use of weapons was not rare. These results mirror, to some extent, findings from American research, which also observed that the most frequently occurring forms of violence on television involved perpetrators using their own bodies to commit violence, such as by hitting, punching, or kicking their target. When weapons were used, handheld firearms were most commonly used (Wilson et al., 1996).

The violence type profiles were similar across terrestrial channels and from one year to the next. For all four terrestrial channels, use of the body in violence, use of handheld weapons, and incidents involving the threat of violence were the three most commonly occurring categories. On the satellite channels monitored in this study, the overall violence type profiles were very much the same again. Use of the body, violence featuring handheld weapons, and incidents involving the threat of violence were the key categories. There were few differences between channels in terms of the most frequently occurring types of violence, nor did the top 10 listings change very much from one year to the next.

Types of weapons confirmed the types of violence findings. Nearly one in two violent acts involved the use of various parts of the body as a weapon (48.6% of acts). This was followed by the use of military weapons (12.8% of acts), the use of handheld weapons in a crime context (6.8% of acts), and the use of a clubbing instrument (4.7% of acts).

The most frequent weapon types of all were the fist or hand (9,801, or 29.5% of acts), use of some part of the body other than the hand or foot (2,428, or 7.3% of acts), and use of a hand gun (1,839, or 5.5% of acts). These three weapon types also occupied the top three places in

1994–1995. These results were consistent with results obtained for American television during the mid-1990s, which showed that the most common form of violence involved perpetrators using their body as a weapon by punching, pushing, tripping, or kicking their target (*National Television Violence Study*, 1997, 1998). The American–British comparisons are examined in more detail in chapter 10.

Weapon type profiles across channels exhibited far more similarities than differences. Use of the body as a weapon was significantly more prevalent on Sky Sports (96.4% of acts) than anywhere else, however, because most violence on this channel involved boxing or wrestling.

Violent acts were classified in terms of whether they represented a first strike by a perpetrator or retaliatory action. For the most part, violence on British television in the mid-1990s was proactive in nature. Nearly 7 of 10 violent acts (69.1%) comprised a first strike, with a little over 1 in 4 (27.8%) taking the form of retaliation. These results were very similar to those from 1994–1995.

Across different terrestrial channels, the previous pattern of violent acts was fairly consistent throughout. Most acts of violence represented a first strike by an aggressor. The same result was found throughout on the satellite channels. The highest proportion of retaliatory actions was found on Sky Sports, where most of the violence took place inside boxing or wrestling matches in which both opponents were engaged in initiating and reacting to violence.

Content analysis cannot reveal anything directly about how viewers will respond to particular violent acts. It can, however, indicate how often acts occur that are regarded as potential causes of psychological distress to viewers or triggers of antisocial behavior among certain members of the audience. Graphic portrayals on American television have been associated closely with the use of weapons such as guns and knives. When these weapons are used, it is often the case that scenes will contain more close-up shots of blood and gore, and pain and suffering on the part of victims of violence (Potter & Smith, 1999). Such scenes are known, via separate audience research studies, to give rise to negative perceptual and attitudinal responses among viewers (Gunter, 1985; Docherty, 1990; Morrison, 1993b).

Chapter **5**

Motives and Consequences of Violence on Television

Criminology has long been concerned with the motives and consequences of crime. Motive is the key to understanding the criminal and thereby to developing effective methods of crime prevention, on the one hand, and treatment and rehabilitation of offenders, on the other. Motive goes hand in hand with consequences. Criminal acts depend on there being a suitable victim who will experience the consequence of crime. Motive and consequence are at the polar ends of the continuum of crime. They are kept apart by "guardians of persons or property" (Hopkins Burke, 2001, p. 45). Such guardians may be the police, private security, individuals or groups such as Neighborhood Watch, physical deterrents such as fencing or lighting, or technology such as closed circuit television. According to Hopkins Burke, the likelihood of crime increases when there is one or more persons present who are motivated to commit a crime, a suitable target or potential victim that is available, and the absence of formal, or informal guardians who could deter the potential offender (p. 45).

Consequences for victims may be immediate or longer term physical or psychological damage to a person and not necessarily unrelated to those outcomes: damage to property, removal of property, covert costs (e.g., the increased cost of goods to cover theft from shops), and changed behaviors. In a major shift from the traditional focus on the offender and the role of the penal system, victimology is now a major part of criminology research and a central part of the British Home Office's strategy for criminal justice. Police and courts increasingly take account of the victim who may seek financial compensation from the perpetrator in certain circumstances. Moreover, sentencing is moving toward an acknowledgment of victims' experiences and needs. Reparation is an increasingly familiar term, especially in juvenile courts where offenders are encouraged or ordered by the court to make amends, if only by apology, to their victims. Other, not dissimilar, processes include the shaming of perpetrators within their communities by making their motives, such as kerb-crawling and soliciting in order to buy sex from prostitutes, public.

THE CONTEXTUAL SIGNIFICANCE OF MOTIVES AND CONSEQUENCES

Motives and consequences color the perceptions of crime, not only of the police and those working in the criminal justice system, but also of the general public whose consensus to the law and its operational processes is essential for social order. Public opinion about the use of violence, for instance, is affected by the degree to which such action is regarded as justified or legitimate. Violence of an official nature, such as that used by the police, may be regarded as more acceptable than similar actions perpetrated by a law breaker (Gamson & McEvoy, 1972). Indeed, police violence may not be regarded as violent at all in certain contexts (Blumenthal, Kahn, Andrews, & Head, 1972).

Motive is central to decision-making processes within the criminal justice system and to the application of the law. Premeditated crime is treated more harshly and more punitively than opportunist crime. In British courts, pleas may be changed from murder to manslaughter, for example, or sentencing may be ameliorated by pleas of "diminished responsibility" or "temporary loss of control" due to provocation (Wykes, 1995). Premeditation is seen as the peak of offending. The planned execution of a crime with deliberate intent is normally viewed more seriously by police, courts, and public, than crimes committed out of opportunism or due to provocation—even when the actual criminal act is identical in each case.

For example, date rape tends to be less frequently reported to the police by victims, less frequently prosecuted, and less successfully prosecuted (Gregory & Lees, 1999). The victim is often viewed as compliant or even preemptive of the crime. The offender may be ascribed motives of friendliness, affection, and sociability that become distorted by the victim's actions, clothing, or familiarity into sexual overtures. Gregory and Lees (1999) pointed out, "The implication here is clearly that this type of rape is of a totally different order from 'real' rape and is due to men misreading signals and being confused" (p. 101). Date rapists' motives are often seen as understandably mistaken sexual goals, given that offender and victim may know each other and have other relationships (e.g., work or mutual friends). The crime (if recognized as such at all) may be ascribed to misplaced opportunism brought about by the interpreting of friendly signals as sexual invitation.

Stranger rape, on the other hand, tends to be much more severely castigated and punished (although prosecution is still relatively difficult to pursue and a guilty verdict is hard to secure unless the consequences are traumatic and the motives clearly predatory and violent). Yet both crimes are broadly the same and the consequences for the victim may be equal. Ironically, it may possibly be even more difficult to recover from date rape, where trust has been abused, physical violation endured, the likelihood of sympathy and empathy may be considerably lessened, and social life dramatically curtailed.

Motive and consequence are therefore twin key aspects to the understanding of real crime. They affect the perception and treatment of criminals and victims by the state and its various criminal justice institutions. Those discourses also filter through to public perceptions about the seriousness of crime, effectiveness, and justice of treatment, and the rights and roles of victims. This process takes place largely through the news media because, despite something of a public panic about crime (especially violent crime), relatively few people actually experience crime (Home Office, 1999).

The harms caused by on-screen violence produce distinct audience reactions. Viewers rate violent acts resulting in serious harmful consequences as more violent than similar acts that produce no such consequences (Gunter, 1985). Among children, the sight of a victim being hurt can generate more anxious responses and encourage more destructive play behavior after viewing has finished (Noble, 1975). Among adults, however, laboratory research into controlled aggressive responding after viewing selected scenes of film violence indicated that violence resulting in an obviously painful outcome for a victim inhibited subsequent aggressive behavior (Goranson, 1970; Hartmann, 1969). The latter reaction, however, was confined to viewers who had not been angered prior to viewing, that is, those who had subsequently exhibited enhanced aggressiveness after watching a violent scene in which the pain and suffering of the victim was depicted (Hartmann, 1969). Hence, the consequences of screen violence represent an important discriminating variable that can exert a direct impact on how audiences psychologically respond to the violence.

Because motive and consequence are central to an understanding of real crime issues, it follows that their portrayal in fiction will also affect the audience's perception of the act being portrayed. That perception may in turn impact on viewers understanding of the "real" analogy. Understanding the way that motive and consequence are part of crime narratives in the mass media may therefore help illuminate the debates around effects. This becomes even more key when the crime is one of violence because violent crime is the one most individuals are least likely to experience directly and therefore they depend on other sources for information about violence. Moreover, violence at its most extreme attracts most condemnation and greatest punishment, so motives and consequences may be key to public acceptance of criminal justice processes and legislation. If violence is portrayed in the media in contexts of justifiable motive or without serious consequence, then there may be reasons to be concerned about the undermining of moral value and increases in violence, or less contentiously the acceptance of violence as relatively normal. Or, if violence is portrayed as linked to pleasure or power, then there may well be reasons for concern, linked to the arguments discussed in chapter 6, about the possible impact of images of sex and violence on real sexual or violent attacks on women, or less overtly on the legitimization of objectifying and subordinating attitudes to women.

MOTIVES AND CONSEQUENCES IN TV VIOLENCE

Most studies of the representation of violence on television have included some form of classification of violence in terms of motives and consequences. From early on, television violence has been characterized by the use of nonlegal methods as often as legal ones. However, this overall pattern could be interpreted to show that the use of violence was frequently legitimized on television (Larsen, Gray, & Fortis, 1963). Certainly, good guys were much less likely than bad guys to use violence, but even good guys did not shrink from deploying actions that could or did cause harm (Gerbner et al., 1979).

On British television, research in the early 1970s indicated that perpetrators of violence were usually on the wrong side of the law, but nevertheless a significant minority of good characters used violence from time to time. Bad guys, however, were much more likely to kill their victims than were good guys (Halloran & Croll, 1972; Shaw & Newell, 1972). During the mid-1980s, Cumberbatch and his colleagues (1987) reported that the most popular motive for televised violence was for evil or destructive purposes, followed by the need for self-preservation. This same study found that violence took place twice as often in a criminal context as in the service of upholding the law.

The consequences of violence have also featured prominently in most content analysis studies of television violence. Gerbner and his colleagues singled out the probabilities of being victimized and especially of being killed as key measures (Gerbner, Gross, Jackson-Beeck, Jeffries-rõz, Signorielli, 1978; Gerbner et al., 1979). During the 1970s, for instance, nearly 4 in 10 violent incidents on peak-time television drama on the American networks resulted in injury or painful consequences for victims. Nearly 4 in 10 of these casualties were fatal. On British television, during this period, more than 3 of 4 violent episodes resulted in some form of pain and suffering (Shaw & Newell, 1972).

METHODS, MOTIVES, AND CONSEQUENCES

These issues informed a particular focus within the current study of television violence, which took account of motives and consequences in broadcast violence. The study's definition of violence embraced motivations and consequences, especially injurious ones, as key elements of the behavior on which it focused. Violence was behavior with the intent to harm. Harmful consequences were a further sign that violence had taken place.

The definition excluded action against goods or property unless that act has consequences for an animate being. Also the act of physical force had to be carried out by an animate being so the violence of a thunderstorm or earthquake, for example, would not be logged or coded in the study. Clearly, with the latter instances, there would not normally be a motivational force underpinning such activity unless perpetrated by some almighty being, with a personality, who used such forces of nature as weapons. Some researchers have included natural catastrophes within the realm of motivated violence on television, arguing that the motive to include such incidents for dramatic effect derived from the program's producer or director (Gerbner & Gross, 1976).

Thus, the acts that were identified and coded in the study could all be discussed in terms of the motives and consequences of agency rather than accident. In each of the years studied (1994–1995 and 1995–1996), and across the terrestrial and satellite channels from which broadcast output was analyzed, the motives and consequences of televised violence were coded wherever possible.

Whereas the quantity of violence found on British television was small in terms of program running time (1.4%), the quality of depictions seems to be what most concerns viewers (Gunter, 1985), and certain kinds of violence resonate particularly dramatically, causing public debate and giving an illusion of a violence-saturated medium (Gunter & Wober, 1988). The violence that draws most protest tends to be set in contemporary and familiar, even familial, contexts: sexual violence, violence involving weapons, violence set in the home, and graphic suffering and assaults on women, children, or an elderly person. In other words, it is realistic violence, or rather violence that is perceived to be realistic, which upsets viewers and draws the attention of the censorship lobby. In this context, perceptions of motives and consequences become central to theorizing what the possible impact of perceptions of broadcast violence might have on audiences. If motives for criminal violence, as opposed to law-keeping or warfare, seem legitimate or at least understandable and consequences of violence appear slight or perhaps even pleasurable for victims, then it would seem reasonable to argue a case for censorship, if only on the grounds of media ethics rather than effects (Stevenson, 1997).

The study teased out motives and consequences of violence systematically, within the broad remit and methodology of its research. Motives were classified in relation to the context of the violence: criminal act, interpersonal violence, upholding the law, defending civil liberties, war/armed force violence, riot or civil unrest, domestic violence, and other. They were also classified according to the perceived goal of the aggressor: evil/ destruction, self-preservation, ambition/power, desire for money, upholding the law, protecting home/family, protecting society, respect for law, sexual, religious, and other.

The consequences of violence were coded in relation to the injury caused to the victim of crime, either directly or indirectly. Ten labeling terms were used: death, mutilation, broken limbs, serious wound, minor wound, stun, bruise, other physical injury, psychological damage, no physical injury, and not codable. Consequences were further evaluated in relation to perceived pain, blood, and horror.

The next two sections review the statistics resulting from the measure of motives and consequences. The discussion then turns to consider motive and consequence in relation to specific concerns around sexual violence, women as victims, domestic violence and the impact of television violence on child audiences. These are the issues that have drawn the greatest attention of some broadcasting critics.

MOTIVES, GOALS, AND TELEVISION VIOLENCE

The patterns of motives of violence changed little between the 2 years of the study. In 1994–1995, criminal motives featured most frequently at 24.7%; this dropped somewhat in the following year to 21.2%. However, interpersonal violence featured highest overall at 23.1% in 1994–1995 and 23.8% in 1995–1996. Other motives featured significantly less frequently; for example, upholding the law came third in each year with 7.6% and 5.9%, respectively. Domestic violence at home scored lowest with 2.4% and 2.6%. In both years, criminal acts featured more often on satellite (26.9% and 23.7%, respectively) than on terrestrial television (18.5% and 21.4%, respectively) (see Table 5.1).

Among the terrestrial channels there were some differences in the motivational context of violence. Criminal contexts featured more frequently on ITV for both years than on the other channels, at about 26% for each year. BBC2 had the least criminal motivation, at close to 15% for each year. Both Channel 4 and BBC1 showed an increased use of

TABLE 5.1

Motivational Context of Television Violence (1994–1995 and 1995–1996)

Context	1994–1995 (%) Terrestrial	1995–1996 (%) Terrestrial	1994–1995 (%) Satellite	1995–1996 (%) Satellite
Criminal act	18.5	21.4	26.9	23.7
Other interpersonal	23.9	22.4	21.9	25.2
Upholding the law	7.5	6.8	8.4	6.8
Defending civil liberties	8.0	7.7	6.4	7.2
War, armed forces	7.6	10.3	4.6	5.0
Civil strife/riot	3.9	2.4	1.8	1.6
Domestic/ at home	3.1	2.4	2.5	2.9
Other/ cannot code	26.9	26.6	27.1	27.6

criminal motivating contexts in their violent material. Channel 4 increased from 15.1% to 20.9% and BBC1 from 16.8% to 23.5% between 1994–1995 and 1995–1996. Satellite channels were more consistent in their use of criminal motivation. All showed crime as a motive between 24% and 29% of the time—except for the cartoon network, which had crime motives only 14.5% of the time.

Interpersonal violence served as the context most systematically on the terrestrial channels with between 19% and 24% of incidents and little variation between years, except for a considerable drop on Channel 4 from 32.8% to 23.1%. On satellite interpersonal violence featured most on the cartoon channel (32.7%) and least on Sky One (17% in 1995–1996). Both UK Gold and Sky Movies showed more portrayals of interpersonal violence between the years of the study, with increases of 7.8% and 7.1% respectively.

Violent motives linked to upholding the law or defending civil liberties featured in about 7% of all violent motivational contexts on both satellite and terrestrial. War as a context was more commonly found on terrestrial channels and increased somewhat between the 2 years of the research.

Civil strife and domestic violence were the least common codable motives, with the controversial realist area of domestic violence featuring only between 1.6% and 4.3% of times on terrestrial television showing violence (which in itself constitutes only 0.7% of all terrestrial broadcasting). So domestic, familial violence is only a tiny proportion of total broadcast material, with rates in each case dropping in the second year, except on ITV where domestically contextualized violence remained stable but minimal at 1.6%. Satellite figures were also low, although perhaps oddly the TNT cartoon channel showed domestic motivations for violence most frequently at 5.1% in 1995–1996. Second came UK Gold with decreasing figures for the 2 years of 4.1% (1994–1995) and 3.5% (1995–1996).

In order to best map and categorize motives, a set of codes were applied to acts of violence that labeled the apparent goals of the aggressor in the incident. These included five broadly positive goals—self-preservation, upholding the law, protecting home/family, protecting society, and respect for law—and five goals that might more readily seem negative reasons to act violently against another person—sexual, religious, evil/destruction, ambition/power, and desire for money (see Table 5.2).

Evil or destructive goals occurred most frequently across all channels, at a rate averaging about 20% of goals, followed by the drive for power or ambition (about 13% of goals on average) and then by the more positive need for self-preservation (about 11% of goals). Although the need for self-preservation showed the biggest drop in occurrences year-on-year from 14.4% of cases to 11.8%. Desire for money also dropped from 7.3% to 5.5% between 1994–1995 and 1995–1996. Sexual motives barely featured (0.9% both years) and religious motives never featured. Comparing terrestrial with satellite channels the same

TABLE 5.2
Aggressor Goals in Television Violence (1994–1995 and 1995–1996)

Goals	1994–1995 (%) Terrestrial	1995–1996 (%) Terrestrial	1994–1995 (%) Satellite	1995–1996 (%) Satellite
Evil/destructive	19.5	21.2	21.4	22.4
Self-preservation	12.4	10.6	14.8	13.1
Ambition/power	13.5	13.5	13.1	12.7
Desire for money	6.7	6.9	7.9	5.5
Upholding the law	6.6	6.7	6.8	6.5
Protect the family home	3.7	6.1	7.4	6.1
Protect society	6.1	7.3	4.2	6.6
Respect for the law	2.3	1.9	2.4	1.7
Sexual	0.8	1.2	0.9	1.0
Religious	0.3	0.3	*	*
Other/cannot code	27.1	23.5	20.8	24.3

Note: * = less than 0.05%

three goals came out on top with the main differences occurring in the goal of self-preservation and desire for money, both of which appeared more frequently on satellite channels. Violence to protect the family or home decreased on satellite but increased on terrestrial channels year-by-year. Violence to protect society increased slightly on both.

The different terrestrial channels showed consistent distribution of goals overall, although there was some rising and falling between the two separate years of recording. Self-preservation goals dropped across all channels. One exception was that ambition/power goals increased slightly on all channels except for Channel 4, which showed a fall from 13.3% to 6.1%.

Evil or destructive goals consistently topped the list for the satellite channels at between 17% and 28% of all coded goals. Only UK Gold showed any significant decrease of the use of this goal for motivating violence, dropping from 23.3% of coded goals to 16.7% in the following year. Almost as if to compensate, Sky One increased depictions of evil or destructive goals from 18.8% in 1994–1995 to 28.4% in 1995–1996. The more positive aggressor goals (e.g., upholding the law, protecting the family, or protecting society) occurred less frequently, but upholding the law showed some increases on all individual satellite channels over the 2 years.

In summary, the data on motives and goals showed interpersonal dispute (23.8%) and crime (21.2%) to be the most common motivational contexts of violence. Both were more dominant on satellite channels (23.7% and 25.2%) in each of the 2 years than they were on terrestrial (21.4% and 22.4%). Terrestrial channels showed more warfare (10.3%) than satellite (5%). BBC2 showed most predilection for war; this channel's 17.3% of violence occurred in war settings, which is symptomatic perhaps for its tendency to screen old war films on weekend afternoons. TNT, the cartoon channel, had fewer crime acts than average (14.5%) and perhaps unsurprisingly given the genre, many more unclassifiable acts (33.9%). Overall, evil and destructive goals were most common (21.3%), followed by the drive for ambition and power (14.2%) and self-preservation (11.8%). These were fairly consistent across all terrestrial and satellite channels with two slight exceptions in that Channel 4 had rather higher than average numbers of goals linked to upholding the law and Sky One had high rates for goals linked to protecting society (13.4%). The following section details the perceived consequences of this range of motivation and goals in broadcast violence.

CONSEQUENCES OF TELEVISION VIOLENCE

Coders interpreted the consequences of violent acts in terms of the nature of damage done to the victim. The following labels were used: death, mutilation, broken limbs, serious wound, minor wound, stun, bruise, other physical injury, psychological damage, no physical injury, and not codable.

In many ways, the most worrisome finding was that 47% of all violence shown in 1995–1996, was not, apparently, in any way harmful or damaging. The "stunning" of victims was the most common result of assault at 14% across all channels, followed by minor wounds at 9% not codable at 8% and death at 7% (although this dropped significantly from the previous year when it stood at 12%). Broken limbs or mutilation were not depicted at all and serious wounds were shown in only 4% of violent scenes. Between the two sample years there was a marked drop in injury depiction resulting from aggression, from 60% to 45%. Findings were consistent across all channels, terrestrial and satellite (see Table 5.3.)

There were some variations in representations of injurious consequences between the terrestrial channels. Channel 4 showed a slight increase in deaths caused by violence between the years (8% rose to 11%), but other channels all showed reduced proportions of deaths: BBC2's death rate fell most from 15% to 8%. All channels also showed increased rates of no injury: Except for Channel 4, whose rate went down slightly from 43% to 41%.

Sky One maintained numbers of deaths between 1994–1995 and 1995–1996 but at a very low rate of 4%. All other satellite channels reduced the proportion of deaths shown. All channels increased the proportion of noninjurious results of violence. This was most dramatic on UK Gold, where no injury could be identified as resulting from 61% of aggression in 1995–1996, as compared to 40% in 1994–1995.

Alongside the injurious consequences of violence, coders also evaluated perceived suffering in terms of pain, blood, or horror. These aspects of injury were rated on a 5-point scale. So, for example, pain was coded

TABLE 5.3
Injury Types (1994–1995 and 1995–1996)

Injury	1994–1995 (%) Terrestrial	1995–1996 (%) Terrestrial	1994–1995 (%) Satellite	1995–1996 (%) Satellite
Death	11	7	12	7
Mutilation	1	*	*	*
Limbs broken	*	*	*	*
Serious wound	5	3	4	4
Minor wound	11	8	11	8
Stun	17	12	15	14
Bruise	9	5	9	4
Other injury	4	5	5	4
Psychological damage	2	2	2	2
No injury	35	47	45	50
Cannot code	9	10	3	7

on a sliding scale from 1 = no pain to 5 = intense pain. Sixty percent of all acts of violence across all channels showed no pain and around 20% showed slight pain. Serious and severe pain (coded 4 and 5) only occurred in an average of 1.5% of violent events. Pain-free consequences increased from 59% to 63% over the 2 years studied. This was more evident on terrestrial (58% increased to 66%) than on satellite channels (60% increased to 62%). BBC2 showed the least pain of all channels in 1995–1996 (73% depiction of pain-free consequences), whereas Sky Movies showed the most painful incidences (35% of consequences), although none of these was severe.

There was also little evidence of blood on screen during 1994–1995 and 1995–1996. Three out of four violent acts (75%) across all channels depicted no blood or bleeding by either victims or perpetrators. Blood was always rare and increasingly absent from televised violence during the years studied and there were no incidences of violence where any consequence showed much blood. In addition, there was not much discernible difference between terrestrial and satellite channels. Depictions of bloodless consequences increased overall from 73% to 76% between the 2 years overall. There were even greater shifts toward not showing blood on three channels: ITV increased blood-free imagery in violent scenes from 53% to 80%. UK Gold increased it from 66% to 84% and Sky Movies increased it from 60% to 71%.

Horror was not significantly in evidence as a consequence of violence. Sixty percent of consequences showed only mild expressions of horror in 1994–1995 and this rose to 63% the following year. Extreme horror barely featured at all as a consequence of violence and there was very little difference between terrestrial and satellite. Among individual channels, BBC2 was the most horror free over the 2 years, whereas BBC1 showed an increase in moderate horror (from 5% to 8%).

So consequences of violence on television, whether physical or psychological, were scarce and slight on British mainstream television during the years studied. Evidence of injury—whether pain, blood, or horror—was similarly minimally apparent. Year-on-year, there were falls in the incidence of injury and of death with the increase in representations of no physical injury increasing more on terrestrial channels (35% to 47%) than on satellite (45% to 50%). Sky Movies (17%) and The Movie Channel (16%) showed the most death or serious injury, but even here the rate of death dropped, on average from 16% to 11%. On the whole, any violence depicted showed little negative effects at all, which may be cause for some concern if aggression is minimalized in seriousness by the failure to indicate realistic outcomes such as damage or distress. Such contextual and consequential representations might support a model of television violence as having "normalizing" effects when violence could come to be seen by audiences as unproblematic, even sometimes legitimate or humorous, and of no great detrimental consequence (Federman, 1997). Much concern about the possible effect of broadcast violence has focused closely on women's experience as victims, or of their fear of crime, or of being subject to everyday harassment and degradation (Stanko, 1985, 1990). The discussion section addresses these concerns, fully expressed in chapter 6, in relation to the screened motives and consequences and also looks at motives and consequences more broadly as a means of analyzing textual violence in relation to effects.

MOTIVES AND CONSEQUENCES OF TELEVISION VIOLENCE: DISCUSSION

Bandura (1973) argued that television is a superb tutor, offering models of aggression and violence to which young people, in particular, might be susceptible. Effects research still sees this as a contentious and disputed claim, not just in relation to young audiences, but also in terms of whether gendered and/or sexualized violence in the mass media supports the reproduction and perpetuation of sexist or even misogynistic attitudes about women. Freedman (1984) felt variables other than a liking for television violence explained aggression and that already aggressively predisposed children chose to watch more violent programs because they were already oriented to violence, not because violent imagery somehow worked to distort normal growing up processes toward aggressiveness. On the other hand, Bailey (1993) interviewed violent young offenders and sex offenders and claimed that watching violence on television was significantly causal in 25% of cases of aggressive offending. Livingstone (1996) reviewed much research on correlations between broadcast violence and violent behavior and concluded that the question of detrimental effects on the viewers of violence has to stay unresolved. Nonetheless, the debate continues and this book attempts to illuminate some issues not by focusing on the audience, but by carefully mapping the volume and content of violent material by which any susceptible audience might be affected.

Central to that content are the depicted motives for violence, which might or might not provide a means of identification or legitimization and so encourage and justify copycat behavior; and consequences, which might deter violence by showing unattractive results or glamorize aggression and make it appear pleasurable and productive. The motives for violent or sexual offences are difficult to understand or explain, unlike theft for gain, for example, where the goal is clearly materialistic. In Western cultures, a certain amount of aggressiveness is a prerequisite for gaining status. Psychologists tend to see it as a survival instinct, which in contemporary culture becomes channeled through education and enculturement into competitiveness, ambition, and drive. For aggression to be criminal, it must be designed to cause harm that is unjustified (Van Eyken, 1987) or, more precisely, be action that aims to inflict injury or harm on a person who seeks to avoid that (Zillman, 1979). This latter definition thus excludes activities like sadomasochism or boxing. For "healthy" aggression to transform to criminal violence requires some kind of acceptance of violence as a means of achieving desired goals, this may be momentary, as in anger, or premeditated, as in armed robbery. The motivation may therefore be negative, that is, the aggressors need to purge themselves of anger or frustration or it may be positive and instrumental as in the use of violence for material gain. For many, these possibilities are curtailed by the knowledge of consequences, which counters the possible gains.

Consequences may be perceived damage to the victim, fear of retribution, fear of the law, or an unwillingness to be viewed as deviating from social norms or codes, whether for moral or conformist reasons. For example, Zillman (1979) argued that signs of pain or injury acted as inhibitors to aggression because the consequences could be seen as untenable. In other words, most individuals learn one way or another that violence toward others is unacceptable and one of the ways in which people learn is through the mass media. Those concerned with the role of the media in this process argue that children are increasingly taught and "baby-sat" by television and for some children the mass media may dominate their socialization. If other influential factors (e.g., parenting, schooling, and moral education) are in some sense not providing appropriate messages about behavior, then television's role becomes critical.

Media theorists of news have long argued that news values, journalistic profiles, and commercial pressure have tended toward the reporting of crimes of sex and violence in graphic and titillating ways (Chibnall, 1977; Soothill, & Walby, 1991). Such news skews crime information available to the general public toward an extreme model, which is of concern because studies have shown that over 50% of people get their information about crime from the mass media (T. W. Smith,

1984). The portrayal in news of crime as typically violent and often sexualized arguably informs fictional representations of crime, which may
also overemphasize dramatic, rare, and damaging[1] crime in order to as-
pire to realism (i.e., the realism of the news accounts that many people
rely on for information about real crime). So, typically, British television crime series (e.g., *The Bill* and *Prime Suspect*) deal with extreme
crime rather than the everyday business of property crime (91% of all
recorded crime in 1997; Home Office, 1999).

The implications of such reporting and fictional portrayal are potentially broad. Certain kinds of deviancy may become amplified in the
public imagination, leading to stereotyping, inappropriate legislation,
and moral panic (J. Young, 1971); such processes can lead to political
consequences (e.g., oppressive policing of Black youths in the inner cities after the "mugging" phenomenon of the late 1970s; Hall, Critcher,
Jefferson, & Clarke, 1978) and may also obfuscate serious but less dramatic crime (i.e., the current focus on dangerous stranger pedophiles
rather than the enormity of child sexual abuse within the family).
Finally, the implications may be less about attitudes and policies and
more about audience behavior. This might be indirect behavior relating
to crime, for example :

> More than half the women interviewed in a study commissioned by the
> Broadcasting Standards Council considered that television and the tabloid
> press increased their fear of crime, with third saying that such reports
> made them "feel afraid." … Only half the sample said they would be willing
> to report crimes and only a quarter said their confidence in the police had
> been increased by watching *Crimewatch UK* (Schlesinger et al., 1991).
> (Jones, 1998, p. 83)

The mass media may impact causally on the actual realization of crime
because of its significant role as *tutor*. In the area of attitudes and behaviors toward violence, the role in understanding and therefore possible
effect of motives and consequences may make the difference between
perceiving violence as abhorrent and unrewarding or as pleasurable and
rewarding.

In real life, motives and consequences are integral to the criminal justice system. They impact both on prevention and punishment and also
on the ways in which victims are treated. On television, motives for violence were criminal in only 24.7% (1994–1995) and 21.2% (1995–1996)
of cases. This meant that over three quarters of the violence shown on
television happened outside of any motivating context that carries
strong cultural connotations of right and wrong. At least if a crime is
committed in a narrative, viewers can draw on their sociocultural

---

[1]Drama, rarity, and negativity are three of the components that Galtung and Ruge
(1965) identified as essential in order for a real event to qualify as newsworthy. Others included repetition, unambiguousness, cultural resonance, sustainability, consonance, fit
with other news events, elite references, and personification.

experience to assess the act portrayed. Crime offers a relatively straight-forward route interpretation. In Foucault's (1975) terms, people learn norms and values through powerful institutional discourses, of which the law, with the demise of organized religion, is probably dominant. So, adult audiences can draw on a powerful set of value judgments from the legal system and the ways in which it permeates their lives to make sense of televised crime. Consequently, television violence linked to crime, if portrayed within the conventions of the legislative framework of the viewing community, may well serve to support a consensus around crime and punishment and an advocacy of policing and the criminal justice system rather than in any sense encourage crime among viewers.

This may not be the case, however, for younger viewers whose models of right and wrong may be less well established than are those of adults or, indeed, for the small proportion of adult viewers who for physiological or psychological reasons are less socially skilled and discriminatory. These more vulnerable groups may lack access to the kind of moral paradigms that would enable them to decode even straightforward crime drama in the preferred way[2]. Rather, they may read televised criminal violence as pleasurable, if only as release of tension, especially if apparent consequences to both perpetrators and victims appear slight, as is suggested by the data from the current study. Or, their own experience may be such that violence seems normal rather than deviant, so televised models simply confirm rather than threaten their own sense of identity. So even if the crime context of television violence was relatively conventional, it could be misconstrued by viewers who were underexposed to sociolegal norms and values, who in other words lacked the necessary tools to comprehend crime stories in ways that uphold law and order.

Crime stories were the context of violence in less than one quarter of the acts logged during this study. In many ways, the crime context of the broadcast material analyzed is of less concern than the way violence featured in frameworks where interpretation was dependent on more elusive discourses than that offered by the law. In particular, violence most commonly occurred in what coders termed interpersonal motivational contexts (around 23% of events) and the dominant goals were evil or destructive at around 20%, or the drive for power/ambition at about 13%. Most victims (73%) and perpetrators were male (77%), most were young adults (57%), and most first–strike attacks were carried out by males (68%). Yet, the portrayed consequences of all this rampant masculinity were minimal. Men were simply stunned by other male aggres-

---

[2]Hall (1973) argued that mass media producers encode events according to the dominant hegemony and viewers will tend to decode them similarly unless the experience of the viewers conflicts with dominance partially or completely. This may occur because some audience members belong to groups who may be excluded from or denigrated by dominant discourses.

sion (18%) or suffered minor wounds (6.7%) with no evident pain, blood, or horror. Much televised violence, mapped in this research, seemed therefore not "realist," but unreal and therefore less worrying in terms of potential copycat behavior.

Television was true to reality in that most real–life violence is carried out by young men on young men (22% of British men from age 16 to 24 were at risk of violence in 1997; Home Office 1999), but it is not true that such violence causes little physical or psychological damage. Making male victimhood invisible in this way has many implications beyond the scope of this study. Some work, for example, has linked increases in young male suicide to the oppressive nature of hegemonic masculinity (Tolson, 1977). But, on television, masculine aggression is offered as nonproblematic for the most part either for the men who act it out or the men who receive it.

Male suffering at the hands of men barely features in television, but also conspicuous by its absence is the depiction of the motives for and consequences of male abuse of women and children, with whom in real life they have intimate familial relationships. In all, 47% of women homicide victims are killed by their own spouse or lover (over 100 women per year), 88% of rapes are carried out by someone known to the victim and 23% of women aged 16–59 claimed to have been assaulted by a current or former partner; Home Office, 1999, p. 15). Men who they know are probably the greatest source of violence for women; on the contrary, men who do not know present the same threat for men. Yet, in 1994–1995 and 1995–1996, only 1.6% and 4.3% of televised violent acts were placed in a domestic context; sex was the motive of male aggression in only 1.5% of acts coded and only 0.9% of acts showed men being violent toward children under age 14. Yet, in 1992, National Society for Prevention of Cruelty to Children (NSPCC) published the report, *Child Sexual Abuse Trends in England and Wales*, on 10,000 children at risk of abuse in England and Wales. This was followed by the Utting Report in 1997, which focused on the large number of runaway abused children who are systematically returned to the abusive environment (Utting, 1997).

Consequently, to conclude the problem with televised violence seems to be at least as much what is not shown as what is shown, particularly in relation to the motives for and consequences of violence. Motives and consequences arguably provide viewers with value hooks on which to hang their judgments of the validity of the material they are viewing. The media may not have the power to tell audiences what to think, but in areas of which they have little personal knowledge the media can certainly provide them with an agenda of what to think about. In the televised violence studied, there are several issues of concern when focusing on the motives and consequences of violence: First, what people are told to think about most is a particular model of male violence and aggression that is young, intra-male, and pro-active; second, violence has goals of destruction and power but virtually no detrimental consequences to those involved; and third, violence that afflicts women and children, often in their own home and delivered by men they know, is barely on the agenda of televised crime. So televised violence is potentially political for similar reasons, but perhaps with different consequences, as imputed by Ericson about the selection and depiction of news in the press: "Deployed stereotypically, explanations of deviance in the news are political. They impute motives, whether noble or blameworthy, which in turn bear justifications and excuses for deviant behavior with specific control implications" (Ericson, Baranek, & Chan, 1991, quoted in Jones, 1998, p. 84).

The politics here was gendered: Traditional models of masculinity, with their rites of passage of male aggression, were reproduced, whereas the ways in which that hegemonic masculinity and its aggression impact on the lives of women and children, and the implications too for men who struggle to conform to its requisite machismo, were barely addressed. For those with no alternative experience of the world or critical willingness to interrogate what they view, the status quo that equates masculine identity with aggression and ignores the consequences was confirmed in this sample of television violence. The effect may be simply that the goals of those motivated to maintain existing norms and roles are satisfied and others will have to live with the resulting consequences.

Chapter 6

Gender and Violence on Television

Studies of television drama and entertainment programs, over many years, have revealed significant gender differences, which are especially pronounced in relation to depictions of violence (Gerbner, 1972; Gerbner & Gross, 1976; Gerbner et al., 1977, 1978, 1979; *National Television Violence Study*, 1997, 1998; Signorelli, 1984). In purely quantitative terms, men tend to significantly outnumber women as aggressors, whereas women are more frequently featured as victims of violence (*National Television Violence Study*, 1998). However, as already indicated in this book, it is the nature of violence as much as its frequency of occurrence that may be most important in the context of its impact on television audiences. The depiction of the sexes as victims or aggressors may convey subtle and sometimes not so subtle social meanings about the relative power of men and women. This chapter considers television violence and gender with specific attention to patterns of victimization and aggression.

Despite the prevailing dominance of male aggression and female victimization, prominent counter examples have attracted considerable public attention. Such gendered violence depictions in the media have drawn attention to controversial forms of violence that society would often rather not have to confront. Much of the violence faced by ordinary people has been regarded as too mundane for film or television.

Films about serial killers, dangerous strangers, and mad, bad women showed to full cinemas and, soap operas featured domestic violence, murders and incest on television. Indeed, it appeared that extreme interpersonal violence had become something of an obsession for the fictional visual media. Some violence was depicted as female, heterosexual, and commonly directed against male suitors, lovers, or spouses (e.g., in the films *Fatal Attraction*, *Body of Evidence*, *Dirty Weekend*, and *Black Widow*). Male violence was depicted in narratives of reasserted masculinity and bonding (e.g., *Fight Club*); highly intelligent, even intellectual, psychosis (e.g., the *Hannibal* films); or terrorism versus high patriotism (e.g., *Clear and Present Danger*). Few mainstream films or television fantasies depicted the grim reality of male violence against women and children in the home, or featured the fact that rape is rarely an attack by a dangerous stranger on a dark city street but is usually committed by someone familiar to the victim.

Women are rarely violent and, in real life, they are most often at risk at home and from men they know (Dobash & Dobash, 1992; Lees, 1993, 1995). In the late 20th century, Faludi (1992) identified, on both sides of the Atlantic, the extent not only of represented disempowerment of women in the mass media but the realized disempowerment through violence in marriage and at home, such that in the United States "in the 1980s, almost half of all homeless women (the fastest growing segment of the homeless) were refugees of domestic violence" (p. 8).

Yet, even though in reality "men provide more menace to the basis of society, it is women who are instructed in how to behave" (Heidensohn, 1986, p. 106) in the stories of sex and violence that comprise such a popular section of our contemporary culture. Frequently, the stories involve the "good" woman protecting her virtue or her family and by her very nature saving one or the other and often both, whereas the "bad" or unnatural woman (i.e., the lesbian, prostitute, nymphomaniac, femme fatale or most recently feminist) causes not only her own downfall but the fall of those around her too. She inevitably, in Heidensohn's terms, gets her just deserts and the good woman is placed on a pedestal (Heidensohn, 1985).

Violent encounters involving men and women in the media often include sexual components. Newspapers, for example, focus disproportionately on sex-related attacks. Sexual assaults are reported far more often than they actually occur. Furthermore, although the greatest proportion of sexual attacks on women are perpetrated by men known to the victims, the news media have been found to prefer reports of stranger violence against women (Carter et al., 1998).

Accounts of violence, often combined with elements of sexuality, make good stories with many of the requisites for fables and folktales—struggle, drama, problem, danger, heroes, villains, good, evil, and resolution (Propp, 1968). They attract and titillate because they offer viewers a glimpse of the taboo of sex, yet also reassure people of the rightness of familiar norms and values. Individuals are reassured because taboo, although depicted as exciting, is also dangerous, sometimes even deadly. In 1976, Foucault explained this double appeal as rooted in the so-called repression of sexuality, which constructed sex as safe and legitimate only in the fertile marital bed during 19th-century

Victorianism,[1] but actually by attempting to do so nurtured fascination with forbidden and risky sexualities in reality and fantasy. Any nonconforming sex became not truly repressed, but secret, illicit, or even criminal and so dangerously attractive.

Representations of sex have long troubled moral conservatism. When such representations are linked to violence, the concern is not just about morality but about actual harm and crime. In particular, this concern foregrounds theories that the representation of violence against women causes, legitimates, or trivializes actual violence against women in real life, and fictional forms are a particular problem because they link violence to sexual pleasure and attraction, support the objectification of women, and so desensitize viewers to the real effects of male aggression. When sexual representation is linked to violence, the apparent popularity of such material with mass media audiences stimulates the concern about media effects that is a major focus of discussion in this book.

This chapter considers the relation between broadcast drama and real gendered violence in order to explore the effects argument specific to media accounts of sex and violence. It examines evidence from the literature on women as victims of violence on television and then presents findings from the study of violence on British television on this subject. It then turns attention to the gender of aggressors on television. The findings from the British study are put into a broader context of what is known about the social and psychological status of female versus male aggressors. Finally, some consideration is given to real-life crime statistics and the extent to which television representations of crime depart from everyday reality.

GENDER, VIOLENCE, AND VICTIMIZATION ON TELEVISION

The victimization of females in scenes of television violence has long been a source of concern. Some believe it sends out the wrong messages about women's position in society and cultivates an unnecessary degree of anxiety among women themselves, especially if they identify with such portrayals (Signorielli, 1984; Tuchman, 1978b).

The extent to which violence is deployed differs markedly between the sexes. Female characters in television drama are far less likely to be depicted as aggressive or to use violence than are males. Traditionally, females have tended to be characterized more often as being emotionally and physically dependent (Butler & Paisley, 1980; Tuchman, 1978b). Analyses of American network prime-time television, over many years, showed that women were disproportiontely depicted as victims of violence (Gerbner & Gross, 1976; Gerbner et al, 1977, 1978, 1979). Similar patterns of male and female involvement in violence have also been

---

[1]See Foucault's discussion of Victorianism and the repressive hypothesis of sexuality in Foucault (1998).

found in other countries (Cumberbatch et al., 1987; Halloran & Croll, 1972; McCann & Sheehan, 1985; Mustonen & Pulkkinen, 1993).

Most content analysis research, however, has not drawn distinctions between the varying degrees or weights of concern that members of the public might attach to individual portrayals of violence depending on the contexts in which they occur and the particular form they take. One exception to this general rule has been research conducted by Potter and his colleagues, who examined through content analysis the representation of male and female perpetrators and victims of violence on American network television (Potter et al., 1995, 1997). These researchers distinguished between different forms and contexts of violence, identifying occurrences of female and male victimization, for example, in episodes involving serious assault, minor assault, theft, verbal aggression, deceit and accidents in news, current affairs, and talk shows. Females were generally less often reported or featured as being victims of violence than were males, regardless of the type of incident. Females were most likely to be on the giving and receiving end of violence in incidents involving verbal aggression.

Audience research has shown that viewers may distinguish between portrayals of violence in terms of their possible significance or meanings they have for those individuals. According to some writers, people have "preformed maps" for schematically classifying aggressive acts. Television viewers use these maps to plot or classify violent behavior in three principal dimensions: physical versus verbal aggression; violence between strangers versus violence between acquaintances, and provoked versus unprovoked violence (Campbell, Muncer, & Gorman, 1993; Muncer et al., 1986).

The significance of such distinctions lies principally in the specific meanings that individual television portrayals or repeated patterns of portrayals of violence against females might convey to different groups within the audience. There is ample evidence that violence against women may be regarded as particularly heinous, and repeated depictions of it may convey the impression that it is a normal fact of life. This could lead some audience subgroups to believe that it is an acceptable way to behave, while generating in others an unnecessary fear or exaggerated perception of personal risk. The closer to everyday life certain television portrayals get, the greater their potential to upset viewers who may identify more strongly with such depictions because of the similarities they have with their own lives and situations. In the case of violence against women, the most common forms that occur in the real world include physical assault, rape, sexual abuse, and incest. Most female victims who have experienced such victimization generally do so at the hands of a male perpetrator who is well-known to them, rather than a stranger (Schlesinger, Dobash, Dobash, & Weaver, 1991). One analysis in Britain, which covered over 30,000 police records, reported that 25% of all violent crimes involved wife assault (Dobash & Dobash, 1992). Another British survey of over 1,000 women found that one in six had reportedly been raped or sexually assaulted, with one in five having had such an experience as a child (Hall, 1997). In the United States, a study of 900 women found that 44% had experienced one attempted or completed rape and 20% had been assaulted during marriage (Stanko, 1985).

Research among British viewers revealed that scenes in which females were targets of violence were rated in more serious terms than scenes in which males were the targets, even though the form of violence was controlled (Gunter, 1985).

The reactions specifically of women to depictions of television violence have indicated that even more complex patterns of reaction can occur that are dependent on the specific nature and context of the displayed violence, particularly when that violence shows women as victims. One characteristic of discussions of violence against women noted by Schlesinger et al. (1992) is a tendency to focus on the victim rather than the perpetrator when seeking explanations for the causes of such incidents or in the allocation of responsibility. This form of discourse tends implicitly to cite women as the makers of their own plight. The female victim is held accountable as much as, if not more so than, the male aggressor. This form of discourse is highly problematic for women.

In a series of in-depth group discussions with women, Schlesinger et al. (1992) invited participants to express their opinions about a number of different depictions of violence against women on television. Reactions were sometimes universal, but on other occasions were dependent on the personal experiences and circumstances of the women interviewed. A depiction of aggression between a husband and wife in a well-known British soap opera produced greater identification from women who had been through such experiences themselves. These women perceived such scenes as more realistic and more disturbing than did women with no such experience in their own lives. At the same time as viewing this type of portrayal as distressing, there was an accompanying opinion that it might have socially positive benefits by making men in the audience realize the vulgar nature of this kind of behavior.

Quite apart from the way viewers might perceive violence against women on screen, there is also concern about female victimization on television because of evidence stemming from research into the attitudinal and behavioral effects of portrayals depicting extreme forms of violence against women, especially when the violence is blended with sexual behavior. There is evidence, for instance, that both males and females report feeling more aggressive after seeing films of sadomasochism and group rape than after seeing a film depicting romantic sex (Schmidt, 1975). Further evidence has shown that young men may display increasingly callous attitudes toward women and more particularly toward victims of rape after a diet of movies depicting violently sexual behavior against female victims (Malamuth, 1981; Malamuth & Check, 1981; Malamuth, Haber, & Feshbach, 1980).

Erotic films equated for their arousal level but varying in aggressive content have been found to lead to differing levels of male–female aggression. When a male views a film depiction of rape and is then given an opportunity in a controlled laboratory context to aggress against a young women who has annoyed him, he inflicts more harm on her because of her association with the female victims in the films (Donnerstein, 1980, 1983). Exposure to films depicting men treating women roughly, often with sexual motives underpinning their portrayed behavior, has been found to produce short-term changes in male attitudes toward women. Young men may become less sympathetic toward the plight of a rape victim in a simulated trial context (D. Linz, 1985) and more relaxed about the seriousness of rape (S. Linz, Donnerstein, & Penrod, 1984)

This evidence indicates that certain portrayals of violence on television, in which women are depicted as victims, are perceptually differentiated by audiences and may produce postviewing changes in attitudes toward women and in male behavior toward them. Bearing this in mind, it is clear that any analysis of the depiction of female victimization on screen should take into account not just the quantity of such portrayals, but also the form they take and context or setting in which they occur.

In recent times, some researchers have acknowledged the need to qualify content analysis studies by suggesting taxonomies of portrayal classification based on the findings of media effects research. If the risk of harmful effects from exposure to televised violence is enhanced by certain qualities inherent in the violence itself or the context in which it is portrayed, such features could be used as weighting factors to differentiate between violent television portrayals. Thus, some portrayals of violence would be classified as potentially more serious or harmful than others. Among the key risk factors listed are the nature of the perpetrator and victim of violence, whether the violence was justified, the types of weapons used, the degree of injury caused to victims, how graphically portrayed is the violence, whether the violence is rewarded or punished, and whether it occurs in realistic or humorous contexts (Federman, 1997; Wilson et al., 1996). Greatest concern is reserved for those violent portrayals that feature two or more of these risk factors in combination.

VICTIMIZATION PATTERNS ON BRITISH TELEVISION

The findings presented in this section focus on the portrayal of females as victims of violence in television drama programing. Attention is devoted not just to the quantity of violent acts in which females were targets or victims, but also to the nature and form such portrayals took and the contexts and settings in which they occurred. This analysis was especially interested in establishing the extent to which certain portrayals occurred that were characterized by a number of critical risk factors, in terms of the way audiences might respond to them. Thus, portrayals featuring violence against females in which serious harm resulted, involving the use of graphic forms of violence (stabbing, strangulation), and those occurring in domestic settings or involving sexual motives on the part of the attacker were of special significance.

General Prevalence of Female Victimization

A total of 1,803 violent acts were found across all drama programing (including televised cinema films) in which females were victims of violence. This represented 10.4% of all the violent acts cataloged in televised films (originally made for the cinema) and drama series and serials on the 10 television channels monitored in this study. Televised cinema films depicted significantly more acts of violent female victimization than other television drama program genres (χ^2 = 1524.0, df = 2, p < .0001). In televised cinema films alone, there were 1,380 acts of female victimization (9.8% of all violent acts coded in films), whereas in drama series and serials there were 423 acts of female victimization (12.7% of all drama series/serial violence). More violent acts featured females as victims in drama series/serials produced outside the United Kingdom (265) than in the United Kingdom (158). Non-U.K. programs also outnumbered U.K.-made programs (907 vs. 491) in the program sample analyzed in this study. This meant that U.K. and non-U.K. drama programs therefore displayed the same rate of acts of violent female victimization (0.3 per program). Cinema films averaged 1.3 acts of violent female victimization per film.

On computing the 10 transmissions that contained the highest number of incidents of violent female victimization, 9 were cinema films, with the remaining member of this group being an episode from a non-U.K.-made drama series. The top 10 programs each contained a minimum of 12 acts of violence aimed at female victims. In total, they contained 152 acts of violent female victimization between them, or 8.4% of all such incidents in the current program sample.

The great majority of female victims was estimated to be between ages 20 and 35 (72.8%), with around one in seven from age 36 to 65 years (13.8%). A small proportion of female victims were in their high teens (6.8%), with smaller proportions in their early teens (1.6%) or pre-teens (2.3%). There were very few elderly (65+) female victims (0.7%, or 13 cases). Most female victims were White (88.8%), with small proportions being either Afro-Caribbean (4.1%) or Asian/Oriental (3.8%).

Form of Violence

Violent acts were classified in terms of the form of violent behavior and types of weapons or instruments of aggression that were used.

Fifty-two separate codes were used to classify violent behavior and 47 codes for instruments of aggression. The most frequently occurring types of violence and weapons of violence over all televised films and television drama are summarized in Table 6.1.

Between 4 and 5 out of 10 violent incidents in which females were targets involved fairly mild pushing and shoving or simply violence that was attempted but not fully followed through. A further 1 in 15 incidents comprised verbal threats, but no actual physical contact. A far from insubstantial number of incidents, however, involved more serious forms of physical violence against women. About 1 in 10 of violent female victimization incidents involved someone shooting at the female target.

There were more than 100 incidents of women being slapped, 80 incidents of women being hit with an object, more than 70 incidents of women being punched, more than 60 incidents of women being strangled, and more than 60 incidents of them being kidnapped. Twenty-five incidents of psychological torture were coded, along with 20 stabbing incidents and 17 instances of rape. Although more than 4 in 10 incidents involved the use of the hands as weapons, well over 200 female victimization incidents involved the use of handheld guns and nearly 30 further incidents involved the use of a rifle. There were more than 60 scenes in which a stabbing instrument was used on a female victim, with two categories of such weaponry featuring among the top 10 instruments of aggression being used against women.

Consequences of Violence

Violent acts were classified in terms of whether they resulted in the victim's death, serious injury, mild injury, psychological damage, or no observable injury. Serious injury might entail serious wounding, muti-

TABLE 6.1
Most Frequently Occurring Forms of Violence

	Violence Types	N	%		Weapon Types	N	%
1.	Push/trip/assault	524	29.1	1.	Hand/fist	801	44.4
2.	Attempted violence	274	15.2	2.	Other body part	213	11.8
3.	Shoot at	171	9.5	3.	Hand gun	154	8.5
4.	Verbal threat	136	7.5	4.	Throw/push	88	4.9
5.	Slap	117	6.5	5.	Pistol	72	4.0
6.	Hit with object	80	4.4	6.	Rifle	28	1.6
7.	Punch	73	4.0	7.=	Boot/foot	22	1.2
8.	Strangle	62	3.4	7.=	Domestic knife	22	1.2
9.	Abduction	61	3.4	9.=	Machine gun	20	1.1
10.	Kick	24	1.3	9.=	Dagger	20	1.1
	Total	1,522			Total	1,440	

lation, or broken limbs. Mild injury generally entailed cuts and bruises or the victim being stunned. The results are summarized in Table 6.2.

The overall pattern to emerge was that violence directed against female characters in televised drama was significantly more likely to result in mild or no injury than serious injury or death ($\chi^2 = 1133.2$, $df = 4$, $p < .0001$). One in two incidents of violence directed at females resulted in no physical or psychological damage to the victim. More than one in five further incidents resulted in minor physical injury only. Serious injury resulted in more than 80 cases and death in nearly 160 cases. Psychological damage was more frequently occurring than either critical or serious physical injury. There were some marked differences between drama genres in the distribution of female victimization outcomes ($\chi^2 = 110.9$, $df = 8$, $p < .001$). Films and non-U.K. drama were more likely than expected as compared with U.K. drama to depict female victims of violence being seriously hurt or killed.

Where serious physical injury or death resulted, perpetrators were most likely to have used either a handgun or pistol (28.5% of cases) or their hands (16.4%) as weapons. In nearly 1 in 10 such instances (9.7%), death or serious injury was caused by a stabbing instrument. There were 18 instances of serious injury or death to a female victim caused by actual stabbing and a further 18 instances when it was caused by strangulation. There were 93 instances coded of female victims being shot. Female victims were most likely to be killed or seriously hurt in scenes involving criminally motivated violence (103 cases, or 43.3% of such scenes). There were 27 instances where serious harm to females occurred in the context of a personal dispute between the female character and another character and just 9 cases of serious harm resulting from domestic violence. Serious harm was most often likely to occur to females in cinema films (201 cases). In televised drama, serious outcomes were much more likely to be shown in non-U.K. productions (30 cases) than in U.K. productions (7 cases).

In a further examination of violence combining a number of high risk factors, there were nine instances where the violence that resulted in

TABLE 6.2
Consequences of Violence Against Females

	All Drama		Films		U.K. Drama		Non-U.K. Drama	
	N	%	N	%	N	%	N	%
Death	158	9.1	137	9.9	3	1.9	18	6.8
Serious injury	83	5.0	66	4.6	4	2.5	13	4.5
Minor injury	413	23.8	312	22.6	43	27.3	58	21.9
Psychological damage	164	9.5	139	10.1	8	5.1	17	6.4
No injury	868	50.0	643	46.6	84	53.2	141	53.2

Note: Unclassified acts not included.

death or serious injury to a female victim was sexually motivated. In five of these cases, the victim was killed. All such incidents occurred in cinema films. The victim was strangled in three cases, punched in two cases, pushed or tripped in two further cases, stabbed in one instance, and kicked in one further instance. Six of these victims were ordinary female citizens, and three were prostitutes. Seven of them were between age 20 and 35 and one was between age 15 and 19. One other was not age classified. Eight of the nine victims were White and one was Black. In five cases, the setting was in the present day, whereas the other cases were depicted in historical settings. The aggressor was male in every instance; in four cases White, in one Black, and in one oriental, with three unclassified for ethnicity. In five cases, the aggressor was between age 20 and 35, in one case between age 36 and 65, and in three further cases the person was unclassified for age.

Motivational Context of Violence Against Females

The motivational context of violence was measured in terms of the dramatic setting of the violence and in terms of the goals of individual aggressors. These results are summarized in Tables 6.3 and 6.4, respectively. Violence against females was most likely to take place in televised films and drama as part of a criminal act. This motivational context accounted for one in three of all cataloged instances of violent female victimization. This was followed in terms of frequency of occurrence by violence that formed part of an interpersonal argument or dispute. The interesting finding was that the third most likely context for violence against females in televised drama was a domestic dispute.

Acts of aggression against female victims were significantly more likely to take place in the context of criminal activity or an argument with another person than anything else ($\chi^2 = 1872.9$, $df = 6$, $p < .0001$). The pattern of distribution of motivational contexts of violence

TABLE 6.3

Motivational Context of Violence Against Females

	All Drama		Films		U.K. Drama		Non-U.K. Drama	
	N	%	N	%	N	%	N	%
Criminal act	596	33.1	431	31.2	53	33.5	112	42.3
Interpersonal argument	527	29.2	407	29.5	44	27.8	76	28.7
Domestic dispute	159	8.8	131	9.5	12	7.6	16	6.0
Uphold/defence of law	64	3.5	46	3.3	9	5.7	9	3.4
Defence civil liberties	29	1.6	25	1.8	2	1.3	2	0.8
War	21	1.2	11	0.8	5	3.2	5	1.9
Civil strife/riot	18	1.0	17	1.2	1	0.6	0	0

Note: Unclassified acts not included.

TABLE 6.4

Goals of Aggressor

	All Drama		Films		U.K. Drama		Non-U.K. Drama	
	N	%	N	%	N	%	N	%
Evil/destruction	477	26.5	377	27.3	42	26.6	58	21.9
Ambition/power	275	15.3	195	14.1	13	8.2	67	25.3
Money	140	7.8	99	7.2	14	8.9	27	10.2
Self-preservation	127	7.0	92	6.7	7	7.0	24	9.1
Sexual	118	6.5	100	7.2	10	6.3	8	3.0
Family well-being	79	4.4	64	4.6	9	5.7	6	2.3
Upholding the law	66	3.7	48	3.5	8	5.1	10	3.8
Societal well-being	29	1.6	21	1.5	4	2.5	4	1.5

Note: Unclassified acts not included.

against females varied significantly across drama subgenres ($\chi^2 = 31.0$, $df = 12$, $p < .01$). Criminal acts were proportionately more frequent with non-U.K. drama than elsewhere, whereas domestic violence was proportionately more likely to be found in cinema films than made-for-TV drama.

Focusing on the goals of the aggressor, violence against female victims was most frequently motivated by evil or destructive goals or by drives for power ($\chi^2 = 911.6$, $df = 7$, $p < .0001$). In more than 300 scenes of violence against female victims, the violence was motivated by positive motives such as the self-preservation of the aggressor, upholding the law, the well-being of society, or the well-being of the aggressor's own family. There were significant differences between drama subgenres in the distribution of aggressor goals ($\chi^2 = 43.1$, $df = 12$, $p < .001$). Evil and destructive goals were proportionately more frequent in cinema films than made-for-TV dramas. Sexually motivated violence was also proportionately more likely to occur in cinema films, and was less frequently occurring than expected in statistical probability terms in non-U.K. drama.

Domestic Violence. There were 159 instances of violence that occurred in a domestic setting. Given the significance of violence "close to home" as a high risk factor in the context of potential audience reaction, the characteristics of these incidents were examined in greater detail. Female victims of violence in domestic disputes were most likely to be from age 20 to 35 (66% of cases), White (94%), and to have been attacked by men (83%). There were a few cases ($n = 25$) when female victims were attacked by members of their own sex. Approaching one in two of these scenes resulted in no observable harm for female targets (45%), one in five (21%) produced minor injury, and one in four (26%) produced psychological harm. Serious injury (three cases) or death (six cases) were fairly rare.

Sexually Motivated Violence. In all, 118 incidents of violence against females were motivated by sexual goals on the part of the aggressor. Most incidents (100) occurred in films originally made for the cinema. In scenes depicting sexually motivated violence, female targets (81%) tended to be young adults (age 20–35) and White (83%). There were 11 cases when female victims of sexually motivated attack were in their teens, from age 15 to 19, and one case in which the victim was between age 12 and 14. In around two thirds of these cases (65%) only mild or no injury resulted. In nearly one in five cases (18%), the harm caused was psychological in nature. Serious harm (four cases) and death (five cases) were relatively rare.

Sex of Aggressor

Across televised films and made-for-television drama, female victims of violence were significantly more likely to be attacked by males than members of their own sex ($\chi^2 = 546.0$, $df = 1$, $p < .001$). Male aggressors accounted for more than 7 in 10 acts of violence against females. In around 1 in 20 cases, female victims were subject to attack by more than one male aggressor. Around 300 incidents were recorded, however, in which females were attacked by members of their own sex. Usually, such incidents comprised one-on-one violence, but in a handful of cases, a female victim was targeted by more than one female attacker (see Table 6.5).

A closer examination of solus male aggressors revealed that they were overwhelmingly likely to attack female victims from age 20 to 35 (76%) or from 36 to 65 years (12%). There were 90 cases in which females who were attacked by male aggressors were between age 15 and 19, and 29 cases in which they were from age 12 to 14. The female victims of solus male aggressors tended to be White (89%) and rarely Black (4%) or Asian/Oriental (5%).

TABLE 6.5

Sex of Aggressor

	All Drama		Films		U.K. Drama		Non-U.K. Drama	
	N	%	N	%	N	%	N	%
Male (solus)	1,282	71.1	1,308	73.2	102	64.6	170	64.2
Female (solus)	385	16.1	296	14.6	35	22.2	54	20.4
Male (group)	99	5.5	68	4.9	8	5.1	23	8.7
Female (group)	11	0.6	6	0.4	2	1.3	3	1.1

Note: Unclassified acts not included.

Solus male aggressors themselves tended to be most often from age 20 to 35 (60%) or from age 36 to 65 (32%). A few were teenagers between age 15 and 19 (32 cases) or between age 12 and 14 (eight cases). These male aggressors were mostly White (85%), rather than Black (3%) or Asian/Oriental (5%).

Solus male aggressors caused no observable physical or psychological injury or harm to their female victims in one in two cases (50%), caused minor injury in more than one in five cases (23%), and caused psychological harm in just over 1 in 10 cases (11%). In a further one in eight cases (12%), male aggressors caused serious injury or death to female victims. In 102 cases (8%), their violence was sexually motivated, and in 15 cases, it took on the form of rape.

In 385 violent incidents aimed at female targets, their attackers were members of their own sex. Female victims who were targeted by female antagonists tended predominantly to be from age 20 to 35 (57%) or from age 36 to 65 (25%). In 19 cases (7%), they were between age 15 and 19 years and there were 4 cases of female victims below age 15. There were three further cases in which female victims were over age 65. Female victims of female aggressors were mostly White (88%). There were 14 cases where female victims were Black and 10 further cases in which they were Asian/Oriental.

The female aggressors in these incidents exhibited a similar demographic profile to their victims. Most were either from the age group 20 to 35 years (62%) or 36 to 65 years (27%). There were 12 cases in which the aggressors were in their late teens (age 15–19) and 6 more cases in which they were children (under age 15). Five cases portrayed female aggressors who were over age 65. Most females who aggressed against their own sex were White (87%). There were 16 cases in which female aggressors were Black and 13 cases in which they were Asian/Oriental.

For the most part, when females attacked members of their own sex, victims were either not observably harmed or injured (42%) or suffered only minor injuries (31%). There were 51 incidents (17.5% of total) in which females caused serious injury or death to other females. Most incidents occurred in the present or recent past (86%).

One final comparison was made between the forms of violence used on female victims by male and female aggressors. Male aggressors used a greater variety of violent forms against female victims than did female aggressors (42 vs. 27). Nonetheless, the most frequently occurring forms of violence were very similar across genders. Among male aggressors, the most frequently used types of violence in scenes featuring female victimization were mild physical assault such as pushing and shoving (30% of incidents) and attempted violence that was not actually successfully followed through (16%). Other relatively frequent forms of violence were shooting a female victim (9%), verbal threats (8%) and slapping the victim (7%). Among female aggressors who targeted female victims, mild physical assault (29%) and attempted violence (12%) again emerged as the two most frequently occurring types of behavior.

These were followed by incidents of slapping the victim (9%), hitting the victim with an object (9%), and verbal threats (8%).

Although there were many similarities in the ways male and female actors attacked female victims, there were some differences of note between genders. Female victims were 10 times as likely, in purely numerical terms, to be strangled by a male attacker ($n = 50$, 4%) as by a female attacker ($n = 5$, 2%). Female victims were much more likely to be abducted by a male aggressor ($n = 35$, 3%) than by a female aggressor ($n = 2$, > 1%). Female victims were psychologically tortured only by males ($n = 19$ case). In contrast, although male attackers narrowly numerically outnumbered female attackers in stabbing their female victims ($n = 11$ vs. $n = 8$), female aggressors were proportionately more likely to stab female victims than were males (3% vs. 1%).

GENDER, AGGRESSION, AND TELEVISION

Next consider patterns of aggression. In purely numerical terms, male aggressors on television outnumber female aggressors by a significant margin (National Television Violence Study, 1998). This pattern has been observed in a number of countries, including Australia, Britain, and the United States (see Cumberbatch et al., 1987; Halloran & Croll, 1972; McCann & Sheehan, 1985). In Britain, in the mid-1980s, Cumberbatch and his coworkers reported that three quarters of aggressors in televised dramatic fiction, for whom gender was identifiable, were male (75.1%) and fewer than 1 in 10 (7.3%) were female. In Australia, McCann and Sheehan reported that the overwhelming majority of aggressors (88.5%) depicted on television, and for whom gender could be identified, were male, with relatively few (11.5%) being female. Female characters also had a greater likelihood of being victims of violence (23.8%).

Some observers noted changes in the way women have been depicted on television in the past few decades. Although evidence continued to surface that women on television generally lacked power in the workplace (Pribram, 1988), signs have emerged that traditional stereotypes have been diluted by alternative depictions of women. More women have appeared in "typically male" occupations (Huston et al., 1992). Indeed, in some popular television series (e.g., *Xena: Warrior Princess* and *Buffy: The Vampire Slayer*), the female leads are very aggressive.

These physically powerful female characters, who are both attractive in a feminine way and quite capable of using aggression and willing to do so, represent a departure from traditional female dramatic roles. In the wider debate about television violence, one important question about these portrayals concerns whether they represent higher than average "risk of harm" behaviors (*National Television Violence Study*, 1997). The significance of such role reversal for female leads in action-oriented television series may also lie in the perception that audiences have of such portrayals and in whether these more assertive or aggressive women represent icons whose presence will have positive benefits for the general image of their gender. Where women get involved in violence as perpetrators, how accepting of this type of characterization are audiences likely to be? In examining this issue further, and in considering its relevance to the classification of violent acts on television, it is perhaps helpful to examine not just how female perpetrated violence is regarded, but also how characteristic it is of this gender.

Gender and Aggression

The significance of violence committed by women on television can be gauged through public perceptions of different types of violent acts. Before looking at this evidence, however, it can be reasoned that public perceptions of female violence will be influenced by the generally accepted behavioral norms for each gender. In other words, the evaluation of female violence is likely to be mediated by whether or not it is regarded as abnormal.

Aggression has traditionally been more closely tied to the male gender role than to the female gender role (Cicone & Ruble, 1978). Aggressiveness, as a male trait, has been highlighted continually by male heroes in literature and popular culture (Fasteau, 1974). Men have been rated as more aggressive than women (I. K. Broverman, Vogel, D. M. Broverman, Clarkson, & Rosencrantz, 1972; Spence & Helmreich, 1978). Men have also been found to display more favorable attitudes than women toward aggression (S. Smith, 1984).

For many years, the traditional female gender role places little emphasis on aggression. Instead, females were characterised primarily as caring and affiliative (Eagly & Crowley, 1986). These attributes favored behaviors that were incompatible with aggressiveness toward other people. Less traditional views of women emerged during the 1970s with the feminist movement, which identified assertiveness as an acceptable female trait. Whereas assertiveness may advocate taking control of situations, this does not necessarily or invariably mean resolving issues through aggressive means (Eagly & Steffen, 1986). Many women have a problem with aggression, and suffer more guilt and anxiety about it than men do (Frodi, Macauley, & Thome, 1977). Women also display greater concern about the consequences of aggression for both themselves and others.

Some aggressive behaviors may be more common in one gender because they are aspects not of gender roles, but of other social roles normally occupied by that gender. Particularly important are military, law enforcement, and contact sports. In these venues, males are more prevalent than females and may receive socialization in aggressiveness. Traditionally, men have also occupied more senior positions in ostensibly nonviolent occupations, but in those positions in which "aggressive-

ness"—in the sense of confidence and assertion of one's will—are important requirements (Eagly & Steffen, 1986).

The magnitude of gender differences may depend on the type of aggression. Across a range of social situations, males are more likely to be
both the aggressor and target of direct physical aggression (Berkowitz,
1993; A. Campbell, 1995; Crick & Grotpeter, 1995; White & Kowalski,
1994). In contrast, gender differences in verbal aggression, although in
the same direction as those for physical aggression, tend to be much
smaller and less gender consistent (Archer, Kilpatrick, & Bramwell,
1995; Buss & M. Perry, 1992; Gladue & Bailey, 1995). Indirect and relational aggression (e.g., spreading malicious gossip, socially excluding
others from the group, destroying another's property, and displaced aggression on objects) can be at least as typical of females as of males
(Bjorkqvist, 1994; Bjorkqvist, Osterman, & Lagerspetz, 1994; Hines &
Fry, 1994). M. B. Harris and Knight-Bohnhoff (1996) found that men
scored significantly higher than women on the Physical Aggression
scale of the Aggression Questionnaire (Buss & M. Perry, 1992), but not
on scales measuring verbal aggression and indirect forms of hostility.

In domestic settings and dating situations, women and men have
been found to show similar rates of violent behavior toward their
spouses (Straus, Gelles, & Steinmetz, 1980). In these situations, women
are as likely as men to admit to slapping their partner or throwing
things (M. B. Harris, 1991; McNeely & Mann, 1990; Sugarman &
Hotaling, 1989). Women are more likely than men, however, to be injured as a result of such violent encounters (Cantos, Neidig, & O'Leary,
1994; Stark & Flitcraft, 1988).

Perceptions of Aggression

Perceptions of television violence involving female as opposed to male
perpetrators are likely to be influenced by more general public opinions
about aggression and gender. Men are more likely than women to endorse the use of violence across a wide range of situations (S. Smith,
1984). Some studies have examined evaluations of violence within domestic and family contexts. In particular, male college students were
more likely than females to approve of marital violence (Finn, 1986).
Elsewhere, young adult females considered a battering incident to be
more violent than did same-age males and were more likely to feel that
the police should be called to such an incident (R. J. Harris & Cook, 1994).

Violence in the family was viewed in more serious terms by females
than by males. Both genders, however, considered violence from a
woman as more acceptable than violence from a man (Koski & Mangold,
1988). Women have been perceived as more responsible than men, however, when one spouse hits another, regardless of whether they are the
victim or perpetrator of the incident. All the same, a wife hitting her husband was seen as far less serious than a husband hitting his wife
(Greenblat, 1983). Females were found to consider acts of emotional and

physical abuse as more severe than did men. Even so, when such behavior was enacted against a child by a mother, it was regarded as less serious than when enacted by the father (Howe, Herzberger, & Tennen, 1988).

One key factor in the judgment of violence resides in the different purposes it serves for each gender. Women tend to view aggression as expressive and a way of dealing with their feelings when they get out of control. Men, in contrast, treat aggression as an instrumental behavior that represents a means of achieving goals and gaining control over situations (A. Campbell & Muncer, 1987; A. Campbell, Muncer, & Coyle, 1992; A. Campbell, Muncer & Gorman, 1993). This difference in orientation toward aggression has been observed to occur among children (Archer & Parker, 1994).

The sex of an aggressor and sex of victim can affect the way aggressive behavior is evaluated. The nature of the violence (e.g., physical, verbal, or indirect aggression) also interacts with gender to mediate these perceptions. Further, whether or not aggression involves same-sex or opposite-sex aggressors and victims (e.g., male–male, female–female, male–female encounters) also makes a difference (Bjorkqvist & Niemela, 1992; Burbank, 1987).

Another finding has more direct relevance to the classification of televised violence according to gender of those involved. Condry and Ross (1985) found that college students rated a video of rough play between two pre-school children as significantly less aggressive when both children were identified as boys than when one or both of them were girls. In a further study, Lyons and Serbin (1986) found that some adults showed a tendency to perceive more aggression in pictures of boys behaving violently than in pictures of girls behaving in a similar fashion.

Consistent evidence has emerged that across a range of situations, aggression perpetrated by males is regarded more negatively and perceived as more serious than aggression from females. Aggression directed toward female targets tends to be evaluated more negatively than aggression toward male targets (M. B. Harris, 1991, 1994, 1995). Although aggression in general may be frowned on by most people (regardless of the gender of aggressor), when required to make a choice, violence perpetrated by a male aggressor is considered as more serious than the same act performed by a female (M. B. Harris & Knight-Bohnhoff, 1996). For instance, honking and rear-ending someone else's car was seen as somewhat more acceptable for a female than for a male. Shoving a neighbor into the bushes was perceived to be more harmful if the aggressor was male rather than female. A male holding someone's head under water was seen as more aggressive than a female doing the same thing.

Gender and Violence on Television

Violent conduct is associated with men rather than women on television. Nevertheless, women may represent up to 1 in 10 aggressors in televised violent interactions (Gunter & Harrison, 1998; *National Televi-*

sion Violence Study, 1998). Furthermore, audience research has indicated that when they are involved in violence as perpetrators, there may be little difference in the degree of seriousness attached to such violent portrayals by viewers. In fact, evidence has emerged that, in certain settings, female violence may be rated as more violent and more distressing than male violence (Gunter, 1985). This finding appears to contradict opinions that have been endorsed about certain kinds of female violence in real-life situations (e.g., Greenblat, 1983; M. B. Harris, 1991, 1994, 1995; Koski & Mangold, 1988). In domestic settings, where an otherwise sociable woman is driven to violence by extreme circumstances, her conduct may be forgiven or at least understood. Even outside of a domestic context, honking and rear-ending someone's car or shoving someone into the bushes who had caused annoyance were regarded as less serious offences for a woman perpetrator than for a man (M. B. Harris & Knight-Bohnhoff, 1996).

Elsewhere, women who engage in criminal behavior may invoke more hostile public attitudes (Buckhart, 1973; McGlynn, Megas, & Benson, 1976). In the basic dichotomy of women into essentially "good" and "bad" types, women who conform to idealized notions of femininity (e.g., gentleness, passivity, etc.) are perceived as basically good, whereas those who turn to crime and violence, and who thereby abandon their femininity, are regarded as deviant and bad. Thus, although a man who gets involved in violence may be partly excused because it is seen as being part of his nature, a woman who gets involved in violence without just cause may be regarded more harshly because she is acting against her nature. Whether a woman who aggresses is forgiven for doing so ultimately depends on the context in which the aggression occurs (M. B. Harris & Knight-Bohnhoff, 1996).

Shifts toward counter stereotyped portrayals of women in prominent television series, in some of which the female lead regularly gets involved in violence, were noted earlier. If the depiction of violence serves as a demonstration of where power resides, is there evidence that women are indeed acquiring more power in televised dramatic narratives? Do televised depictions of violence reflect the previously indicated gender distinctions in the display of violence? Do women resort to violence primarily to protect themselves or others and when they have no other alternative course of action? Do men, in contrast, more often than women, display violence for instrumental purposes such as personal gain?

GENDER, AGGRESSION, AND VIOLENCE ON BRITISH TV

The findings presented in this section derive from an analysis of the portrayal of women and men as perpetrators of violence in televised drama programs (including films, drama series, and serials) on British television. The main focus is placed on women as perpetrators of violence on screen, but a parallel analysis of men as perpetrators of violence is presented for comparison purposes.

Amount of Female and Male Violence

It was expected that female perpetrated violence would be much less prevalent than male perpetrated violence in television drama programs. The findings upheld this expectation. A total of 1,680 violent acts were located that were perpetrated by a lone female character and 11,840 violent acts were found that were perpetrated by a lone male character. Violence perpetrated by females aggregated to 153.5 minutes of program running time, as compared with 1,350.6 minutes for violence perpetrated by males. A total of 625 programs were found that contained violence perpetrated by a female and 1,273 in which violence was perpetrated by a male.

In programs that contained female violence, there was an average of 2.7 acts of female violence per program. This compared with an average of 9.3 acts of male violence in programs that contained any male violence. On average, programs containing female violence displayed 15 seconds of female violence, whereas programs with male violence displayed 64 seconds of such violence. Thus, not only were there far fewer acts of female violence overall than acts of male violence, but when female violence did occur, it tended to be much briefer in duration than male violence.

Instrumentality of Female and Male Violence on TV

It was also expected that female violence would more often be expressive, whereas male violence would be instrumental in nature. This hypothesis was explored through an analysis of the status and goals of aggression and was supported in part by the findings.

The status of aggression was represented in terms of whether the violence represented a "first strike" by the perpetrator or retaliation against someone or something else that had instigated the violence. A similar, majority proportion of all female perpetrated (70.2%) and male perpetrated acts of violence (67.7%) were first strikes. Between one in four and one in three acts of female (26.5%) and male (30.2%) violence represented some form of retaliatory action. An independent samples comparison was nonsignificant ($\chi^2 = 0.13$). Thus, when female characters were engaged in violence as perpetrators, they were just as likely as male perpetrators to have instigated the violence and were proportionately less likely to be simply retaliating against another's aggression.

Ten specific categories of aggressor goals were used to distinguish the behavior of aggressors in terms of their dramatic objectives. These categories were aggregated into two superordinate categories of behavior that reflected: (a) goals that were positive and mostly reactive and protective (family well-being, societal well-being, upholding the law, respecting the law, and self-preservation) and (b) acts of violence performed for self-centered, antisocial, instrumental reasons (destructive and evil violence, ambition/power oriented, acquisition of money, sexual reasons, religious reasons) (see Table 6.6).

Although there was little difference between genders in the extent to which perpetrated violence was pursuant of expressive or protective goals, female violence was proportionately much less likely to be motivated by selfish and instrumental goals. An independent sample chi-square analysis indicated that this difference was significant (χ^2 = 82.1, df = 1, p < .001). This result was consistent with Hypothesis 2.

FORM OF VIOLENCE

A further prediction was that female perpetrators would be proportionately more likely to use parts of their own body (e.g., hands and feet) or unconventional weapons (i.e., objects to hit with or throw) rather than conventional firearms as compared to male perpetrators. The reasoning for this was that female violence was more likely to be expressive and reactive than instrumental and premeditated. The use of conventional firearms might be more expected in the case of preplanned violence than spontaneous outbursts, during which protagonists might reach for or use any weapon that came to hand. It was also anticipated that females and males would be equally likely to use verbal aggression.

The type of violent behavior perpetrated by female and male aggressors was classified according to more than 40 behavioral categories. The 10 most frequently occurring behavioral forms of violence for each gender are shown in Table 6.7. The 10 most frequently detected categories accounted for 88% of all female perpetrated violent acts and 87% of all male perpetrated violent acts. The most salient point to emerge from an examination of this table is the degree of similarity across genders in respect to most frequent forms of behavior, the proportion of total violent acts they represented, and the rank order of many of these violent behaviors. Nine out of 10 most frequently occurring forms of violent behavior were common to female and male aggressors. The only

TABLE 6.6

Goals of Aggressors

	Female Aggressors		Male Aggressors	
	N	%	N	%
Expressive, protective goals	727	43.2	4,464	37.7
Selfish, instrumental goals	454	27.1	4,929	41.7
Other/unclassifiable	497	29.6	2,442	20.6

*Less than 0.5%

TABLE 6.7

Most Frequently Occurring Behavioral Forms of Violence

	Female Aggressors			Male Aggressors	
Form of Violence	N	%	Form of Violence	N	%
Push/trip	338	20.1	Push/trip	2,367	20.0
Shoot	228	13.6	Shoot	2,309	19.5
Attempted violence	202	12.0	Punch	1,513	12.8
Hit with object	187	11.1	Attempted violence	1,463	12.4
Slap	158	9.4	Hit with object	954	8.1
Kick	126	7.5	Kick	533	4.5
Punch	108	6.4	Verbal threat	525	4.4
Verbal threat	66	3.9	Slap	231	2.0
Property damage	31	1.8	Stab	193	1.6
Throw object	26	1.5	Property damage	192	1.6

difference in the list composition was the presence of throwing an object in the female list and of stabbing in the male list.

For purposes of further analysis, these most frequently occurring types of aggression were divided into four categories: direct aggression using the body (pushing/tripping, punching, kicking, slapping), direct aggression using conventional weapons (shooting), direct verbal aggression (verbal threat), and indirect aggression (property damage, throwing an object). The frequency counts of violent acts falling into these categories for females were 730, 228, 66, and 57, and for males were 4,644, 2,309, 525, and 294. Among these prominent categories of violence alone, the distribution for females was 67.5% (direct aggression using body), 21.1% (direct aggression—conventional weapons), 6.1% (verbal aggression), and 5.3% (indirect aggression). For males, the distribution was 59.8% (direct aggression using body), 29.7% (direct aggression—conventional weapons), 6.8% (verbal aggression), and 3.8% (indirect aggression). An independent sample chi-square analysis indicated these distributions to be significantly different ($\chi^2 = 40.6$, $df = 3$, $p < .001$). This result reflected the greater likelihood of use of the body as a weapon among female than among male perpetrators of televised violence and a lesser likelihood for females to use conventional weapons as compared with males. Females were also marginally more likely than males to use forms of indirect aggression, and both genders were equally likely to use verbal aggression.

These results offered some support for the view that male perpetrators were more likely to use conventional weapons, which are the more common instruments of preplanned violence. Females, in contrast, were relatively more likely to use their body as a weapon. The data were also consistent with the hypothesis that both genders were depicted as equally likely to use verbal aggression.

Gender of Victims

Victims of male and female perpetrators of violence were distinguished in terms of their gender. One point of interest was whether females were more likely to be violent against their own sex or the opposite sex. Female aggressors and male aggressors both tended to be more violent against male victims (74.8% and 80.3%, respectively) than against female victims (18% and 10%, respectively). It is apparent, nevertheless, that females were more likely to be violent toward their own sex than were males. An independent sample chi-square revealed that the victim gender distribution did differ significantly between male and female perpetrators of violence ($\chi^2 = 87.9$, $df = 1$, $p < .001$).

VIOLENCE AND GENDER: THE REAL WORLD

Crime has very often been theorized as either caused by or at least exacerbated by the mass media and particularly by the portrayal of fictional sex and violence (see Tracey & Morrison, 1979, on the National Viewers and Listeners Association). In that context, it is worth noting that recorded crime figures rose consistently from the 1940s until 1992 in England and Wales during the vast increase in mass media sources (i.e., terrestrial television, video, satellite and cable television) after the end of World War II. Yet, overall figures have dropped each year since 1992 during the rapid growth of, and accompanying anxiety about, satellite television and the World Wide Web. The most recent data available on crime in the United Kingdom, for the period 1996–1997, details a drop in crimes recorded by police of about 8.4% (Home Office 1999, p. 9). (The Home Office report also notes that, in the same year, crime also dropped in the United States by 2.4%, whereas The Netherlands saw the highest overall rise in relation to other available national statistics, at 13.5%.) So, during the period immediately following the dates material was broadcast and recorded for analysis during the violence study, crime as a whole seemed to be on the wane in both the United Kingdom and United States, somewhat confounding, at first glance, any claim for media effects at a time of burgeoning media sources and audiences (see Table 6.8).

But, although crime appeared to be reducing in England and Wales during the period of the broadcast violence studies (1994–1996), closer inspection of the figures shows increases in two significant areas: numbers of acts of violence against the persons rose by 5% and reports of sexual offences rose by 6% between 1996 and 1997. The overall drop was largely a result of fairly dramatic reductions in robbery (–15%), vehicle crime (–14%), and burglary (–13%), which overwhelmed the much lesser volume and smaller increase in violence. Violent crime constituted 8% of all recorded crime and includes sexual offences. These made up 10% all recorded violent crime and 0.8% of all recorded crime for 1996–1997:

TABLE 6.8
U.K. Home Office: Violence and Gender (1996–1997)

Suspect	Rape Victim*	Male Homicide Victim (N = 426)	Female Homicide Victim (N = 224)
Intimates/lovers	43%	8%	47%
Acquaintances	45%	33%	11%
Family		13%	21%
Stranger	12%	31%	13%
No suspect		16%	9%

Note: Data from Home Office Digest, October 4, 1999. Crime period 1996–1997.
   *Victims of rape are not identified by gender. Male rape was only recognized as such from the 1994 Criminal Justice and Public Order Act. Gregory and Lees (1999, p. 116) found 150 reported male rapes as compared to 5,000 reported rapes of females in 1996. For the purposes of this chapter, rape victims are therefore presumed to be female.

> Nearly two-thirds of the violent crimes were minor wounding. There were 739 offences initially recorded as homicide in 1997; homicides and more serious offences of violence accounted for 7% of violent crimes and 0.5% of all recorded crime. 6280 rapes were recorded against females and a further 350 against males; 18670 indecent assaults were recorded against females and 3500 against males. In 1997 firearms were recorded as having been used in 0.3% of recorded crimes; 5% of robberies and 1% of offences of violence against the person. (Home Office, 1999, p. 4)

Moreover, "Overall the risks of being the victim of violence are greater for men (6.1%) than women (3.6%)" (Home Office, 1999, p. 15) and that risk is greatly exacerbated by youth. In these cases, 21% of male victims and 9% of female victims were in the 16 to 24 age group. In the context of domestic violence, the gender balance of these figures changed significantly. During 1994 (the most recent available figures for domestic violence), 5% of both men and women claimed to have experienced assaults and 1% of men and 2.5% of women said they had been actually injured. Yet surveys indicate that "of married women 28% had been hit by their husbands and 33% hit or threatened with physical violence. The proportion rises to 63% among women who are separated or divorced" (Home Office, 1999, p. 15).

The relationship of perpetrators and victims of violent crime is only available for homicide and rape. The gender of the victim is available only for homicide. Of 426 males killed in 1996–1997, 31% were killed by strangers, 33% by a person known to them, 13% by family, and only 8% by a spouse or lover. Of the 224 female victims, 13% were killed by strangers, 11% by a person known to them, 21% by family, and 47% by

their spouse or lover. Serious violence is most likely to result from an attack by someone known to any victim. In the case of women, this is
most likely to be within the domestic and familial context (68%). A similar pattern exists with rape, where only 12% of rapes were committed
by someone unknown to the victim; 45% by acquaintances, and 43% by
intimates. There is no gender breakdown. (See Table 6.2).

Between 1987 and 1997 there was an increase of 134% of those serving time for rape, even though where prosecutions for rape are brought,
as few as 10% led to conviction in 1996 (http://www.rapecrisis.co.uk/
page44.html). Even the reporting of rape merely represents the tip of an
iceberg as "only 8% of raped women ... reported the assault to the police"
(Segal, 1990, p. 242). There was also an increase of 38% of prisoners for
other sexual offences and an increase of 27% for violent sentences. Offender profiles show "more than 1 in 4 males but only 1 in 10 females
admitted to offences of violence. 1 in 4 males and 1 in 6 females admitted
offences of vandalism or arson" (Home Office, 1999, p. 22). There were
48,800 prisoners in England and Wales during the period from June
1996 to June 1997. Twenty-one percent of the prison population is
serving time for violence and 8% for sexual offences.

Figures from the United States show that measures for gendered violence in the United Kingdom are not uniquely British, but show patterns
of real crime that compare broadly with those in the United States: "On
average each year, women experienced over 572,000 violent victimiza-
tions committed by an intimate, compared to approximately 49000 incidents committed against men" (BJS, 1994).

As in the United Kingdom, it is the young who are most vulnerable:
"Women aged 20–34 had the highest rates of violent victimization attrib-
utable to intimates (16 per 1000 persons) of any age group" (BJS, 1994).
Bureau of Justice Statistics show that, in 1991, 7% of the 328,000 prisoners in state penitentiaries were in jail for violent offences against intimates. Of these, 35% were convicted of murder, 30% of assault, and 25%
had committed rape or other sexual assault. As in the United Kingdom,
intimate violence is not always reported; over 18% of victims did not report the incident, as compared to only 3% for those abused by strangers
(BJS, 1994). In addition, "More than 90 women were murdered every
week in 1991—9 out of 10 were murdered by men" (Committee on the
Judiciary, U.S. Senate, 1992, p. 2). It was further reported that "of the
5745 women murdered in 1991, 6 out of 10 were killed by someone they
knew. Half were murdered by a spouse or someone with whom they had
been intimate" ("When Violence Hits Home," 1991).

In real life, in the United Kingdom and the United States, women are
most at risk of violence from men with whom they have had previous
sexual relations, often in their own homes. That risk may be assault,
rape, or murder. Men, on the other hand, were far more likely to experience violence at the hands of strangers in both countries. One major difference in violence between men and women in the United States
compared to the United Kingdom is that the ready availability of guns in

the United States leads to some 62% of intimate killings resulting from shooting. Even American women use guns: according to the FBI's Supplemental Homicide reports for 1992, 61% of murdered husbands or ex-husbands were shot to death in the United States. In the United Kingdom, women tend to use knives (often just from the household kitchen) and men use their hands.

It is curious that factual reporting of such real gendered crime in the newspapers has included gratuitous journalistic descriptions of violence against women; popular newspapers often show apparently salacious interest in rape; reporting focuses on the female victim's "attractiveness" or "flirtatiousness"; the press fail to report on the masculinity at the heart of such violence or reflexively recognize the dangers for justice of prejudicial accounts of crimes (Heidensohn, 1986; Lees, 1995; Wykes, 1998, 2001). Yet, there has been no call to censor such reporting of real crime, despite its possible implications for the criminal justice process, its potential effects on readers, and the ongoing pressures to censor fictional accounts of sexual titillation and violence. The only time there has been a call to censor the British press related to the portrayal of gender was when British MP. Clare Short called for an end to the British popular newspaper *The Sun's* daily page 3 photograph of a topless model:

> In 1986 MP Clare Short introduced a Parliamentary Bill to ban the use of the Page Three pin-up girl on the grounds that it was embarrassing and degrading for women. In the heated debates which followed—in parliament, in the media and around the country—the relationship of women's sexualised image to women's public presence became an issue, which divided feminists as well as the public at large. (Holland, 1998, p. 18)

Page 3 still appears—every day—and there has been little further outrage about newspaper representations of sex or violence. Yet, in contrast, broadcasting and film fiction is constantly scrutinized in the search for causes of social ills. The following discussion considers the validity of that accusatory scrutiny by comparing real and fictional gendered violence.

CONCLUSIONS

An analysis of gendered violence in drama programing on British television was reported in this chapter. This analysis examined the role of gender in the perpetration of violence and the representation of female victimization in screen violence. A sample of 2,220 drama programs recorded from 28 days of television output yielded 1,803 violent acts with female targets. A total of 1,680 violent acts were perpetrated by a lone female character, as compared with 11,804 perpetrated by a lone male character.

The broad definition of violence meant that a wide variety of on-screen behaviors were cataloged, with much of this aggressive behavior being mild in nature. The analytical framework was not untypical for this type of research and had been harmonized with violence definitions used in other major studies of this sort (see Cumberbatch et al., 1987;

Federman, 1997). Following the suggestions of other commentators (e.g., Wilson et al., 1996), the current analysis closely scrutinized the attributes of violent acts as much as the sheer quantity of violence. In particular, attention was focused on the occurrence of violence characterized by high risk factors. These are attributes of violence—such as form, context, outcomes, and perpetrators—that have previously been shown to mediate audience reactions (see Greenberg & Gordon, 1972a, 1972b, 1972c; Gunter, 1985; Van der Voort, 1986). Given concerns about violence directed against women (Stanko, 1985), these factors were deemed to be of special significance in an examination of televised depictions of female victimization.

The present analysis indicated that the great majority of violent acts in which females were victims could be classified as potentially low risk in terms of many vital attributes. At the same time, however, violent portrayals did emerge that combined a number of potentially high risk elements within the same scene. Furthermore, certain programs were found (usually films originally made for the cinema) that contained relatively high numbers of acts of female victimization.

Presence of High Risk Attributes

The major risk factors explored in this analysis comprised the form of violence along with the instruments of aggression used by perpetrators of violence, the consequences of violence, and the motivational context of violence. These factors have previously been shown to mediate viewers' perception of on-screen violence (Gunter, 1985; Gunter & Furnham, 1984), and their identification with the action that can in turn influence the severity of emotional and behavioral reactions to television violence (Lagerspetz et al., 1978; Noble, 1975; Potter, 1999; Turner & Berkowitz, 1972).

Another important feature linked to the realism of violence that operates through the psychological mechanism of identification is the closeness to home of the violence. Violence that occurs in domestic settings, for example, may be more likely to strike a chord with viewers because of the increased likelihood that such settings and the anger displays, arguments, and overt aggression depicted in them, resemble situations with which they are familiar in their own lives (D. G. Perry & L. C. Perry, 1976). This analysis of drama programing on mainstream British television revealed a significant number of acts of violent female victimization that occurred with a domestic context. These incidents were most likely to occur in films, and were rare in British-produced or American-produced made-for-TV drama programs. Most incidents involved a woman being attacked by a man, with both usually in the young adult age group of 20 to 35 years. Although these raw statistics may seem worrisome on the surface, further analysis indicated that it was rare for other significant risk factors to be associated with such scenes. For instance, serious physical injury to the victim was rare, occurring in only a handful of cases.

Another motivational factor of concern when mixed with violence is sexual behavior. Depictions of sexually motivated violence have been found to have pronounced effects on the attitudes of male viewers toward women and more especially toward rape victims (Donnerstein, 1983; D. Linz, 1985). More than 100 instances of sexually motivated violence against females were found in this analysis, most of which occurred in films. In the current analysis, the great majority of the female targets were young women between age 20 and 35 years, with just a handful of cases emerging in which the victims were teenagers. Fifteen cases of rape emerged from the analysis of scenes in which the violence against females was classified as sexually driven or occurred in a sexual context. Despite these statistics, there were just four cases in which serious physical injury was caused to the victim and five more cases in which the victim was killed. These occurred in a comprehensive analysis of television output on 10 channels covering 28 days sampled over a period of 12 months. All incidents occurred in films originally made for the cinema.

Another key risk factor that mediates audience reactions to televised violence is the degree of harm or injury caused to victims. Viewers are more disturbed by scenes of violence in which victims are seriously hurt or killed. Further, the behavioral impact of televised violence on viewers has also been shown to be enhanced, under certain circumstances, by depicting the pain and suffering of victims (Baron, 1971a, 1971b; Hartmann, 1969). The current analysis showed that the greater majority of violent acts in which victims were female suffered either mild injury or no injury at all. Nevertheless, female victims were killed in 9% of the violent incidents in which they were targeted and seriously hurt in a further 4%. In numerical terms, the latter two types of outcome comprised a total of 241 scenes of violence, spread over 28 days of output on 10 television channels. Although the overall distribution of violence against females indicated that it was generally mild, serious consequences occurred in one in seven cases. However, this finding is counterbalanced by the fact that, statistically speaking, fewer than one such incident occurred per channel per day.

Perpetrators and Their Methods Against Female Victims

Female victims were most likely to be attacked by male aggressors. In a significant number of cases, however, females were attacked by members of their own sex. In general, the violence aimed at female targets was mild. Female targets were victims of mild physical assault such as pushing and shoving, attempted violence that failed to connect, or verbal threats. Even so, the third most likely form of violence in scenes of female victimization involved females being shot at. Even more dramatic was the finding that strangulation was among the 10 most frequently used forms of violence against females. More than 60 acts of violence involved a female victim being strangled. One form of violence about which viewers are concerned is stabbing (Gunter, 1985). This study found that stabbing incidents involving female victims, however, were rare.

Elsewhere, it has been observed that females are more likely to be involved in verbal aggression than any other form of violence (Potter et al., 1995, 1997). This research found that verbal threats were among the most frequently occurring forms of violence in scenes of female victimization, although not the most frequent. However, male aggressors and female aggressors were equally likely to use verbal threats against female victims. More broadly, male aggressors used a wider variety of forms of violence when attacking female victims than did female aggressors.

Female victimization represents a visible, but not predominant, form of violence in televised films and drama programs on mainstream British channels. Around 1 in 10 violent incidents in these programs featured a female victim. Interest in the representation of violence on television in the past has often been framed within a cultivation effects perspective, whereby stereotyped patterns of portrayals on screen are believed to shape public beliefs about the real-life occurrences of those on-screen entities (see Gerbner & Gross, 1976; Gerbner et al., 1978, 1979). The representation of female violent victimization cataloged in this study was not generally prevalent or serious enough to warrant concern about its capacity to cultivate fear of victimization among females in the audience. Moreover, the majority of such acts of violence was not characterized by high risk attributes of the sort hypothesized to enhance adverse audience reactions (Wilson et al., 1996). Female targets of violence on screen tended to predominantly to be young physically robust females, rather than more vulnerable subgroups, such as the very young or very old. Although a minority of these incidents were characterized by attributes known to enhance severe perceptual or emotional responses in viewers, these risk factors tended to occur singly rather than in dangerously high combinations.

Female Aggressors

Within the drama genre on British television, males were seven times as likely to perpetrate violence as were females. Female violence occurred in half as many drama programs and films as did male violence. Further, when male violence occurred, it tended to be more prolonged than was female violence. On average, male violence occupied four times as much running time as female violence in those programs that contained any male or female violence. The dominance of male aggressors in mainstream television drama programs in Britain is consistent with findings from the United States (*National Television Violence Study*, 1997, 1998).

Whereas the quantity of male violence far exceeded that of female violence, however, the significance of any female violence that does occur may stem more from its character than from the quantity. Gender differences have been observed in the extent to which males and females use aggression (Berkowitz, 1993; A. Campbell, 1995; White & Kowalski, 1994). It is not, however, simply the case that aggressiveness is conceived to be primarily a male trait. Whereas men have exhibited a greater readiness to use physical aggression than women (Buss & M. Perry, 1992; M. B. Harris & Knight-Bohnhoff, 1996), gender differences in reported use of verbal aggression (Archer et al., 1995; Gladue & Bailey, 1995) and indirect aggression (Bjorkqvist, 1994; Bjorkqvist et al., 1994; Hines & Fry, 1994) are slight.

Certainly, as far as viewers are concerned, prior research has indicated that reactions to female- and male-perpetrated violence can differ markedly (Gunter, 1985). Other research on public perceptions of gender involvement in violence, beyond the media context, has revealed that the way aggressive behavior is evaluated can depend significantly on the sex of the aggressor and sex of the victim (Bjorkqvist & Niemela, 1992; Burbank, 1987). Gender stereotypes appear to play an important role in shaping people's responses to aggressive acts and their opinions toward the perpetrators of violence in different situations (Eagly & Steffen, 1986; R. J. Harris & Cook, 1994).

The current analysis revealed many similarities in the nature of violence perpetrated by female and male actors. Nevertheless, some interesting and occasionally significant differences did emerge in the gender distribution of particular types of violence. There was a tendency for female perpetrators to display their aggression in expressive and reactive contexts in the service of self-preservation or the protection of self and others. Thus, although there was no overall difference in the distribution of "first strike" versus retaliatory acts of violence by gender, female aggression was nevertheless dominated by a need to respond to a source of threat. In contrast, male aggression was more frequently driven by selfish, instrumental goals, such as the acquisition of power, status, and money. These findings were consistent with earlier work highlighting the primarily instrumental nature of male aggression and expressive nature of female aggression (A. Campbell & Muncer, 1987; A. Campbell et al., 1992, 1993).

In terms of the form of the violence, male and female violence exhibited similar overall profiles. Even so, female aggressors were more likely to use their body as a weapon and less likely to use conventional firearms when compared with male aggressors. Both genders were equally likely to display first strike aggression, as distinct from retaliatory aggression, so it was not the case that women were mostly drawn into violence as a form of retaliation or self-defense having been provoked first by someone else.

Once involved in an aggressive altercation, female actors often turned to similar forms of aggression as male aggressors. These generally involved the use of a part of the body as a weapon, such as the hand or foot. Proportionately, male aggressors shot their victims to a greater extent than did female aggressors, but for both genders, shooting a victim was the second most popular form of violence.

On comparing the distribution of female and male aggressors within particular violent forms with the overall gender distribution of violent acts in television drama programs, female aggressors were found to be more likely than male aggressors to engage in slapping and kicking in their aggressive behavior. The prevalence among violent women on television to use expressive and reactive forms of violence (e.g., slapping someone) or indirect, displaced aggression (e.g., throwing objects) was consistent with earlier reports of women demonstrating these types of aggression in actuality, especially in domestic or romantic situations (M. B. Harris, 1991; McNeely & Mann, 1990; Sugarman & Hotaling, 1989). There was equal use of verbal aggression by women and men. This pattern confirmed earlier self-report evidence from men and women (Buss & M. Perry, 1992).

Male actors were more frequently involved in violent interactions as both perpetrators and victims than were female actors. Even so, there was a marked difference in the degree to which perpetrators of television violence victimized their own gender. Women were proportionately more likely to commit violence against their own gender than were men. The tendency of females to turn on their own gender has been observed among children, although such aggressiveness is often manifest in the form of social exclusion, malicious gossip, and verbal remarks rather than actual physical altercations. Lagerspetz, Bjorkqvist, and Peltonen (1988) found that girls would be more likely to exclude newcomers from a group more than boys, especially during initial social interactions. The real significance of gender of perpetrator and gender of victim resides in the ways such scenarios are likely to be perceived by the television audience. Research has shown that aggression from males is rated more seriously than aggression from females across a range of situations. Furthermore, aggression directed toward females is rated more negatively than aggression directed toward males (M. B. Harris, 1991, 1994, 1995). Research with television scenes has indicated, however, that such perceptions can also be mediated by other factors, such as the realism of the violence and its geographical location. Under some circumstances, female aggression may be rated in more serious terms than male aggression, especially when the violence is untypical (Gunter, 1985).

What emerged from this analysis, therefore, was that gender differences in involvement in violence on television can be defined quantitatively and qualitatively. Males are much more likely to be involved in violence as aggressors and victims than are females. In many respects, female and male violence is similar in nature. However, where significant differences did occur, they revealed subtle distinctions in the nature of the violence involving each gender. Females involved in violence as aggressors are more likely than males to display expressive and reactive forms of aggression concerned principally with protecting themselves or others, and are less likely than males to display instrumental aggression in the service of personal gain.

Gendered Violence: Television Versus Reality

This chapter has focused on the depiction of violence involving women either as victims or aggressors. Traditionally, most attention has been devoted to the way women are depicted as victims on television. The prevalence of violence on television has been cited in connection with factors thought to contribute to public fear of crime (Gerbner et al., 1978; 1979; Wober & Gunter, 1988). Despite the public uproar about an increasingly violent and crime ridden society, often allegedly fueled by television and film violence, the vast majority of crimes in Britain are nonviolent, with just 8% involving some violence. Moreover, despite the emphasis on fear of crime, reports of fear are low or described as quite erroneously felt: "18% of women and 3% of men felt very unsafe on the street at nights; while 3% of women and 1% of men felt unsafe at home at night. Women aged 60 and over felt most unsafe; 31% said they felt very unsafe on the streets at night" (Home Office, 1999, p. 12).

Although the press emphasize attacks on women by strangers (Dobash & Dobash, 1992), women are most at risk at home from people they know and the elderly are at least risk of any kind of violence at all. It may be that, in fact, if there is any effect from broadcast violence, then it is to construct an artificially anxious populace among those who should be least anxious or, in the case of women, promote anxiety about something other than the likely source of risk. Those who are actually at risk from dangerous strangers on the streets (21% of young men, age 16–24, were deemed at risk of violence according to the 1998 British Crime Survey) appear to be largely oblivious to the threat, in as much as only 3% of men admit to any fear. This seems even more odd when broadcast representations of victims are examined because these show men as being at greatest risk of becoming victims of violence. Seventy-nine per cent of the victims of male aggressors on television were coded as male, as were 75% of the victims of female aggressors. Also, 52% of victims of male violence and 53% of victims of female violence were between age 20 and 35. Add to these figures the fact that on television about one third of all violence where gender was a clear variable occurred in the city and that 29% of male violence and 37% of female violence was interpersonal rather than offered in a war or criminal context, young men should be very afraid on the street.

In contrast, women were victims of male violence in 11% of acts on television and victims of female violence in 18% of occurrences. Male violence was depicted on television as most usually meted out by a criminal (18%), situation character (14%), police officer (8%), member of the armed forces (7%), and in only 1 in 20 cases, by an domestic assailant (5%). Yet, in real life, women are most at risk from rape and extreme violence at home and/or from men they know "intimately." Moreover, rape by men accounted for only 0.1% of male violence on television in the material broadcast in 1995–1996, whereas for the following period in real life sexual offending rose by 6% and "6280 rapes were recorded against females and a further 350 against males" (Home Office, 1999, p. 4). Of those rapes, 43% were committed by intimates and 45% by acquaintances and, in cases where violence toward women ended in murder, 47% of suspects were the woman's spouse or lover.

Consequently, the model of threat to men offered by television drama in the period of the study was relatively similar to the kind of violence men might encounter in reality. In both instances, young men are at risk in the city from other young men who are probably strangers. It is interesting that when asked about their fear of crime, young men do not seem to recognize this threat: "Indeed on the face of the evidence frequently discussed in the fear of crime debate, it could be argued that it is (young) men who behave irrationally given their greater exposure to risk from crime and their lower reported levels of fear of crime" (Walklate, 2001, p. 92).

Irrationality may not, however, be the most accurate description of such male refusal. Rather, hegemonic masculinity with its constructions of men as strong, controlling, risk taking, and resourceful (Connell, 1987) suggests men may well either deny or simply not recognize fear because it conflicts with the most pervasive cultural expectations of what it means to be a man. Simply, to be fearful is not to be masculine and, in addition, a certain amount of aggression is very much the mark of manhood (T. W. Smith, 1984). Also, few depictions of violence on television actually show much in the way of really harmful results, contributing to the construction of masculinity as secure, powerful, and aggressive, although not necessarily in a negative way.

Depictions of women's experience of violence on British television during 1995–1996 seemed conversely neither to comply with their real experiences nor to particularly promote the kind of sexual attacks for which the mass media and film are blamed. The broadcast material seemed to focus not on women's everyday experience of violence (Stanko, 1990), but rather masculinized women by placing them in violent situations that are more likely to be the site of male-on-male violence (i.e., crime, the street, and strangers). In fact women's real vulnerability to violence (i.e., rape and aggression from men they know at home) was almost made invisible on television (Tuchman, 1978b). Nor was there very much evidence of the area, much publicized in the 1990s, where provoked and battered women have killed assailants, who are usually their spouses or lovers, in the context of domestic violence (Wykes, 1995). Instead, women, as often as men, tended to appear as primary attackers rather than retaliators.

The actual volume proportions of broadcast gendered violence did roughly correspond with real crime statistics (1,680, or 12.4% of violent acts by lone women, and 11,840 violent acts by lone men; women's violence occupied 153.5 minutes of airtime and men's violence occupied 1350.6 minutes). Such figures reasonably mirror real crime statistics, which show that 83% of all "convicted or cautioned offenders in 1997 were male" (Home Office, 1999, p. 24) and in a study of young people and crime, only 1 in 10 females admitted to violence (Home Office, 1999, p. 22). However, the nature of the portrayed violence differed significantly between the genders. The masculine model of violence appeared to more or less confirm real male violence and victimhood and the feminine model appeared to contradict and deny both real female violence and real female victimhood. The contradictory images included women shown getting into serious trouble by emulating male behaviors. Curiously, this happened often and continues to happen in films or television drama that show women as police officers (e.g., *Blue Steel* and *Prime Suspect*), perhaps because the police officer is such an unassailable icon of masculinity (Reiner, 1992). So, in a sense, the effect of such representations may be similar to that theorized for images of male violence—a reenforcement of traditional femininity or, as Heidensohn (1986) argued, women were being instructed in how to behave as proper respectable women.

Perhaps what is more worrying is the potential effect of the missing discourses of gendered violence in the sample analyzed. Audiences were not shown the truth of women's victimization, both in terms of sexual assault and physical violence, at the hands, literally, of men with whom they have had intimate relationships, often in the supposed safety of their own homes. The effect is to leave intact myths about marriage, family, and home and to leave unchallenged men's power within these institutions.

Again, in essence, what is achieved by nondisclosure in the context of women and violence serves the interests of hegemonic masculinity. In terms of the effects lobby, representations of violence and gender in the early 1990s actually served the interests of conservatism rather than challenging or threatening the moral order. They underpinned the gender norms and values of the moral right by upholding the status quo of gender relations. And, in that sense, the concerns from radical feminism about the possible effect of sex and violence on the screen may also be upheld by the data from the study, not because people are being bombarded with increasingly pornographic representations of violence against women, but because the extent and nature of already real and present violence against women is not being portrayed, let alone critiqued.

So, in terms of the effect of gendered violence in broadcast fiction during 1995 and 1996, audiences were being taught a lesson not so much about violence but about gender. Such a possible effect suggests that the normalizing theory of television should be more focused on the ways in which programs replicate, legitimate, or obfuscate existing conditions in the social organization of gender, which maintain injustice, oppression, and cruelty rather than focus (as much research on the mass media and violence does) on the desensitizing effect of the familiarity of images of crime and violence as possibly instigating new or increased criminality or perversion.

Chapter **7**

Children and Violence
on Television

A great deal of concern is reserved for the involvement of children in television violence. Although research has shown that television is not invariably bad for children, it has also shown that television can, and does, influence children to some extent. Television interacts with children in both a positive and negative manner (Potter, 1999) and it follows that its effects can be either good or bad depending on how the medium is used (Gunter & McAleer, 1997). Problematically for researchers, policymakers, and parents, the effects on the young are rarely simple or direct. Questions relating to children and television violence are often exacerbated by violent events that occur in society, which seem to be linked to screen violence. In Britain, the links made during the trial between the killing of 2-year-old James Bulger in 1993 and alleged viewing by his 10-year-old killers of the video *Child's Play 3* is often cited as an example of how children growing up in a "violent video culture" can become violent themselves (Barker & Petley, 1997). Even though it is unlikely that the murderers actually saw that particular video, their exposure to similar types of video has been viewed as a type of electronic "child abuse" (Buckingham, 1997; Newson, 1994).

A direct causal link between screen violence and aggressive behavior is still a hotly disputed issue, and a body of opinion based on partial and impressionistic research findings exacerbates fears about the response of children to screen violence. Often the most vociferous opinions have derived from antitelevision lobby groups whose own empirical findings, although loudly trumpeted in the media, seldom stand up to close critical scrutiny. One of the most substantive concerns rests on the assumption that children are exposed to massive amounts of violence on television during the pre-adult years and such experience may condition in many of them a pro-violence mentality or exaggerated fear for their own safety. This chapter examines the extent to which British television screens violent material and the likelihood that children will be exposed to this material. Further, the analysis considers the extent to which children may be exposed to material that might disturb them or is likely to encourage them to emulate what they see.

PERSPECTIVES ON EFFECTS

Three perspectives have dominated thinking about the relation between children and the media. These have resulted in a simplistic account of the likely dangers of television and have led to what Barker (1997, p. 13) called "common sense" knowledge about the media. These perspectives have focused on the influence of television on behavior, thought processes, and beliefs and attitudes (Buckingham, 1993a). Questions about dangers of television viewing are almost inevitably questions about children and television violence. Such questions also draw attention to the role and responsibilities of the media and its regulators to ensure that children are protected from the potential harm that television viewing may do them. Often, concerns about the effects of television violence can be seen as part of a broader anxiety about increased conflict in society or fears that social order is disintegrating. Arguments relating the media to wider social ills, or bad or disturbing behavior in children, are typically based on presumed effects of television viewing and ignore the complexity and sophistication of adults and children's understanding of television messages.

A second major area of concern about children and television focuses on the effects of television on children's thought processes. The emphasis here is centered, not on the content of television, but on the nature of the activity of viewing itself. Television is seen to somehow lure children into only seeking to engage in entertainment. This then encourages their brains to work at a lower level, destroys their ability to engage in intelligent thought processes, and reduces their attention span and linguistic skills. The concern here is that children consequently become passive acceptors of media messages (Winn, 1977).

Postman (1989) argued that television is primarily responsible for the "disappearance of childhood," where the medium has led to a blurring of the distinction between adulthood and childhood. The exposure of youngsters to television means that adults can no longer keep children ignorant of adult knowledge. According to this view, children who watch television copy the behavior of adults at the expense of their own sense of identity and may even become increasingly discontented and less well behaved. There is a problem with claims relating to these types of influences of television on children and the fears that this will lead to a breakdown in social order because researchers have been unable to prove a causal connection between television and these broader social and behavioral developments.

A third major area of concern about children and television focuses on the influence of television on children's attitudes and beliefs, rather than on their behavior or thought processes. The media are seen here as a mechanism through which the ruling class maintains its ideological domination of subordinates. For some, the media are regarded as propagating attitudes, which children may adopt, either consciously or unconsciously. Notwithstanding the fact that many of the attitudes and values shown on television may indeed be unsuitable for children, it is the perception of television as a mechanism for ideological domination that is problematic. Such views are based around the idea that the audience is an innocent victim of a powerful propaganda tool, whereby the media are able to impose particular attitudes and values on a passive audience. Such a view is simplistic because it ignores the active participation of viewers in making meaning and interpreting media messages, and fails to recognize the complex processes involved in cultural consumption of media products (Hall, 1981). This view also fails to consider other, and perhaps more powerful, sources of influence on children like parents, school, and their friends.

Although the perspectives outlined ignore the complexity and sophistication of children's understanding of television messages, make assumptions about the passivity of children's viewing, and are often based on partial or impressionistic evidence, they provide a seemingly plausible "explanation" about the relation between children and television. These perspectives, notwithstanding the differences in terms of their areas of concern, also serve to exacerbate parental and policymakers' anxiety about the relation between children and television violence.

Consequently, children are consistently seen to be those who are likely to be most at risk from television violence. The common view is that children lack the skills to understand the messages from television in the same way as adults. The approach to children's relationship with television is generally a pessimistic one, whereby children should be protected (Buckingham, 1997; Clifford, Gunter, & McAleer 1995).

As Hodge and Tripp (1986) pointed out, however, children can also foster a positive relation with television, whereby television provides an opportunity for cognitive growth and new educational experiences. Research has shown that children do not simply sit passively and watch the images on the screen, absorbing everything and anything that is presented without question or interpretation. They often actively select what to watch and also place their own meanings on programming and advertising content. Some programs are designed to inform and educate, whereas others are made to entertain. But entertainment programs may also cultivate an awareness of certain aspects of life and social problems. Programs made to inform may also need to be entertaining in order to win and maintain their audience. There is a body of academic research evidence, which demonstrates the positive learning potential of television programs with a direct educational intention (e.g., *Sesame Street*, *Play School*, and *Rainbow*; Gunter & McAleer, 1997).

Clifford et al. (1995) argued that both the positive and negative views of the relation children foster with television have some truth in them. Television can be a positive tool in the education of children, which may be used to educate and inform them. Conversely, television may be misused and will consequently be more likely to misinform, mislead, and act as a bad influence on children.

A key to the concern about children's relation with television is based on the knowledge that cognitive processing is related to age. Developmental psychologists, in particular Piaget, have shown that the minds of children develop cognitively between birth and age 12 via a number of distinct stages and during these formative years children of different ages have differing abilities to process television content. Very young children and babies show interest in the movement and sounds on the television screen, but it is not until age 6 that children develop the ability to make sense of story lines (Kodaira, 1990). By age 12, they are seen to be cognitively mature, although there is a growing research evidence to show that adults also continue to develop cognitively (Potter, 1999). Thus, children may display initial attention to the television screen as early as 6 months old (Hollenbeck & Slaby, 1979), and establish regular viewing patterns by age 3 or 4 (Huston et al., 1983). Very young children below age 8, however, are often unable to make links between a character's violent behavior on screen and the motives, which may have been established at some earlier point in the story (Collins, 1973, 1983). By age 10 to 12, children have developed an understanding of characters' motives for their actions and can make links between on-screen actions and the story events that caused them to happen (Van der Voort, 1986).

Cognitive theory has been criticized for being too compartmentalized (Potter, 1999). Indeed, it is not possible to consistently demonstrate that children of a particular age will be at the same development stage. Other factors, such as socioeconomic status and family background, affect children's development. Van der Voort (1986) showed that children from a lower socioeconomic background would be more likely to identify with violent characters than children of a higher socioeconomic status. He also showed that not all children of the same age relate to television in the same way. He identified differences in preference for violence, perception of reality, and the level of identification with different characters. Furthermore, the relations within the family are significant, with abused children more likely to watch violent television and to identify with the perpetrators of violence (Heath, Bresolin, & Rinaldi, 1989). Children growing up in stressful family environments may receive less support from their parents or siblings and could be more vulnerable to the effects of media violence than those growing up in calm, supportive family environments or those with strong values against violence (Borduin, Mann, Cone, & Henggeler, 1995; Heath et al., 1989; Tangney, 1988; Tangney & Feshbach, 1988).

It is worth noting that research has shown that despite claims that children are today spending far too much time watching television, they are by no means the heaviest viewers. Adults (except those in the 18–24 age group) spend more hours watching television than children. Children watch a mixture of programing, with *Mighty Morphin Power Rangers*, cartoons, *Byker Grove, Grange Hill*, and Saturday Disney being favorites, but they also like to watch a wide variety of programs made for adults (Independent Televison Commission, 1996). Many of these are nonviolent family-centered sitcoms, showing that violence is not the only way to attract child viewers (Cantor, 1994). Many programs that children choose to watch, however, are action and adventure programs, such as *Knight Rider, The A Team*, and reality programs dealing with crime themes and often containing real-life violence. Children do distinguish between program types, however, favoring adventure and crime drama above the more violent law enforcement programs (Van der Voort, 1986). Furthermore, among those programs targeted specifically at child audiences, especially those shown on Saturday mornings, the most popular tend to be those containing violence—particularly cartoons (Stipp, 1995).

When children watch television is an important question and is becoming more so as television broadcasting hours continue to expand. The main concern is about children staying up late at night to watch television, often watching programs deemed to be unsuitable for them by regulators. Viewing figures produced for the television industry in Britain show that substantial numbers of children watch television until quite late (ITC, 1996). The data show that 1 in 24 6-year-olds are watching television between 10 p.m. and 11 p.m. and around 1 in 5 10- to 15-year-olds are still up at this time on the average weekday. Children are watching most from 4 p.m. until about 11 p.m. On Saturday night, the numbers of children viewing increase.

Analysis of the amount of violence on television, which may have an impact on children, therefore needs to consider programs specifically made for children as well as other programs aimed at adult viewers that children may be viewing. The type and amount of violence located in programs involving children in violence are significant, because research has shown that children tend to identify more closely with characters who are near to their own age (Potter, 1999). The analysis presented in this chapter therefore examines children's programs showing children as aggressors or victims of violence, as well as programs not specifically made for children that involve children in violence.

VIOLENCE ON PROGRAMS INVOLVING CHILDREN

Violence has been previously noted as a prevalent feature of programs aimed at children. In the United States, for instance, Saturday morning cartoons and noncartoon action shows made for young viewers were found to be among the most violent programs on network television (Gerbner et al., 1978, 1979, 1980a). In this case, the violent nature of programs was measured simply in terms of numbers of violent acts without any further qualification of violence according to the dramatic context or setting in which it occurred.

On British television, Cumberbatch and his colleagues found that cartoons (54%) were far more likely to contain violence than noncartoon programs (14%) aimed at children. Even when violence was registered for noncartoon programs, often these programs were magazines that contained many different items (e.g., music, comedy, games, interviews), among which were cartoons. Much of the violence in these programs occurred in the cartoons or cartoon extracts embedded in them. When all cartoon material was excluded, fewer than 5% of children's programs contained any violence. Indeed, cartoons contributed about one tenth of all the violent acts counted on the four major (terrestrial) channels in Britain in 1986 (Cumberbatch et al., 1987).

Interpreting the significance of findings such as those already reported depends on how significant cartoon violence is considered to be in the context of children's reactions to screen violence. Research evidence has indicated that adults, teenagers and children make distinctions between violent portrayals on the basis of program genre and the context in which violence occurs (Gunter, 1985; Hodge & Tripp, 1986; Howitt & Cumberbatch, 1974). Despite their tender years, by age 9, children recognize the fantastic nature of cartoons and respond to them differently from noncartoon programs that may present violence in a more realistic fashion (Buckingham, 1993a; Hodge & Tripp, 1986).

Although cartoons can be categorized as a special category of entertainment in which hostile acts may not be perceived by viewers as representing true "violence" in the everyday sense, another type of children's program has been the source of concern, despite its fantasy nature. Action shows featuring fantastic human heroes and villains or animated characters with human persona (e.g., the *Teenage Mutant Ninja Turtles* and the *Mighty Morphin Power Rangers*), have been criticized for encouraging children to emulate the violent actions routinely displayed by lead characters. Other dramas that have grown out of video games, such as *Mortal Kombat*, have been a source of equal dismay among critics of televised violence.

Such television shows are believed to exert powerful effects on children because they represent part of a wider marketing mix that includes spin-off merchandise, such as toys and games with which children can interact and role play. For some time, researchers have observed an increase in the extent of superhero play themes among very young children (French, Pena, & Homes, 1987; Jennings & Gillis-Olion, 1980; Kostelnik, Whiren, & Stein, 1986; Paley, 1984). The increased presence of toy action figures, associated with popular children's television action series, may be contributing to this trend (French & Pena, 1991).

Any analysis of violence on television involving children must therefore keep in mind that particular types of violence may have special significance for young viewers because of links between programs and commodities with which children, as young consumers, are invited to engage. Equally, a predominance of violence in cartoons may be less of a cause for concern.

VIOLENCE AND CHILDREN ON BRITISH TELEVISION

The analysis of young people and violence began with a calculation of the overall extent to which children and teenagers were involved in violence on British television. In this case, children were characters depicted on screen as involved in violence whose age was estimated to be age 14 or under. Teenagers were actors involved in violence whose age was estimated at between age 15 and 19. Table 7.1 summarizes the age distribution of aggressors and victims across all program genres. Results are shown for the 2 years of the study.

Both aggressors and victims of violence on television were most likely to be young adults between age 20 and 35, with around 40% being older than this. Children represented around 1.8% and 2% of aggressors and victims, respectively, across the 2 years. Teenagers were involved in violence somewhat more frequently, representing around 4.5% and 4.4% of aggressors and victims, respectively, across the 2 years.

Table 7.2 uses an aggressor–victim ratio to show that, once involved in violence, children under age 14 are relatively more likely to be portrayed as victims than as aggressors. All other age groups, except old adults in the 1996 sample, once involved in violence, were relatively more likely to appear as aggressors. Such a finding is socially significant because it indicates a particular pattern of representation of children in

TABLE 7.1

Percentage and Number of Victims and Aggressors Across All Programs

	Aggressors				Victims			
	1995		1996		1995		1996	
	N	%	N	%	N	%	N	%
Child (up to age 14)	326	1.5	675	2.0	370	1.7	795	2.4
Teenager (age 15–19)	1,183	5.6	1,158	3.5	1,016	4.8	1,279	3.9
Subtotal	1,509	7.1	1,833	5.5	1,386	6.5	2,074	6.3
Young adult	10,827	51.1	14,372	43.3	10,060	47.5	13,957	42.1
Middle-aged adult	4,239	20.0	6,607	19.9	4,162	19.7	6,020	18.2
Old adult	149	0.7	139	0.4	142	0.7	163	0.5
Mixed ages	656	3.1	1,800	5.4	1,453	6.9	2,154	6.5
Unclassified	3,791	18.0	8,417	25.5	3,968	18.7	8,800	?
Total	21,171	100.0	33,168	100.0	21,171	100.0	33,168	

TABLE 7.2

Aggressor–Victim Ratio

	1995	1996
Child (up to age 14)	0.88	0.85
Teenager (age 15–19)	1.16	0.91
Young adult	1.08	1.03
Middle-aged adult	1.02	1.10
Old adult	1.05	0.85

violent situations, whereby they are relatively more likely to be portrayed as victims than as aggressors.

Violence in Children's Programs

The 2-year study into television violence, from which this book draws its data, classified children's programing into two categories: general children's programs and children's cartoons. More than one half of children's programs that contained violence were noncartoon shows in 1995 and nearly 7 in 10 fell into this category in 1996 (see Table 7.3). Hence, cartoons were markedly less likely to contain violence than noncartoon programs aimed at the child audience.

The amount of program running time occupied by violence was calculated for children's programs across all the channels monitored. In total, the running time was 433.5 minutes in 1994–1995, amounting to 1.5% of total television programing, and 990.2 minutes in 1995–1996, amounting to 2.6% of television programing overall. Twenty percent of the violence in children's programs occurred on terrestrial television channels, with the rest located on the satellite channels.

Although an increase in violence in children's programs between 1995 and 1996 may offer some cause for concern, the figures only provide a limited picture of the nature of violence on television. To take the analysis further, it is necessary to consider the characteristics of violence that audience research has revealed as important mediators of viewers' reactions to televised violence.

TABLE 7.3

Percentage of Total Violent Programs Contributed By Different
Children's Genres

Children's Program Genre	1995	1996
Cartoons	45.0	30.6
General children's programs	54.0	69.4

Genre and Children's Involvement in Violence

An important question concerns how often children are shown as aggressors and how often they are shown as victims in children's and nonchildren's programs. This information may be used to ascertain if there are variations in the amount of times children are involved in violence in particular genres. The genre distribution of such incidents is important because the appearance of child aggressors or victims in more realistic contexts may have a more profound impact on young viewers than violent incidents involving children in obviously fantasy settings (cf. Lagerspetz et al., 1978; Noble, 1975).

Table 7.4 shows that violence involving children either as aggressors or victims was most likely to occur in films originally made for the cinema (678 aggressor incidents, 601 victim incidents) or in children's programs (633 aggressor incidents, 605 victim incidents). Across other major drama and factual genres, incidents involving children either as perpetrators of violence or as victims were relatively rare.

TABLE 7.4

Programs Containing Violence Involving Children as Victims and Aggressors Across All Genres

	Children as Aggressors				Children as Victims			
	1995		1996		1995		1996	
	N	%	N	%	N	%	N	%
Children's cartoons	109	7.2	405	22.1	173	12.5	480	23.1
Other children's programs	524	34.7	465	25.4	432	31.2	396	19.1
Cinema	678	44.9	698	38.1	601	43.4	867	41.8
U.K. series	21	1.4	12	0.7	18	1.3	16	0.8
Non-U.K. series	24	1.6	29	1.6	29	2.1	62	3.0
U.K. long series	12	0.8	24	1.3	17	1.2	29	1.4
Non-U.K. long series	37	2.5	23	1.3	37	2.7	30	1.4
Made for TV films	30	2.0	30	1.6	35	2.5	30	1.4
National news	20	1.3	1	0.1	6	0.4	2	0.1
Current affairs—politics	10	0.7	1	0.1	10	0.7	1	*
Current affairs—consumer	12	0.8	4	0.1	2	0.1	3	0.1
Documentary	7	0.5	9	0.5	4	0.3	8	0.4
Regional news	3	0.2	–	–	3	0.2	–	–
Sport	1	0.1	20	1.1	–	–	18	0.9
Other cartoons/animation	4	0.3	13	0.7	4	0.3	13	0.6
Pop videos	2	0.1	43	2.3	1	0.1	49	2.4
Situation comedy	1	0.1	9	0.5	2	0.4	10	0.5
Chat show	2	0.1	13	0.7	2	0.1	11	0.5
Other								

Realism and Violence Involving Children

An important element that should be considered when assessing the likely impact of screen violence on children is the degree of identification a viewer has with the victim or aggressor. The degree of identification is related to the amount of realism portrayed in the violent scene. Certain elements in media narratives cue viewers about reality, when the character is of the same age, has the same traits, the same name or appearance as someone in real life, or when there is familiarity of setting (Gunter, 1985). Children are likely to identify with younger victims and aggressors due to age and other similarities. This identification with television characters may be further intensified by the realism of the setting or geographic location of the violence.

Gunter and Furnham (1984) showed that a contemporary setting makes the violence seem more realistic and serious and increases viewer identification with the characters involved in the violence. Therefore, violence in westerns, science fiction, and cartoons was perceived by viewers to be less serious regardless of the nature of the violent act or the consequence of it. Gunter and Furnham argued that the more a program simulates real life for the viewer in relation to its historical setting (the time period the program is about), physical location (inner city, urban, suburban, etc.), or the country where the act of violence takes place, the more likely a viewer will be disturbed by the violence. Furthermore, in more realistic settings, viewers exhibit greater sensitivity to other features, such as the form of the violence and its consequences for victims when judging the seriousness of violent incidents.

To examine the seriousness of televised violence for children in terms of its perceived realism, therefore, the content analysis conducted here classified violent incidents in terms of their *historical setting*. Violence shown in contemporary settings has a more profound impact on audience reaction than violence shown in other historical settings (Gunter & Harrison, 1998). Gunter (1985) argued that contemporary violence is seen to be the most serious, followed by violence set in the past, and finally, the least serious, violence in the future. Although graphically depicted violence even when shown in a futuristic setting may still be disturbing, it would be perceived as far more upsetting if it were set in a contemporary context.

In both children's and nonchildren's programing, the greatest proportion of violence was shown in the present (see Table 7.5). However, a clear difference emerges between children's and nonchildren's programing in terms of the location of the rest of the violence. Children's programs tended to contain a high percentage of violence set in the future. In contrast, most noncontemporary violence in nonchildren's programs was located in the past. Further, for a marked percentage of violent incidents in children's programs, it was not always easy to determine the time period in which the violence was depicted. This finding signified that a further proportion of the violence in children's programs occurred in

TABLE 7.5

Historical Setting of Violence in Children's Programs Compared with the Historical Setting of Nonchildren's Programs Involving Children in Violence

| | Children's Programs | | | | Nonchildren's Programs | | | |
| | 1995 | | 1996 | | 1995 | | 1996 | |
Setting	N	%	N	%	N	%	N	%
Distant past	52	4.3	104	6.0	315	18.9	195	9.0
Past (1900–1980)	38	3.1	190	10.9	446	27.2	609	28.0
Present (1980s/1990s)	518	41.9	839	48.1	847	51.1	1,290	59.9
Realistic future	212	17.1	226	13.0	5	0.3	7	0.3
Distant future	299	24.1	145	8.3	14	3.4	41	2.0
Other	2	0.2	–	–	–	–	–	–
Unclassified	117	9.5	121	13.9	16	1.0	19	0.9

unrealistic settings for which there was no obvious time code. Consequently, children's programs, in contrast to nonchildren's programs, locates a high proportion of their violence in settings that may be rather less realistic and, in consequence, less disturbing for young viewers than that shown by nonchildren's programing.

The *geographical location* of violence on television is also significant in relation to viewer reaction. A key factor is the proximity of the violence to viewer's own home. Previous research found that British viewers were more likely to be concerned about violence located in British programs than about those situated in American programs (Gunter, 1985; Gunter & Furnham, 1984). Portrayals of violence situated in locations closer to home for viewers tend to be rated as more serious.

The greatest proportion of violence in both children's and nonchildren's programs occurred in an American setting (see Table 7.6). More than one half of all violence in children's and nonchildren's programs was situated in the United States across the 2 years of analysis. Britain was the second most likely location of violence in children's and nonchildren's programs. Children's programs, however, depicted a lower percentage of violence in Britain than did nonchildren's programs and contained a higher proportion of violence located in more fantastic geographical settings, such as outer space or other worlds. Much children's program violence occurred in cartoon settings where the geographical setting was uncertain.

Realism of Characters

As children develop cognitively, they are better able to make judgments about whether the screen violence is occurring in a realistic or unrealistic setting. The ability to make this distinction means that the older chil-

TABLE 7.6

Context of Violence in Children's Programs Compared with the Context of Nonchildren's Programs Involving Children in Violence

| | Children's Programs | | | | Nonchildren's Programs | | | |
| | 1995 | | 1996 | | 1995 | | 1996 | |
Context	N	%	N	%	N	%	N	%
Great Britain	75	6.1	94	5.4	249	15.2	382	17.7
USA	681	54.9	918	52.6	826	49.9	1,588	59.9
Europe	43	3.5	50	3.4	44	2.7	126	5.4
Other N. America	1	0.1	19	1.0	18	1.1	21	0.9
Africa	–	–	10	0.5	12	0.7	15	0.6
Middle East	4	0.4	10	0.6	8	0.5	24	1.1
India/Asia	–	–	6	0.4	15	0.9	32	1.5
Oriental	1	0.1	–	–	180	10.8	51	2.5
Australasia	10	0.9	3	0.1	102	6.2	82	7.6
Central/S. America	–	–	–	–	11	0.6	23	1.0
Other parts of the world	2	0.1	19	1.1	21	1.3	69	3.2
Other planet	87	7.1	40	2.3	9	0.5	1	*
Other (Sci-fi)	35	2.8	38	2.2	7	0.4	4	0.2
Cartoon	233	18.9	424	20.9	15	0.9	3	0.1
Unclear	50	4.1	50	2.8	65	3.8	29	1.4
Unclassified	17	1.4	539	6.6	75	4.4	11	0.5

dren get, the more unlikely it becomes that they will be influenced by violence in unreal, animated, or fantasy settings (Potter, 1999). Young viewers tend to show more intense responses to human-type screen characters than to animated or cartoon characters (Cantor, 1994; Osborn & Endsley, 1971; Surbeck, 1975). Arguably, however, once children are able to make such a distinction they are more vulnerable to fear or other types of reactions to more realistic violence on television. Van der Voort (1986) found that children's reactions change as they develop. Younger children will respond to fantasy or unrealistic violence, whereas older children become more responsive to realistic violence and less concerned by fantasy or unrealistic violence. As children develop, they are better able to make format distinctions between programs that guide other reactions they might have to characterizations. Thus, children may dismiss the relevance to everyday reality of cartoons because they recognize that they are animated and hence different in type from programs featuring human characters (Buckingham, 1943a).

In the current analysis, a distinction was made between the realism of characters in scenes in which children were featured as aggressors or victims. This distinction was applied across children's programs and nonchildren's programs. Table 7.7 shows that for many of the scenes in which children were involved in violence in children's programs, both

TABLE 7.7

Status of Aggressor and Victim in All Programs Containing Violence
Involving Children

| | When the Aggressor Is a Child | | | | When the Victim Is a Child | | | |
| | 1995 | | 1996 | | 1995 | | 1996 | |
	N	%	N	%	N	%	N	%
Realistic character								
Children's programs	140	22.1	439	50.5	120	19.8	185	21.1
Nonchildren's programs	569	65.0	872	90.6	542	69.4	1,082	90.3
Subtotal	709	47.0	1,311	71.5	625	45.1	1,261	60.8
Fictional character								
Children's programs	493	77.9	429	49.3	484	80.0	68	78.7
Nonchildren's programs	307	35.0	88	9.1	239	30.6	106	8.8
Subtotal	800	53.0	515	28.2	758	54.7	804	38.8
Unclassified	–	–	5	0.3	3	0.2	9	0.4
Total	1,509	100.0	1,833	100.0	1,386	100.0	2,074	100.0

the aggressor and the victim were clearly fictional characters. The exception occurred in 1996, when child aggressors in children's programs were equally likely to be depicted as clearly fictional/fantasy characters or realistic characters. In contrast, violence involving children occurring in nonchildren's programs more often portrayed the child aggressor and victim as a realistic character. These differences in realism between characters in different program genres are important. On the one hand, children may identify with and copy the activities of a superhero in a fantastic setting, and, on the other hand, very realistic portrayals of violence involving a child may also lead to close identification of the child viewer with the violence occurring on screen. In the latter case, children may find it particularly disturbing, especially if it is very realistic. In particular, children may be particularly influenced by violent portrayals involving their own age group on television and by the perceived similarity to themselves (Potter, 1999).

In children's programing, the character involved in violence is often a young superhero (e.g., the *Teenage Mutant Ninja Turtles*, *Buffy the Vampire Slayer*, and the *Mighty Morphin Power Rangers*). The role of the hero or superhero in children's programing has been seen to have great influence on children who often play out the heroic scenes again themselves. Erickson (1977) argued that such play is important because it helps children to understand the society within which they live and their own role within it. It also may help children to understand their own place in the power structure (Elkind, 1981). Bandura and Walters (1963) showed that the perceived prestige of the hero is likely to attract children to incorporate that hero into their own pretend play. Identification with characters can also be stimulated by their attractiveness (Hoffner &

Cantor, 1985). Concerns have arisen because children often emulate the violent exchanges that occur between characters. The question here is whether the aggression shown by children playing out the encounters of their superheroes is really aggression or whether it is merely play. Goldstein (1998) argued that the defining feature of boys at play is their lack of intent to harm each other. There is a huge difference between pretending to shoot someone and trying to actually injure someone. Thus, there is an important distinction between real aggression and aggressive play behavior that is usually ignored in most of the media effects literature.

Although most viewers identify with heroes in television narratives, identification is particularly marked with younger viewers. Children in particular are likely to identify with superheroes. Such characters are attractive to children, always winning the particular battle they fight, and using a form of violence that seems to be justifiable within the program context (Liss, Reinhardt, & Fredriksen, 1983). Indeed, some writers have observed that with the advent of television children's play themes, heroes, and role models have changed (French & Pena, 1991). For preschoolers, in particular, the role models adopted in fantasy play historically were family members and other real people in the community, such as teachers, doctors, firefighters, shopkeepers, and so on (F. Caplan & T. Caplan, 1973; Hartley et al., 1952). By middle childhood, age 7 to 11, children were observed to have moved on from pretending to be real-life characters to adventure themes associated with more distant fantasy characters (F. Caplan & T. Caplan, 1973). Today, however, by preschool age, children were found to be adopting fantasy heroes as role models in their pretend play behavior (French & Pena, 1991). Television fantasy characters had come to replace real figures as role models in children's local environment.

Consequently, concern has been raised that children may be particularly influenced by the superheroes who consistently appear in children's television programing. Indeed, reports have appeared of children copying the actions of superheroes such as the *Mighty Morphin Power Rangers* and the *Ninja Turtles* (Boyatzis, Matillo, & Nesbitt, 1995). This phenomenon is not new: Japanese superhero dramas, which became very popular in Japan in the 1960s, issued a broadcast warning "don't kick like this hero does" (Kodaira, 1998a, p. 84). The *Mighty Morphin Power Rangers* was inspired by Japanese programs and released in the United States in 1993. The release of the program created controversies over its depiction of violence in Canada and Europe in mid-1990s (Kodaira, 2000). Concern has arose primarily from accidental harm children inflicted on one another when trying to copy their heroes' martial arts kicks and punches. It is important, however, to draw attention here to the distinction identified by Goldstein (1998) that injury is generally a consequence of imaginative and daring play, and not of aggressive behavior with intent to harm.

Problematically, the rationale for the violence in such fantasy-based programs appears to be presented to the viewer as being legitimate, because the superheroes generally react to a violent perpetrator and only become aggressors in order to protect each other, other innocent victims, or society. Such violence is portrayed as an extension of the political order, and the activities of the superhero are often concerned with maintaining the status quo through the use of defensive and protective violence. A normative judgment is made here, which implies that certain types of violence are politically acceptable and, for the program makers, are "suitable" forms of violence for children to watch and copy.

The violence shown in *Mighty Morphin Power Rangers* is highly stylized, with the majority being kicking and punching that results in no physical injury the majority of the time. The villains in such programs tend to be monsters or anthropomorphized animals, or are presented as other nonhuman creatures. The narrative structure of the program ensures that the death or destruction of a nonhuman creature is acceptable and does not challenge viewers' sensibilities in the same way as the death or serious injury of a human or a hero. The normative order of this cultural construct is very conservative. The reinforcement of such social and cultural messages via use of iconography is a common theme throughout many children's fantasy programs.

The *Mighty Morphin Power Rangers* had a big male and female following, arguably because the female main characters are, rather unusually, as violent as the male ones (Cantor, 1994). The violence, however, usually tends to be highly choreographed and copies a form of martial arts. The result is unrealistic and improbable.

In a further analysis of characterizations, child aggressors and child victims were further classified in terms of the dramatic roles they occupied in both children's and nonchildren's programs. The results are summarized in Tables 7.8 to 7.11. Three character types emerged as the most commonly appearing child aggressors in children's programs. These were fantasy (human) characters, cartoon (human) characters, and schoolchildren (see Table 7.8). These three dramatic role types accounted for over 80% of the aggressor types. This finding underlined the prevalence of nonhuman characters in many children's programs and the presence of superheroes or fantastic characters. It also illustrated the presence of children as aggressors, again underlining the likely amount of identification children are likely to find with characters committing violence in programs made for children.

Similarly, the character types who featured most often as aggressors tended to figure most commonly as victims. Consequently, child victims appearing in programs made for children tended to be cartoon characters, fantasy characters, other nonhuman characters or schoolchildren. Again, two types of identification may occur with both the superhero and the child victim, and may serve to legitimate subsequent reactive and protective violence (see Table 7.9).

TABLE 7.8
Top 10 Most Common Types of Aggressors in Children's Programs (1995–1996)

	1995			1996		
		N	%		N	%
1.	Fantasy character	193	30.5	Cartoon—human	308	35.4
2.	School child	191	30.2	Fantasy character	208	23.9
3.	Cartoon—human	115	18.2	School child	186	21.4
4.	Martial arts	64	10.1	Cartoon—animal	60	6.9
5.	Cartoon—animal	38	6.0	Martial arts	26	3.0
6.	Situation character	23	3.6	Cartoon—other	17	2.0
7.	Robot	3	0.5	Situation character	16	1.8
8.	Petty criminal	2	0.3	Robot	12	1.4
9.	General public	1	0.2	Monster	6	0.7
10.	Cowboy	1	0.2	Member of public	5	0.6

Whereas some cartoon characters appeared in nonchildren's programs, a larger proportion of realistic characters were present here than in children's programs. The most commonly occurring child victim and aggressor in nonchildren's programs was the school child, followed by a situation character or someone in a nonspecific domestic role (see Tables 7.10 and 7.11). The situation character was used in the coding schedules to refer to characters not defined in terms of occupation or role type, but appearing in a variety of settings. The pattern that emerges from the top 10 child aggressor and child victim character types in nonchildren's programing is that those who are involved in violence are generally both aggressor and victim. Violence involving children in nonchildren's programs also tends to be portrayed by real-

TABLE 7.9
Top 10 Most Common Types of Victims in Children's Programs (1995–1996)

	1995			1996		
		N	%		N	%
1.	Fantasy character	193	31.9	Cartoon—human	358	40.9
2.	Cartoon—human	155	25.6	Fantasy character	181	20.7
3.	School child	134	22.1	School child	159	18.2
4.	Cartoon—animal	42	6.9	Cartoon—animal	78	8.9
5.	Martial art	39	6.4	Cartoon—other	25	2.9
6.	Situation character	26	4.3	Situation character	20	2.3
7.	Cartoon—other	8	1.3	Martial art	14	1.6
8.	General public	2	0.3	Nobility/royalty	8	0.9
9.	Monster	1	0.2	Monster	6	0.7
10.	Robot	1	0.2	Supernatural power	6	0.7

TABLE 7.10

Top 10 Most Common Types of Aggressors in Nonchildren's Programs
(1995–1996)

	1995			1996		
		N	%		N	%
1.	School child	303	34.6	School child	365	37.9
2.	Situation character	126	14.4	Situation character	156	16.2
3.	Cartoon-animal	105	12.0	Domestic person	108	11.2
4.	Tribal people	60	6.8	Martial art	97	10.1
5.	Rioter	41	4.7	Member of public	43	4.5
6.	Petty criminal	33	3.8	Petty criminal	34	3.5
7.	Domestic character	28	3.2	Cartoon—human	34	3.5
8.	General public	20	2.3	Vigilante—non-legit.	14	1.5
9.	Sport person	18	2.1	Criminal—serious	8	0.8
10.	Vampire	17	1.9	Nobility/royalty	4	0.4

istic characters in realistic settings. Again, the age of the child victims
and aggressors may result in children identifying with the aggressors
and victims of violence.

Motives and Consequences of Violence

Identification of characters involved in violence on television is important, given that viewers' response to violence is related to the types of
characters involved. Research has generally taken two approaches,
namely, to analyze violence committed either by law enforcers or by

TABLE 7.11

Top 10 Most Common Types of Victims in Nonchildren's Programs
(1995–1996)

	1995			1996		
		N	%		N	%
1.	School child	319	40.8	School child	447	37.3
2.	Situation character	147	18.8	Situation character	223	18.6
3.	Cartoon—animal	70	9.0	Domestic person	174	14.5
4.	Petty criminal	34	4.4	Martial art	63	5.3
5.	General public	24	3.1	Member of public	61	5.1
6.	Domestic character	22	2.8	Petty criminal	52	4.3
7.	Rioter	22	2.8	Cartoon—human	37	3.1
8.	Tribal people	18	2.3	Sports person	32	2.7
9.	Vampire	15	1.9	Nobility/royalty	11	0.9
10.	Sports person	13	1.7	Vigilante—nonlegit.	8	0.7

other legitimate forces and criminals (Cumberbatch et al., 1987; Gunter & J. Harrison, 1998). Audiences may discriminate between violence committed by "good" characters and violence committed by "bad" characters. Public definitions of violence typically reflect the perceived legitimacy of the act (R. C. Brown & Tedeschi, 1976; Kane et al., 1976). Thus, people may exhibit remarkable tolerance for legitimized violence, but not for unjustified coercive actions. This means that the public may accept violence used by the police in the line of duty (Blumenthal et al., 1972; Gamson & McEvoy, 1972; Lincoln & Levinger, 1972). On television, viewers have been found to discriminate the seriousness of violent acts on the basis of whether the perpetrators were fictional police or fictional villains. However, the nature of the perpetrator in this case interacted with the setting and location of the action to determine audience response. In American settings, British viewers judged police violence as less violent than that perpetrated by criminals. In contrast, police violence in a British setting was regarded as more violent than similar incidents performed by villains (Gunter, 1985).

A key part of becoming a discerning viewer who can decode television messages is to be able to consider the motives and values of aggressors. Crucially, this ability increases with age. Once the motives of violence have been evaluated, a viewer is better able to make a judgment about the justification of the violence. There is a lack of clarity about the precise cognitive process that occurs when a viewer makes such a judgment, but it is likely that a viewer considers a character's motive for a violent act in terms of moral culpability (Mees, 1990). The motives and values of aggressors and the victims are important elements in relation to the viewer's judgment about whether or not the violence is justified. Potter (1999) argued that a causal path may exist between the motive, justification, and disinhibition in a viewer.

Consequently, the type of motive that influences an act of aggression on screen may influence the viewers' justification of the violent act, which in turn may influence a viewer's disinhibition about the violence they have just witnessed. Disinhibition can occur when a viewer believes that a motive legitimates an action or reaction on screen and, consequently, that the violence is justified (Potter, 1999). Of concern is the idea that certain types of violence may be perceived as justifiable by children because it is being committed by an attractive character or superhero with whom they identify. The causal link between this perception and consequent activity is unclear in terms of long-term consequences, but in the short term it is more likely to result in children trying to emulate the "justified" violent activities of superheroes.

The current analysis examined the distribution of motives for violence among those incidents in which the perpetrators of violence were children. A comparison was made between children's programs and nonchildren's programs. There was a stark contrast in the motives of child aggressors in children's programs and nonchildren's programs. In the former, child perpetrators of violence acted out of positive, altruistic motives or self-preservation much more often than out of selfish, greedy, or antisocial motives. In nonchildren's programs, child aggressors were far more likely to act out of selfish reasons (see Table 7.12).

In addition to the motives of violence, the consequences that follow it have been shown to represent important discriminating features that can determine audience response. Children have been found to display more pronounced and negative emotional reactions to violent television scenes in which victims are obviously hurt (Noble, 1975). Teenage and adult viewers perceive violent scenes in which victims are shown to suffer in far more serious terms (Greenberg & Gordon, 1972b; Gunter, 1985). Similarly, effects studies have shown that when violence is shown to have no consequences, viewers are less likely to feel inhibited in acting aggressively (Potter, 1999).

Quite apart from the reactions of victims of screen violence, another criterion children may use to evaluate the consequences of violence is whether or not the aggressors receive a reward or a punishment for their actions. Bandura (1973) argued that absence of punishment for a violent act may have serious consequences, because it may encourage the viewer to learn to behave in a similar manner. Potter (1999) argued that a viewer's interpretation of justification for a violent act may be linked to the idea of reward. Often, a character is rewarded when the goal of violence is portrayed as legitimate. In children's programs,

TABLE 7.12

Goal/Motive of Aggressors in Children's Programs Containing Violence Compared with the Goal/Motive of Aggressors in Nonchildren's Programs Involving Children in Violence

| | Children's Programs | | | | Nonchildren's Programs | | | |
| | 1995 | | 1996 | | 1995 | | 1996 | |
Goal/Motive	N	%	N	%	N	%	N	%
Upholding the law	6	0.9	12	1.4	14	1.6	4	0.4
Well-being of the family	33	5.2	81	9.3	159	18.2	126	13.1
Well-being of society	200	31.6	266	30.6	34	3.9	74	7.7
Respect for the law	11	1.7	8	0.9	13	1.5	4	0.4
Subtotal	250	39.4	367	42.2	220	25.2	208	21.6
Self preservation	220	34.8	208	23.9	202	23.1	172	17.9
Desire for money/goods	12	1.9	18	2.1	25	2.9	30	3.1
Ambition for power	32	5.1	87	10.0	124	14.2	120	12.5
Religious goals	–	–	–	–	3	0.3	–	–
Evil/destructive goals	14	2.2	54	6.2	108	12.3	111	11.5
Sexual goals	1	0.2	2	0.2	7	0.8	15	1.6
Subtotal	59	9.4	161	18.5	267	30.5	276	28.7
Other	101	16.0	124	12.3	168	19.2	250	26.0
Unclassified	3	0.3	10	1.1	19	2.2	57	5.9

superheroes gain praise or even more adoration from their fans, further legitimating their violent activity. Harmful consequences of violence must be considered in relation to their intensity, whereby some types of violence are seen to be worse or more harmful than others.

The consequences of televised violence involving children were classified in terms of their seriousness in physical terms for victims, with a further distinction being made for damage or suffering of a psychological nature. Again, comparisons were made between children's programs and nonchildren's programs. Table 7.13 shows that in both children's and nonchildren's programs, the majority of acts of televised violence involving children (i.e., over 80%) resulted in little or no physical injury. Over the 2 years of analysis, only in a small minority of cases were children seriously hurt or killed. Serious injury and death were twice as likely to occur in nonchildren's programs as in children's programs.

There are different schools of thought on the implications of showing different consequences of violence. On the one hand, audience research has shown that viewers are more likely to react to depictions of a great deal of pain or suffering on the part of the victim and that this may be distressing for the viewer (Gunter, 1985, Gunter & J. Harrison, 1998). On the other hand, it is believed that only when the viewers are exposed to the less pleasant consequences of violence can they have a sense of the horror or suffering it can cause. In a further analysis of consequences of

TABLE 7.13

Consequences of Violence in Children's Programs Containing Violence Compared with the Consequences of Violence in Nonchildren's Programs Involving Children in Violence

| | Children's Programs | | | | Nonchildren's Programs | | | |
| | 1995 | | 1996 | | 1995 | | 1996 | |
Consequence	N	%	N	%	N	%	N	%
Death	24	2.0	32	3.7	88	5.4	51	2.4
Mutilation	2	1.0	14	0.8	4	0.2	3	0.1
Broken limbs	2	1.0	1	*	1	*	–	–
Serious wound	30	2.4	15	0.9	57	3.4	61	2.8
Sub-total	34	31.7	29	1.7	62	3.6	64	2.9
Minor wound	103	8.3	97	5.6	231	13.9	254	11.8
Stun	208	16.8	229	13.1	473	14.5	225	10.7
Bruises	81	6.6	87	5.0	174	10.5	162	7.5
Sub-total	392	31.7	413	23.7	878	38.9	641	30.0
Psychological damage	18	1.5	45	2.6	52	3.2	73	3.2
No physical injury	845	53.5	1,231	58.6	773	43.6	1,223	53.0
Other	91	7.3	113	6.5	57	3.4	58	2.8
Unclassified	18	2.7	111	6.4	28	1.6	124	5.8

violence, violent acts were classified according to the amount of blood displayed, the degree of visible pain on the part of the victim, and in terms of an overall rating of "horror" (see Table 7.14).

Research has shown that viewers are particularly sensitive to graphic scenes that involve suffering, great pain, or large amounts of blood. Such graphic portrayals engage emotions more strongly than nongraphic portrayals (Ogles & Hoffner, 1987). Table 7.14 shows that an evaluation of the qualities of violence involving children in both children's and nonchildren's programs in terms of the degrees of associated pain, horror, and bloodshed indicates that portrayals of an extreme or graphic nature are rarely depicted when children are involved. Only 12 nonchildren's programs showed scenes accompanied by a high degree of bloodshed and fewer scenes involving high amounts of pain or of a horrific nature. On the one hand, this might be cause for comfort, given that graphic scenes involving children in the full horror may be ex-

TABLE 7.14

The Amount of Blood, Pain, and Horror Inflicted by Child Aggressors in Programs Containing Violence

| | Children's Programs | | | | Nonchildren's Programs | | | |
| | 1995 | | 1996 | | 1995 | | 1996 | |
Dramatic Detail	N	%	N	%	N	%	N	%
Blood								
No blood	589	93.0	763	87.7	623	71.1	740	76.8
A little blood	7	1.1	3	0.3	31	3.5	58	6.0
Some blood	1	0.2	2	0.2	6	0.7	10	1.0
Quite a lot of blood	–	–	–	–	9	1.0	1	0.1
Much blood	–	–	–	–	3	0.3	–	–
Cannot code	34	5.4	102	11.7	204	23.3	154	16.0
Total	633	100.0	870	100.0	876	100.0	963	100.0
Pain								
No pain	505	79.8	633	76.2	577	65.9	601	62.4
A little pain	98	15.5	14.2	16.3	141	16.1	247	25.6
Some pain	4	0.6	3	0.3	26	3.0	27	2.8
Quite a lot of pain	3	0.5	–	–	10	1.1	6	0.6
Intense pain	–	–	2	0.2	2	0.2	–	–
Cannot code	21	3.3	60	6.9	120	13.7	82	8.5
Total	633	100.0	870	100.0	876	100.0	963	100.0
Horror								
Mild	542	85.6	587	67.5	600	68.5	628	65.2
Slightly horrific	69	10.9	224	25.7	121	13.8	228	23.7
Some horrific scenes	7	1.1	8	0.9	9	1.0	3	0.3
Horrific	1	0.2	–	–	9	1.0	3	0.3
Very horrific	–	–	2	0.2	2	0.2	–	–
Cannot code	12	1.9	49	5.6	125	14.3	55	5.7
Total	633	100.0	870	100.0	876	100.0	963	100.0

tremely disturbing to children, particularly if they identify with the victim. On the other hand, it could be argued that children rarely see serious consequences of violence involving either their own age group, superheroes, or fantasy characters.

Form of Violence

Viewers are known to find graphic scenes of certain types of violence disturbing, such as stabbing, strangulation, hanging, mutilation, or torture (Gunter & J. Harrison, 1998). In this context, the type of violent act undertaken, the type of injuries (see previous consequences) suffered by the victim, and the type of weapon used may all serve to disturb child viewers, particularly if the victim or aggressor is a child with whom they can identify. An analysis of violent acts involving children was undertaken to reveal the most popularly occurring forms of violence and frequently used instruments of aggression. Tables 7.15 and 7.16 show the top 10 weapon types used in scenes of child violence in children programs and nonchildren programs, respectively.

These 10 weapon types accounted for over 90% of the violence in children's programs over the 2 years analyzed. The most common weapons were the fist or the hand, karate or other body part, or a futuristic weapon (e.g., a laser). These 10 weapon types accounted for 88% of the violence in nonchildren's programs over the 2 years analyzed. Child aggressors in nonchildren's programs were most likely to use their hand or fists as a weapon. In contrast with children's programs, child aggressors in nonchildren's programs also used more realistic weapons such as handguns and rifles rather than more futuristic laser weapons. This difference reflects the varying program compositions of children's programs and nonchildren's programs. The former featured far more dramatic violence in animated and fantasy (often futuristic) settings.

TABLE 7.15

Types of Weapons Used by Child Aggressors in Children's Programs Involving Children in Violence

	1995			*1996*		
		N	*%*		*N*	*%*
1.	Karate	142	22.4	Hands/fist	181	20.8
2.	Hands/fist	119	18.8	Karate	157	18.0
3.	Boot/ kick	75	11.8	Other weapon	125	14.4
4.	Other weapon	67	10.6	Laser	91	10.5
5.	Laser	60	9.5	Boot/kick	71	8.2
6.	Other body part	33	5.2	Other body part	45	5.2
7.	Vehicle	24	3.8	Throw/push	32	5.2
8.	Sword	23	3.6	Sword	31	3.6
9.	Stick	13	2.1	Other projectile	22	2.5
10.	Explosive	13	2.1	Bow and arrow	17	2.0

TABLE 7.16
Types of Weapons Used by Child Aggressors in Nonchildren's Programs Involving Children in Violence

	1995				1996	
	N	%			N	%
1. Hands/fist	280	32.0	Hands/fist		363	37.7
2. Other weapon	99	11.3	Other weapon		83	8.6
3. Karate	80	9.1	Boot/kick		80	8.3
4. Sword	70	8.0	Karate		78	8.1
5. Other projectile	52	5.9	Throw/push		68	7.1
6. Boot/kick	47	5.4	Other body part		62	6.4
7. Hand gun	43	4.9	Stick		47	4.9
8. Other body part	40	4.6	Hand gun		27	2.8
9. Stick	34	3.9	Other projectile		26	2.7
10. Rifle	20	2.3	Sword		16	1.7

In addition to the weapon types and instruments of aggression used by child aggressors, the analysis also examined the different forms of violence in which children became involved on screen. Once again, this analysis was conducted for children's programs and nonchildren's programs (see Tables 7.17 and 7.18). The most common form of violence used by child aggressors in children's programs were pushing, kicking, shooting with a laser gun, punching, or hitting with an object. Whereas child aggressors in nonchildren's programs employed similar tactics, there were also incidents of stabbing and shooting with a handgun in nonchildren's programs. This may be problematic. Gunter (1985) showed that scenes involving stabbings or shootings were perceived to be far more violent and disturbing by viewers than scenes depicting fistfights.

TABLE 7.17
Types of Violence Used by Child Aggressors in Children's Programs Involving Children in Violence

	1995				1996	
	N	%			N	%
1. Push/trip	135	21.3	Push/trip		211	24.3
2. Kick	121	19.1	Kick		108	12.4
3. Shoot at	84	13.3	Shoot at		108	12.4
4. Hit with an object	73	11.5	Attempted violence		90	10.3
5. Punch	72	11.4	Hit with an object		77	8.9
6. Throwing	23	3.6	Punch		56	6.4
7. Fall/thrown	17	2.7	Throwing		34	3.9
8. Attempted violence	17	2.7	Bullying		30	3.4
9. Explosion	13	2.1	Use of a trap		26	3.0
10. Verbal	11	1.7	Explosion		21	2.4

TABLE 7.18
Types of Violence Used by Child Aggressors in Nonchildren's Programs Involving Children in Violence

1995			1996		
	N	%		N	%
1. Push/trip	183	20.9	Push/trip	299	31.0
2. Hit with an object	124	14.2	Punch	114	11.8
3. Verbal	96	11.0	Hit with an object	84	8.7
4. Kick	95	10.8	Attempted violence	8.1	8.4
5. Punch	91	10.4	Kick	74	7.7
6. Shoot at	59	6.7	Shoot at	45	4.7
7. Throwing	37	4.2	Throwing	37	3.8
8. Slap	24	2.7	Aggression in sport	33	3.4
9. Stab	22	2.5	Verbal threat	26	2.7
10. Aggression in sport	20	2.3	Slap	23	2.4

CONCLUSIONS

Research has shown that television interacts with children in a positive and negative manner (Potter, 1999) and its effects can be either good or bad depending on how the medium is used (Gunter & McAleer, 1997) and how well it is regulated. There is understandably a great deal of concern about the involvement of children in violence on television and about the portrayal of violence in programs aimed specifically at children. Public anxieties about television violence, in the context of the protection of children, stem from concerns about effects on youngsters (e.g., imitation of risky conduct, triggering of aggression impulses, desensitization, and enhanced fear).

Parents and teachers have expressed concerns about the possible role played by television in the conditioning and encouragement of destructive, antisocial, or potentially harmful behavior performed by children. Such concerns should not be diminished because they are important. Yet, it is equally important to understand and acknowledge the varying levels of sophistication children bring to the viewing situation and in their ability to identify causes of misbehavior. Children do not automatically accept, let alone copy, everything they see on television, nor do they invariably identify with character portrayals or regard them as having relevance to their own lives (Buckingham, 1993a, 1993b, 2000; Gunter & McAleer, 1997).

The current research indicated that although violence does form a part of children's programing on British television, much violence was located in a small number of children's programs (see also Gunter & J. Harrison, 1997, 1998). In examining the involvement of children in violence on television, it emerged that across programs, in general, children become involved, either as aggressors or victims of violence, infrequently (see Tables 7.19 and 7.20). Young male adults initiate most televised violence,

TABLE 7.19

Top 10 Violent Children's Programs Where a Child Is the Aggressor

Program Title	Number of Violent Acts	TV Channel	Time Shown
Mighty Morphin Power Rangers	29	ITV	(During GMTV)
Mighty Morphin Power Rangers	18	Sky One	4:30 p.m.
Mighty Morphin Power Rangers	18	Sky One	8:00 p.m.
Mighty Morphin Power Rangers	13	Sky One	8:00 a.m.
Mighty Morphin Power Rangers	13	ITV	(During GMTV)
Mighty Morphin Power Rangers	13	Sky One	5:30 p.m.
Super Human Samurai Squad	12	Sky One	8:30 a.m.
VR Troopers	12	ITV	(During GMTV)
Mighty Morphin Power Rangers	11	ITV	(During GMTV)
Mighty Morphin Power Rangers	11	Sky One	8:00 a.m.
Mighty Morphin Power Rangers	11	Sky One	6:00 p.m.
Mighty Morphin Power Rangers	11	Sky One	8:00 a.m.
Mighty Morphin Power Rangers	11	Sky One	4:15 p.m.

and the majority of victims also derive from this demographic group. Only a small number of young children under age 15 are shown as aggressors (1.8%) and victims (2%), with teenagers between age 15 and 19 accounting for 4.5% of the aggressive acts and constituting 4.5% of the victims. Despite these low figures, concerns about the effect of television violence on the very young will remain and are centered around a belief that their children's immaturity may make them more likely to react to television violence in an undesirable or unpredictable way.

The purely descriptive statistics of content analysis do not directly shed any light on how young viewers might respond to or be influenced

TABLE 7.20

Top 10 Violent Children's Programs Where a Child Is the Victim

Program Title	Number of Violent Acts	TV Channel	Time Shown
Mighty Morphin Power Rangers	36	ITV	(During GMTV)
Mighty Morphin Power Rangers	22	Sky One	5:30 p.m.
Mighty Morphin Power Rangers	22	Sky One	8:00 a.m.
VR Troopers	18	ITV	(During GMTV)
Basic	15	ITV	(Cartoon during GMTV)
Teenage Mutant Ninja Turtles	15	Sky One	10:30 a.m.
V R Troopers	12	ITV	(During GMTV)
The Whipping Boy	12	TNT	6:00 p.m.
Basic	11	ITV	(Cartoon during GMTV)
James Bond Junior	10	Channel 4	9:50 a.m.

by televised violence. The implications of these data need to be considered in the context of audience research, which has more directly investigated the way viewers react to different forms of violence on television. Such research has shown, for instance, that viewers can make refined perceptual distinctions between acts of violence on screen on the basis of their form, perpetrator and victim characteristics, underlying motives, observable consequences, and proximity to the lives of viewers (Gunter, 1985; Hodge & Tripp, 1986; Van der Voort, 1986).

Children's emotional and behavioral reactions to television violence are also sensitive to the nature of on-screen portrayals (Noble, 1975). Another key factor is the degree to which young viewers identify with the perpetrators of violence (Bandura & Walters, 1963). Children make distinctions between violence from realistic and fantasy settings, although the ease with which this occurs varies with the age of the child. There may be confusion about whether or not the people on television are "real," especially among very young children age 6 or less. By age 7 or 8, however, although some confusions still persist, most children can generally discriminate between human and animated characters on screen (Dorr, 1983). As they grow older, children become more sophisticated in the kinds of judgments they can make about programs. They become more skilled at "reading" narratives and special production effects (Dorr, 1983). They also begin to make comparisons between what they see on television and the experiences from their own lives (Hawkins, 1977).

Implications for Effects on Children

It is worth reflecting on the descriptive findings of this content analysis in relation to research with young viewers on how they respond to television portrayals. The research reported here has revealed a lot about the nature of television violence, especially violence involving children. It has revealed that much of the violence found in programs aimed at the child audience took place in unreal or fantasy settings, involving either animated or fantasy characters. Very often these fantasy heroes had superhuman powers or might transform from ordinary looking human characters into costumed alter egos with special abilities. Thus, much violence in programs targeted at young audiences had a fairy-tale quality to it. Given that much of this content in terms of its setting was removed from the everyday reality of children, it is reasonable to assume that it represented the type of material unlikely to give rise to unpleasant, disturbing or fright reactions in children.

Programs aimed at children rarely depicted serious consequences as following from acts of violence involving children. Serious or fatal injury to victims in violence featuring children was more likely to be found in nonchildren's programs, but even here it was relatively rare. There are mixed viewpoints concerning whether any dilution of the potentially harmful consequences of violence is a good or bad thing. According to one argument, it is necessary to show the real consequences of violence when portrayed on television so that children learn that violence can cause serious harm to those on the receiving end. In turn, this might in turn cause children to reflect on the possible outcomes of their actions before behaving violently themselves. Another view purports that graphic depiction of the horror and damage of violence may be excessively upsetting for children and they should therefore be protected from such images. On the current evidence, the pattern of violence involving children on television found in this study would suggest that the second position has been privileged by broadcasters.

The form of violence is another significant area of concern. Research has shown that viewers, in general, exhibit greater sensitivity to certain forms of violence (e.g., violence featuring sharp instruments like knives) than they do to others (Gunter, 1985). Also, children may be tempted to copy some unusual forms of violence if they fall within their means and physical capabilities (Bandura, 1973). In the current research, evidence emerged that violence involving children on screen is likely to take on certain forms that might invite children to emulate what they see. In particular, use of superheroes in children's programing is likely to foster a good deal of identification from the child audience (French & Pena, 1991). The fantasy genre encourages character identification from both male and female viewers: the *Mighty Morphin Power Rangers*, in particular, shows female teenage heroines successfully engaging in numerous violent scenes. Children have been observed to copy the martial arts actions of the characters in such television series (Boyatzis et al., 1995). Although this may occur in a play context more often than in real life (cf. Goldstein, 1998), there is still the possibility that children could accidentally cause injury to themselves or others in performing these movements.

A further problem arises from the way the violence may be perceived by a young audience. There is concern about the capacity of some children's programs to provide undesirable examples to young viewers because they depict lead characters with whom children can identify. Identification can occur especially when viewers perceive some degree of similarity between themselves and characters on screen or when on-screen characters have attractive attributes (e.g., prestige, status, or ability) that render them desirable role models. Moreover, the program narrative may be structured in a way that makes violence and dramatic action a natural part of the program. Superheroes inevitably engage in reactive violence in order to protect themselves, society, or other innocent victims and, after a struggle, always win the battle. The program narrative presents the violence enacted by the superhero as being justifiable or legitimate violence. Legitimate violence is portrayed as a necessary part of the political and social order, whereby the activities of the superhero are often concerned with maintaining the status quo through the use of defensive and protective violence. Program makers appear to assume that such violence is a "suitable" form of violence for children to watch and copy.

The motives that underlie violence have significance because they indicate whether or not the violence was justified. The justification that attaches to acts of violence on screen can, according to some researchers, play a significant part in mediating whether screen depictions are used by young viewers to justify their own aggressive tendencies (Berkowitz & Alioto, 1973).Whereas the motives of superheroes and other child aggressors often seem to legitimate violence, child aggressors in nonchildren's programs often have motives that are more destructive or show an ambition for personal power. The use of child aggressors and victims in programs made for children and the adult audience may be some cause for concern, given that children are more likely to identify with a character from their own age group. Violence that is evil or destructive, but that goes unpunished or is rewarded, or that has little or no consequence, may be particularly attractive to children (see Bandura, 1973; Potter, 1999).

Summing up, examination of the nature and extent of violence in children's and nonchildren's programs has shown that violence involving children is relatively rare on the small screen. A good deal of the violence is unlikely to disturb or frighten child viewers, but there nonetheless remains the possibility of character identification among young viewers. Such identification with young victims and aggressors may influence the reaction children have to the violence they see. Furthermore, the use of fantasy program settings as a means to screen legitimate violence aimed at young viewers is problematical because they appear to justify and glamorize the use of violence and aim to make violence appear particularly attractive to young viewers. Often the violence goes unpunished, or results in no apparent consequence for the victim, potentially increasing the possibility of a disinhibition effect.

Steering young children away from fantasy-based, exciting, fast-paced programing is likely to be highly problematical and program makers are unlikely to be persuaded to change a successful programing format. The solution may lie in further education of children. Education might help children to understand the implications of the types of violence they encounter and consider the motives and values of the aggressors and victims and, consequently, put them in a position to make a critical judgment about the justification for the violence.

Chapter 8

Violence in Soaps

Soap operas represent one the longest running and most consistently popular broadcast entertainment genres. The name "soap" in "soap opera" derived from the sponsorship of daytime serials in the United States by manufacturers of household cleaning products, such as Proctor and Gamble, Colgate-Palmolive, and Lever Brothers. Originally a radio phenomenon, soap operas later became firmly established on television. Initially, soap operas were regarded as a solution to an advertising problem. How could radio be used during daylight hours to attract the largest audience of potential consumers of certain products? However, as social scientists began to apply their early methodologies to the analysis of the genre, it became clear that soaps represented much more, in social and cultural terms, than vehicles for advertising (R. C. Allen, 1985).

Soaps represented a fictional world into which millions of listeners (and eventually viewers) plunged everyday. Although a fictional genre, the power of soaps derived from their focus on everyday problems involving characters who were portrayed as real people. Indeed, the realism of soaps was noted early on. In 1939, an article in *Newsweek* defined soap opera as a type of drama that brings "the hard-working housewife the real life adventures of real people." (p. 8)

Not surprisingly, given their popularity and realistic qualities, soaps soon came under criticism for promulgating potentially harmful social and psychological side effects among members of their audiences. In March 1942, New York psychiatrist Louis Berg told the Buffalo Advertising Club that listening to soap operas caused "acute anxiety state, tachycardia, arrhythmias, increase in blood pressure, profuse perspiration, tremors, vasomotor instability, nocturnal frights, vertigo, and gastrointestinal disturbances" (quoted in Thurber, 1948, p. 309). Such conclusions were based on clinical observations rather than systematic social scientific research evidence linking social and psychological conditions specifically to exposure to soap operas.

Much of the earliest social scientific research on soap operas, dating from the 1930s, focused on who listened (and watched) and why, with relatively little attention given to effects. The first studies indicated that soaps drew audiences from across the social spectrum (Beville, 1940). However, the early indications were that this was a genre preferred by women more than by men (R. C. Allen, 1985). One study that did examine effects of soap opera listening found that regular listeners scored lower in terms of imagination, were less spontaneous, and held more stereotyped beliefs about interpersonal relations as compared with nonlisteners (Warner & Henry, 1948).

Between the early 1950s and early 1970s, there was little academic research carried out on soap operas (Katzman, 1972). By the 1970s, this situation changed with the emergence of research exploring the content of soaps and the way they represented aspects of social reality. Extensive textual analyses of soap operas began to unravel a complex set of social and cultural meanings that were conveyed by the genre and linked, among viewers (with the genre by now firmly established on television), to perceptions of social reality (Cassata & Skill, 1983).

The long-running nature of soap operas means that they can develop plot lines, character personalities, and histories or relationships among characters in a more elaborate fashion than any other dramatic genre. Often, they are community based, family and relationship centered, contemporary, and realistic. Although fictional, real life provides the template for much that viewers encounter on screen:

> In order to be convincing, television soap operas often try to blur the gap between real time and story time; for instance, a *Brookside* episode may start in the morning with characters meeting over breakfast, follow characters through the day and end with families meeting again over dinner. By the evening the events being shown on screen may be happening at the same time as the audience is watching them. Events in soap operas may parallel 'real' events and seasons; for instance, Christmas celebrations of popular soaps often show the characters themselves celebrating Christmas. (O'Sullivan et al., 1998, p. 54)

Such parallel narratives in familiar settings like the bar, school, local square, community, street, market, or park make a soap opera especially credible as an entertainment form. Familiarity repeated readily becomes part of everyday culture and gains what Levi-Strauss (1958) called mythic quality. Soap opera is contemporary folktale and part of the attraction is its predictability. Just as in Cinderella stories, such the film *Pretty Woman*, where the audience knows the poor girl will get her prince, in soaps, "knowing" the outcome is part of the pleasure and power of the text. Another aspect of pleasure is understandability; it is satisfying to be able successfully to read the plot. Yet another source of enjoyment is identification (, 1991). Soaps feature ordinary people in ordinary contexts who sometimes become embroiled in extraordinary, although never too extraordinary, events: "In the same way as we recognize our own live as stories, so we recognize that these fictional stories reflect our own lives, or our projected desires and fantasies, the social world we inhabit and our place in it" (Geraghty, 1991, p. 57). Soaps can confirm or comfort, or even explain and educate (Liebes & Katz, 1990).

Apart from theorizing the implications of such qualities, the large audiences soaps draw are, in themselves, reasons to consider the potential for effects. The combination of their typically large audiences and potentially powerful effects-related attributes of soap narratives made this genre particularly interesting to the current study. This interest was stimulated by research linking greater potential for effects on viewers of easy identification with characters and the familiarity and realism of settings (Buckingham, 1993a; Gunter, 1985). This interest was exacerbated by an increasing tendency for British soaps to tackle contentious contemporary issues often linked to morality, sexuality, and crime. These themes made violent content more likely and brought soap opera to the attention of the pro-censorship lobby in the United Kingdom, whose remit presupposes a direct link between broadcast material of a sexual or violent nature and real sexual deviance or violent crime.

SOAP AUDIENCES

Pleasure helps explain the popularity of soap opera. Soaps appeal to a variety of social groups, including the less well educated and the better educated, those with relatively low financial income and the affluent, and women and men (Greenberg & Rampoldi-Hnito, 1994). Long-running U.K.-produced series (e.g., *Coronation Street*, *Brookside*, *Eastenders*, and *Emmerdale*) attract millions of regular viewers. Each is screened two or three times per week and features a weekend "compendium" program. Despite a skew toward women viewers:

> A week's survey of television viewing in 1990 discovered that soap operas featured in five out of ten of the top ten programs watched by women but also three out of ten of those watched by men (Beere, 1991, pp. 54–55). In Britain the soap opera *Eastenders* was deliberately conceived by the BBC in 1985 to appeal to a male as well as female audience. The purpose of this was unashamedly commercial: to lure a young unisex audience away from the attractions of ITV programming. (Macdonald, 1995, pp. 70–71)

Coronation Street is featured in numerous Web sites, including one provided by its production company Granada's site (http://www. coronationstreet.co.uk/coronationstreet/40_index.html), which not only offers story lines and information about stars from some 40 years of transmission, but also hosts a chat room and sells a large range of spin–off products (e.g., videos and books). *Coronation Street* is Britain's longest running soap. It is more than a soap; it is a whole commercial operation and regularly gets reported as if "real" in the British tabloid press. Viewing figures for this highly popular serial hover at around 15 million. Table 8.1 provides a summary of viewing figures for the major U.K. television soaps in 1999.

Tables 8.2 and 8.3 show the terrestrial viewing figures of U.K. programs for 1996 and 1999. In each case, the soaps on the major channels, *Coronation Street and* , attracted between 13 million and 20 million viewers for peak episodes. *Brookside* runs on the less established and mainstream Channel 4 and attracts fewer viewers, but has created much controversy for its most contentious story lines (e.g., one on infertility treatment and abortion within the same family). Alongside the U.K.-made soaps, British viewers are also offered a range of Australian series. The two most popular at the time of the violence study were *Neighbors* and *Home and Away*.

SOAP SYNOPSES

The seduction of soaps is very much their ordinariness. To watch is effortless because it is like watching ourselves reflected back to us. Settings are familiar; characters are knowable; events are everyday; emotions are all too human; joys and tragedies occur just as in real life, if rather more frequently than most people thankfully experience.

Brookside (Channel 4) is set in a pleasant modern suburb of Liverpool in Brookside Close. Houses are neat, well tended, and owner occupied.

TABLE 8.1
Soap Opera Audiences (United Kingdom, 1999)

Rank	Channel	Approximate Number of Viewers (millions)	Program
1	ITV	16.38	Coronation Street (Mon)
2	ITV	15.62	UEFA Champions League Final
3	ITV	14.6	Coronation Street (Wed)
4	ITV	13.81	Coronation Street (Fri)
5	ITV	13.29	Coronation Street (Sun)
6	BBC 1	12.44	Eastenders (Mon)
7	BBC 1	11.92	Eastenders (Tue)
8	BBC 1	11.53	Eastenders (Thu)V
9	ITV	10.5	Emmerdale (Thu)
10	ITV	10.11	Emmerdale (Tue)
11	ITV	9.71	Emmerdale (Fri)
12	ITV	9.58	Where the Heart Is
13	BBC 1	8.91	Eurovision Song Contest 1999

Note: Data from May 24–30, 1999. Retrieved from http://www.appleyardfamily.demon.co.uk/Peter/ViewFig.html

TABLE 8.2

Top 20 Programs for All Terrestrial Channels (1996)

Rank	Title	Channel	TX date	Audience (millions)
1	Only Fools and Horses	BBC1	12/29/96	24.3
2	Coronation Street	ITV	2/28/96	19.8
3	Casualty	BBC1	2/24/96	18.1
4	Eastenders	BBC1	10/7/96	17.9
5	A Touch of Frost	ITV	2/4/96	17.6
6	Heartbeat	ITV	12/8/96	17.6
7	One Foot in the Grave	BBC1	12/26/96	17.5
8	Football: England vs Germany	BBC1	6/26/96	17.5
9	You've Been Framed	ITV	10/27/96	17.3
10	National Lottery Live	BBC1	1/6/96	16.6
11	London's Burning	ITV	10/13/96	16.6
12	The Bill	ITV	1/26/96	16.4
13	News	ITV	10/20/96	16.1
14	Jurassic Park	BBC1	12/25/96	15.7
15	Grandstand	BBC1	6/22/96	15.6
16	The Vicar of Dibley	BBC1	12/25/96	15.1
17	Ballykissangel	BBC1	3/20/96	15.0
18	Football: England vs Spain	BBC1	6/22/96	14.9
19	Emmerdale	ITV	2/8/96	14.8
20	Inspector Morse	ITV	11/28/96	14.8

Note: Retrieved from BARB/RTS/BFI contact: *feedback@bfi.org.uk* http://www.bfi.org.uk/facts/stats

There are local shops, a garage, a hairdresser, and a club, all of which feature in the story lines. Characters are varied but relatively prosperous lower middle to middle class working people. There are trades people, teachers, a window cleaner, business people, doctors, students, and schoolchildren. There are families, couples, and singles—most are White but there are key roles played by Black actors. Most are also heterosexual, although recent storylines featured a gay relationship ruined by one partner's promiscuity, the first screened lesbian kiss, and a lesbian love affair. Another story line featured a crisis in one of the serial's resident families with a late-thirties mother having treatment for infertility while, at the same time, trying to deal with the terrible irony of her teenage daughter's unplanned pregnancy:

> Diane has an announcement to make. She tells her assembled family that Adele has decided to keep the baby. Steve is surprised, Anthony is delighted. Steve wonders if Adele's sure that's what she really wants. Adele's uncomfortable with all the discussion. Diane, Marty and Brigid discuss what's going to happen with Adele. She suddenly flips, she's fed up of everyone talking about it. Brigid tells Diane that maybe Adele's baby could be a blessing in disguise, but Diane wants a baby of her own. Mick arrives and

TABLE 8.3
Top 20 Programs for All Terrestrial Channels (1999)

Rank	Title	Channel	TX date	Audience (millions)
1	Coronation Street	ITV	3/7/99	19.8
2	Who Wants to Be a Millionaire?	ITV	3/7/99	19.2
3	Heartbeat	ITV	2/28/99	17
4	A Touch of Frost	ITV	3/21/99	16.8
5	Eastenders	BBC1	1/7/99	15.7
6	Champions League Final—Man Utd v. Bayern Munich	ITV	5/26/99	15.6
7	Walking with Dinosaurs	BBC1	10/4/99	15
8	Football: Euro 2000 Play Off: England v. Scotland	ITV	11/17/99	14.6
9	The Vicar of Dibley	BBC1	12/27/99	14.4
10	Now You've Been Framed	ITV	11/7/99	13.0
11	Emmerdale	ITV	1/10/99	13.4
12	Golden Eye	ITV	3/10/99	13.2
13	TV Nightmares	ITV	1/9/99	13.1
14	Casualty	BBC1	2/13/99	13.1
15	Mission Impossible	ITV	12/26/99	12.8
16	Neighbors from Hell	BBC1	1/7/99	12.8
17	Before They Were Famous	BBC1	12/25/99	12.2
18	Lost for Words	ITV	1/3/99	12.2
19	Stars in Your Eyes	ITV	6/5/99	12.2
20	Police, Camera, Action	ITV	1/6/99	12

Note: Retrieved from BARB/RTS/BFI contact: feedback@bfi.org.uk http://www.bfi.org.uk/facts/stats

> Marty tells him to do one. Mick tells him that he's already informed Leo and he wants to help as much as he can, that he wants to come home to get things sorted. Marty thinks he gets it—he'll pay up but won't get his hands dirty. Diane insists if they all work together they can make it work. (http://www.brookie.com/, July 6, 2001, *Brookside*)

Other social issues, many with violent themes, have included domestic violence, spouse murder, hit-and-run vehicle drama, male-on-male fighting, child abuse, children killed in car accidents, and drug-related violence.

Coronation Street () is set in a terraced street in Manchester. It is a predominantly White, working-class story set around the public house, "The Rover"s Return; the corner shop, "The Cabin"; and the local underwear factory, "Underworld." "Corrie," the most traditional of the U.K. soaps, has had scandalous stories, including the transsexual Harold becoming Hayley and then having a relationship with Roy of the local café, "Roy's Rolls." Recently, the death of a prominent and long-standing character, Alma, from cancer, after she missed a smear/pap test and was not followed up by the local Health Authority, has played into the anxieties of women in contemporary Britain. Less violent than *Brookside*, *Coronation Street* has nonetheless featured incidents of rape, male physical violence, and a great deal of verbal aggression.

Eastenders is set in London's East End with its mythology of gangs, low life, and criminality. Narratives rarely take place outside of the context of the central location of Albert Square, with the pub (the Queen Victoria), local café, car sales shop, fish and chip shop, and garage repair shop as featured settings. Oddly, *Eastenders* takes an occasional holiday with a group of characters going away to Paris or Spain, for example, and being filmed in situ. Again, this mirrors the lifestyle of the audience at a period when package holidays abroad are very much normal and everyday. Predominantly working class in character, *Eastenders* has several rogues who live on the edge of or outside the law. It focuses quite heavily on young adult and teenage characters in sexual and familial situations. Determinedly controversial, the program currently foregrounds the story of a heterosexual man with HIV and has featured rape, attempted murder, manslaughter, vehicle death of a child, euthanasia, male violence, teenage pregnancy, and drug-related violence.

Emmerdale (ITV) is set in idyllic countryside in Yorkshire and is very much a tale of country folk. It focuses on farming, village life, and family. It too is very traditional in terms of character and plot and is rarely sexually controversial beyond some infidelity. Violence in the series is often comical or at least not terribly damaging, but there have been depictions of fighting between father and son and between neighbors. There are several incidences of men fighting each other over women. There is a great deal of verbal aggression and a frequent sense of menace and brutishness in the program.

The Australian soaps are much less aggressive and foreground stories about young characters. *Neighbors* is based on a community in a modest Australian town and filmed in the local café, bar, outdoors, or in characters' homes. It is very family focused and rarely controversial, although it does tackle death quite frequently, presumably to enable characters to leave the program. *Home and Away* is a more bawdy soap opera set near the sea in Summer Bay and featuring sand, surf, and sex. The local diner called "The Cabin," school, hospital, beach, and a large home of foster children are the key spaces where the action takes place. The fostering theme allows a steady stream of actors to come and go and serves the soap's focus on teenage lifestyle well. Stories focus on adolescent sex, health, education, parenting, and youth crime. Accidents rather than violence are the motifs for drama.

Soaps have been the focus of research attention for some time now; in fact, in the last 20 years, "soap opera has moved from being an object of academic and popular contempt to a major area of media study" (Marris & Thornham, 1996, p. 354). Scholars of feminist cultural studies take notice of the dominant place occupied by women in soap audiences and the everyday domestic and communal content of the programs. The focus has been on what soap means to audiences and the political or other implications of the narratives and characterization. Although this work has mainly been concerned about implications for gender norms and roles, some of the theory and findings bear on concerns about violence in broadcasting and its possible effects.

ANALYZING SOAP

Geraghty (1981) mapped the structure of soap operas to try to begin to understand their appeal through textual analysis. She found an organization of material that "establishes base which becomes increasingly familiar to its audience while maintaining sufficient flexibility to be able to present apparently different situations. It provides us with the feeling of an unwritten future while giving necessary access to the past. We are constantly left wondering what will happen next—occasionally with a real cliffhanger" (Geraghty, 1981, p. 369). Soaps are attractive, she argued, because they balance repetition and change and cement them with gossip.

Modleski (1996) also focused on text in order to try to explain the pleasure of viewing. She identified themes of family, community, and domesticity, which connected the viewer with the text because they "accord closely with the rhythms of women's work in the home" (Modleski, 1996, p. 375). Yet, the texts also provide escapism, which helps make bearable that everyday business by providing a fantasy of the desirable family or desirable community. So women's real needs and anxieties may be addressed, providing means of identification and understanding, but they may also be distorted toward a rather conservative and conforming myth. Modleski's reading is a political one that is critical of the mass cultural provision for women that is characterized by soaps and her call is to try to find ways of meeting women's needs that are "more creative, honest and interesting than the ones mass culture has supplied" (Modleski, 1996, p. 279). There is an underlying assumption here about the potential of soap to affect the audience, in a way, which in the case of women legitimates and even aggrandizes their everyday position in the world. So soaps may be acting to maintain a gender status quo, which includes women's subordination.

In the early 1980s, Dorothy Hobson focused less on the text and more on the soap audience when she wrote *Everything stops for crossroads: Watching with the audience. Crossroads* was broadcast on independent television from 1964–1988 (Hobson, 1982). It was based on a motel in the British Midlands and the lives of those who worked there. It has recently been revamped in an updated version and is back on the screens of daytime television, with some original cast members. Hobson focused on the way women and their families positioned themselves in relation to the characters and stories and sought to add value to both the phenomena of soap and the status of those who enjoyed watching them by combating the elitism that surrounded discussions of the serial's cardboard sets and appalling acting. She found close identification between viewers and characters; viewers embedded themselves in "stories of everyday life and it's 'ups and downs', problems and pleasures; the inclusion of personal, moral and emotional matters is an integral part of the genre" (Hobson, 1982, p. 392).

However, fans were critical of, rather than engaged with the story and challenged many of the outcomes and experiences portrayed to them. Women drew on their own lives in their interpretation of the text and were readily dismissive if a broadcast event or act did not seem to "fit." According to Hobson (1982), "Sometimes storylines are touchstones for experiences which the viewers have and which they see reflected in the serial" (p. 395). Hobson viewers did not respond to stories that were too far removed from their own knowledge, that is, they were not in any sense "propagandized" into new attitudes or behaviors. Rather:

> It seems that the myth of the passive viewer is about to be shattered. They do not sit there watching and taking it all in without any mental activity or creativity. It seems they expect to contribute to the production which they are watching and bring their own knowledge to augment the text. Stories, which seem almost too fantastic for an everyday serial, are transformed through a sympathetic audience reading whereby they strip the story line to the idea behind it and construct an understanding on the skeleton that is left. (Hobson, 1982, p. 396)

Hobson's view was of an active audience that creatively deals with broadcast material rather than passively absorbs it. Moreover, the creativity of that experience for audiences is a vital part of the attraction of soap and its ability to maintain large viewing figures.

The soap audience has become an integral part of broadcasters' planning and program design. Audiences are valuable for broadcasters because they can be sold to advertisers and used by public service broadcasting to justify license fee collection. When *Eastenders* was launched in 1985, it was certainly part of the BBC's need to justify public funding by keeping a mass audience happy, but it was also an attempt to reinvent the BBC with a new symbol in place of its "rather staid and middle-class 'Auntie' image" (Buckingham, 1996, p. 356). "In addition *Eastenders* sought to extend the traditional audience for British soaps, which is weighted towards women and the elderly" (Buckingham, 1996, p. 357) by having young and strong male characters. It treated social issues openly and won a significant teenage audience. That large heterogeneous audience has become a vital part of U.K. public service broadcasting's self-justification and the goal of other channel's soaps.

This switch from women's genre to a more inclusive model of social life in British soaps is best represented by *Brookside*. Although Macdonald (1995) pointed out that a conservative, feminine model of gender norms and roles still tends to dominate the characters and narratives, for example, even when paid work and men's roles are featured, these tend "to fit into the paradigm of domesticity and personal relationships more normally associated with the private sphere" (p. 69).

Feminist academic work has raised the cultural status of soap opera but has not resolved the value of its content. Soaps do address the everyday, personal, and ordinary issues that are often diminished or invisible in other cultural and entertainment spheres (Tuchman, 1978b), but not always in radical or transforming ways that might support change and growth in women's lives. They give a voice to women's lives, but it is not generally a liberating voice. But, remember that the largely (still) female audience is not a duped and quiescent one. It does not have the power to interrupt the consensual flow from the box and if that flow represents oppressive male practices such as domestic violence, rape, bullying ,and aggressive sexual jealousy without offering hope for change, if it is not possible to argue that soap operas cause damage, then it might at least be claimed that they do not actively seek to prevent it.

AUDIENCES AND SOAPS

Much academic work done on soap texts has been qualitative and interpretative, sometimes even anecdotal with little close reference to or analysis of the actual broadcast data. A few audience studies have attempted to address more directly the qualities of the genre that underpin its appeal for viewers. Wober and Fazal (1994) reported a study of British viewers' opinions about the two Australian soap operas already mentioned, *Neighbors* and *Home and Away*. They related viewers' ratings of each program along a range of descriptive attributes, such as perceptions that the acting was good, there was little bad acting, there was a benevolent atmosphere, and the program was not behind the times. Higher ratings statistically predicted greater audience enjoyment of each serial. The descriptive attributes used in this study, however, were derived not from viewers but from a combination of the researchers' own intuitions about soap operas and an analysis of reviews of each serial by prominent television critics. Indeed, the researchers in this case found that the critics' perceptions that these serials were popular because they were moral tales was not supported by the opinions of viewers themselves. The morality aspect of each serial did not emerge as a major predictor of general audience appreciation.

Taking this work further forward, Gunter (1997) presented a study of the qualities volunteered by viewers that underpinned good soap operas in which the attributes used to rate soaps were first generated by viewers themselves. This study used a combined approach of initial soap assessments via a program analyzer and follow-up focus group discussions to generate attributes that for viewers defined the essential features of soap operas. Then, in a later stage, these attributes were developed into rating scales and presented to panels of home viewers of particular soaps who were asked to provide evaluative ratings of episodes they had viewed.

The key defining features of soap operas were realism (characters and settings), established characters with known histories, the presence of conflict and confrontation to create tension and drama, an ability to identify and get involved with characters and events, a degree of coherence among the different story lines and the way they are integrated within episodes, high technical professionalism in production, a mix of characters offering contrasts, and an optimal number of running plot lines (although not too many to follow). Realism, tension, identification, technical professionalism, and optimal balance among plots were consistent predictors of intended future viewing of soap operas.

Ultimately, however, a perspective is needed that can combine a sophisticated analysis of audiences' readings of soaps with an equally elaborate mode of textual analysis that reveals the complexities of plot lines and character development that typifies the genre. Liebes and Livingstone (1994) made some advance toward this position by combining a number of perspectives in an analysis of television soap operas from Britain and the United States. Essentially, they adopted three techniques: a study of viewers using closed questionnaires and a quantitative analysis of soaps, a reception analysis of viewers' commentaries on soaps and a literary analysis of the text of soaps, and an analysis of the narrative characteristics of soaps, including a detailed assessment of relationships between the dramatic characters. The latter analysis examined in detail the characters who were related by blood, marriage, or romance and the story lines that brought the characters together or kept them apart. This technique was regarded as more sensitive than a standard content analysis that would have counted the numbers of characters appearing from different categories. Instead, Liebes and Livingstone mapped out the kinship relations among soap characters in the form of family trees. Comparisons were then made at this level between British and American soap operas.

The research revealed that characters were linked mostly through family ties in American soaps, whereas community ties were more important in British soaps. In American soaps, stories focused heavily on young adult characters or characters for whom romantic entanglements were always within reach, and children and the elderly were relatively ignored. The exception to this rule were mothers in leading families who tended to have central roles and might become romantically involved. Indeed, the romantic activities of these mother figures could serve as a source of tension, especially when they competed with their own daughters for the same man. In British soaps, in contrast, mothers rarely enjoyed romance in that sense and certainly not with a man of a different generation. This study demonstrated the value of a qualitative approach that was used to draw kinship maps indicating how characters within dramatic narratives bonded to create a social structure.

VIOLENCE IN U.K. SOAPS ON TELEVISION

In the current study, programs were classified by genre. Two particular categories, long-running U.K. series or serials or non-U.K. long-running serials or series, comprised programs of the type commonly termed "soap opera." In all, 84 soap opera episodes were captured by the study conducted in 1995–1996, including 43 made in the United Kingdom.

To put the soap opera findings in a broader context, in the 1995–1996 analysis of U.K. television output, more than 1 in 10 programs that contained violence (11%) were drama. Overall, most violence occurred in broadcast cinema films (43% contained violence). Among output on the nonthematic channels—BBC1, BBC2, ITV, Channel 4, Sky One, and UK Gold (this excludes movie channels, cartoon, and sport)—23.4% of violent programs were U.K. soaps and 19% were non-U.K. soaps. Thus, on these generic channels, long-running drama series or serials accounted for about 42% of all programs containing violent scenes in 1995–1996.

In this analysis, 23.4% of drama programs containing violence on the six generic (nonthematic) channels were U.K.-produced soaps and 19% were non-U.K. soaps. Of these channels, BBC2 was most likely to screen soaps with violent content: 90.9% of the channel's non-U.K. serials and 80% of U.K. serials had some violent content. However, BBC2 was responsible for only 21.3% of total screened soap violence. The main commercial channel, ITV, screened most soaps terrestrially at 39.3% of its drama output, and 84.7% of these programs contained violence; 48.4% of it was in U.K.-produced programs. The UK Gold satellite channel offered 77.6% of all screened violent soaps and of that material, some 81.8% depicted violence; 52.8% of that was in U.K. material.

U.K. long-running serials also scored highly for the frequency of violent events within programs, particularly on BBC2, where an average 12.3 incidences per program accrued at the rate of 11.7 acts per hour. These findings, however, are ameliorated to some extent because BBC2 also showed the least soaps of all channels at only 6.1% of its total output of violent drama, as compared to 20% at ITV.

This study was concerned not just with rate of incidents of violence but also the distribution of violence in drama to enable a comparison between genre and the length of time viewers were exposed to violent material. Violent material actually decreased in rate of occurrence in non-U.K. series across all broadcasters during 1994–1996 but remained stable for other drama across the whole spectrum. However, a comparison shows some significant shifts from 1994–1995 to 1995–1996 in

TABLE 8.4

Distribution of Violent Sequences in Soap Operas by Channel

% per Channel	Non-U.K. Soaps, 1994–1995	Non-U.K. Soaps, 1995–1996	U.K. Soaps, 1994–1995	U.K. Soaps, 1995–1996
BBC1	9	2	20	2
BBC2	18	12	2	8
ITV	11	7	4	9
Channel 4	10	7	6	6
Sky One	47	31	3	–
UK Gold	14	8	41	47
All Channels	18	11	13	14

TABLE 8.5

Distribution of Minutage of Violence in Soaps by Channel

% per Channel	Non-U.K. Soaps, 1994–1995	Non-U.K. Soaps, 1995–1996	U.K. Soaps, 1994–1995	U.K. Soaps, 1995–1996
BBC1	16	1	5	1
BBC2	12	8	1	5
ITV	9	8	1	18
Channel 4	6	23	2	21
Sky One	55	35	32	0
UK Gold	13	8	35	42
All Channels	19	14	8	15

that violent incidences in U.K. soaps on UK Gold, BBC2, and ITV all increased slightly, whereas violence on BBC1 soaps decreased from 20% to 2% (see Table 8.4).

As a whole, the time occupied by violent output increased across the 2 years of the research by 17% over all drama output,[1] but the gross percentage of violence in minutage remained steady at 1.4% of all satellite output time and increased a fraction from 1.2% to 1.4% for terrestrial output. Curiously, although BBC1 showed fewer soaps with violent scenes, the overall minutes of violent activity in U.K. soaps across all channels went up from 4% to 5%. Table 8.5 shows the breakdown of genre, channel, and running time for dramatic violence. Overall, there were fewer minutes of violence on non-U.K. soaps between the two temporal periods of coding (19% drops to 14%) and more time spent on violence in U.K. soaps (8% rises to 15%). Only Channel 4 shows increases in minutes of broadcast violence for U.K. soaps (2% rises to 21%) and for

---

[1]This was due largely to the inclusion in the second year of research of the output from TNT/Cartoon Network.

non-U.K. soaps (6% rises to 23%). But again, the total of violent text as a percentage of all drama output is very tiny: 0.6% is the highest on UK Gold for U.K. soaps, followed by 0.4% on Sky One for non-U.K. soaps.

None of the six most popular long-running soaps figured in the top 10 drama programs (not including cinema films, which are overwhelmingly the most violent) containing violent acts. The only soap to figure at all was the Australian late night broadcast *Prisoner Cell Block H*, which took the second spot with 34 incidents (the top film *Demolition Man* had 167 acts lasting 15.9 minutes). *Prisoner Cell Block H*, a soap drama about a women's prison, gained cult status toward the end of its run, particularly among gay audiences. It also came into the ratings for minutes of violence in nonfilm drama at sixth position (4 min.).

The coders did find violence in soap operas, albeit very little when compared to other genres and in terms of the general volume of output (e.g., films made for cinema). But much concern about soaps has focused less on the volume of violence and more on its realistic context and familiar characterization, two aspects that inform an empathy model of effects. In other words, the easier it is for viewers to identify with and feel sympathy for actors and actions, the more likely they are to either learn new or to confirm existing beliefs and attitudes. Realistic contexts and justified violence are thought to be two particular risk factors in the potential for depictions to cause harm (Federman, 1997).

In soaps, dramatic violence tended to be set in familiar contexts, either in the present (52.7%) or recent past (23.8%) also 28.5% of acts in drama were set in Britain and 34.5% were set in the United States. The most common type of violence found in broadcast drama was realistic physical aggression: pushing, tripping, punching, kicking, and slapping (39.8%); and using hands, fists, or other body part (37.5% of weapons). The second most common type was shooting (24.3%) with handguns (8.4%)—that is, "realistic" interpersonal shooting, at least in American culture, as opposed to the use of science fiction weaponry or weapons of war. Although 28.5% of such acts in drama occurred in criminal motivational contexts, 27.2% happened in interpersonal and domestic contexts. The goals of some 80% of all violent acts in film and drama were destruction, personal ambition, and power or monetary gain, yet in nearly one in two cases (48.2% in drama) violence was not shown to cause any obvious physical harm or mental distress and any consequences that were shown were slight. Only 1.3% of dramatic violence had sexual motives and only 8.6% of dramatic violence ended with death. More than three in four drama programs (78%), which includes soap operas, showed no blood; 63.6% of violence in drama showed no pain; and 60.6% did not represent any kind of horror. So the nature of violence shown in drama was familiar in context and form—that is, realistic—but the consequences were unrealistic. This was "cleaned up" violence, which quite possibly mitigated the act by obfuscating the damage that physical attack, of even a fairly trivial kind, usually causes. Realistic violence was being depicted but with unrealistic results.

Characterization was a second possible effects risk factor to consider. In drama, generally aggressors were more likely to be male (78%) than female (12.4%). Males were more likely to be victims (73.6%) and females were less often victims (13.2%). Both these sets of figures broadly correlate with figures for real violence (Home Office, 1999)[2] and so are realistic. The age range for perpetrators and victims was also close to real. Most were between age 20 and 35 (52.9% in drama in the case of perpetrators and 50.5% in the case of victims). Perpetrators and victims were also depicted as White in about three quarters of incidences. In other words, the characters biologically in terms of race, gender, age, and ethnic profile match real-life criteria for "people" involved in violence. In social terms, drama shows various characters: criminals, 20.4%; nonspecific situation characters, 13.2%; the armed forces, 10%; police, 9%; and domesticity, 5.1%. Victims are similarly distributed. Only a small portion of victims and perpetrators are nonrealistic (e.g., spacemen), accounting for 3.8% of aggressors and 3.6% of victims. Drama includes plays, made-for-TV films, and short series, as well as soaps. But, of noncinema drama, it is soaps, both British and non-British, that offer nearly two thirds of all drama programs with violence.

VIOLENCE IN MOST POPULAR SOAPS

To explore this further, a smaller substudy focused on the six soaps that were most popular during the mid-1990s: *Coronation Street*, *Brookside*, *Eastenders*, and *Emmerdale* (U.K. produced) and *Neighbours* and *Home and Away* (Australian). Each has been long running, with *Home and Away* the only one off the air since the study. It returned to Channel 5 in July 2001. The soaps were recorded on one day a week (Monday in Week 1; Tuesday in Week two, etc.) for 28 weeks between July 1995 and June 1996. Recording began at 6 a.m. and finished at 6 a.m. the following day. Output was collected from ten channels: terrestrial channels—BBC1, BBC2, ITV, Channel 4; and satellite—Sky One, UK Gold, Sky Movies, The movie Channel, Sky Sports, and TNT/The Cartoon Network.

Soaps not only offer realism and identification, but they are also repetitive over a long period of time. The cumulative effect of viewing, particularly if the process begins in early childhood, has been widely researched (Huesmann, Lagerspetz, & Eron, 1984; Sheehan 1986). An accumulation of violent imagery in repeated, long-running programs like soaps might therefore give legitimate cause for concern. This may be exacerbated with soap operas because of the familiar contexts and characters involved in the programs that encourage emotional bonding between viewer and viewed (Gunter, 1985). If violence is seen as part of the everyday on screen, then it may be more readily accepted or even in-

---

[2]Chapter 6 discusses crime data from the U.K. Home Office for the relevant period in relation to broadcast gendered violence.

stigated in real social situations. A study of soaps in the United States (Greenberg & Busselle, 1996) suggested, for example, that increased violence associated with sexual activity on screen might relate to increased sexual violence in reality. The substudy of the current research project looked at 84 episodes of the six most popular soaps broadcast in 1995–1996 and sought to tease out and map violence in the genre so as to establish whether or not such drama might be implicated in off screen violent behavior.

The 84 episodes analyzed included 43 from British soaps and 41 from Australian soaps. Fifteen British and six Australian episodes contained violence. Thus, British soaps appeared to offer nearly three times the violence of Australian soaps. This was confirmed by measures showing that the British sample portrayed 40 acts as compared to only 11 in the Australian; moreover, the British violence occupied 3.9 minutes, as compared to 1.4 minutes in non–British material; and each British episode showed five acts per hour in violence-containing programs, as compared to only 2.1 per hour in the Australian material. Yet, in both cases, the violence minutage in total program running time was equal at only 0.8% of running time; this was only slightly more than one half the 1.39% average violence depiction for the total broadcast hours of the whole study and lower than the figure of 1.04% achieved when boxing and wrestling were removed from the total hours figure. So, in terms of volume alone, soap violence seems of less consequence than program violence across the whole spectrum of televized material. Even where violence did occur, it was only briefly on screen—at most, less than 9 seconds worth in each of eight episodes of the British soaps.

Alongside measures of quantification of violence, soaps were coded in terms of the form of violence, motivation, consequences, and characterization. The most common form of violence was some kind of unarmed physical assault (47.5% in U.K. soaps and 45% in Australian soaps). U.K. soaps included 17% of attacks with an object, but the most common instrument of aggression was the fist or hand in all instances (47.2% of U.K. violence and 63.6% of Australian violence). Most violence was interpersonal involving two individuals and escalating from verbal abuse to physical violence. The British incidents included two acts of domestic violence and two criminal acts; the Australian episodes included one representation of domestic violence and no crime contexts.

Little of the violence showed any significant consequences. Half the incidents in U.K. soaps resulted in very minor physical damage (56.6%) and two cases showed psychological harm. An additional 32.1% of incidents showed no negative consequences at all. This was exceeded in the Australian soaps, where 54.5% of cases showed no damage; four cases only showed minor injury and there was one act of violence that resulted in psychological trauma.

As in drama, more generally and in real life, most characters involved in violence as either victims or perpetrators were male. Nearly 7 in 10 (69.8%) of acts in U.K. soaps and all acts in the non-U.K. soaps were executed by men. Just over 7 in 10 (71.7%) of victims in U.K. soaps and over 8 in 10 (81.8%) in Australian soaps were men. In British soaps, women were overrepresented both as perpetrators and victims of violence (24.5% and 22.4%, respectively) compared to both drama broadly and real female violence, which constitutes less than 10% of all violence in the United Kingdom (Home Office, 1999). Australian soaps featured no aggressive women, but 18.2% of victims were women. Most violence was male on male (86.5% in British material and 81.8% in non-U.K.). Female violence tended to be against another female (61.5% in U.K. soaps only), but a surprising 38.5% of acts were women against men, perhaps related to the domestic violence story lines involving battered women who retaliate or kill (*Brookside*).

Aggressors and victims in Australian soaps tended to be younger than in British soaps, perhaps because they are broadcast during the daytime and early evening. These time slots are likely to attract younger audiences and so it makes sense to feature stories about young people. The similarity in age groups between aggressors and victims demonstrated a high rate of intra-peer group violence among young people. Three quarters of teenage violence in the Australian soaps was directed at members of their own age group. In British soaps, two thirds of young adult violence was aimed at other young adults.

Viewing the episodes helped illuminate these findings with more qualitative readings of the violence they portrayed. The soap violence is described briefly beginning with the series that showed the most violence during the study period.

Emmerdale contained 24 acts of violence in the seven episodes that were analyzed. Much of this violence was found in a special hour-long show that featured the climax to a series of ongoing tensions and conflict between family members and close neighbors. The main story was focused on one male character whose affair with both a married woman and her daughter had ruined several relationships. In a major scene, the man's father insults the married woman and the two wrestle to the ground, punches are thrown and threats uttered, and both characters sustain black eyes and bruising. Female relatives witness the fight and there are graphic sound effects. As part of the same story, the wronged husband threatens his unfaithful wife and grabs her roughly. A second incident is more lightweight, involving a male character hitting a female by accident instead of the punching bag he is exercising on. She responds with a punch that knocks him to the ground. One third was also more humorous, involving a women's wrestling match and a rather overenthusiastic crowd. Further episodes featured male-on-male insults and taunting and stone throwing between young men over a young woman. Although sometimes light in tone, the serious violence depicted was realistic, interpersonal, and to some extent legitimated by the context of infidelity.

Brookside came second in the table of violence. It has been characterized, and continues to be renowned for, controversial and topical story lines. However, the episodes recorded fell outside the narratives showing the most violence and there were only a few incidences of uncontrolled anger: seven violent acts in four episodes. Three of these acts occurred in one scene and involved two women. The acts were verbal abuse, pulling at each other and tearing of clothing, and slapping. This happened in public and others became verbally involved. A further act tinged graphic expletives and anger with humor in a case of mistaken identity. Several more instances involved grabbing between a spurned woman and her lover, mild scenes of a schoolboy fight, and a verbal threat.

Eastenders depicted six acts of violence, three in one scene in a public house, which involved two male characters pushing and punching each other. A second episode featured two aggressive acts again in the public house, "The Queen Vic." This time, the action took place between a barmaid and a male customer but was limited to verbal threats.

In *Coronation Street*, the public house, "the Rover's Return," also featured as a context for violence. This again involved men, but this time there were merely verbal threats and provocative actions. A further event in the public house, which has comic overtones, occurred between a man and woman. The woman pushed the man to the floor after he challenged her boyfriend's behavior.

Neighbors had no violence in the episodes recorded for analysis, there were 11 violent acts in the 6 episodes of *Home and Away*. Although generally mild, two did occur in contexts of sexual harassment and domestic abuse—although no graphic evidence of these was portrayed. Three violent acts occurred in a scene were a teenage girl accused her mother's boyfriend of harassment. There was no physical violence, but threatening and intimidating behavior was shown. The domestic violence action was shown as flashback and showed bruising, raised fists, a wrecked room, but no physical contact. Other incidents were mild. So, although the contexts for violence did seem quite disturbing, only viewers' imaginations could visualize any actual activity.

IMPLICATIONS FOR AUDIENCE RESPONSES

In the current study, the violence in the most popular soaps watched by millions in the United Kingdom appeared to be low in volume, contemporary and realistic in context and characterization, largely male on male, involved bad language, fisticuffs, rough stuff rather than knives and guns, and did not seem to cause much damage. So to what extent should the public, politicians, researchers, and television regulators be concerned about the potential of soap operas to either promote or condone violence among viewers?

Concern about soap violence seems at first glance to be misplaced. The total of violent soap text as a percentage of all drama output is very tiny; 0.6% was the highest on UK Gold for U.K. soaps, followed by 0.4% on Sky One for non-U.K. soaps. Although there were differences between U.K. and non-U.K. soaps in that U.K. material had more violence per program and more minutes of violence, the overall percentage of violent minutage per program running time in U.K. and non-U.K. soaps was identical at 0.81%.

Moreover, the nature of the violence that was portrayed was relatively innocuous. Most soap violence was just males strutting and fretting around the communities in which they live. Most aggression was intra-male, among peer group members of similar age and of general characteristic. Of this, the worst acts were punching and pushing and the cause seemed most often to be either jealousy, sexual possessiveness, or protectiveness (not always justified in any of the cases). Other male-on-male aggression tended to be more humorous. Female aggression tended to be verbal, often dealing with either male sexual overtures or misbehavior, or female sexual competition or criticism of family mores or members. Occasionally, the consequences rather than the act were depicted, leaving viewers to intuit women's violence. What was rare was any apparent serious outcome to any form of aggression. This was "cleaned up" violence, which quite possibly mitigated the act by obfuscating the damage that physical attack, of even a fairly trivial kind, usually causes. Even real verbal abuse can cause terrible distress and anxiety. These things were not screened in the soaps recorded and analyzed in the violence study. Realistic violence (ordinary, loud, male, and crude) was being depicted but with unrealistic results. And that may be a reason for concern.

First of all, consider the sheer volume of the soap audience, which necessarily increases the possibility of vulnerable or susceptible viewers being subject to potential effects. Clearly, these effects may be valuable rather than destructive. Soaps increasingly act as information conduits educating audiences about issues such as adult literacy schemes, drug-related problems, sexuality, sources of support for abuse or rape victims, parenting, consumer rights, and active citizenship. Second, their potential to inform in a way that is understood and accepted may well be increased by the nature of soap's content. Macdonald (1995) pointed out, "Soap operas, unlike the rest of television drama, clearly do focus on the everyday and on personal relationships dramatized principally through talk rather than action" (p. 68). The potential for effective rhetoric is clearly greater when viewers feel they are viewing their own lives represented back to them on the small screen. In this context, it may be that even relatively small amounts of violence may have more potential effect than, for example, violence in science fiction or violent drama set in the far distant past or in cartoons or between nonhuman characters (Federman, 1997).

It may also be that some members of viewing groups (e.g., children) are susceptible to even small amounts of realistic violence, particularly when it is depicted in settings that are "close to home" (Gunter, 1985). Work on children viewing television suggests they are most susceptible to examples of behavior on screen, which are perpetrated by members of their own age group (Noble, 1975) and virtually no depicted violence in televised soap is acted out by children.

Women too have been theorized as susceptible to images of violence against women. This has been seen as raising anxiety levels (D. G. Linz, Donnerstein, & Penrod, 1988; S. Linz, Donnerstein, & Penrod, 1984). It also might promote an unnecessary sense of vulnerability and fear of crime, given women's relatively low victim status in real life (Home Office, 1999). However, there did not seem to be any excessive focus on women as victims in television soap. Although slightly overrepresented in this role in British soaps, victimization is quite likely to be at the hands of tongues of other women as opposed to physical male violence or sexual attack. Further, this slight overfocus, compared to real data, on women as victims, is more than compensated for by an overrepresentation of aggressive women—nor is this major cause for concern in terms of effects, because women feature as attackers in under 10% of real violent crime (despite the pessimistic predictions of Adler, 1981, on the possibility that feminism would lead to more aggressive women).

Perhaps what is of most concern in the violent content of soaps is what they do not show and do not attempt to deal with. Little is made of the consequences of violence. Even trivial abuse, bullying, and verbal aggression have detrimental effects. Yet, on screen, these are not shown. Nobody portrays the kind of real injuries that can be inflicted by a fist or foot. The effect is a kind of endorsement of everyday aggression, especially between males, which replicates and leaves uncriticized a rather brutish kind of everyday masculinity—particularly in relation to male sexual competitiveness, patriarchy within the family, and male social power. That brutishness in those contexts has real-life implications for women and children. Soaps might not promote new or different violence, and do not actively challenge or seek to change the ongoing, ordinary, everyday exercise of male power that characterizes so many of the social, familial, and sexual relationships in both the United Kingdom and the United States.

Chapter 9

News Values and Violence

Television news broadcasts dramatic and violent events occurring around the world. Giddens (1984) argued that such reporting may affect the viewer's basic sense of ontological security, given that this sense of security is based on whether or not they are safe, whether their family is safe, or whether society is safe. Much violent news featured on television revolves around issues of conflict, including crime, violent civil disturbances, terrorism, or war, or is concerned with natural or man-made disasters and accidents. The dilemma for television journalists is how much can and should be shown without alarming, upsetting, or offending viewers (Gunter & J. Harrison, 1998). For the public and news editors alike, the amount of coverage given by news broadcasts to real-life violent incidents, their aftermath, as well as the way they should be covered, raises difficult issues relating to sensibilities, tastes, and values. Both editorial and public views about how the news on television should cover violent events vary with the type of story, the geographical location of the event, the nature of the event concerned, and the types of people who are involved.

Given that a good deal of news containing violence is about conflict and disaster, it is useful to examine what determines news value for the journalist. International comparisons of broadcast news profiles have confirmed that violence and conflict represent a staple diet of news around the world (A. A. Cohen & Bantz, 1984). In the United States and Britain, for instance, conflict items frequently featured reports of physical aggression and in around one in five cases actually showed acts of aggression on screen. Physical aggression was more likely to be reported and shown with foreign rather than with domestic items. Thus, violent news tended to be emphasized more in geographically remote rather than geographically proximal locations.

The character of violence in factual programing has been examined by other researchers, mainly in the United States. Here, factual programs have been found generally to contain less violence than fictional programs and much violence that occurs in factual programs is described rather than shown (Lichter & Amundsen, 1992). Reality programs (including news programs) have been found to exaggerate the extent to which violent crimes are solved (Oliver, 1994). Later research on reality programs, conducted as part of the National Television Violence Study between 1994 and 1996, found that more than one half the news and public affairs programs monitored (52% in 1994–1995 and 56% in 1995–1996) contained no violence, over one in five during the same time period contained visually depicted scenes of violence (26% in 1994–1995 and 17% in 1995–1996), and one in four contained verbal reports or descriptions of violent events (22% in 1994–1995 and 28% in 1995–1996) (Danielson et al, 1996; *National Television Violence Study*, 1998). The same investigation found that violent scenes in the news were equally divided between those depicting no harm to participants and those depicting harm. Three quarters of all characters involved in violence in factual programs were men.

It is important to understand the criteria employed by broadcast journalists in their coverage of events because television is the most trusted source of news information (Gunter & Winstone, 1992; ITC, 2000). News broadcasters have an important role to play in ensuring that the news media present an accurate and undistorted picture of violent events. Ideally, these events should be put into context and present the viewer with enough information to make a discerning interpretation of the events being portrayed.

Evidence produced by Philo (1993) in Britain has shown how news coverage can distort audience perceptions of conflictual events. The Glasgow University Media Group conducted a set of interviews with members of the public following the British coal miners' strike of 1985 and found that 54% of those questioned believed that the strike was violent in nature, whereas those who had taken part in picketing or knew someone who had been involved, believed the strike to have been predominantly peaceful. The crucial difference between the two sets of interviewees was their reliance or nonreliance on television news for information, where television news appears to have produced a distorted picture relating to the violent nature of the strike. The public tends to believe that the levels of violence in society are much higher than the actual chance of their being victimized. Klijn (1999) considered whether this could be due to the large output of reports about violence in the news. Klijn went on to paraphrase B. Cohen (1963), who argued that the media are clearly successful in telling the public that violence is important because it often reports violent events. However, the media are less good at telling people why the reporting of violence is important, what causes violence in society, and what should be done about it. The reason that television news covers violent events and the way it covers them relates to the constituent features of newsworthiness and journalistic practice.

NEWS VALUES AND NEWS SELECTION

Journalists believe there is a strong similarity between their own news values and those of the audience (Sparkes & Winter, 1980). However, the news values that attract the attention of the audience and are also perceived to be newsworthy by journalists may actually inhibit proper viewer comprehension (Klijn, 1999). The audience tends to find stories interesting if they are human interest stories, show conflict or controversy, cover unusual happenings, cover events that are news, are happening now, and are culturally and geographically relevant.

A range of news factors identified by various writers (Bell, 1991; Galtung & Ruge, 1965; Ostgaard, 1965; Sande, 1971; Tunstall, 1971) have been used to define the properties of news stories that audiences will find appealing enough to watch. News factor analysis is content-based research that attempts to examine the way in which "a property of an event ... increases its chance of becoming 'news'" (Sande, 1971, p. 222), that is, increases its chance of being selected and used by a news organisation. Analysts working within this perspective tend to concentrate on identifying news factors they believe are inherent in an event and would influence journalists making a choice of which event to select.

Further studies have assessed the importance of the news factors identified by Galtung and Ruge and identified some additional factors that increase the likelihood of an event being reported. These can be briefly summarized as follows: In television news, the possession of film of the event increases the newsworthiness of the event (Tunstall, 1971); the more facts and figures that can be reported, the more likely the event is to become a news story (Bell, 1991); and, once a story is in the news, tangential stories are more likely to be reported (Fowler, 1991).

News factor studies have concentrated on news attributes as causal agents in the news selection process, where news is published because it contains particular properties and because of a consensus as to the significance of these qualities. This view of news selection is apolitical because it excludes the possibility of intent by journalists in their publication of stories, and ignores the needs of the audience in assessing news value. Here journalists are believed to select news events simply on the basis of the particular combination of news factors inherent in an event. From this perspective, the audience and the journalist are not seen to be employing a conscious or unconscious desire to meet a political, personal, or institutional goal.

By using news factors as a criterion of news value it is not difficult to show why a violent event might become news. The journalist simply chooses the story because it contains certain inherent properties. In summary, events are more likely to be reported in television news programs if they have good pictures/film; if they contain short, dramatic occurrences that can be sensationalized; if they have novelty value; if they are open to simple reporting; if they occur on a grand scale; if they are negative or contain violence, crime, confrontation, or catastrophe; if they are either highly unexpected, or contain things that would be expected to happen; if the events have meaning and relevance to the audience; if similar events are already in the news; if they contain elite people or nations; or if they allow an event to be reported in personal or human interest terms (Bell, 1991; Galtung & Ruge, 1965; J. L. Harrison, 2000; Ostgaard, 1965; Sande, 1971; Sparkes & Winter, 1980; Tunstall, 1971). Although news factors are useful as an indication that certain properties inherent in an event influence news selection, they do not tell everything about how and why news values are constructed.

Television news values are also shaped by other forces operating in the broadcasting sector: deregulation, technological developments, increasing competition for audiences within the broadcasting sector, and the new commercialization of the television news environment. Changes within the broadcasting environment are, as is discussed later, driving television news values toward an increase in live, dramatic, and sensational news coverage.

News values also reflect the remit and goals of news organizations, the constraints of the television medium, and importantly, of the routines, values, and norms of journalistic practice. A shared belonging to the profession provides journalists with a set of skills, values, pressures, constraints, and expectations within which they practice journalism. Tuchman (1978a) showed how journalists employ a set of routinized conventions in choosing and selecting news to cope with a variety of problems and pressures. These pressures are multifarious, including problems of time and space limitations, financial, bureaucratic, and legal restrictions, logistical difficulties, and the particular demands of the television medium itself (e.g., the need for visuals). Tuchman argued that news values are constructed via the routinization of journalistic practice. Consequently, journalists have to provide news that fits into specific templates and time slots.

VIOLENCE AS A NEWS VALUE

Recognition of news value inherent in an event, coupled with the adoption of a set of journalistic practices and skills that amount to a routinization of journalistic practice, ensures that a similarity exists in the format of news stories. Furthermore, the reliance by journalists on facts and figures to supplement the story helps to create some uniformity of structure and content of broadcast journalism (Tuchman, 1978a). Different studies of individual television newsrooms have highlighted similar types of procedures, structures, routines, pressures, and constraints (see Burns, 1969; Epstein, 1973; J. L. Harrison, 2000; Schlesinger, 1987; Tuchman, 1978a). A very high consensus has been found between news editors in ranking and use of 50 stories (Ward, 1973). Research conducted by Clyde and Buckalew (1969) in the United States found that both press and television news editors valued stories involving conflict, high impact and geographical proximity.

Consequently, violent events have news value because they contain many news factors identified by researchers (Bell, 1991; Galtung & Ruge, 1965; Ostgaard, 1965; Sande, 1971; Sparkes & Winter, 1980; Tunstall, 1971). Furthermore, violent events complement the nature of journalistic practice by fitting into the news template in a way that is impossible for complicated issues and events. Such features of violent events enhance their news value and the probability that they will be reported.

Stories have greater news value if they exhibit cultural and geographical proximity, meaning a variety of story types may have interest to the audience. If a country is not a former colony or close to home, often its news value is determined by mass destruction, genocide, famine, or war. Therefore, for a country such as Rwanda or Ethiopia to get onto British news, there must be a significant amount of violence or death occurring. When J. L. Harrison (2000) questioned a journalist concerning why Rwanda had been off the news agenda for several weeks, despite growing evidence of genocide, the reply was, "To be honest I'm not that sure why Rwanda has gone off the agenda, probably because it is not Europe, or a former colony" (BBC1 Editor, TV News Programs, 3/5/94). This phenomenon has been described as McLurg's law. Schlesinger (1987, p. 117) came across this law when he was observing at the BBC in the mid-1970s. It was expressed to him as "one European is worth twenty-eight Chinese, or perhaps two Welsh miners worth one thousand Pakistanis." Here journalists indicate that there is a direct relation between the amount of violence needed to make a story newsworthy and the geographical location of the event (see Galtung and Ruge's, 1965, news factor, "cultural proximity").

Journalists agree that violence is an important staple of news coverage (J. L. Harrison, 2000). Violence may occur through criminal activity, war, terrorism, civil unrest, or disasters or accidents. In all these cases, the graphic nature of the consequences of the event are generally shown to the viewer. In this sense, analysis of violence on television cannot simply consider the way journalists report the event itself, but also how they subsequently use the event to provide news.

The coverage of crime by the BBC is very carefully considered and their priority is to avoid causing panic or fear in the population by distorting facts, or giving a false impression of the frequency of criminal acts. Many journalists working for the BBC's News and Current Affairs Directorate are aware of the danger of creating moral panics, or of blaming certain groups for the subversion of cultural mores.

Regional news often covers a high percentage of violence-, law-, and crime-related stories (J. L. Harrison, 1997). Consequently, stories about crime need to be carefully monitored to ensure that coverage of a plethora of crimes in a small regional locality does not become distorted. One study of Yorkshire Television's weekday, regional news magazine, *Calendar News*, found it was more oriented to light and trivial stories, but the majority of stories about violent crime appear in the short news belts during its subregional opt outs. The roll call of deaths and crime often turns into a long list, and could be particularly alarming to people because the news in this part of the program is much more localized (often just relating to one main city and two or three towns). There is often little or no attempt to analyze or explain the context of the crimes or violent occurrences, because there is insufficient time allocated for elaboration within the bulletin. After having observed in the *Calendar News* newsroom, Hetherington (1989) also commented on this phenomenon: "There are days when *Calendar* seems to depend too much on short news items, with a bias towards crime, misfortune and catastrophe" (p. 61).

The coverage of war has long been an important part of journalistic activity. Coverage of distant wars that do not involve British citizens or soldiers often receive a different type of coverage than those involving British nationals. In the case of the latter, the climate of opinion is often influenced by the military, which considers television as possibly dangerous in its ability to lower morale. The media, in particular, was blamed for the U.S. public's growing disillusionment with the Vietnam War. Such concerns have been heeded in television news coverage involving British soldiers. In the case of the Falklands War of 1982, the film shown on British television was often weeks old and no pictures of casualties were shown until after the ceasefire (Philo, 1993). The coverage of the Gulf War in 1991 was characterized as a "clean" war and television news was later criticized for its view that killing could be managed and controlled (Philo & McLaughlin, 1995). In 1999, the lessons learned about the failure of precision bombing raised doubts about the coverage of the Kosovo crisis, leading to uncomfortable revelations about the mistakes made by the allied forces and indicated the consequences of those errors for the Serbian and Kosovan public. Because audiences react more strongly to violence that is geographically or culturally relevant, a news editor must therefore ascertain whether it is appropriate to show the same kind of detail for each country.

In contrast, coverage of war in countries that do not involve Britain directly will focus, often in graphic detail, on the immediate aftermath and scenes of destruction. Consequently, coverage of conflict in South Africa, East Timor, Israel, the Balkans, Sudan, and Rwanda have often contained images of the maimed, injured and dead. During the Rwandan genocide of 1994, news editors carefully edited the film they received of the murder of many Tutsis, but showed in graphic detail the piles of dead bodies and some injuries sustained by the victims.

The coverage of the Bosnian conflict in 1993 was handled differently. The coverage of a massacre in Bosnia was reported by a variety of news programs on April 23, 1993 (J. L. Harrison, 2000). ITN's *12.30pm News* reported that "in Bosnia, scenes of horror met British troops when confronted with a Muslim village destroyed by the Croats" and "in Bosnia, sickening evidence of the murder of Muslim citizens by Croat forces has been uncovered by British forces," with the added caution that "you will find the pictures in this report particularly disturbing." BBC1's *One O'clock News* showed film of burned houses and, like ITN, focused in on a curled burned hand of a corpse on the staircase. In both cases, the film was carefully edited to ensure that the audience did not see more than a fleeting glimpse of the burned bodies. Martin Bell of the BBC indicated that the BBC's mission was to protect the audience from scenes that were judged to be too graphic when he said, "what happened here can frankly not be shown in any detail—there is a roomful of charred bodies and they died in the greatest of agony" (BBC1's *One O'clock News*, April 23, 1993). Even past the nine o'clock watershed, the BBC still did not allow the audience to see inside the cellar. In contrast, ITN's *News at Ten* showed more lingering shots of the bodies in the cellar and a variety of shots of the burned hand (and arm) on the stairs. ITN introduced this news report with the caution that "we must warn you that our report by Paul Davies contains pictures of those burnt bodies. They are deeply disturbing images which illustrate the horror of the Bosnian War" (ITN's *News at Ten*, April 23, 1993). The difference between the BBC's coverage and that of the commercial news operator seems to indicate that, in this instance at least, the public service broadcaster was less concerned to use attention grabbing devices than the commercial broadcaster.

VIOLENCE IN THE NEWS AND AUDIENCE RESPONSE

Violence occurring in the news must be treated with care because viewers are known to respond more profoundly, emotionally and behaviorally, to scenes of real-life violence on television (Berkowitz & Alioto, 1973; Noble, 1975; Potter, 1986, 1999). Even during wartime, although people are curious to learn the latest news of a conflict, especially when their own country is involved, they still express concerns about inclusion in the news of graphic images depicting the carnage of war (Wober, 1982). Indeed, viewers are prepared to tolerate certain images of war and not others. During the Gulf War in 1991, British viewers felt that it was right to show pictures of the aftermath of the bombing of the bunker/shelter in Baghdad, but were much less supportive of the decision to show captured coalition pilots paraded before the cameras by the Iraqis when these servicepeople were clearly in some distress (Morrison, 1992). The same study found that although people exhibited a degree of tolerance toward scenes showing the outcomes of war, they were less willing to accept close-up shots of the dead or dying. This was true both in respect to British and Iraqi casualties.

In addition to military conflicts, violence in the news can occur on a domestic front in the form of civil disturbances. During the 1980s, Britain experienced a series of urban riots in major inner-city areas. The nightly television news bulletins almost routinely relayed pictures to the public of street fighting between rioters and police, overturned cars set on fire, and mobs causing vandalism to property. The majority of the public (83%) felt that such outbreaks of violence were unjustified no matter what the social conditions of the rioters in their neighborhoods. Viewers were concerned (68%), as a result of seeing television pictures, about the apparent inability of the police to control these disturbances, and many (61%) felt there was a danger of possible copycat effects following such news coverage (Gunter & Wober, 1988).

Although natural disasters and accidents were not classified in this study as violent events, the nature of the event itself and subsequent reporting may have some impact on the audience. In particular, Cantor and Nathanson (1996) found that children show a tendency to be upset by natural disasters, although their reaction tends to decrease with age. Despite the claims by many journalists that news is of an unpredictable or ad hoc nature, relatively few accidents and disasters appear in television news on a regular basis. Consequently, major accidents, particularly those that occur in one's own country, are very well covered (and in the era of 24-hour news, often overcovered) and become part of the national psyche.

Journalists generally report on the aftermath of a violent event, often giving graphic descriptions and analyses of the way in which the deaths occurred. If film is unavailable, reconstructions are generally made using moving graphics. However, viewers are highly sensitive to graphic scenes in such reconstructions and research has shown that they raise fear and anxiety among the audience (Wober & Gunter, 1990). The Austrian funicular train tragedy of November 2000 was only reported after the event, but the violent nature of the deaths that occurred in the tunnel were speculated on and described in some detail by television journalists. Today many events are captured on personal video cameras and the footage of the disastrous event is used many times by the television news media while they are trying to find out more details of the story. Consequently, more drama and violence can be brought to viewers' screens. Viewers saw footage of the Concorde crash in France in July 2000 and the plane crash in Taiwan in November 2000.

Another context in which violence occurs in the news is in relation to reporting of third world famine. Often famine is linked to war or violent civil unrest and, in that sense, can involve various forms of interpersonal violence. Audience research has shown that the nature of the story also affects the audience's reaction. The audience is more likely to tolerate distressing images from a famine than other kinds of film about victims of violence, disaster or accident (BBC Training Video, 1993). Michael Buerk's memorable coverage of the famine in Ethiopia on October 23, 1984 referred to the event as a "biblical famine, the closest thing to hell on earth." Although the coverage was distressing and showed dying children and adults in some detail, the response was one of compassion. Such pictures have been used to good effect to raise money for charities. Charities and aid agencies acknowledge the crucial role of the media in covering emergencies and will encourage the media to cover events as they unfold (Benthall, 1993). Technological developments have allowed journalists to capture events as they occur, converting a distant third world country disaster into high drama. Consequently, coverage of the floods in Mozambique in 2000 resulted in a strong response from other countries with many donations made by television news viewers. However, a careful balance always needs to be struck when covering international disasters. Aid agencies are concerned about compassion fatigue, from overexposure of such disasters, and the journalists are concerned that the viewers will sometimes become "upset and angered over scenes of suffering" (BBC, 1996, p. 41) or by overuse of visual clichés (BBC Training Video, 1993).

NEWS VALUES, VIOLENCE, AND AUDIENCE AWARENESS

It is not only in relation to public opinion that broadcasters must take care in their inclusion of violent elements in the news, but also in the context of its potential impact on audience comprehension of news. Numerous studies have reported that broadcast news often fails to get its information through effectively to viewers and listeners. Large quantities of televised news, especially, do not penetrate the psyche of audiences (Gunter, 1987a; Robinson & Levy, 1986). Quite apart from a failure on the part of viewers to pay sufficient attention to broadcasts, there are factors within news productions themselves that contribute to such information losses. Content attributes are among the key program factors that are relevant here.

The presence of violence in the news has been identified as a factor that can affect audience memory for broadcast news. Results have not always been consistent, however. Israeli children were found to remember television news items better when they were "emotionally loaded." This meant that those items preclassified by the researchers as "happy," "sad," or "violent" were better recalled after the broadcast than were items designated as emotionally neutral (A. A. Cohen, Wigand, & R. P. Harrison, 1976). This research failed, however, to separate effectively the possible effects on news recall of specific content attributes (e.g., violence) from other production treatment variables (e.g., whether or not an item was accompanied by film footage).

More controlled experimental studies conducted under laboratory conditions have shown that violence in televised news can impede recall of the factual details of stories for some viewers, but enhance it for others. In particular, the gender of the viewer is important here. Male viewers have been found to exhibit better recall of news story content than female viewers immediately after exposure when the narrative is accompanied by film footage depicting violence (Furnham & Gunter,

1985; Gunter, Furnham, & Gietson, 1984). In another experimental study in which male and female viewers were shown a news story depicting horrific killings in El Salvador, the presentation of violent film footage impaired the uptake of information from the story. This effect was almost accounted for by the performance of female viewers, however (Berry & Clifford, 1985). These authors recommended that such is the negative effect of violent film on audience retention of news narratives, that images of violence should be separated from the narrative when the words carry important detailed information.

REGULATING FOR VIOLENCE IN THE NEWS

The foregoing review has indicated that conflict and violence are staple news values of journalists and violent events are more likely to be shown if they are closer to home. Journalistic choice of news values predisposes news content towards disturbing the viewer. It is therefore important to ascertain whether the presentation in the news meets the requirements of broadcasters' own policies about news violence.

In most broadcasting systems, regulation of broadcast content in both factual and fictional programs has been the key to protecting the audience from possible effects of television violence. Regulators draw on the argument that repeated viewing of violence on television may desensitize the viewer to real-life violence. There is such a concern, but research has shown that audiences are able to distinguish between fictional and factual programing. Viewers watch each type of programing with a different set of expectations and reactions (Morrison & McGregor, 1993).

A further concern that underwrites regulatory frameworks is the possibility of the viewer being encouraged to make an aggressive response to the violent images shown on television. Although some researchers have argued that a clear causal link has been established between violent images on the screen and subsequent violent behavior (Bandura, D. Ross, & S. A. Ross, 1963a) the experimental context within which such a link was established has been highly criticized (Gauntlett, 1995).

A third concern underpins regulation, namely, the idea that those who watch a lot of television may develop a distorted view of the world. Gerbner (1988) argued that, in particular, the depiction of a violent world interacts with the viewer's concerns and fears about society. Gerbner's studies have been subject to criticism by British researchers and an attempt to replicate his study in the United Kingdom was unsuccessful (Gunter, 1987). Nonetheless, these three concerns, underpin the regulatory code of practice in the United Kingdom, whereby the key rationale is to protect children and other vulnerable members of society from harmful or disturbing images. Problematically, television news covers the actual event in detail (if the cameras are there on time, the viewer may even be able to see the events unfolding) and may dwell on the immediate consequences, but does not always go into depth about the contextual nature of the occurrence. The method of coverage reflects journalistic interest in capitalizing on intense moments of action or drama that create exciting television viewing and then to move on to the next dramatic event. As Tuchman (1978a) observed, television news usually makes unrest or disruption in the world order seem to be continuous rather than sporadic.

The independent television sector in Britain is regulated by the Independent Television Commission, which is required in Section 7: (1a) of the Broadcasting Act 1990, "to draw up, and from time to time review a code giving guidance as to the rules to be observed with respect to the showing of violence, or the inclusion of sounds suggestive of violence, in programs included in licensed services, particularly when large numbers of children and young persons may be expected to be watching programs."

The BBC (1996), considered that although "there is much confusing and inconclusive research into whether or not there is a relationship between violence on television and in society" there is "a balance to be struck between the demands of truth and the danger of desensitizing people" (pp. 74–75). Given that "the volume of harrowing and distressing material now available to newsrooms could dominate news programs gratuitously if not well handled," the BBC believes they have a responsibility to "step back and think about its impact" (BBC, 1996, p. 74). Consequently, as a public service broadcaster, the BBC has a set of guidelines that it must follow in gathering, editing, and producing the news. The BBC's *Producers' Guidelines* codify public service values into the BBC's Editorial Values: impartiality, accuracy, fairness, fair representation of different people and cultures, editorial integrity and independence, respect for privacy, respect for standards of taste and decency, avoiding the imitation by viewers of antisocial and criminal behavior shown in television programing, safeguarding the welfare of children, and independence from commercial interests. Its own regulation of the way it shows violence in the news is further codified and reinforced by in-house training and guidance notes for producers. In 1993, the BBC conducted an in-house study and produced a document called "Guidelines for the portrayal of violence on BBC TV." This document, along with the BBC's *Producers' Guidelines* (first published in 1993 and updated in 1996), are issued to producers. A video is used for internal training purposes, originally produced in 1991 and updated in 1992 and 1993 to adhere to strict rules about how they show violent incidents in television news. There are some similarities and differences between the two that reflect the differences between public service and commercial news imperatives.

The BBC's *Producers' Guidelines* recognize that factual violence shown in the news can be more distressing to viewers than that shown in fictional programs (BBC, 1996, p. 74), which accords with research findings (Morrison & McGregor, 1993). The BBC considers that audiences expect violent scenes in news to serve a moral or social point in contrast to stylized violence that may be acceptable in entertainment programing. Editors are urged to consider carefully the material they have gathered to ascertain whether the violence they wish to show is appropriate within its context. This has consequences for the amount and type of detail that can be shown. Producers and directors are also reminded that they must take care when violence involves situations close to the audience's own experiences, women and children portrayed as victims, scenes of domestic and sexual violence, scenes of extreme or sustained violence of any sort, and scenes of suicide or attempted suicide. The consequences of violence must also be shown in order to avoid sanitizing events. Weapons (e.g., knives, hammers, or pokers) or methods of violence that are easily available and may be imitated must be shown carefully. The BBC enjoins its journalists to consider the time of day when violence is shown (or when trails of forthcoming programing are shown), with particular care taken before 9 o'clock. Incidents being covered live are seen to need particular care whereby "commentary must not be alarmist" and "descriptions of horrific events should be measured so that the horror is conveyed without being exploited" (BBC, 1996, p. 13).

The concern here is with the impact of the violence on the viewer and the possibility of a cumulative effect if violent scenes are shown close together or repeated frequently. In this instance, the editors and producers are reminded that "a bulletin needs to be considered as a whole, for its total impact on the audience, and not simply as a series of isolated stories" (BBC, 1996, p. 75). The BBC cautions against journalistic instinct to use a good piece of library footage over and over again when updating the story. It argues that this can result in images that become stereotypes, boring the audience or desensitizing it to the nature of the violence. Occasionally, the BBC feels such usage is justified if it informs the viewer. Consequently, the video of the beating endured by Rodney King from the Los Angeles Police on March 3, 1991, was repeatedly shown in the run up to the trial of the police involved. In this case, the BBC felt that the footage was necessary to remind viewers of the event and to help them better understand the views of the people of Los Angeles and the issues raised in the trial. The BBC encourages the use of clear warnings to prevent the audience from being taken by surprise. The BBC is also very careful about coverage of the aftermath of violence, taking care not to show too many scenes of emotional relatives or grief-stricken victims and cautions that "the use of violence should never be gratuitous" (BBC, 1996, p. 77).

The ITC program code (section 1.6) provides detailed guidance for compliance by terrestrial, cable, and satellite licensees (ITC, 1991). In the main, it urges caution, and advises editors and producers to cut material rather than risk offending or upsetting the audience. The ITC will review complaints made about a program and view an item after it has been screened, and unlike the BBC, it does not have the mechanisms in place to review programs before they are screened. The BBC operates a system of referral upward in the case of doubt about the suitability of scenes. Consequently, the BBC news journalists are much more likely to spend time agonizing over whether to show a particular violent scene or dramatic event than those in the independent sector.

In Britain, television news is highly regulated and news editors are aware of the variety of issues that must be addressed when covering violent events and their aftermath. Journalists are made aware of the fact that television audiences vary widely and their reactions, values, opinions, and psychological makeup will influence which types of violence are acceptable or unacceptable to them, and that factual violence can be more disturbing to viewers than fictional violence. News editors have to try to establish a middle ground, neither desensitizing nor alienating the audience while ensuring that in their democratic role as truth-tellers, they do not distort or oversanitize events. The analysis of data collected between 1994 and 1996 will consider, in the context of wider editorial decision making, whether television news journalists in Britain adhere to their own editorial policy when covering violent events.

VIOLENCE IN BRITISH TV NEWS PROGRAMS: 1994–1996

Television news in this analysis comprised two program categories: national news and regional news. In total, 930 national news programs and 284 regional news programs were content analyzed over the 8 weeks of monitoring in 1995–1996. In the previous year's analysis, 474 national news programs and 156 regional news programs were monitored. All coded national news programs were broadcast on the terrestrial channels and all regional news programs were broadcast only on BBC1 and ITV. Over the 8 weeks, 23.4% of all news programs monitored contained some violence, which was located in 284 programs.

National news contained more violent acts, sequences, and minutage than regional news. Over 66 minutes of violence were shown in national news over the 8 weeks. In contrast, regional news only broadcast 3.5 minutes of violence during that time. National news coverage contained 746 violent acts and regional news contained 51 such acts. Likewise, there were 549 violent sequences on national news and 29 sequences in regional news. In comparison with the amount of violence found throughout all television programs during the period monitored (1.39% of program running time), violence in television news accounts for just 0.01% of the total program running time.

NATURE OF VIOLENCE IN TV NEWS

Although television news may show a relatively small amount of violence when compared with the rest of television programing, the nature of that violence may be more significant than its quantity in relation to its impact on the audience. The following sections examine what types of violence portrayed on news programs.

Setting of News

Not surprisingly, the majority of the violence in news programs (90.2%) was located in the present day. A small proportion (3.7%) of violent acts was located in the recent past (between 1900 and 1980), and a very small percentage of violent acts was located in the distant past (0.5%) and the future (0.4%), with slightly more located in the distant future (0.8%). This finding is not unexpected because the rationale of television news is to cover current events.

When violence does occur in the news, it is more likely to be shown on screen with events that are geographically distant from where the viewers themselves live (A. A. Cohen & Bantz, 1984). The location of violence is important in the context of how viewers respond. Violence that is close to home is perceived in more serious terms by viewers (Gunter, 1985). As part of the current study, the analysis of news violence investigated the extent to which it occurred in particular physical settings, such as the city or the countryside, and where it was geographically situated.

Most violence occurring in television news occurred in the inner city (49%). Smaller amounts of violence were located in a small town (11.4%), a rural environment (10.4%), or suburbia (4.4%). Violence shown in television news tends to occur in cities and, consequently, may resonate with a high percentage of the population.

In relation to its geographical location, most violence shown was located in Britain (43.1%), Europe (18.7%), or North America (5.4%). Discrepancies occurred between 1995 and 1996, with 1995 showing more violence in India–Asia (5.7%) than in 1996 (1.8%). Conversely, slightly more violence was shown in Australasia (5.7%) in 1996 than in 1995, which accounted for 0.8% of the violent acts shown. These findings contrast with earlier research, indicating a preference among broadcasters, internationally, to show violence on screen for geographically distant rather than proximal events (A. A. Cohen & Bantz, 1984). This aspect of the nature of news coverage of violent or disruptive events may have important consequences for audiences. The public has concerns about violence in the news and their anxieties are especially likely to be aroused in connection with stories involving ordinary people, in domestic settings, close to home (Morrison, 1993a).

Form of Violence

An earlier chapter observed that the form of violence on television has important implications for how viewers react to it. Graphic, close-up violence, especially when it features sharp instruments, causes viewers considerable anxiety (Gunter, 1985). Therefore, it was important to examine this aspect of violence as it occurs in the news.

The most common type of violence shown on the news was mild pushing or tripping, but a high percentage of shootings were also shown. The other most prevalent types of violence occurring in news programs were throwing, bombardment, sports aggression, punching, and hitting with an object (see Table 9.1). A variety of weapons of violence were shown in news programs. Most violence occurred using a fist or hand (29.6%), throwing or pushing generally (10.3%), or military weapons (7.8%). Shootings involved the use of a machine gun (4.2% of acts), rifle (2.8%), or hand gun (0.9%). With the exception of the use of the fist or hand as a weapon, few weapons shown in the news are easily accessible to the audience.

Motives and Consequences

The reasons underlying violence and the consequences that flow from it represent critical features that influence the way audiences judge the seriousness of violence (Gunter, 1985). The justification for violence and the degree of observed pain and suffering of victims can also mediate behavioral reactions to screen violence, affecting the likelihood of aggression in viewers following exposure (Goranson, 1970; Hartmann, 1969; Meyer, 1972).

In the current analysis, little of the violence occurred in a domestic setting. The context of violence in the news was generally war or civil strife. This is important because violence occurring in a domestic setting is known to be particularly disturbing to viewers (Gunter, 1985; Schlesinger, Dobash, Dobash, & Weaver, 1991) (see Table 9.2).

TABLE 9.1

Top Ten Types of Violent Act

	1995			1996	
	N	%		N	%
Push/trip	115	24.4	Push/trip	113	33.7
Shoot at	63	13.3	Shoot at	56	16.7
Throwing	51	10.8	Sport aggression	32	9.6
Bombardment	45	9.5	Punch	23	6.9
Hit with object	40	8.5	Hit with object	20	6.0
Punch	29	6.1	Throwing	19	5.7
Sport aggression	27	5.7	Damage to property	14	4.2
Explosion	16	3.4	Bombardment	11	3.3
Verbal abuse	13	2.8	Explosion	8	2.4
Cruelty	7	1.5	Attempted violence	8	2.4

TABLE 9.2

Context of Violence in News

	1995		1996	
	N	%	N	%
War	101	21.4	60	17.9
Civil strife	149	31.6	83	24.8
Criminal act	32	6.8	12	3.6
Upholding the law	48	10.2	74	22.1
Defending civil liberties	23	4.9	19	5.7
Domestic violence	2	0.4	–	–
Other inter-personal violence	34	7.2	37	11.0
Other violence	73	15.5	32	9.6
Uncoded	10	2.1	18	5.4
Total	472	100.0	335	100.0

Audiences are concerned when programs show graphic images of real-life violence or consequences of violence (Morrison, 1993). Here, the public tends to sympathize primarily with the victim rather than with the news editor's priorities (Shearer, 1991). Consequently, television news coverage needs to be sensitive to the distress of the victims and not dwell on prolonged suffering or give graphic detail about the type of injuries sustained. In fact, injuries caused by violence on the news tended to be mild, involving no physical injury or only a minor wound or bruising. Crucially, few deaths were shown (see Table 9.3). A survey quoted by Shearer (1991) showed that 78% of British viewers felt it was unacceptable for television news to show scenes from a major incident in which the dead or seriously injured were recognizable.

TABLE 9.3

Type of Injury in News Containing Violence

	1995		1996	
	N	%	N	%
Death	22	4.7	3	0.9
Broken limb	1	0.2	2	0.6
Serious wound	18	3.8	6	1.8
Minor wound	67	14.2	25	7.5
Stun	29	6.1	17	5.1
Bruise	51	10.8	22	6.6
Psychological damage	7	1.5	1	0.3
No physical injury	141	29.9	129	38.5
Other	42	8.9	11	3.3
Uncoded	94	19.9	119	35.5
Total	472	100.0	335	100.0

Coders were also required to rate the dramatic detail of the violence acts in relation to the extent that violent acts were thought to be bloody, painful, and horrific. The ratings were made along a 5-point scale, where 1 indicates no blood, pain, or horror and 5 means there was a great deal of blood, an extreme degree of pain suffered by the victim, and the scene was horrific in nature. Most acts (68.9%) were rated 1 for blood, pain (54.7%), and horror (52.8%). A lot of blood, extreme pain, or horror was not recorded, with a rating of 4 recorded in less then 1% of the violent acts. This is a key finding, because in Britain few people are willing to accept close-up shots of the dead or dying (Gunter & J. Harrison, 1998).

Perpetrators and Victims

The perpetrators and the victims of violence in news were mainly while males, either alone or in a group and between age 20 and 35. Women, children, and the elderly were rarely shown to be perpetrators or victims of violence in the news (see Table 9.4). These findings are consistent with American data showing that 8 of 10 perpetrators and 2 in 3 victims of violence in factual programs were male (with very similar distributions specifically for news and public affairs programs). Eight in 10 perpetrators and over 7 in 10 victims of violence on American factual shows were from age 21 to 44, and around two thirds of perpetrators and victims were White (Danielson et al., 1996; *National Television Violence Study*, 1998).

The demographic distribution is an important finding, because women or the elderly may be particularly disturbed and made to feel vulnerable by certain kinds of realistic violence. Children may be particularly disturbed by violent incidents containing children of their own age. Research has shown that children are particularly prone to identification with their peers. Children may be particularly influenced by violent portrayals involving their own age group on television and by the perceived similarity to themselves (Potter, 1999).

CONCLUSIONS

British news exhibits geographical proximity for a high percentage of the population. This reflects the nature of news and news values. News becomes more newsworthy when it is closer to home and more dramatic. However, the proximity of news events, the realistic nature of the news, and the likelihood that situations close to the audience's own experiences may be shown, encourages journalists to take care in their portrayal of events.

There are few occasions where women and children are portrayed as victims. During the period studied, there were no scenes of extreme or sustained violence of any sort shown to the audience. Although journal-

TABLE 9.4
Demographic Representation of Aggressors and Victims

	Aggressor (%)		Victim (%)	
	1995	1996	1995	1996
Age				
Child (up to 14)	0.9	0.3	0.5	0.3
Teenager (15–19)	3.7	–	0.9	0.3
Young adult (20–35)	46.8	49.9	36.7	44.8
Middle-aged adult	5.0	5.4	4.4	9.3
Mixed age	14.7	15.2	25.0	18.8
Uncoded	28.9	29.3	32.6	26.6
Sex				
One male	29.4	41.5	21.1	40.9
One female	1.8	2.7	5.3	6.3
Group male	38.3	32.5	24.3	15.8
Group female	0.5	1.2	–	–
Group mixed	15.9	8.1	23.4	15.2
Other	–	–	0.9	–
Uncoded	14.0	14.0	25.0	21.8
Ethnic Origin				
White U.K.	26.8	21.2	20.6	26.6
White U.S.	4.8	2.1	3.7	1.5
White other	16.1	43.6	9.6	34.3
Black U.K.	1.1	3.9	1.6	0.9
Black U.S.	–	1.2	–	2.1
Black other	1.4	0.3	0.9	0.9
Asian	7.1	2.7	5.7	2.1
Oriental	–	–	–	2.1
Mixed group	22.2	1.8	25.2	4.5
Other human	0.7	–	0.5	–
Animal	1.8	1.5	3.4	1.2
Uncoded	17.9	21.8	28.7	23.9

ists are aware of, and make it an editorial policy to show, the consequences of violence in order to avoid sanitizing events, they do not appear to do so in a way that will invoke distress from the audience. Weapons (e.g., knives, hammers, or pokers) or methods of violence that are easily available and may be imitated were rarely shown in the news.

Clearly, violence can be represented in the news in a variety of ways. Sometimes, the news crew can capture a violent event as it actually happens. This is relatively rare because news crews often arrive at a location because something has just happened. In an era of rolling news and 24-hour coverage, cameras are more likely to capture concurrent events relating to the original violent event and are able to show the consequences of the occurrence in a more detailed and graphic way. This removes the discretion about editing violence from the screens from the immediate remit of the editor and producer and may subject the audience to a rather more graphic depiction.

External environmental factors occurring in the broadcasting environment are forcing news organizations into a reevaluation of their news priorities in the light of economic pressures, technological developments, globalization of media industries, and the growing competition for audience share. Consequently, is there any evidence that news editors include violence gratuitously to attract audiences? As discussed earlier, the construction of news values is influenced by a variety of forces. A key factor in determining news value is the growing need to deliver large audiences to advertisers.

Crucially, the need to attract larger audiences may be influential in relation to the portrayal of violence in television news. Klijn (1999) examined the differences in portrayal of violence between public service news providers and commercial news organizations. Klijn found that public service broadcasters tend to focus on issues and report news in context, whereas commercial broadcasters were more event led. Using a list of attention versus comprehension attributes present in television news, Klijn was able to ascertain that public service broadcasters were less likely to try to grab the audience's attention, but would seek instead to enhance viewer comprehension.

Klijn, however, identified two main factors that may reduce public service commitment to comprehension enhancement in favor of attention grabbing, and encourage commercial broadcasters to continue to develop attention grabbing formulas. First, the need to hold an audience's interest is intensifying in a highly competitive digital marketplace. Commercial broadcasters are under great pressure to use ever-increasing dynamic formats and images to attract the audience. Public service broadcasters are increasingly concerned about their own audience share, as they often have to justify their own funding arrangements in relation to audience size. It is likely that both commercial and public service broadcasters will take steps to increase the dramatic and attention grabbing nature of their news, consequently increasing the number of dramatic stories. As violence has been strongly correlated with audience interest and attention, it is likely that greater use of violent stories will occur. Furthermore, the way that the violent events are portrayed by the news organizations is significant.

If broadcasters seek to make the news more entertaining and attention grabbing, then it is possible that the contextual, explanatory, and less dramatic factors relating to events will be omitted. Dramatic violent incidents lend themselves to easy reporting because they can be presented as a discrete package. Generally, television news needs to be event focused due to the short amount of time devoted to story telling on each program (Shoemaker & Reese, 1996). Problematically, such events do not occur in a contextual vacuum and the more difficult issues and historical background may be sacrificed in the editorial process that operates within the constraints of time, cost, space, and the pressure to increase ratings. Iyengar (1991) provided empirical evidence to show that USA network news is event focused and does not concentrate on themes or issues (see also Klijn, 1999). Iyengar argued that an act of violence, such as a terrorist attack, when shown as a single event is more likely to produce an audience reaction that blames individuals and calls for stronger punishment. In contrast, news using thematic frames results in the likelihood of a different reaction from the audience, whereby the causes are attributed to societal forces and result in a call for societal solutions. Problematically, event focused news that concentrates on single acts of violence may reduce social responsibility, leading to a focusing of blame on individuals and a lack of understanding about the role of society in relation to the violence that has occurred. The nature of television news is that it will prioritize geographical and cultural proximity of the event to the audience, contain realistic violence, and is likely to show situations close to the audience's own experiences. Nonetheless, analysis of data from 1994–1996 has shown that editors do take care in their portrayal of violent events on screen.

Nonetheless, there is pressure on television news journalists to make news increasingly relevant to the audience so that it resonates with audience experience and to make it more exciting in order to sustain audience interest. Dahlgren (1995) argued that television news is changing. His analysis of tapes of transmissions from 10 or 15 years ago indicated that there has been an increasing popularization of television journalism. Journalists themselves are torn between a professional ideology that privileges hard political news and information and the economic and commercial requisites of broadcasting institutions. Accessible news is often less intellectually challenging than news stories containing esoteric political or economic information, or that exists beyond the viewer's own worldview and experiences. News relevant to the audience encourages viewers to make connections between their own everyday experiences and that which appears on television. As a consequence, overidentification with victims of violence may occur, as audiences increasingly relate to personalities in the news.

As news becomes more dramatic and is available 24 hours a day, the news values that stress violence and conflict could increasingly become a preferred editorial choice. This can bring problems. As Hume (1996) pointed out, in the United States, the trend for television news organizations to go down-market and produce news based on a "if it bleeds it leads" philosophy began to backfire when the journalists realized that each successive news bulletin needed to be more sensational than the last in order to retain viewers. Two shootings and a murder on one night could only be surpassed by four shootings on the next. Organizations competing with each other for this type of news have found it increasingly difficult to meet the expectations of audiences under these circumstances. Furthermore, the increasing drive to provide "live" news from the scene may exacerbate audience interest in a story, but may result in confusion and misunderstanding of the news if contextual information is not simultaneously provided. Lack of understanding about violent events in the news may have consequences for public perceptions and fears about violence in society. The question to be answered asks how television news journalists can retain viewer attention while retaining viewer comprehension in a climate of increasing commercialization and growing competition.

Chapter 10

Violence on Television in Britain and the United States

The research reported in this book has examined the depiction of violence on television in Britain. The current volume is based on the second of two projects funded by the U.K. broadcasting industry in the mid-1990s. A similar project, which also examined the representation of violence on television, was launched simultaneously in the United States. The National Television Violence Study (NTVS) was sponsored by the National Cable Television Association and covered three television seasons (1994–1995, 1995–1996, 1996–1997) (see *National Television Violence Study*, 1997, 1998, 1999). The British study covered the first two of these three television seasons in Britain.

The National Television Violence Study investigated the effectiveness and use of program advisories and the impact of educational broadcast messages with antiviolence themes among children and adolescents. However, the highest profile part of the project was its examination of the portrayal of violence on television. Two separate teams investigated the representation of violence in drama and entertainment output (including reality programs) and in news and factual output on American television.

During the planning stages of both projects, researchers exchanged information and participated in a dialogue about a range of important issues concerned with the measurement of television violence. There was a broad consensus that previous content analysis research in this area failed sufficiently to represent the significance of context in relation to violence. The focus on quantitative measurement of violence led to approaches that treated all violence as equal in weight regardless of its form, setting, or context. Yet, audience research indicated that viewers' perceptions of television violence and their emotional and behavioral reactions to on-screen violent depictions were sensitive to such factors. If advances were to be made in the assessment of violence as it appears on screen, then, it would be important for such attributes to be represented with any content analytic framework.

The American researchers involved with the main part of the content analysis component of the NTVS conducted a comprehensive literature review prior to the design phase of the project in order to identify the kinds of program content features that could form the basis of a system of classification of television violence. This review of past research encompassed studies of behavioral effects of screen violence, emotional reactions to violent portrayals, and audiences' perceptual discriminations among violent depictions. Much weight was attached to research on behavioral and emotional effects because such research was indicative of the harm that watching televised violence could cause to some viewers or to society. Whereas viewers may differ in their personal opinions about which actions can be defined as violence or about whether they find certain violent depictions more acceptable than others on television, the crucial consideration was whether or not violent entertainment caused social or psychological harm.

Although some observers have equated violence with good drama (Baldwin & Lewis, 1972), the scientific evidence on whether violence enhances entertainment value is far from conclusive (Diener & DeFour, 1978; Diener & Woody, 1981; Hamilton, 1998). In contrast, more consistently damning evidence has emerged concerning the potentially harmful side effects of regular viewing of media violence (Friedrich-Cofer & Huston, 1986; Huesmann & Miller, 1994; Paik & Comstock, 1994).

In a further review of the evidence, the NTVS identified three particularly key types of effect in relation to which the different form and context of televised violence were important: learning aggression, enhanced audience fear, and desensitization to violence (Wilson et al., 1996). Across these types of effect, a range of contextual factors were isolated from the literature as having significance as mediators of audience response: the nature of the perpetrator of violence and the nature of the victim of violence, realism of the setting, reason or motive for violence, the means or form of violence (including the presence of weapons), the extent and graphicness of violence, the consequences of depicted violence for victims (including the amount of pain and suffering visibly shown), rewards and punishments for violence, and humor associated with violence.

Past research indicated that these factors could independently or jointly operate to reduce or enhance the effects of media violence. Such effects might include increased or decreased likelihood of imitating screen violence among viewers (Bandura, 1973, 1986, 1994), increased likelihood of aggression being triggered by screen violence (Berkowitz, 1984, 1994; Berkowitz & Rogers, 1986), greater likelihood of aggressiveness being socialized over time (Huesman, 1986; Huesman & Eron,

1986), greater likelihood of desensitization to violence (Cline et al., 1973; Drabman & Thomas, 1974; Thomas, 1982; Thomas, Horton, Lippencott, & Drabman, 1977), and greater or lesser likelihood of enhanced fear of victimization (Bryant, Carveth, & D. Brown, 1981; Gerbner & Gross, 1976; Gerbner, Gross, Morgan & Signorielli, 1994; Wober & Gunter, 1988).

The NTVS therefore committed to a research design in which the incidence of violence on television would not merely be counted in the fashion adopted by earlier studies (Gerbner, 1972; Gerbner & Gross, 1976; Greenberg et al., 1980; Smythe, 1954), it would also apply a further level of analysis based on so-called risk factors in order to distinguish between televised violence that did or did not pose potential high risk of causing harm to audiences. In this case, harm was defined in terms of whether specific violent portrayals comprised attributes known to serve as active trigger points for adverse audience reactions such as increased aggressiveness or increased fear (Wilson et al., 1996).

THE UNITED STATES AND BRITAIN COMPARED

The remainder of this chapter compares violence on television in Britain and the United States, drawing on the NTVS analyses for 1994–1995 and 1995–1996 and the British television violence content analysis study that covered the same 2 years. Because these two research projects were conducted independently, rather than as a joint operation, there were differences between them methodologically, as well as in terms of the programs analyzed, which limit the comparisons. The projects used different program sampling techniques and different coding frames. Nevertheless, early information exchanges between the research teams meant that some degree of harmonization was achieved on certain measures. The definition of violence used in each case contained common elements. There was some common ground also in relation to basic units of analysis. Finally, both projects used a number of common or similar contextual attributes to classify violent portrayals.

Program Sampling

Both the American and British projects amassed the largest program samples ever studied for violence content. In the NTVS, the 1994–1995 program sample comprised 3,185 programs and the 1995–1996 sample comprised 3,235 programs. Each sample represented in excess of 2,500 hours of content. The 1994–1995 U.K. sample comprised 5,607 programs (4,715 hours of content) and the 1995–1996 sample comprised 7,237 programs (6,254 hours of content). These program samples were assembled in different ways, however.

The NTVS sampled programs from 23 television channels, covering the main commercial networks, independent broadcast channels, a public broadcast service, basic cable, and premium cable channels. The U.K. study sampled programs from the four terrestrial broadcast channels (equivalent to the U.S. networks) and from a selection of satellite broadcast channels. A total of eight channels were covered in 1994–1995 and 10 channels in 1995–1996.

In both years, the NTVS created a composite week of programs for each channel covered, using a random sampling frame through which programs were selected from over a 20-week period in total, stretching from October to June for each wave of the study. The sampling procedure used a modified version of equal probability of selection method (EPSEM). With this method, every program had an equal chance to appear in the sample (Kunkel et al., 1995). This procedure began by selecting time slots rather than programs. Two half-hour time slots (defined by hour of day and day of week) were randomly selected for each channel during each week that sampling occurred. Once a time slot was selected, the *TV Guide* was consulted and the program corresponding to that time slot was entered into a scheduling grid several days before the target week of programing began. Programs were retained in the sample in their entirety, regardless of the number of time slots they occupied. This meant that if a 90-minute program was selected that began at 10:30 p.m., it would be included in its entirety, even though the selection at that point had been made only for the 10:30 p.m. to 11:00 p.m. slot. This sampling procedure produced a 7-day composite week of programing for each channel.

The U.K. study used a less sophisticated sampling frame due to constraints of funding and time tabling for the projects. Although a random start point for each program sample was used, in 1994–1995, 28 days of television output on eight channels was sampled in four blocks of seven consecutive days (real weeks), over a period stretching from October to February. In 1995–1996, the sampling frame was modified. Once again, 28 days of television output were sampled (for 10 channels), but composite weeks were used instead of real weeks. These composite weeks were constructed over 7-week spells by choosing a Monday from one week, Tuesday from a second week, and so on, through to Sunday from the seventh week. The sampling spells stretched over a total period spanning July of one year to June of the next. In total, television output was sampled from 28 weeks over a 12-month period. The NTVS sampled programs over 17 hours per day, from 6:00 a.m. to 10:59 p.m.—although if a program sampled in the last 30-minute slot of the day ran beyond 11:00 p.m., as noted earlier, it was included in its entirety. The U.K. study, in comparison, sampled and videotaped programs around the clock, for 24 hours a day. The NTVS excluded certain categories of program (religious programs, game shows, "infomercials" or home shopping material, and instructional programs). The UK study included all program content, and excluded only television advertising from the analysis.

Definition of Violence

Any content analysis study of television violence must begin with a definition of the on-screen behavior that is to be coded. For the NTVS, "Violence is defined as any overt depiction of a credible threat of physical force or the actual use of such force intended to physically harm an animate being or group of beings. Violence also includes certain depictions of physically harmful consequences against an animate being or group that occur as a result of unseen violent means" (Kunkel et al., 1995, p. I-48).

It is notable that the definition of violence covers a range of acts, including credible threat, behavioral acts, and depictions of harmful consequences of unseen violence. Such distinctions did not mean that any of these acts should be regarded as being of equal seriousness or equivalent in terms of potential harmfulness. Nevertheless, it was clear, from conceptual development work, that such broad distinctions had merit and represent a dominant aspect of the way on-screen violence could be differentiated.

A credible threat was an overt behavior that threatened the use of violence. The behavior, in this case, could be verbal or nonverbal. Perpetrators verbally threatened to harm a target person, or their behavior indicated they were clearly taking up a threatening stance against that person. A behavioral act was an overt action that used physical force against another, with an intention to cause harm to the victim. Harmful consequences scenes comprised depictions of the victims of violence when the violence was clearly implied, but not portrayed overtly as it occurred. These were scenes depicting the physical aftermath of violence. If the violence leading to the aftermath was also shown, they were aggregated together as a single violent action, categorized in terms of the characteristics of the overt physical behavior that caused the aftermath.

The NTVS definition of violence focuses on the action of animate beings and does not include naturally occurring acts of violence, such as lightning strikes, tornadoes, or volcanic eruptions. In this last respect, it represented a departure from the earlier work of Gerbner and his colleagues (Gerbner, 1972; Gerbner & Gross, 1976; Gerbner et al., 1977, 1978, 1979, 1980a), who for many years produced an annual report of the status of violence on American network television. Gerbner justified the inclusion of natural violent phenomena on the grounds that they were acts of violence deliberately included by producers to add to the drama. As such, they were not "naturally" occurring in a purely dramatic sense, and should therefore be considered in the same light as interpersonal acts of violence between television characters. For the NTVS, it was essential that an inanimate being should also be the target of aggression for an incident to qualify as violent within their analytical framework. Violence directed by a human aggressor against an inanimate object was not counted.

In the U.K. study, the basic definition of violence, although not word for word the same, bore a number of similarities to the NTVS definition. Although this definition has been given before (see chap. 2), it is worth repeating to make the comparison with the American study. Violence was defined as "any overt depiction of a credible threat of physical force or actual use of physical force, with or without a weapon, which is intended to harm, or intimidate an animate being or a group of animate beings. The violence may be carried out or merely attempted, and may or may not cause injury. Violence also includes any depiction of physically harmful consequences against an animate being (or group of animate beings) that occur as a result of unseen violent means."

Comparing the two definitions, common elements are the inclusion of credible threats of violence, as well as actual physical depictions of intentional harmful behavior. There is also an instruction to include depictions of the harmful consequences of violence even though the actions that produced them may not have been visibly shown at the same time. In the British system, naturally occurring violent scenes were also excluded from the analysis.

Units of Analysis

Most content analysis studies focus on the counting of acts of violence. The emphasis on contextual features, however, led the NTVS to devise a measurement system that assessed violence at three levels. The basic unit of measurement was the violent interaction. This was also referred to as the PAT, which represented an interaction between a perpetrator (P) who performs a type of act (A) directed at a target (T). A perpetrator could be a single individual acting alone or a group acting in unison. At the slightly higher level, or scene level, analysis took account of related series of violent behaviors, actions, or depictions of harmful consequences of violence that occurred without a significant break in the flow of the actual or imminent violence. A scene could contain one or a number of consecutive PAT interactions. At a third level, or program level, analysis focused on the entire program and assessed, in particular, the extent to which violence was punished. Individual PATs might go unpunished, but at the end of the program the bad guys might be apprehended and punished for their misconduct. The NTVS researchers believed the higher levels of analysis above the PAT were important from the perspective of representing certain contextual features that might not be detected at the individual act level, but might nonetheless have an important bearing on how audiences might respond to the program as a whole. Within the U.K. study, the basic level of measurement was the "violent act." A secondary level of analysis was also used, called a sequence analysis, which was equivalent to the NTVS scene level of assessment. The latter measure, however, did not prove to add significantly to the violent act data and more emphasis was placed instead on the measure of amount of program running time occupied by violence in the U.K. study.

Contextual Measures

The NTVS researchers emphasized the importance of context in assessing television violence. A basic quantitative analysis of the numbers of violent acts needed to be further qualified in terms of the nature and setting of the violence if such findings were to have value in the wider arena of social policy and media regulation. Although knowledge of the amount of violence on television was significant in relation to certain longer term effects such as desensitation, concerns about the imitation, triggering, and fear-arousing effects of television violence focus more attention on the nature of the violence to which viewers are exposed.

At the PAT level, the NTVS classified violent interactions in terms of the motives or reasons for the violence, the means of violence and especially the use of weapons, the consequences (harmful or otherwise) for victims or targets, the amount of pain and suffering, and the presence of sexual violence. At the scene level, violence was broken down in terms of whether it was punished, graphic, bloody, and placed within a humorous context. At the program level, judgments were made about the level of realism, whether or not it was animated, and the overall pattern of punishments at the end of the program. In addition, perpetrator and victim character variables were included such as gender, age, ethnicity, and dramatic role type.

Within the U.K. study, a number of contextual features were recorded about violent acts in the same way. The distribution of violence by genre provided a broad indication of the level of violence in realistic as distinct from fictional contexts. In addition, violent incidents were categorized in terms of motives of aggressor, consequences for victims, form of violence and use of weapons, graphicness of depiction of pain and suffering, presence of blood, and physical and geographical setting. Perpetrators and victims were classified in terms of gender, age, ethnicity, and dramatic role type.

COMPARISONS OF TELEVISION VIOLENCE

As we have seen, there were a number of key areas in which the NTVS and British studies of television violence differed. Fortunately, there were a number of measures both studies had in common or in relation to which there were sufficient similarities that cross-study comparison can be attempted. The comparisons reported in this chapter are based on published NTVS data that have been made available in a series of books and papers produced by the NTVS researchers since their project's onset.

Comparisons can be made on a purely quantitative level of the amount of violence on television in total and its distribution across the television schedules. On a more qualitative level, comparisons can be made between the extent to which violence on screen is associated with specific motives or reasons, specific consequences, specific instruments of aggression, and particular types of perpetrator and victim.

Quantity of Violence

At a quantitative level, comparisons can be made between American PAT scores and British violent act scores and in terms of the proportions of programs containing any violence at all. Further quantitative comparisons, using these measures, can also be made concerning the distribution of violence across channels and selected program genres.

The basic quantitative measure of television violence used in both studies was a count of violent interactions involving single or group perpetrators attacking single or groups of victims. At this point, it is relevant to remember that the NTVS analyzed a composite week of programs (i.e., 7 days) from 23 television channels, whereas the British study analyzed 4 real weeks of output (28 days) from 8 channels in the first study (see Gunter & J. Harrison, 1998), and 4 composite weeks (28 days) of output from 10 channels in the second study. Hence, the volume of total program content analyzed was different in each case. Further, the American study operated on the basis of a 17-hour day, whereas the British study operated on a 24-hour day.

Despite these differences, as a starting point, it is interesting to examine the total volume of violence coded in each study. Another complication here, however, is that the NTVS provided only a general indication of the number of violent interactions cataloged each year. In its initial report on the 1994–1995 analysis, it was stated that "a total of more than 18,000 violent interactions were observed in our sample of programming" (Kunkel et al., 1995, p. I-81). The exact number of violent acts was not stated. For the 1995–1996 analysis, Wilson et al. (1996) did not state a total PAT count at all in their initial results chapter (Results, Year 2 Data), but later in the Years 1 and 2 comparisons chapter, they stated that: "In Year 2, more than 18,500 violent interactions were observed" (p. 103).

The British study reported 21,170 violent acts for 1994–1995 (see Gunter & J. Harrison, 1998), and as reported in chapter 3 of this book, a total of 33,161 violent acts were found in the 1995–1996 analysis. Whereas the British study examined more days of television output than the American study, it analyzed programs from fewer channels. A common denominator might be found in terms of the number of channel days analyzed. In the American study, 161 channel days (23 channels by 7 days) were analyzed in 1994–1995 and 1995–1996. In the British study, 224 channel days were analyzed in 1994–1995 (28 days by 8 channels) and 280 channel days were analyzed in 1995–1996 (28 days by 10 channels). Even here, the comparison is not exact, because the American study used a 17-hour day, whereas the British study used a 24-hour day. Although given the overrun in the NTVS of programs selected for the 10:30 p.m. to 11:00 p.m. slot, the actual average hours per day occupied by selected programs probably exceeded 17 hours. Furthermore, some British channels took a 2- to 3-hour break in the middle of the night, so that not all channels operated a 24-hours-a-day service during the periods of study. So, assuming an approximately equal "day" for both studies, the average number of violent interactions per channel day on American television was 113.4 (taking the total counts as 18,000 and 18,500), compared with 106.5 per channel day on British television across the 1994–1996 period. Thus, the average rate of violent interactions was slightly higher on American television than on British television.

The second major quantitative measure on which U.S.–U.K. comparisons can be made is the prevalence of violence on major television schedules, as evidenced by the percentage of programs analyzed that contained any violence at all. The overall results, summarized in Table 10.1, revealed a greater prevalence of violence on American television than on British television in the mid-1990s. These overall figures disguise dramatic differences between channels in both countries in the prevalence of violence.

A further comparison can be made between the four major networks in the United States (ABC, CBS, Fox, NBC) and the four terrestrial broadcast networks in the United Kingdom (BBC1, BBC2, ITV, Channel Four). The NTVS reported that 44% of coded programs on the networks in 1994–1995 contained violence. In 1995–1996, this figure increased to 54%. The British television violence study reported that 28% of programs coded on the four terrestrial broadcast networks in 1994–1995 contained violence, a figure that increased marginally in 1995–1996 (31%).

In both the United States and Britain, the highest prevalence of violence occurred on premium movie channels. On the premium cable channels analyzed by the NTVS (Cinemax, HBO, Showtime), the great majority of programs analyzed contained violence (85% in 1994–1995 and 86% in

TABLE 10.1

Prevalence of Violence on American and British Television

	% of Programs with Violence	
	1994–1995	1995–1996
American television	57	61
British television	37	45

1995–1996). A similar result was found in Britain for the satellite broadcast subscription movie channels (Sky Movies and The Movie Channel), with 80% of programs analyzed in 1994–1995 and 84% in 1995–1996 containing violence. The greater similarity in the results for encrypted movie channels than for open-access, nonsubscription channels probably reflects the greater similarity across these channels in their program composition. Cable and satellite movie channels in the United States and Britain draw their content from similar sources (i.e., mainly Hollywood) and, indeed, often show the same movies. The established networks in each country show more distinctive domestic products produced for home viewing markets. Although there may be some overlap in programing (with British channels importing many American television series), the distinctiveness of their respective schedules is reflected in the differences in violence prevalence scores.

Some program genre comparisons can also be made in terms of prevalence of violence. Although the American and British projects used their own genre classification systems, both studies presented prevalence of violence results for drama series and serials, movies, and children's programs. Around 9 in 10 televised movies (91%) contained violence on American television, compared with over 8 in 10 (85%) on British television. American drama programs (74%) were much more likely to contain violence than were British drama programs (49%). American children's programs (68%) were also more likely to contain violence than were British children's programs (50%). However, the difference between American and British children.s programs could be accounted for by the stronger presence of noncartoon programs for children in the British schedules. On examining cartoon programs aimed at children in Britain, an average of 64% contained violence. This result is much closer to the American finding. (Figures presented here for British children's cartoons are for 1995–1996 only, the only year in which The Cartoon Network was analyzed.)

The third quantitative measure on which trans-Atlantic comparisons can be made is the saturation of violence in programs. This measure examines the breakdown of violence-containing programs in terms of the numbers of violent interactions they contain. In both projects, computations were made of the proportions of programs that contained just a few violent acts or large numbers of violent acts. The divisions that were reported were not exactly the same across the two studies, so the comparisons are not exact. Furthermore, the comparison is restricted to 1995–1996 data. For this year, the American study reported that 41% of violence-containing programs showed between one and three violent interactions, whereas 59% had four or more violent interactions. In 1995–1996, the British study reported that 51% of violence-containing programs included between one and five violent acts and that 49% had six or more.

At the upper end of the scale, the American study reported that 30% of violent programs in 1995–1996 contained 9 or more violent interactions, and during the same year, the British study reported that 33.5% of violent programs contained 10 or more violent acts. Hence there appears to be considerable similarity between Britain and the United States in the proportion of violent programs that fall into the very violent category on this measure. It is also noteworthy that the range over which the amount of violence within violent programs varied was far greater in Britain than in the United States. On this indicator, comparable data were available for both years. The range from least to most violent programs in the United States was 1 to 88 (1994–1995) and 1 to 99 (1995–96). For Britain, the equivalent scores were 1 to 171 (1994–95) and 1 to 167 (1995–1996).

Attributes of Violence

Comparisons can be made between the NTVS and British television violence study in terms of the nature of perpetrators and victims of violence, the weapons of violence, the reasons for violence, the consequences of violence, and the graphicness of violence. The nature of these comparisons is more precise on some measures than others.

Perpetrators of Violence

The perpetrators of violence comparisons can be made in respect to their breakdown into individual versus group perpetrators, their gender, age, and ethnicity. The NTVS identified a perpetrator for each violent interaction (PAT), as did the British study for each violent act. Involvement of different types of perpetrator was weighted according to the violent interactions for which they were the instigators. One initial classification of perpetrators was into single individuals acting alone versus groups acting in unison. In the British study, this individual versus group distinction was made at the same time as the gender classification. Hence, perpetrators were categorized as males acting alone, females acting alone, males acting in a group, and females acting in a group. These are the figures with which comparisons with the American data are made here.

In 1994–1995, 2 of 3 perpetrators of violence on American television were individuals acting alone (67%), as compared to more than 7 in 10 perpetrators of violence on British television (72%). In 1995–1996, 7 of 10 (70%) perpetrators on American television and just over 7 of 10 (73%) on British television were individuals. The distribution of solus and group aggressors was similar across studies.

The distribution of perpetrators by gender was very similar across the American and British studies. On American television, around 3 in 4 aggressors were male (78%) and 1 in 10 were female (10%). On British television, the distribution was almost the same (male, 77%; female, 9%)

over the 1994–1996 period. The remaining perpetrators (around 13%–14% in each study) were of unknown gender.

There was a very similar distribution of perpetrators by age. The age divisions used in both studies were near enough the same to render direct comparisons on this attribute. The results are summarized in Table 10.2. Perpetrators were divided into children, teenagers, adults, and the elderly. Around three quarters of all perpetrators were adults in the age 21 to 64 range on American television. A somewhat smaller, although still clear, majority of perpetrators fell into this age band on British television. Relatively few perpetrators of violence fell into either the very young or very old age bands on American television and on British television.

Assessments of the ethnicity of perpetrators of violence were made by the American and British studies, but some ethnic categories used in each case were different. Nonetheless, direct comparisons can be made in broad terms of the proportions of perpetrators who were White, Black, or other. These findings are summarized in Table 10.3. On both American and British television in the mid-1990s, White perpetrators of violence were dominant. Among minority perpetrator groups, Blacks were most prevalent as perpetrators of television violence in both countries, although Asian and Hispanic characters were not far behind on U.S. television and Asian/Oriental characters featured almost as frequently on U.K. television.

Targets of Violence

As with perpetrators of violence, targets or victims of violence were categorized by gender, age, and ethnicity, and also in terms of whether they

TABLE 10.2

Age Distribution of Perpetrators of Violence

	% of Perpetrators	
	1994–1995	1995–1996
American television		
Child (0–12 years)	2	4
Teen (13–20 years)	5	6
Adult (21–64 years)	76	74
Elderly (65+ years)	1	1
Unknown	16	15
British television	–	1
Child (0–11 years)	7	4
Teen (12–19 years)	71	63
Adult (20–64 years)	1	*
Elderly (65+ years)	21	31

* less than 0.5%

TABLE 10.3

Ethnicity Distribution of Perpetrators of Violence

	% of Perpetrators	
	1994–1995	*1995–1996*
American television		
White	76	73
Black	5	5
Asian	3	3
Hispanic	2	4
Native American	3	1
Middle Eastern	1	3
British television		
White	66	59
Black	5	5
Asian/Oriental	5	4
Other	24	32

were alone or in a group. In 1994–1995, on both American and British television, 69% of targets of violence were individuals. In 1995–1996, these percentages increased slightly to 71% on American television and 70% on British television.

The great majority of targets of violence on American (75%–76%) and British television (72%–73%) in 1994–1995 and 1995–1996 were male, with 1 in 10 or fewer being female (America: 9%–10%; Britain: 8%–9%). In fact, the gender distribution of targets was very close to that for perpetrators in both countries.

The age distributions of targets of violence observed similar patterns on American and British television, but larger proportions of targets were identified as adult in the American research than in the British research. A substantially higher proportion of targets of violence were not clearly classifiable in terms of age in the British study than in the American study (see Table 10.4). Once again, the victim of violence distribution mirrored the perpetrator of violence distribution.

The ethnic distribution of targets of violence exhibited a similar pattern on American and British television, as did the ethnicity of perpetrator of distributions. The great majority of targets of violence throughout were White. The minority target groups were led by Blacks, followed by Asians and Hispanics on American television and by Asians on British television (see Table 10.5).

Presence of Weapons

The form of violence on television is important to how audiences react. This factor is significant due to the so-called weapons effect, whereby the mere sight of a weapon such as a knife or a gun has the capacity to

TABLE 10.4

Age Distribution of Targets of Violence

	% of Targets	
	1994–1995	*1995–1996*
American television		
Child (0–12 years)	3	4
Teen (13–20 years)	7	7
Adult (21–64 years)	72	72
Elderly (65+ years)	1	1
Unknown	17	16
British television		
Child (0–11 years)	–	1
Teen (12–19 years)	7	5
Adult (20–64 years)	67	60
Elderly (65+ years)	1	1
Unknown	25	33

enhance the aggressive behavior of a person who has already been an-gered. Evidence for this effect, however, has been mixed, with some studies supporting its existence (Berkowitz & LePage, 1967; Caprara, Renzi, Amolini, D.Imperio, & Travaglia, 1984) and others failing to do so (Cahoun & Edmonds, 1984, 1985; Halderman & Jackson, 1979). Per-haps more significant as an indicator to content analysis research are findings that viewers make perceptual distinctions between scenes of vi-olence on the basis of the types of weaponry present (Gunter, 1985).

Both the American and British studies included a classification of tele-vised violence in terms of weaponry. The NTVS distinguished between

TABLE 10.5

Ethnicity Distribution of Targets of Violence

	% of Targets	
	1994–1995	*1995–1996*
American television		
White	77	75
Black	6	5
Asian	3	3
Hispanic	2	4
Native American	2	1
Middle Eastern	1	2
British television		
White	63	57
Black	5	5
Asian/Oriental	5	5
Other	27	34

natural means of violence (perpetrators use their body as a weapon), handheld firearms, conventional weaponry (knife), unconventional weaponry (use of nonviolent objects as weapons, throwing or hitting with household objects), heavy weaponry, and bombs. The British study distinguished 48 basic-level weapon types, which were reduced to 11 broad categories: body, gun (military), gun (handheld), other shooting instrument (e.g., bow and arrow), knife/stabbing instrument, throwing instruments, clubbing instruments, vehicle, animals, other electrochemical means (electricity, gas, chemicals), and other varied weapon types.

On reclassifying the British weapon types to match the American weapon types, a comparison can be made between the distribution of different forms of violence in each case. Both studies categorized violence in terms of use of the body (hand, fist, foot, head) as a weapon, use of handheld firearms, heavy weaponry, and bombs/explosives. The American "conventional" category was compared with the British knife/stabbing category, and the American "unconventional" category was compared with the British clubbing, throwing, use of vehicle, and use of animal as weapon categories (see Table 10.6).

The results show that the prevalence of violence of "natural means" using the body as a weapon was similar on American and British television, and in both instances was the most common form of violence on screen. The frequencies of occurrence of the other violent forms varied to some extent between British and American television, with incidents featuring handheld firearms being more commonplace on American television, and the use of heavy military-type weaponry being more frequent on British television.

Reasons for Violence

For every violent interaction, coders in both studies assessed the reason or motive for the perpetrator.s aggression against a particular target. The significance of this contextual feature stems from the fact that audience judgments about screen violence take into account a character's

TABLE 10.6

Forms of Violence on American and British Television

Weapon Type	American Television 1994–1995 (%)	British Television 1994–1995 (%)	American Television 1995–1996 (%)	British Television 1995–1996 (%)
Natural means (Body)	40	45	41	49
Handheld firearm	25	10	23	7
Unconventional weapon	20	13	19	13
Conventional weapon	8	7	8	4
Heavy weaponry	3	11	3	11
Bombs	2	2	3	2

motives. The degree of intent to do harm and lack of thought about consequences affect the opinions of onlookers about aggressors (Mees, 1990). Whether or not the violence is justified also makes a difference to audience reactions. The justification for violence is often linked to its reward. Rewarded violence may appear more attractive and even more justifiable (Ball-Rokeach, 1972). In the end, whether or not violence is justified may depend on the observer's own moral philosophy (Rule & Ferguson, 1986). Regardless, violence that is legally sanctioned may be regarded as more acceptable and therefore as "less violent" than violence conducted for illegal reasons. Even then, there must be a sense that legalized violence (i.e., that perpetrated by the police) is equitable and does not go beyond the bounds of what is necessary in the circumstances (Gunter, 1985).

Both the American and British studies of television violence classified occurrences of violence in terms of reasons and motives. Only a few cross-study comparisons are possible, however, because different systems of motive/reason classification were used in each case. The NTVS divided violence into that motivated by personal gain (30% of violent interactions across 1994–1996), protection of life (25%), anger (25%), mental instability (5%), retaliation (2%), and other (14%). The British study used a number of categories of personal gain, referred to distinctively as ambition, power, and money. Together these accounted for an average of 21% of violent acts over the 1994–1996 assessment period, fewer than the proportion noted in the American research. It also used a series of categories (self-protection, family protection, and protection of society) that are the near equivalents to the American study's "protection of life" category. Together these categories accounted for 24% of violent acts, almost the same proportion as that observed in the NTVS.

Both studies also classified the amount of violence motivated by sexual reasons. In both cases, fewer than 1% of violent incidents were coded as sexually motivated across the period of assessment (1994–1996).

Consequences of Violence

The consequences of violence refer to the harm and pain that result from violent interactions. The importance of this variable stems from its capacity to influence audience reactions at behavioral, emotional, and perceptual levels. Watching images of someone being hurt in a violent altercation has been found to enhance the subsequent aggressive responding of the observer in a laboratory setting (Goranson, 1970; Hartmann, 1969). However, some depictions of pain and suffering can induce anxiety reactions and cause more destructive play behavior in young viewers (Noble, 1975).

Perceptually, viewers define incidents of violence in which someone gets hurt as more violent than incidents in which no one is visibly harmed (Greenberg & Gordon, 1972b; Gunter, 1985). Furthermore, the stronger the degree of harm that results, the more violent a scene is perceived to be (Gunter, 1985).

The NTVS coded this aspect of violence at the interaction (PAT) and program levels. The British study coded them at the interaction (act) level only. For harm, the NTVS coded the amount of physical injury actually depicted on screen and the amount of likely injury that would have occurred if the violence had been enacted against a human in real life. Both measures had four possible values: none, mild, moderate, and extreme. Coders also had a fifth option indicating that the target was not visibly shown on screen.

The British study used several categories ranging from death, through serious injury, mild injury, psychological damage, to no injury at all. Table 10.7 presents comparative results for the two studies. In this case, the categories of death, serious wound, broken limbs, and mutilation from the British study were classified as equivalent to "extreme" harm as used in the NTVS. Minor wound and stun/bruise categories in the British study were treated as equivalents to "moderate" and "mild" harm in the American research. Because no American equivalent for "psychological harm" was indicated, this category was omitted from the comparisons made here.

Targets were not shown a similar number of times in both studies, and the no observable harm category was the most frequently occurring in each instance. The distributions of cases of serious, moderate, and mild harm were also very similar across the British and American studies.

Another consequence of violence coded in both studies was the degree of pain and suffering displayed on screen by victims of violence. The American research classified pain as none, mild, moderate, extreme, or target not shown. A 5-point degree of pain scale was used in the British

TABLE 10.7
Harmful Consequences of Violence on American and British Television

	1994–1995 (%)	1995–1996 (%)
American television		
Target not shown	3	8
Extreme harm	18	17
Moderate harm	12	11
Mild harm	22	20
No harm	44	44
British television		
Target not shown	4	8
Extreme harm	19	11
Moderate harm	11	9
Mild harm	29	26
No harm	36	47

study. A score of 1 was regarded as equivalent to "none" in the American scale, 2 was equated to "mild," 3 and 4 were equated to "moderate," and 5 was equated to "extreme." There was also a target not seen ("don't know") category. The comparative results are shown in Table 10.8.

The overall distribution of results was similar across the American and British studies. Most violent incidents depicted either no pain or only mild pain on the part of victims. There was a somewhat greater likelihood of the no pain category being used and a smaller likelihood of the extreme pain category being used by coders in Britain.

Graphic Nature of Violence

The American television violence research coded violent interactions in terms of the explicitness of the violence and in terms of the amount of blood and gore shown on screen. The British study also coded the amount of blood shown on screen. The American study classified the depiction of blood and gore as "extreme," "moderate," "mild," and "none." The British study used a 5-point scale and a "don't know" option. Translating the British ratings into the American classifications—treating 5 as "extreme," 3 and 4 as "moderate," 2 as "mild," and 1 and "don't know" as "none"—allows for cross-study comparisons. These comparisons are summarized in Table 10.9. As with the distribution of harmful and painful consequences of violence, the distribution of blood and gore was similar across both studies. In the great majority of instances, there was no blood and gore associated with violent interactions. Extremely graphic violence of this kind was a rarity, especially on British television.

TABLE 10.8
Pain Consequences of Violence on American and British Television

	1994–1995 (%)	1995–1996 (%)
American television		
Target not shown	8	7
Extreme pain	6	7
Moderate pain	7	8
Mild pain	30	29
No pain	49	49
British television		
Target not shown	9	10
Extreme pain	1	*
Moderate pain	8	6
Mild pain	24	21
No pain	59	63

* less than 0.5%

TABLE 10.9
Blood and Gore in Violence on American and British Television

	1994–1995 (%)	1995–1996 (%)
American television		
Extreme	3	2
Moderate	6	5
Mild	6	6
None	85	86
British television		
Extreme	*	–
Moderate	3	1
Mild	8	4
None	88	85

CONCLUSIONS

This chapter has attempted to make some direct comparisons between violence on television in Britain and the United States. It was fortuitous that two major studies were funded in both countries at the same time in the mid-1990s and notification of the existence of both of these projects occurred to their respective research teams in time to enable an exchange of views to take place during their planning stages. Differences in budgets, time constraints, and project requirements asserted by sponsors meant that a precise match in terms of methodology was not possible. Nevertheless, a number of common measures did emerge within similar overriding definitional frames of reference. The account presented here represents the first attempt at drawing direct comparisons between the results of these two projects on those measures they had in common or on measures that were very similar in nature. Despite differences in their respective program sampling techniques, both projects eventually compiled the largest videotaped television archives ever to be analyzed as part of a single project in this field. Furthermore, the basic quantitative measures were similar enough to permit direct comparisons between the two countries. The NTVS eventually ran for 3 years, whereas the British project ran for just the first 2 of those years. Data comparisons were made for that period (1994–1996).

Overall, American mainstream television was more violent than British mainstream television in terms of the proportion of programs containing any violence and in terms of the average rate at which violent incidents occurred per day. American terrestrial channels had a higher percentage of violent programs than British terrestrial channels. However, the difference between the two countries on this measure virtually disappeared when comparing violence levels on satellite or cable subscription movie channels. The latter findings were not too surprising.

The movie channels in both countries draw significantly in each case from the same production source—Hollywood. Thus, they might be expected to exhibit a considerable degree of content overlap. The terrestrial channels, in contrast, contain much more indigenous national programing and schedule compositions, which vary in terms of violent genre representation.

Although the American terrestrial television schedules may contain more violent programing than their British counterparts, the average violence saturation levels of violence-containing programs did not vary that much between the two countries. In other words, there was no strong tendency for violent programs on American television to be a great deal more violent, in terms of average numbers of violent acts, than violent programs on British television. Indeed, the most violent programs cataloged on British television during this period of analysis were more violent than the most violent programs cataloged in the American study. But, there was very little to choose between the two countries in terms of the proportion of violent programs that contained 10 or more violent acts.

The quantity of violence on television is not the only indicator of television violence. Further, it may not even be the best such indicator. From the perspective of the audience, the nature of the violence is often more significant. A program containing just one graphic portrayal of violence could be judged by viewers as more violent than a program containing 20 nongraphic portrayals. Viewers' judgments about the seriousness of television violence is highly context dependent (Gunter, 1985; Potter, 1999; Potter & Smith, 1999). The effects that televised portrayals of violence may have on viewers' attitudes or behavior are also mediated by contextual factors within programs (Comstock & Strasburger, 1990; *National Television Violence Study*, 1997; Paik & Comstock, 1994; Potter, 1999).

Principal among these contextual factors is the realism of the setting in which a portrayal takes place and how graphically it is presented. Graphic portrayals, in turn, can be defined in terms of a range of other features such as the type of perpetrator, type of victim of violence, weapons used, and the outcome of the violence for those involved (Potter & Smith, 1999).

Those involved in violence on American and British television tend to be young adult, White males, whether they appear as perpetrators of violence or victims. Despite concerns about television violence and children, few children are featured in incidents of violence on television. Likewise, the elderly were not often present during on-screen violence. Ethnic minorities were much less prevalent than Whites in all forms of violence, reflecting their lower visibility on television. When they did appear, however, they were no more likely to be victims of violence than perpetrators. Therefore, was no indication that they were proportionately more at risk once involved in violence.

The forms of violence are important in relation to audience reactions to screen violence (Gunter, 1985), and also in connection with behavioral reactions of viewers subsequent to viewing (Berkowitz & LePage, 1967; Leyens & Parke, 1975). Whereas a majority of violent acts on both British and American television involved the use of weapons, the most prevalent single type of violence involved the use of the perpetrator's own body (i.e., hand or fist, foot, knee, head, etc.). The use of weapons of some form was slightly more prevalent on American television than on British television. In particular, the use of handheld firearms was markedly more prevalent on American television than British television. This may reflect the greater prevalence of guns in American society.

The degree of harm caused by violence is a significant factor in relation to audience's perceptions of violence (Gunter, 1985; Gunter & Furnham, 1984). It can also mediate viewers' subsequent displays of aggression after viewing screen violence (Goranson, 1970; Hartmann, 1969). On both British and American television, most violent portrayals produced either no visible harm to victims or only mild physical effects. Even so, around one in four violent incidents resulted in moderate to extreme harm befalling victims. Hence, harmful violence was far from rare on mainstream television in both countries. Harm could follow from violence, but graphic depictions of pain and suffering or of blood and gore were fairly rare. This was especially true of British television on which scenes of violence in which victims were judged to display extreme pain or in which there was lots of blood and gore were virtually nonexistent.

This comparison of violence on British and American television has revealed a number of similarities between the two countries in the degree to which violent programs are violent and in the nature of that violence on a number of important attributes. In addition, however, there were some differences between the two countries. American television has a higher proportion of violent programs than British television overall, but on subscription movie channels such differences diminish to virtually zero. But although movies on American television are not significantly more likely to be violent than those shown on British television, American drama series and children's programs are more likely to contain violence than their British counterparts. When violence does occur, however, the perpetrators are young, White, adult males who are more likely not to harm one another than to cause serious damage, and will be highly likely to hit someone with a part of their own body. In the United States, an aggressor is far more likely to shoot at his target than in Britain.

Chapter 11

Violence on Television
and Helping the Audience

This book has discussed the way violence is represented on television. It has presented findings from a large research project that comprised the second stage of a program funded by the broadcasting industry in Britain. Although concerned primarily with providing broadcasters with a descriptive account of the amount, nature, and distribution of the occurrence of violence on mainstream terrestrial and satellite television channels available to British viewers, the findings have been considered within a wider context of public opinion and media effects. Research into viewers' attitudes toward television programs and television portrayals and into the effects that viewing experiences might have on viewers' attitudes and behaviors is important here because it can add greater depth to otherwise dry, descriptive data about television output.

On the subject of television violence, viewers have frequently been found to hold very firm opinions. They may be for it or against it. However, public attitudes have also been observed to exhibit sensitivities to the nature and form of portrayed violence (e.g., Gunter & Stipp, 1992; Gunter & Wober, 1988). It is not simply a case of people being either for or against the showing of violence on television. This is not a black or white issue, but one with many shades of grey. Viewers' opinions about televised violence can vary significantly with the physical form it takes, the type of behavior displayed, the reasons for the violence, the consequences for those involved, the nature of the perpetrator and victim and the relationship between them, and the setting in which the action takes place (see Greenberg & Gordon, 1972b, 1972c; Gunter, 1985; Hodge & Tripp, 1986; Van der Voort, 1986).

In a similar vein, evidence on the effects of televised violence has indicated that viewers may experience short-lived or lasting changes in attitude to aggression or in their own aggressive dispositions as a function of exposure to violent screen portrayals (Geen & Thomas, 1986; R. M. Kaplan & R. D. Singer, 1976). The effects literature has also shown, however, that the strength of postviewing psychological changes in viewers can often depend on the nature of the observed violence. The features that have been found to shape public perceptions of televised violence—particularly the context in which the violence is shown, the nature of the perpetrators and victims, their reasons for bring involved in violence, and the consequences of such involvement for them—can also mediate postviewing effects of screen violence on viewers (*National Television Violence Study*, 1997; Potter, 1999). Thus, to understand fully the implications of descriptive studies of the representation of violence on television, it is vital to consider what is known about audiences' reactions to it. Not only does this add a fresh perspective on the classification of violent television content, it is important in regard to interpreting the possible policy implications of content analysis research into television violence for broadcasters and their regulators.

THE POLICY CONTEXT

This chapter considers the relevance of research into the representation of violence on television in relation to wider social policy debates about how best to help the audience to make informed judgments about their viewing needs. Ensuring that the audience is well informed in advance about the content of television programing is an important element of the regulation of media content, and generally takes the form of program ratings, advance warnings to parents, and of information about programs in electronic program guides. Debates about how to provide information for audiences most effectively vary in different countries. This chapter draws on debates that have been conducted in the United States, Australia, and Europe.

Future regulation of television content in general is open to question due to the rapid growth of television channels. The proliferation of digital, cable, and satellite channels has resulted in a more confusing array of program choices for the audience and a more complex task for regulators trying to ensure that content requirements are met. In the contemporary broadcasting climate there has been growing concern that children may have easier access to unsuitable material given the increasing range of channels available to them (Gunter, 2000).

Consequently, there have been, to differing extents, discussions in Europe, the United States, and Australia about how best to protect children. Two key strategies to protect children have traditionally been to require programers to display ratings for programs and to limit the showing of violent programs to times when children are not viewing (Potter, 1996). A key part of this strategy has been to provide viewers with better information about programs in advance. In theory, better information should be helpful to parents and allow them to make better judgments about the suitability of programing for their children. Problematically, the basis for television content classification in these countries is open to some doubt because it is founded on an unclear understanding of audience psychology and the effect that censorship of material has on young viewers' desire to watch violent programing.

Furthermore, academic scholars have begun to examine more closely the context in which violence takes place on television (*National Television Violence Study*, 1997, 1998; Potter, 1999; Potter & Smith, 1999). There is growing interest in the complexity of audience responses to different types of contextual cues, meaning that blanket restrictions on access to violent programs using content classifications and ratings are probably insufficient and sometimes irrelevant as a means of protecting the audience. This chapter begins with an overview of the way broadcasters have used restrictive scheduling practices and labeling systems in Britain, Australia, and the United States. Such practices are deployed as a form of consumer protection, providing a default filter designed to safeguard the interests especially of younger viewers and those of a more sensitive disposition. The discussion leads to an illustration of the problems with such classifications.

CONSUMER PROTECTION IN BRITAIN

Broadcasters in Britain have used restrictive scheduling as a means to protect children from unsuitable material for many years. The Independent Television Commission (ITC) and the British Broadcasting Corporation (BBC) have comprehensive and explicit codes of practice on the portrayal of violence, sex, and bad language on television, as well as for taste and decency. Program makers know these codes and must obey them. If the code is breached, then the ITC will intervene, possibly with a sanction (e.g., a public apology or a fine). The ITC rules go back to the basics and ask program makers to consider why violence has to be portrayed on the screen. They impose a duty to consider its role and nature, how it is portrayed, what effect it may have, and whether there is any danger of imitation or emulation.

Violence, sex, or bad language in a program is subject to the overriding requirements of the Family Viewing Policy (or the "watershed" as it is more commonly known). No program shown before 9 p.m. may be unsuitable for children to watch. After 9 p.m., programs with progressively less suitable (i.e., more adult) material may be shown, and it may be that a program will be acceptable at 10:30 p.m. that would not be suitable at 9 p.m. There is a degree of greater flexibility in terms of scheduling for premium subscription channels, available via satellite or cable (e.g., the BSkyB movie channels in Britain), whose accessibility to children is assumed to be more restricted due to payment barriers on premium channels. For this reason, a dual watershed system operates, with divides at 8 p.m. and 10 p.m.. The 8 p.m. watershed on subscription channels is equivalent to the 9 p.m. watershed on open-access terrestrial channels, and permits the showing after 8 p.m. on subscription channels of programs that would not be permitted until 9 p.m. on nonsubscription channels. The 10 p.m. watershed on subscription television channels permits the showing of adult material that would probably not be allowed at all on nonsubscription channels, or only allowed following heavy editing. ITC research (1999) has shown that most British parents say they are aware of the 9 p.m. watershed on the nonsubscription channels, but far fewer viewers are fully cognizant of the 8 p.m. and 10 p.m. scheduling divides on subscription channels. Further, viewers do express concerns and some parents, politicians, and pressure groups still believe there is too much violence on television and that children are at risk.

Broadcasters in Britain have adapted cinema film and video ratings to provide ratings for televised films. The British Board of Film Classification (BBFC) is responsible for classifying films for theater and video distribution. Film classifications are largely age based ("12," "15," and "18"), but also make reference to the role and responsibilities of parents ("PG"—parental guidance, whereby films may be viewed by children under age 12, provided they have a parent with them; not recommended for children under 8 years even with a parent present). The BBFC does take into account a range of factors concerning the form and context of portrayed violence in determining what should be permitted for public viewing and what classification should be applied. However, the guidelines relating to the regulation of the distribution of films and their classification has been influenced by public and political lobbying often triggered by violent incidents in society.

In one of Britain's most notorious murders, 2-year-old James Bulger was abducted from a shopping mall in Liverpool by two 10-year-old boys, led to a railway line, hammered to death with an iron bar, and then cut in half by a train. There were suggestions that a horror film about a demonic doll, *Child's Play 3*, helped inspire the crime. No evidence was presented that either boy had seen it, but the father of one had rented it shortly before the murder took place. More disturbing anecdotal evidence emerged from another case in which a gang in Manchester tortured a 16-year-old girl, set her on fire, and left her dying. One of the perpetrators allegedly repeated the menacing *Child's Play 3* catch phrase, 'I'm Chucky, wanna play?' The murder of James Bulger did not merely sicken the country's conscience, it stirred the government and Parliament to action. The Prime Minister at that time, John Major, called on parents to keep a closer eye on their children's viewing. Subsequently, the BBC and the ITC, which regulates Britain's commercial channels, issued new guidelines urging producers to be much more cautious.

A series of amendments were made to the Video Recordings Act in the belief that video films needed stricter ratings than cinema films because children were likely to have easier access to the former. Harsher standards were in any case applied by the BBFC whenever a film was transferred to video. A film rated as "12" for theater showing, automatically became a "15" when transposed to videotape. The Bulger case, however, resulted in a tougher attitude toward the implementation of the movie ratings, such that a number of movies were, at that time, denied classifications, rendering them outlawed. On television, an even stricter regulatory regime applies than that imposed on cinemas or videos. As with cinema films, the ratings used for films destined for showing on broadcast television are generally age based, with other content advisories indicating that parental guidance is required or that the film contains sex, violence, or bad language. However, a greater amount of footage may end up on the cutting room floor before films are broadcast, especially on the nonsubscription channels.

CONSUMER PROTECTION AT THE EUROPEAN LEVEL

At a European level, audiovisual policy is still developing, having to overcome the reluctance of different Member States to relinquish national control and the consequent differing levels of regulation in different Member States. It was the concern with the creation of an internal market in television broadcasts that led to an emphasis on market mechanisms as the driving force in the development of the information society, as epitomized in the 1994 Bangemann Report. Technological development—which has led to cross-frontier satellite broadcasting, increasing choice through the growth in digital channels, increasing commercial pressure, and convergence of broadcasting and telecoms—has an impact on the ability of the Member States to control the quality of programing within their borders. Mitchell (1998) argued that such factors will lead to a pressure to relax existing provisions that aim to protect children. The Television Without Frontiers Directive (1989) and the Amended Directive (1997) provided that Member States should regulate the broadcasters within their own jurisdiction Thus, it was thought that each broadcaster would be subject to only one level of broadcasting regulation, reducing duplicate regulation. Problematically, the country from which a program is broadcast sets the regulatory rules for which it alone is responsible. Member States are not allowed to block direct transmissions from other European Union countries, although Member States have the power to temporarily suspend (usually after a problematic program has been transmitted) programs that infringe on the provision of Article 22. The Amended Directive created stronger and more precise rules to protect minors against television programs containing pornography and gratuitous violence (Articles 22, 22a, and 22b), providing further clarification for Member States wishing to take steps to prevent the transmission of incoming broadcasts. In practice, these amendments to the directive only served to highlight the difficulties in trying to harmonize standards in a complex multicultural environment (see J. L. Harrison & Woods, 1999) and often do not succeed in preventing incoming transmission until after it has been broadcast.

Certain Member States have complained about the entry of unsuitable material into their territories. For example, Sweden has sought to prohibit advertising aimed at children. In the United Kingdom, there have been several cases in which the national regulator has sought to make a proscription order seeking to ban the input of pornographic broadcasting[1]. The European Parliament attempted to add 103 amendments to the Television Without Frontiers Directive, in particular the European Parliament tried to extend the power of Member States to block transmissions. The latter was rejected by the Commission and Council of Ministers and only a few of the European Parliament's amendments were accepted (Mitchell, 1998). The Amended Directive Article 22(b)2 states that the Commission, within 1 year, should conduct an inquiry into further measures of protecting children and the feasibility of the V-chip, setting up content rating systems and encouraging a European-wide family viewing policy. As Mitchell (1998) pointed out, however, this is undermined to some extent by Recital 41, which states that none of the measures need to be implemented before the program is broadcast. Clearly, once the program has been broadcast, the damage may have already been done.

In 1999, the European Commission, under obligation, carried out its inquiry into the desirability, practicability, and effectiveness of the V-chip and program content rating systems as a way of improving parental control over television (European Commission, 1999). The commission dismissed the use of the analogue V-chip, indicating that the V-chip technology used in the United States and Canada was not feasible in Europe due to the different levels of technological developments across Europe. Concerns were also raised by the Commission regarding technological blocking devices, perceiving them as "upstream censoring" that may violate freedom of expression. Furthermore, the practical difficulty of imposing a uniform labeling scheme across different Member States was recognized. Although the Commission recognizes that different and new forms of technological development across Europe are interfering with established patterns of parental control of children's viewing, it points out that digital technology, once established, will offer a much higher level of protection of minors,, due to use of pin numbers and encryption.

---

[1]Red Hot Television, TV Erotica, Rendez-Vous Television, Satisfaction Club TV, Eurotica Rendez-Vous, Eros TV have been proscribed in the United Kingdom. S.177 Broadcasting Act 1990 enables the Secretary of State to declare a foreign satellite service as unacceptable. One broadcaster lodged an action before the Court of First Instance to challenge the commission's decision that the U.K.'s actions are in conformity with Community law. See Case T-69/99 *Eurotica Rendez-vous Television Danish Satellite TV A/S v Commission*, Proceedings of the ECJ 10/99.

Consequently the Commission recognizes that Europe is currently in an interim phase and that measures should be taken to protect children. The Commission recommends that specific efforts to provide information about content should be made via analogue and digital electronic program guides. Descriptive ratings should be used rather than evaluative ratings, because the former are seen by the Commission to provide greater levels of information for parents, enhancing their choice, and to be better at overcoming cultural differences. The future for the protection of minors within the European context will emerge as a compromise from a set of tensions: between economic and cultural policy imperatives, between the different European institutions (indeed the European Parliament has generally taken a stronger line on the need to protect minors than either the Council of Ministers or the Commission; Mitchell, 1998), between the Member States and the European institutions, and between different Member States who seek to retain differing levels of regulatory autonomy.

CONSUMER PROTECTION IN THE UNITED STATES

In the United States, concerns about the link between parental and academic concerns about screen violence and aggression and the policy initiatives enacted by the government are more coherent. Policymakers rely on numerous academic studies claiming to have established a causal link between screen violence and behavior. In such studies, researchers have argued that television violence can lead to desensitization, approval of aggression, aggressive behavior, and fears about the world being a dangerous place (Donnerstein et al., 1994; Gerbner, Gross, Morgan, & Signorielli, 1994). D. R. Roberts (1998) explained that ratings in the United States have become a major social and political issue in the 1990s. Concerns about the levels of violence on television have occurred at the same time as advances in technology that have enabled the broadcast media to experiment with new and more graphic and realistic ways of portraying violence. This, coupled with the dramatic rise in teenage violence and crime in American society and the belief that screen violence and aggression are linked, has elicited renewed debate in the United States. Problematically, control by regulatory authorities must be carefully counterbalanced against the requirements of the First Amendment, which guarantees freedom of speech and the press. The limitation of First Amendment freedoms is generally supported by the public and policymakers when these freedoms are limited for the greater good of the public (Hoffner et al., 1999). This view has been exemplified in government measures to try to limit the negative effects of television violence.

Congressional hearings have been regularly held since the 1950s to discuss television violence in response in part to public concerns about the effects of screen violence (Kunkel, 1997). In the early 1990s, Congress took a renewed interest in television violence (Hoffner et al., 1999). The numerous debates and bills that have resulted from legislative proposals on television violence in the United States can be placed into three separate groups: family viewing hours, content ratings requirements for programs, and blocking devices (Potter, 1996). In 1997, under pressure from Congress, the television industry implemented a voluntary code for rating program content. It did so under the threat that a code would otherwise be imposed by the Federal Communications Commission (FCC), the industry regulator (Hoffner et al., 1999). The new ratings system was to be used in conjunction with the V-chip which the Telecommunications Act of 1996 required to be placed in all new television sets starting from 2000.

The V-chip is a device that allows viewers to block programs based on their rated levels of specified content (e.g., violence, sex, bad language) and is designed specifically to enable parents to block programs they think are unsuitable for their children. The introduction of the V-chip in the United States raised concerns from many quarters. It will take several years to ensure that a V-chip is in every home because people do not necessarily replace their television sets regularly. Often, the old family set finishes up in a child's bedroom. In consequence, the next generation of children are not going to be protected by such a device in the United States. A further problem anticipated by the mandatory instalment of the V-chip was the requirement for someone to rate programs for violence. Potter (1996) argued that there was little agreement on an explicit definition of violence either in political or academic literature and the ratings that emerged from the television industry are problematical.

The television industry's ratings system, which was designed to help parents make informed choices, has been controversial from its inception. The television rating system used in the United States is based on the Motion Picture Association of America (MPAA) ratings scheme. The rating system was created by members of the television industry, but critics felt that the ratings lacked the information about which parents were most concerned (Chen, 1999). In July 1997, the industry's original age-based rating system was modified to include symbols that would inform parents whether the programs contained fantasy violence (FV), which applies mainly to children's programs, Violence (V), sexual situations (S), coarse language (L), and suggestive dialogue (D) (Salvoza, 1997).

CONSUMER PROTECTION IN AUSTRALIA

Program classifications for commercial television stations in Australia were initially devised by the Australian Broadcasting Tribunal (ABT). The ABT was replaced in 1992 by the Australian Broadcasting Authority (ABA), which has been working to replace the age-based television classifications with a system that includes more information about the content of the programs following the results of a project undertaken by ABA and the Office of Film and Literature Classification (OFLC) which revealed that viewers desired more than age-based information in order to make informed viewing decisions.

PROGRAM RATINGS SYSTEMS

Age-based categories for rating programs are used in Britain, the United States, and Australia. In each system, they are related to, or based on, the system used originally for cinema films. In Britain, the BBFC uses three age specifications: 12, 15, and 18. Satellite, cable, and digital television use the 15 and 18 age restrictions on premium movie channels. In the United States, the MPAA uses two age divides at 13 and 17. American television uses more classification divides, identifying the ages 7, 14, and 17 as particular barriers for children's viewing. In Australia, the OFLC uses two age specifications, 15 and 18. Australian television ratings suggest a program is suitable for all children, for primary school-children, that parental guidance is needed, or that the program contains adult-only material.

The use of age-related ratings systems as the only means to identify the suitability of a program for children raises problems. Age-based categories make specific assumptions about the psychology of the television audience that may not be valid (Gunter, 2000). They assume that there are distinct types of reactions to violent content depending on the age. Kunkel (1997) argued that such ratings represent an inadequate understanding of child development. Furthermore, they also fail to identify sufficiently the violent content attributes that are known to affect viewers' responses to the programs they are watching.

In the United States, researchers and parental groups have challenged the use of an MPAA-based system for television ratings. The main criticism has been that the system tends to treat all children as a homogenous group, when they are likely to be psychologically diverse (Wilson, D. Linz, & Randall, 1990) and they include little descriptive information about what type of content warrants the age-based advisory. Problematically, the decision to rate a program suitable or not suitable for a particular age group is often based on very subjective and judgmental criteria. However, different families may have different concerns about the level and nature of violence in a television program that are unique to their own values or their judgment of the specific needs of their own child. This renders a universal standard for all children of the same age irrelevant (Potter, 1996). Consequently, the broad nature of a warning may make it almost worthless (Wurtzel & Surlin, 1978). Kunkel (1997) likened such warnings to a weather forecast where viewers are told that bad weather is approaching, but not informed about the type of weather to expect.

Research has shown that cognitive processing is related to age, whereby the minds of children develop cognitively between birth and age 12 and that during these formative years, children of different ages have differing abilities to process television content (Potter, 1999). Very young children and babies show interest in the movement and sounds on the television screen, but it is not until children become older that they develop the ability to make sense of story lines (Kodaira, 1990). Children under age 8 are more likely to be attracted to the superficial surface features of the program (Gunter, 2000). Older children are seen to be cognitively more mature and likely to be able to follow more complex story lines (Potter, 1999).

Age-based rating systems classify programs according to the amount of violence they contain. The assumption here is that more violence is worse than less violence and therefore, to protect a child, a higher age threshold must be placed on programs according to the amount of violence they contain. However, this does not take into account the nature of the violence or the context in which it appears (Kunkel, 1997), nor does it consider that children of a younger age group may actually be less concerned by certain types of violence (because the violent is covert and needs a more sophisticated reading of the story line) than older children.

There is a growing body of research evidence that age-based ratings may invoke audience reactions that are the opposite of those intended (Gunter, 2000). This is especially the case when children are involved (Bushman & Stack, 1996). To illustrate this effect, Chen (1999, p. 4) cited psychological reactance theory research conducted by J. W. Brehm (1966), S. S. Brehm and J. W. Brehm (1981), and Wicklund (1994), which states "the act of threatening to restrict or take away an individual's freedom to act will motivate the person to restore that freedom by actively seeking to engage in the proscribed activity." The labeling of programs with age-based restrictions rather than providing descriptive nonjudgmental information may create a boomerang effect, whereby children are actually more attracted to material simply because it is restricted. This phenomenon is also known as the "forbidden fruit" effect (Cantor & Harrison, 1996; Kunkel, 1997). Children may perceive a loss of personal freedom, especially when advisories delegate control to another party. Advisories such as "parental discretion advised" (D. R. Roberts, 1998) may actually encourage children to watch restricted shows regardless of the content of the program (Chen, 1999).

The incorporation of informational advisories into the age-based ratings scheme has resulted in a combination of two different types of labels. The first is an evaluative system and the second is an informational system. In contrast to the subjective, judgmental evaluative ratings system, informational labeling systems do not seek to make judgments regarding for whom the content is appropriate. This means that parents are left to make decisions about what type of content is suitable for their child based on the information given. Consequently, the comprehensibility and usefulness of the information becomes more important as a guide to viewing decisions. Chen (1999) drew an analogy between the content labeling of programs and nutritional labeling that provides information about the content of food without making judgments about whether or not a person should eat it. The revised television ratings in the United States now use descriptive advisories to specify the type of content that programs contain. A particular audience reaction may be provoked by the provision of this kind information. A "tainted fruit" explanation derives from information-processing theory (Gunter, 2000) and is based on the assumption that more information about a program may repel viewers from watching if they confront material that makes them feel uncomfortable or is not of interest.

D. R. Roberts (1998) argued that informational advisories that indicate a program contains violence may repel or attract viewers. Further, whether an advisory is prohibitive and age based or descriptive and informative, the latter may still be interpreted as an attempt to control content and lead to reactance. Research has shown that gender may also play a role in reactance. Morkes, Chen, and D. F. Roberts (1997) found that boys between 10 and 14 were more likely to find programing attractive in direct relation to the severity of the rating, whereas girls tended to use ratings information to avoid violent content.

The feedback from parents using informational systems has been relatively positive, with their use of television ratings as a guide to their child's viewing increasing from one third to two fifths of the population between 1997 and 1999 (Chen, 1999) in response to the use of more information in ratings systems. Research conducted in 1992 into parents' attitudes toward ratings information by the ABA and OFLC in Australia reiterates the importance of information-based systems. Similarly, in the United States, the revised television parental guidelines added content information to age-based evaluative ratings to be used in conjunction with the V-chip. However, in both cases, the adjustments have been made in direct response to concerns about parents' ability to make informed viewing choices for their children. Several studies have shown that children and adolescents also use ratings to make program choices (Cantor & K. Harrison, 1996; Chen, 1999; Kunkel, 1997; Morkes et al., 1997). Whereas evaluative age-based ratings are likely to engender a reactance effect making programs appear to be forbidden fruit, information systems (especially when used with parental locking devices such as the V-chip) may also provoke some reactance. Nonetheless, informational nonjudgmental content-based advisories seem to be less likely to provoke reactance from children and should give parents the opportunity to discuss content issues with their children (Roberts, 1998).

PUBLIC OPINION ABOUT RATINGS AND CONTROL

The debate about censorship and regulation of the media has been a long-standing one, particularly in the United States. Davison (1983) suggested that there is a tendency to attribute greater media effects on others than on themselves. He referred to this perception as the "third person effect," arguing that it might play a role in policy decisions, with some people endorsing lighter regulation of broadcasting content based on their belief that other people are more susceptible to harmful media effects than themselves.

Studies have looked at a variety of variables that might account for this phenomenon. Social structural factors such as age (Perloff, 1996) have been shown to be a predictor of the third person effect, whereby people believe that life experience provides them with more information and knowledge than it does young people. Other predictors of the third person effect (e.g., education, gender, number of children, and media use) have been examined. One investigation found that women perceived greater effects of television on others than they did on themselves and were more concerned about television violence than men (Moore & Saad, 1993). Lasorsa (1989) predicted that if people believe they have political knowledge, even if that is only a perception, then the third person effect is fueled.

Support for policies recommending the censorship of both violent and sexual content are often grounded in people's concerns about adverse effects on others (Fisher et al., 1994). Gunther (1995) found that willingness to censor material is motivated by a desire to protect society from the adverse effects of media content on other people. The third person effect has been linked to a greater willingness to support restrictions on television violence and pornography (Rojas et al., 1996). The question arises here as to whether policymaking is based on the wrong kind of perceptions that derive from personal prejudices and beliefs.

Research has shown that certain groups such as women, the elderly, and religious groups are especially likely to support censorship of violent television more than others on the basis that it is harmful to society (Fisher et al., 1994; Gunther, 1995; Rojas et al., 1996). Clearly, people from different backgrounds or different geographical locations may have different views on media violence and censorship. As lobbying for greater regulation and censorship necessarily poses a challenge to freedom of speech, it is vital that it is not based on false or unrepresentative perceptions or on bogus pseudo-scientific claims.

THE EFFECTS DEBATE AND VIOLENCE CLASSIFICATION

The debate about the effects of television violence has reached different points in the United States and Europe. Researchers in the United States, in particular, have claimed that the debate is closed given their belief that they have proven that a causal link exists between violence on television and viewer reaction. Their claim that television violence leads to desensitization, imitation, and fear has been broadly accepted in the United States and underpins both public policy and public debate about the problems of violence on television. However, the question about effects of television violence has been further complicated by new emphasis on the importance of context. This new focus gives rise to a whole new raft of uncertainties about the way audiences respond to violence on the screen and should be taken into account when discussing issues of censorship, warnings, advisories, and content ratings.

Consideration of research literature that analyzes television violence elicits widely varying research findings and thinking. Potter (1999) pointed out that there is a great deal of disagreement on basic definitional issues, such as the way in which violence should be defined, what constitutes an effect resulting from exposure to screen violence, and what factors lead to which effects. Potter argued that policymakers need help and information in order to understand how best to program the V-chip and to provide effective guidance for parents about how to control and improve the viewing experience of their children. In order to generate confident conclusions that are useful to policymakers, many areas of violence scholarship need to be reconceptualized. Two areas that have elicited a challenging new approach to this understanding of screen violence are the importance of context and the levels of analysis used by media scholars when monitoring violent output from television.

Few systematic attempts were made to analyze the context in which television violence takes place until the mid-1980s, but by the mid-1990s many studies recognized the importance of the characteristics of screen violence in addition to the frequency of violent incidents shown (see Potter, 1999). Contextual characteristics are those used by viewers to construct meaning when watching screen violence, although there is still a good deal of doubt about how the contextual information they see is actually processed. Some writers have drawn on schema theory that helps to explain how templates are used to guide perceptions. Fiske and S. E. Taylor (1991, p. 139) referred to interpretative schemas as "people's cognitive structures that represent knowledge about a concept or type of stimulus including its attributes and the relationship among the attributes." Researchers are showing greater interest in making an attempt to understand which forms of contextual characteristics have the most effect on viewers and the "script" used by viewers to understand television programs. Potter (1999, p. 85) referred to scripts as "patterns of contextual information." When viewers see contextual characteristics in a television program, their personal mental script is accessed to help them interpret the information cued by those characteristics. However, each individual viewer will have a different script or schema, resulting in different perceptions of the images viewed. Consequently, interest in the contextual characteristics of television narratives is an attempt to understand the complex nature of television viewing and through this, to try to identify which contextual elements in a violent program are likely to have the most negative effects on viewers.

Potter (1999) examined 7 contextual cues in some detail, but argued that these could be extended to over 40 characteristics that may affect viewing in some way. An important contextual factor is the extent of reward or punishment shown in relation to violent activity (see Bandura, 1973). The consequences of violence are another important factor. Mees (1990) identified three types of harm: distress, legal harm, and moral guilt. Other empirical studies have indicated that reinforcement of violence on the screen can lead to a disinhibition effect (Bandura, 1965; Bandura, D. Ross, & S. A. Ross, 1963a; Rosekrans & Hartup, 1967).

In contrast, studies have shown that if violence is punished, the aggression of viewers may be inhibited (Comstock, Chaffee, Katzman, McCombs, & D. Roberts, 1978). When there is no observable negative consequence from a violent act the viewers are not likely to feel inhibited in responding to the violence aggressively (Berkowitz & Rawlings, 1963), whereas a victim who shows pain has been shown to cause inhibition in viewers (Swart & Berkowitz, 1976). A further contextual cue that affects how viewers interpret screen violence is one of motive. Mees (1990) showed that viewers consider characters' motives in terms of moral culpability, or whether the violence enacted is offensive or defensive (Potter, 1999). Linked to the motives and values of the perpetrator and the victim is the degree of justification a viewer will feel for the violence they enact. Retaliation for a violent act appears to be a motive that is most justifiable to viewers, but is consequently more likely to lead to disinhibition. However, viewers' interpretation of justification may also be linked to the idea of reward (Potter, 1999).

The realism of the violent portrayal is an important contextual cue. Viewers are more likely to identify with a perpetrator or victim when the character has similar traits to the viewer or when portrayals seem to be true to life or are similar to their own environment (Gunter, 1985). Consequently, the setting of the violence, the historical period in which it takes place and the geographical location in which it takes place, can all provide narratives that cue viewers about the reality of the violent portrayal (Gunter & J. Harrison, 1998). Children have differing responses to the realistic nature of violence. As children develop cognitively, they are better able to evaluate whether the screen violence is occurring in a realistic or unrealistic setting. Children as young as age 3 to 5 are able to understand that cartoon violence is not realistic violence (Potter, 1999). Once children are able to make a distinction between realistic and fantasy violence, their responses to violence will change.

Another important contextual characteristic is the level of identification a viewer has with the characters involved in violence. Liss et al. (1983) showed that children are likely to identify with superheroes. In general, most viewers will, from time to time, identify with certain characteristics of screen characters. The attractiveness of the character's appearance (Hoffner & Cantor, 1985) and the perceived similarity to the viewer (Potter, 1999) are likely to influence viewer reaction. However, viewer identification with characters is extremely subjective, with different viewers identifying with different characters.

Finally, the use of humor in portrayals of television violence has been found to be problematic because it can lower viewer inhibition. Furthermore trivialization of violence through humor may make imitation of the violence easier and more attractive. Bandura (1973) argued that easily imitated acts of violence are more likely to be copied by viewers than violence that is more difficult to emulate. However, judgment about what is humorous can vary because each individual may have a different perspective and approach to humor (Potter, 1999).

CONTEXTUAL FEATURES AND VIOLENCE CLASSIFICATION

Although scholars have identified a variety of contextual factors that gain viewer attention (see *National Television Violence Study*, 1997, 1998; Potter, 1999; Potter & S. L. Smith, 1999; D. R. Roberts, 1998), there is still uncertainty about how many contextual cues exist and how they work in combination. Furthermore, there is a need to consider which ones are dominant or whether some cancel others out. Potter (1999) pointed out that it is vital to study the way in which viewers' interpretative schemas are constructed in order to understand how the cues inter-relate and how they lead to effects.

At the time the research reported in this book was being carried out, the National Television Violence Study (NTVS) was being conducted in the United States. Its aim was to assess violence on television by taking "a public health approach to the issue, treating violence as a partially preventable social ill" (National Television Violence Study, 1997, p. 1). Researchers took the view that the report should aim to encourage more responsible television viewing. In addition to a large-scale analysis of the representation of violence on television, this study also considered whether violence ratings and advisories could alter viewer choices in programing and how antiviolence messages in programing can best be portrayed.

Prior to its analysis of violence in television output, however, the study reviewed research literature on the effects of media violence. In so doing, its researchers identified three broad categories of effect on the viewer: desensitization, (see, e.g., Cline et al., 1973; D. G. Linz, Donnerstein, & Penrod, 1988), imitation (see Bandura, 1965), and fear (see Cantor, 1994; Gerbner, Gross, Morgan, & Signorielli, 1994). In relation to each of these effects, it was possible to identify specific features within violent portrayals that had been found to act as mediating variables that could facilitate certain types of audience response. These format and context features were then offered as a preliminary blueprint for a taxonomy to classify violent portrayals on television (*National Television Violence Study*, 1997). The British study has been mindful of these distinctions between violent portrayals in its interpretation of program output (see also Gunter & J. Harrison, 1998).

Given that in the United States the effects of television violence on viewers appears to be extant and well known, researchers have moved on to develop new and more interesting research. New research has concentrated on the identification of contextual factors within media content that appear to make a difference to audience responses. Furthermore, the NTVS recognized that not all violent portrayals are equal in regard to the risk they pose to viewers. Consequently, the same portrayal of violence may elicit different effects on different audiences, causing fear in some but aggression in others. For example, a documentary or factual program may contain violent scenes, but the message of the program is likely to be different from an action program that may glamorize violence. The NTVS draws on academic research, recognizing that contextual cues influence audience reactions to a violent portrayal (Bandura, 1986).

Dissatisfaction with existing analyses of the way in which context might influence audience response led the NTVS team to conduct their own exhaustive review of the literature. Their analysis led them to develop a set of contextual factors that they assessed as being those that influence audience reactions to violence on television. They identified nine factors: the nature of the perpetrator, the nature of the target, the reason for the violence, the presence of weapons, the extent and graphicness of the violence, the degree of realism of the violence, whether the violence is rewarded or punished; the consequences of violence and whether humor is involved in the violence (see *National Television Violence Study*, 1997, pp. 20–21). The study concluded that each identified factor either increased or decreased the probability that a violent portrayal is a risk to viewers either in relation to the likelihood of learning from the act (imitation), desensitization, or fear responses (D. R. Roberts, 1998).

Different studies of television violence have looked at different narrative levels (see Potter & S. L. Smith, 1999) in order to see how important contextual cues are portrayed across the different narrative levels. They identify the three levels as the microlevel, which concentrates on the brief incidents of violence; larger narrative units, or sequences, in which more than one violent act occurs; and the macrolevel, or entire program. Contextual information can be examined at each level in order to obtain a clearer picture about the portrayal of violence in the program. The narrative structure of a program is important in relation to the effects identified in academic studies.

Potter and S. L. Smith (1999) used NTVS data that considered violence at three narrative levels—the program, the scene, and the act—to compare the contextual cues at the macrolevel with those at the microlevel.

They compared two contextual cues: harm to the victim and punishment to perpetrators. They argued that when the two sets of contextual cues match on certain contextual characteristics, then there is a consistent pattern of context across levels. Consistency across levels of narrative in a program is likely to reinforce viewer interpretations. Conversely, where there is inconsistency across levels, child viewers are likely to become confused. For example, perpetrators who commit several violent acts in which they are unpunished may, to a child, seem to tell the whole story, even if the perpetrator is punished at the end of the program by being sent to jail. In other words, the perpetrator is only punished at one level and a young child is unlikely to be able to make the connection between the micro- and macrolevels of the narrative structure (see Collins, 1983; Collins & Wellman, 1982).

Perplexing as this might be to some viewers, Potter and S. L. Smith (1999) found that there is more consistency than inconsistency across the different levels. Always this may avoid confusing young people, the message that was consistently portrayed was that violence is frequently unpunished and socially acceptable. This message is reinforced across the narrative cues. This may be problematic. Social cognitive theory indicates that individuals are more likely to imitate behavior seen on screen when those behaviors are either rewarded or not punished (Bandura, 1994).

Potter and S. L. Smith (1999) argued that consistency across narrative cues results in a higher likelihood that viewers will construct the same meaning from the violence in the program. For example, the violence may have a pro-social tone where it is seen to be wrong and is punished. In contrast, the perpetrators may be free from punishment or even rewarded. In the latter case, the message is that consistent violence will eventually lead to a positive outcome. Potter and Smith found that the contextual cue on harm and pain to victims reinforced in viewers the idea that violence is bad and will harm a victim. In contrast, on punishment to the perpetrators, the message was that violence is condoned and generally free from punishment. Consequently, there is inconsistency across narrative levels for different contextual cues.

The finding of lack of punishment to perpetrators led Potter and S. L. Smith (1999) to reevaluate the previous defenses of television violence, particularly in children's programs. They contested the claim by some program makers that the message of television is a pro-social one whereby perpetrators are punished. They argued that because many analyses of violence have often concentrated on one, or at most two, of the narrative levels of violence, the results are open to question. As violence often goes unpunished, and there is sometimes a decoupling of narrative levels, violence shown in programs that claim to have a pro-social agenda may still lead to disinhibition.

Potter and Smith's finding reinforces D. R. Roberts' (1998) analysis of NTVS data whereby violence in entertainment programs often goes unpunished. Roberts considered further contextual cues in relation to the different messages across different narrative levels, finding that violence in entertainment programs seldom results in pain or consequences and is often humorous. Roberts showed that the way these contextual cues are presented is likely to increase the possibility of viewers learning to be more aggressive, fearful, or desensitized. He also concluded that the contextual factors inherent in much of American television programing are precisely those that increase the likelihood of negative consequences among young viewers, and argued that the NTVS results show how not to produce programing for children.

Drawing on his concerns about the importance of the role of contextual cues in eliciting a response from viewers, Roberts adapted five contextual factors from the NTVS to draw up an advisory system for computer games. He was asked for help by the Software Publishers Association and developed an informative ratings system for the Recreational Software Advisory Committee (RSAC). Roberts identified particular contextual cues as important: namely, the nature of the target (victim), the stance of the target (threatening or nonthreatening), the consequence to the victim, depiction of gore and blood, and the consequence to the player (i.e., whether the player is rewarded or not rewarded for aggressive behavior). Roberts argued that these types of contextual cues could be used in a television rating system for the V-chip. He purported that the information provided would be relatively detailed and relevant, but would still be simple enough for both labelers and parents to use. The key to making the system work would be to have program makers rate their own program subject to a questionnaire, which is open to public scrutiny. If this method were to be adopted, then it would have an advantage over the existing industry-based voluntary code, because it would place decision-making power back into the hands of parents, who would have sufficient information to make an informed decision specific to the needs of their own child (D. R. Roberts, 1998). In addition, such a method presumes children are different from each other and allows parents to judge their capabilities and, finally, there would be consistency across labeling. Labeling would be objective and open to public scrutiny.

VIOLENCE ON BRITISH TV: ANY CAUSES FOR CONCERN?

The research reported here deployed a number of measures of televised violence. Clearly, it is possible to place varied interpretations on how much violence British television contains. Overall statistics can give an impression of large quantities of violence that permeates most parts of the mainstream television schedules. However, it is equally valid to emphasize the finding that small numbers of programs account for significant proportions of violent portrayals and most programs with violence contain only small amounts. One of the most important points to be made in this book, and increasingly by other researchers who have studied the representation of violence on television, is that it is essential to examine the nature, form, and context of violent portrayals. This type of analysis is especially crucial when wishing to draw certain policy or regulatory conclusions from research of this kind.

The *National Television Violence Study* (1997) drew on research recognizing that contextual cues influence audience reactions to a violent portrayal. The study developed a set of contextual factors that they assessed as being the ones that influence audience reactions to violence on television. These were outlined as having a predicted impact on three outcomes of exposure to media violence: learning aggression, fear, and desensitization.

The nature of perpetrator and the level of viewer identification with that character are important factors in predicting outcomes of exposure to media violence. Work by D. G. Perry and L.C. Perry (1976), for example, showed that male undergraduates who identified with the victor of a filmed prizefight were subsequently more aggressive than those who imagined they were the loser. Further research showed that viewer identification with the hero may increase aggressive behavior (Leyens & Picus, 1973; Turner & Berkowitz, 1972). Identification with a character may also be encouraged when the character is perceived to have attributes in common with viewers themselves. This perception may be in relation to characteristics such as sex and age (Jose & Brewer, 1984). For example, Hicks (1965) found that children are more likely to engage in aggression after watching a violent child on the screen than by watching an adult being violent. The *National Television Violence Study* (1997) considered that the nature of the aggressor is important in relation to imitation and learning aggressive behavior.

The studies conducted by the University of Sheffield found that the characters most likely to be aggressors predominantly were solus males. In the 1994–1995 study, solus male aggressors accounted for 62.3% of the aggressors and in 1995–1996 they accounted for 65% of the total aggressors. Men acting in groups as aggressors accounted for a further 14.5% and 11.8% respectfully. This may prove problematic in relation to viewer identification, particularly if young males overempathize with the most common perpetrator of violence on television.

The nature of the victim or target is also important in relation to viewers' response to the violent act. Again viewers react to perceived similarities in characteristics and to the heroic status of the television character. However, in contrast to viewer responses to aggressors, the *National Television Violence Study* (1997) considered that similarity of the victim to oneself is more likely to stimulate a fear response rather than imitation or learning of aggression. Here, the concern is that victimization may convey a particular message to the viewer about who has the most power and control in the world of television and stimulate concerns about who may be at greatest risk in the real world (Gunter & J. Harrison, 1998). The studies conducted in Britain, however, showed that the characters most likely to be involved as victims of violence were again solus males. In the 1994–1995 study, solus male victims accounted for 60.1% of the aggressors and in 1995–1996 they accounted for 62% of the total aggressors. Men being victimized in groups accounted for a further 11.9% and 11.1% respectfully. Clearly, women were not victimized in screen portrayals of violence and do not seem to be portrayed as being particularly vulnerable (Gunter & J. Harrison, 1998).

The age of the victim is also significant, because the majority of the victims were young or middle-aged adults. Thus, vulnerable groups such as children, teenagers, or the elderly were not portrayed predominantly as victims of violence. This finding is significant because it reduces the risk of a fear response to the majority of screen violence from those vulnerable groups.

The goal or motivation for the violence is an important contextual cue in relation to influencing a viewer's likelihood of learning or imitating aggression. The *National Television Violence Study* considered that violence portrayed as being justified has been shown to encourage viewers to behave more aggressively than those who saw less justified violence (see, e.g., Hoyt, 1970), whereas unjustified violence reduced the aggressive response from viewers compared to a control group who had no information about the motive (see, e.g., Geen, 1981). However, the *National Television Violence Study* (1997) indicated that it is possible that unjustified violence may be more frightening to viewers than legitimate or altruistic violence, stimulating a fear response. The content analyses conducted on British television indicated that the majority of violence shown on television during the period analyzed was unjustified. In 1994–1995, 43% of the violence shown was unjustified and in 1995–1996, 42% of the violence was coded as being unjustified. In contrast, 34% and 31% of the violence was seen to be justified in 1994–1995 and 1995–1996 respectfully (Gunter & J. Harrison, 1998; see also chap. 5).

The presence of weapons is of concern to researchers. In particular, weapons such as knives are more likely to stimulate aggression in viewers because they are conventional weapons. It is possible that the viewer may have stored the use of knives as a violent image in their memory and violence using such a familiar and traditional weapon may have a so-called weapons effect on audiences (*National Television Violence Study*, 1997, p. 26). However, the studies conducted in Britain showed that in 1994–1995 only 2% of all violent acts coded involved some form of stabbing. In 1995–1996, this figure fell to 1% of all violent acts. In 1994–1995, only 1% of violent acts involved cutting of the victim and in 1995–1996 this fell to just 0.3% of all violent acts shown. Consequently, usage of weapons such as knives, which might raise concern in relation to stimulating aggression in viewers, is rare in television portrayals of violence. In both the 1994–1995 and the 1995–1996 studies, only 2% of violent acts involved the use of a dagger or knife (Gunter & Harrison, 1998; see also chap. 4).

The extent and graphicness of the violence may influence audiences by provoking all three outcomes to exposure to media violence indicated in the *National Television Violence Study*: learning aggression, fear, and desensitization. Concern has been raised about the impact of repeated violence or extensive portrayals of violence on viewer desensitization. The *National Television Violence Study* (1997) considered evidence that exposure to extensive scenes of violence, within a single program or across numerous programs, results in decreased arousal and sensitivity to violent scenes. This desensitization effect occurs in both children and adults and may result in heightened aggression. However, the *National Television Violence Study* (1997) also pointed out that exposure to very graphic and extensive scenes of violence may also stimulate a fear response. The extent to which prolonged and graphic violence may stimulate a fear response, aggression, or a desensitization response is still uncertain and requires further research.

Evaluations of the graphicness of portrayals of television violence on British television showed that very offensive or potentially distressing scenes of violence were very rare. A measure of the magnitude of pain suffered by the victims, the degree of bloodshed, and the horrific nature of the programs showed that viewers were given few opportunities to witness violent acts that showed extreme pain, bloodshed, and horror. In 1994–1995, only 41 programs were found to contain at least one violent act coded as showing extreme suffering on the part of a victim. Twenty-two programs contained at least one act with a lot of bloodshed and 39 programs contained at least one act thought to be really horrific in nature. In 1995–1996, 44 programs contained depictions of extreme suffering, only 6 programs showed a lot of bloodshed, and 46 programs contained one act thought to be really horrific. Throughout the studies, only a very small number of programs showed three or more such acts and these depictions of violence were generally found in movies that were broadcast late at night. So viewers of British television are rarely exposed to the type of realistic violence that is most likely to stimulate aggression, desensitization, or a fear response.

The realism of screen violence may be problematic, for both adult and child viewers, both in relation to encouragement of an aggressive response and in relation to a viewer's fear reaction. The *National Television Violence Study* (1997) discussed studies showing that adult viewers are more emotionally aroused by realistic violence scenes, namely, those that appear to have actually happened, than if the scenes are perceived as fictional (e.g., see Geen, 1975). Comparison of reaction to animated and human violence led Hapkiewicz and Stone (1974) to conclude that the human or realistic violence led to more aggressive behavior than animated violence. Realistic violence may also frighten children more than animated or fantasy violence, particularly in relation to older children. However, very young children may perceive cartoons and fantasy programs to be realistic.

Clearly, the genre in which the violence is portrayed is an important variable affecting the way that viewers respond to violence and is linked to distinctions viewers can make between realistic and unrealistic violence (Gunter & J. Harrison, 1998). In studies of British television between 1994 and 1996, violence was found to occur mainly in fictional drama programs, with only 8% of all violent acts occurring in factual programs in 1994–1995; this figure fell to 2.1% in 1995–1996. These results indicate that violence in highly realistic settings that are known to cause viewers greater concern occurs rarely on British television.

The types of contextual cues identified by the *National Television Violence Study* (1997, 1998) that might have consequences for viewer response to violence (i.e., learning aggression, fear, and desensitization) raise some concern in relation to British television programing. However, comparison of the British data with the contextual cues to which audiences may respond indicates that audiences in Britain are not overly exposed to the type of violence that might provoke a problematic response from viewers. Analysis of the rather descriptive data elicited from a study of television output has been used here to consider more closely the effects that viewing experiences in Britain might have on viewers' attitudes and behaviors. This closer analysis of television output data and the potential response from viewers has allowed for a fuller understanding of the likelihood of viewer's reactions to British television output and the appropriateness of classification methods of violent television content. Such an understanding enables further interpretations of the way in which television content analysis data can be used in informing future policy decisions relating to regulation of television output.

CONCLUSIONS

Debates about provision of information to parents in the form of warnings, advisories, ratings, or electronic program guides have reached different levels in Australia, Europe, and the United States. In the United States, the policy debate about television violence is grounded in the assumption that it does have an effect on viewers. This position has encouraged strong endorsement of using technology to facilitate greater parental control of children's viewing via the mandatory installation of a V-chip in new television sets. It has also led to calls for an amended industry program ratings code to provide parents with better age-related guidance and higher quality information about the content of programs. The debate about the usefulness of the information ratings continues.

In Europe, the changing broadcasting environment has brought with it new types of technological distribution through cable, satellite, and digital technologies. Regulation of spectrum scarcity in the European context is becoming unfeasible. In Europe, satellite technology has encouraged cross-frontier broadcasting, which has brought with it issues of jurisdiction and censorship, and highlighted the problems of trying to achieve standardization across a multicultural environment. Consequently, in Europe, discussion about the V-chip and the consequent program rating guide has been postponed until digital distribution is complete. It is unlikely that the blocking of broadcast material via the V-chip will be permitted in Europe because it is seen to infringe on the principles of freedom of expression and the idea of a single European market. Interim measures are being taken to try to improve parental information about programs. In Australia, the debate about the inadequacies of age-rated guidance for parental choice is well developed, and an information-based rating system has been adopted. In Europe, the United States, and Australia, the idea of a watershed, or safe harbor, to protect children has also been widely adopted.

Although regulatory measures have been adopted to different extents in different parts of the world, the debate about the usefulness of information provided for parents in advisories and ratings has been questioned. Consequently, the assumption by some researchers in the United States that the effects of television violence have been established must now be reconsidered by the growing emphasis on the importance of context. Researchers have shown that certain contextual characteristics (e.g., harm to the victim, punishment, justification of violence, motives, realism, identification with characters, and the use of humor in violent portrayals) elicit different responses from viewers. The complexity of the interrelations between the different contextual cues, their number, which ones are most important, and the reaction of different viewers to different cues throws into question the feasibility of consistent regulation for violent content. The range of uncertainties raised means that a good deal more research is needed in order to provide practical empirical evidence to policymakers in order to prevent draconian regulation that is both ineffective and unnecessary. Researchers have already shown that age-based advisories can have the effect of turning programs into forbidden fruit for younger viewers, especially young male viewers. Furthermore, as D. R. Roberts (1998) pointed out, the different narrative levels inherent in a violence-containing program mean that programers who claim to produce programs of a pro-social nature for children may in effect be perpetuating very negative messages. A good deal of public debate about the dangers of television violence is elicited from third person effects, which it would indicate that consideration of policy and regulation needs to be reevaluated to take into consideration further empirical evidence.

Bibliography

Adler, F. (Ed.) (1981). *The incidence of female criminality in the contemporary world*. New York: NYUP.

Allen, J., Livingstone, S., & Reiner, R. (1997). The changing generic locations of crime in film: A content analysis of film synopses, 1945–1991. *Journal of Communication, 47*(4), 89–101.

Allen, R. C. (1985). *Speaking of soap operas*. Chapel Hill: University of North Carolina Press.

Aluja-Fabregat, A., & Torrubia-Beltri, R. (1998). Viewing of mass media violence, perception of violence, personality and academic achievement. *Personality and Individual Differences, 25*, 973–989.

Archer, J., Kilpatrick, G., & Bramwell, G. (1995). Comparison of two aggression inventories. *Aggressive Behavior, 21*, 325–342.

Archer, J., & Parker, S. (1994). Social representations of aggression in children. *Aggressive Behavior, 2*, 101–114.

Atkin, C., Greenberg, B. S., Korzenny, F., & McDermott, S. (1979). Selective exposure to televised violence. *Journal of Broadcasting, 23*, 5–13.

Bailey, S. (1993). Fast forward to justice: Violent visual imaging and serious juvenile crime. *Criminal Justice Matters, 11*, 6–7.

Baldwin, T. F., & Lewis, C. (1972). Violence in television: The industry looks at itself. In G. A. Comstock & E. A. Rubinstein (Eds.), *Television and social behavior: Reports and papers: Vol. 1: Media content and control* (pp. 290–373). Washington, DC: U.S. Government Printing Office.

Ball-Rokeach, S. J. (1972). The legitimation of violence. In J. F. Short, Jr. & M. E. Wolfgang (Eds.), *Collective Violence* (pp. 100–111). Chicago: Aldine-Atherton.

Bandura, A. (1973). *Aggression: A social learning analysis*. Englewood Cliffs, NJ: Prentice-Hall.

Bandura, A. (1986). *Social foundations of thought and action: A social cognitive theory*. Englewood Cliffs, NJ: Prentice-Hall.

Bandura, A. (1994). Social cognitive theory of mass communication. In J. Bryant & D. Zillmann (Eds.), *Media effects* (pp. 61–90). Hillsdale, NJ: Lawrence Erlbaum Associates.

Bandura, A., Ross, D., & Ross, S. A. (1963a). A comparative test of the status envy, social power and secondary reinforcement theories of identificatory learning. *Journal of Abnormal and Social Psychology, 67,* 527–534.

Bandura, A., Ross, D., & Ross, S. A. (1963b). Imitation of film–mediated aggressive models. *Journal of Abnormal and Social Psychology, 66,* 31–41.

Bandura, A., & Walters, R. H. (1963). *Social learning and personality development.* New York: Holt, Rinehart & Winston.

Barker, M., & Petley, J. (Eds.) (1997). *Ill effects: The media/violence debate.* London: Routledge.

Baron, R. A. (1971a). Aggression as a function of magnitude of victim's pain cues, level of prior anger arousal, and aggressor-victim similarity. *Journal of Personality and Social Psychology, 18,* 48–54.

Baron, R. A. (1971b). Magnitude of victim's pain cues and level of prior anger arousal as determinants of adult aggressive behaviour. *Journal of Personality and Social Psychology, 17,* 236–243.

Baxter, R. L., Piemer, C. D., Landini, A., Leslie, L., & Singletary, M. W. (1985). A content analysis of music videos. *Journal of Broadcasting & Electronic Media, 29,* 333–340.

BBC. (1996). *Producers' guidelines.* London: BBC.

BBC Training Video. (1993). "Violence in the news." Presented by Peter Sissens, London, BBC.

Bechtel, R. B., Achelpohl, C., & Akers, R. (1972). Correlates between observed behaviors and questionnaire responses on television viewing. In E. A. Rubinstein, G. A. Comstock, & J. P. Murray (Eds.), *Television and social behavior: Vol. 4. Television in day-to-day life: Patterns of use* (pp. 274–344). Washington, DC: U.S. Government Printing Office.

Bell, A. (1991). *The language of news media.* Oxford: Basil Blackwell.

Benthall, J. (1993). *Disasters, relief and the media.* London: Tauris.

Berkowitz, L. (1970). Aggressive humour as a stimulus to aggressive responses. *Journal of Personality and Social Psychology, 16,* 710–717.

Berkowitz, L. (1971). The "weapons effect," demand characteristics and the myth of the compliant subject. *Journal of Personality and Social Psychology, 20,* 332–338.

Berkowitz, L. (1984). Some effects of thoughts on anti- and prosocial influences of media events: A cognitive-neoassociation analysis. *Psychological Bulletin, 95,* 410–427.

Berkowitz, L. (1990). On the formation and regulation of anger and aggression: A cognitive neoassociationistic analysis. *American Psychologist, 45*(4), 494–503.

Berkowitz, L. (1993). *Aggression: Its causes, consequences, and control.* Philadelphia: Temple University Press.

Berkowitz, L. (1994). Is something missing? Some observations prompted by the cognitive-associationist view of anger and emotional aggression. In L. R. Huesmann (Ed.), *Aggressive behavior: Current perspectives* (pp. 35–57). New York: Plenum.

Berkowitz, L., & Alioto, J. T. (1973). The meaning of an observed event as a determinant of its aggressive consequences. *Journal of Personality and Social Psychology, 28,* 206–217.

Berkowitz, L., & LePage, A. (1967). Weapons as aggression-eliciting stimuli. *Journal of Personality and Social Psychology, 7,* 202–207.

Berkowitz, L., & Rawlings, E. (1963). Effects of film violence on inhibitions against subsequent aggression. *Journal of Abnormal and Social Psychology, 66*(3), 405–412.

Berkowitz, L., & Rogers, K. H. (1986). A priming effect analysis of media influences. In J. Bryant & D. Zillmann (Eds.), *Perspectives on media effects* (pp. 57–82). Hillsdale, NJ: Lawrence Erlbaum Associates.

Berry, C., & Clifford, B. (1985). *Learning from television news: Effects of presentation factors and knowledge on comprehension and memory.* Research Report. London: North East London Polytechnic and Independent Broadcasting Authority.

Beville, H. M. (1940). The ABCD's of radio audiences. *Public Opinion Quarterly, 4,* 195–206.

Bjorkqvist, K. (1994). Sex differences in physical, verbal, and indirect aggression: A review of recent research. *Sex Roles, 30*(3/4), 177–188.

Bjorkqvist, K., & Niemela, P. (1992.). New trends in the study of female aggression. In K. Bjorkqvist & P. Niemela (Eds.), *Of mice and women: Aspects of female aggression.* San Diego, CA: Academic Press.

Bjorkqvist, K., Osterman, K., & Lagerspetz, K. M. (1994). Sex differences in covert aggression among adults. *Aggressive Behavior, 20,* 27–33.

Bureau of Justice Statistics. (1994). Violence against women: A national crime victimization survey report. Retrieved from http://wwwsilcom.com/~paladin/madv/stats.html

Blank, D. M. (1977a). Final comments on the violence profile. *Journal of Broadcasting, 21*(4), 287–296.

Blank, D. M. (1977b). The Gerbner violence profile. *Journal of Broadcasting, 21*(4), 273–279.

Blumer, H. (1933). *Movies and conduct.* New York: Macmillan.

Blumenthal, R., Kahn, R., Andrews, F., & Head, K. (1972). *Justifying violence: Attitudes of American men.* Ann Arbor, MI: Survey Research Center, Institute for Social Research, University of Michigan.

Borduin, C. M., Mann, B. J., Cone, L. T., & Henggeler, S. W. (1995). Multisystematic treatment of serious juvenile offenders: Long-term prevention of criminality and violence. *Journal of Consulting and Clinical Psychology, 63,* 569–578.

Boyanowsky, E. O. (1977). Film preferences under condition of threat: Whetting the appetite for violence, information or excitement? *Communication Research, 4,* 133–144.

Boyanowsky, E. O., Newtson, D., & Walster, E. (1974). Film preferences following a murder. *Communication Research, 1,* 32–43.

Boyatzis, C. J., Matillo, G. M., & Nesbit, K. M. (1995). Effects of the Mighty Morphin Power Rangers on children's aggression with peers. *Child Study Journal, 25,* 45–55.

Brehm, J. W. (1966). *A theory of psychological reactance.* New York: Academic Press

Brehm, S. S., & Brehm, J. W. (1981). *Psychological reactance.* New York: Academic Press.

Broadcasting Standards Council. (1993). *Monitoring Report II.* London: Author.

Broverman, I. K., Vogel, S. R., Broverman, D. M., Clarkson, F. E., & Rosenkrantz, P. S. (1972). Sex-role stereotypes: A current appraisal. *Journal of Social Issues, 28*(2), 59–78.

Brown, J. D., & Campbell, K. (1986). Race and gender in music videos: The same beat but a different drummer. *Journal of Communication, 36*(1), 94–106.

Brown, R. C., Jr., & Tedeschi, J. T. (1976). Determinants of perceived aggression. *Journal of Social Psychology, 100,* 77–87.

Bryant, J., Carveth, R. A., & Brown, D. (1981). Television viewing and anxiety: An experimental examination. *Journal of Communication, 31*(1), 106–119.

Buckhart, K. (1973). *Women in prison.* New York: Doubleday.

Buckingham, D. (1993a). *Children talking television: The making of television literacy.* London: Falmer.

Buckingham, D.(1996). *Eastenders:* Creating the audience. In P. Marris & S. Thornham (Eds.), *Media studies: A reader* (pp. 355–361). Edinburgh, UK: Edinburgh University Press.

Buckingham, D. (1997). Electronic child abuse? Rethinking the media's effects on children. In M. Barker & J. Petley (Eds.). *Ill effects: The media/violence debate* (pp. 32–47). London: Routledge & Kegan Paul.

Buckingham, D. (2000). *After the death of childhood: Growing up in the age of electronic media.* Cambridge, UK: Polity Press.

Burbank, V. (1987). Female aggression in cross-cultural perspective. *Behaviour Science Research, 21,* 70–100.

Burns, T. (1969). Public service and private world. *The Sociological Review Monograph, 13,* 53–73.

Bushman, B. J., & Stack, A. D. (1996). Forbidden fruit versus tainted fruit: Effects of warning labels on attraction to television violence. *Journal of Experimental Psychology: Applied, 2*(3), 207–226.

Buss, A., Booker, A., & Buss, E. (1972). Firing a weapon and aggression. *Journal of Personality and Social Psychology, 22,* 296–302.

Buss, A. H., & Perry, M. (1992). The aggressive questionnaire. *Journal of Personality and Social Psychology, 63,* 452–459

Butler, M., & Paisley, W. (1980). *Women and the mass media.* New York: Human Sciences Press.

Cahoun, D. D., & Edmonds, E. M. (1984). Guns/no guns and the expression of social hostility. *Bulletin of the Psychonomic Society, 22,* 305–308.

Cahoun, D. D., & Edmonds, E. M. (1985). The weapons effect: Fact or artifact? *Bulletin of the Psychonomic Society, 23,* 57–60.

Campbell, A. (1995). A few good men: Evolutionary psychology and female adolescent aggression. *Ethology and Sociobiology, 16,* 99–123.

Campbell, A., & Muncer, S. (1987). Models of anger and aggression in the social talk of women and men. *Journal for the Theory of Social Behavior, 17,* 489–512.

Campbell, A., Muncer, S., & Coyle, E. (1992). Social representation of aggression as an explanation of gender differences: A preliminary study. *Aggressive Behavior, 18,* 95–108.

Campbell, A., Muncer, S., & Gorman, B. (1993). Sex and social representations of aggression: A communal-agentic analysis. *Aggressive Behavior, 19,* 125–135.

Cantor, J. (1994). Fright responses to media productions. In J. Bryant & D. Zillmann (Eds.), *Responding to the screen: Reception and reaction processes* (pp. 169–197). Hillsdale, NJ: Lawrence Erlbaum Associates.

Cantor, J. (1998). Children's attraction to violent television programming. In J. H. Goldstein (Ed.), *Why we watch: The attraction of violent entertainment* (pp. 88–115). New York: Oxford University Press.

Cantor, J., & Harrison, K. (1996). Ratings and advisories for television programming. In *National television violence study scientific papers 1994–1995* (III-1–III-50). Studio City, CA: Mediascope.

Cantor, J., & Nathanson, A. I. (1996). Children's fright reactions to TV news. *Journal of Communications, 46*(4), 139–152.

Cantos, A. L., Neidig, P. H., & O'Leary, K. D. (1994). Injuries of women and men in a treatment program for domestic violence. *Journal of Family Violence, 9*(2), 113–124.

Caplan, F., & Caplan, T. (1973). *The power of play.* New York: Anchor.

Caprara, G. V., Rentz, P., Amolini, P., D'Imperio, G., & Travaglia, G. (1984). The eliciting cue value of aggressive slides reconsidered in a personalogical perspective: The weapons effect and irritability. *European Journal of Social Psychology, 14,* 313–322.

Carlson, M., Marcus-Newhall, A., & Miller, N. (1990). Effects of situational aggression cues: A quantitative review. *Journal of Personality and Social Psychology, 58*(4), 622–633.

Carter, C. (1998). When the ordinary becomes extraordinary. In C. Carter, G. Branston, & S. (Eds.), *News, crime and gender* (pp. 219–232). London: Routledge & Kegan Paul.

Cassata, M., & Skill, T. (1983). *Life on daytime television: Tuning-in American serial drama.* Norwood, NJ: Ablex.

Center for Media and Public Affairs. (1994). *Violence in prime-time television.* Washington, DC: Author.

Chen, H. L. (1999, May). *Young adolescents' responses to evaluative and informational labelling systems for TV.* Paper presented at the International Communications Association Conference, San Francisco, CA.

Chibnall, S. (1977). *Law and order news.* London: Tavistock.

Cicone, M. V., & Ruble, D. N. (1978). Beliefs about males. *Journal of Social Issues, 34*(1), 5–16.

Clark, D. G., & Blankenberg, W. G. (1972). Trends in violent content in selected mass media. In G. A. Comstock & E. A. Rubinstein (Eds.), *Television and social behavior: Vol. 1, Media content and control* (pp. 188–243). Washington, DC: U.S. Government Printing Office.

Clifford, B. R., Gunter, B., & McAleer, J. (1995). *Program evaluation, comprehension and impact: Television and children.* Hillsdale, NJ: Lawrence Erlbaum Associates.

Cline, V. B., Croft, R. G., & Courrier, S. (1973). Desensitization of children to television violence. *Journal of Personality and Social Psychology, 27,* 260–265.

Clyde, R. W., & Buckalew, J. K. (1969). Inter-media standardisation: A Q-analysis of news editors. *Journalism Quarterly, 46,* 349–351.

Coffin, T. E., & Tuchman, S. (1972). Rating television programs for violence: A comparison of five surveys. *Journal of Broadcasting, 17*(1), 3–20.

Cohen, A. A., & Bantz, C. (1984, May). *Social conflicts in TV news: A five-nation comparative study.* Paper presented at the annual conference of the International Communication Association, San Francisco.

Cohen, A. A., Wigand, R. T., & Harrison, R. P. (1976). The effects of type of event, proximity and repetition on children's attention to and learning from television news. *Communication Research, 3,* 30–36.

Cohen, B. (1963). *The press and foreign policy.* Princeton, NJ: Princeton University Press.

Cole, J. (1995). *The UCLA television violence report.* Los Angeles: UCLA Center for Communication Policy.

Cole, J. (1996). *The UCLA television violence monitoring report.* Los Angeles: UCLA Center for Communication Policy.

Collins, W. A. (1973). Effect of temporal separation between motivation, aggression, and consequences: A developmental study. *Developmental Psychology, 8*(2), 215–221.

Collins, W. A. (1983). Interpretation and inference in children's television viewing. In J. Bryant & D. R. Anderson (Eds.), *Children's understanding of television: Research on attention and comprehension* (pp. 125–150). New York: Academic Press.

Collins, W. A., & Wellman, H. M. (1982). Social scripts and developmental patterns in comprehension of television narratives. *Communication Research, 9*, 380–398.

Commission of the European Communities. (1989). *Television without frontiers directive* (89/552/EEC).

Commission of the European Communities. (1994). *Europe and the global information society: Recommendations to the EC (the Bangemann report)*. Brussels: European Commission, May 24, 1995.

Commission of the European Communities. (1997). *Television without frontiers amending directive* (97/36/EC).

Commission of the European Communities. (1999). *Study on parental control of Television broadcasting communication* (COM[1999] 371—1999/2210[COS]).

Committee on the Judiciary. U.S. Senate. 102nd Congress. (1992, October). *Violence against women*.

Comstock, G., Chaffee, S., Katzman, N., McCombs, M., & Roberts, D. (1978). *Television and human behavior*. New York: Columbia University Press.

Comstock, G. A., & Strasburger, V. C. (1990). Deceptive appearances: Television violence and aggressive behaviour. *Journal of Adolescent Health Care, 11*(1), 31–44.

Condry, J. C., & Ross, D. F. (1985). Sex and aggression: The influence of gender label on the perception of aggression in children. *Child Development, 56*, 225–233.

Connell, R. (1987). *Gender and power*. Cambridge, UK: Polity Press.

Crick, N. R., & Grotpeter, J. K. (1995). Relational aggression, gender, and social-psychological adjustment. *Child Development, 66*, 710–722.

Cumberbatch, G. (1989). Violence and the mass media: The research evidence. In G. Cumberbatch & D. Howitt (Eds.), *A measure of uncertainty: The effects of the mass media* (pp.31–59). London: John Libbey.

Cumberbatch, G., Lee, M., Hardy, G., & Jones, I. (1987). *The portrayal of violence on British television: A content analysis*. A report for the British Broadcasting Corporation. Applied Psychology Division, Aston University.

Dahlgren, P. (1995). *Television and the public sphere*. London: Sage.

Danielson, W., Lasorsa, D., Wartella, E., Whitney, C., Campbell, S., Haddad, S., Klijn, M., Lopez, R., & Olivarez, A. (1996). Television violence in "reality" programming: University of Texas, Austin study. In *National Television Violence Study, scientific papers, 1994–1995* (pp. II-1–II-55). Los Angeles, CA: Mediascope.

Davison, W. P. (1983). The third person effect in communication. *Public Opinion Quarterly, 47*, 1–15.

Diener, E., & DeFour, D. (1978). Does television violence enhance program popularity? *Journal of Personality and Social Psychology, 36*, 333–341.

Diener, E., & Woody, L. W. (1981). TV violence and viewer liking. *Communication Research, 8*, 281–306.

Dobash, R., & Dobash, R. (1992). *Women, violence and social change*. London: Routledge & Kegan Paul.

Docherty, D. (1990). *Violence in television fiction*. London: John Libbey.

Dollard, J., Doob, L. W., Miller, N. E., Mowrer, O. H., & Sears, R. R. (1939). *Frustration and aggression*. New Haven, CT: Yale University Press.

Dominick, J. R. (1973). Crime and law enforcement in prime-time television. *Public Opinion Quarterly, 37*, 243–250

Donnerstein, E. (1980). Aggressive erotica and violence against women. *Journal of Personality and Social Psychology, 39*, 269–277.

Donnerstein, E. (1983). Erotica and human aggression. In R. Geen & E. Donnerstein (Eds.), *Aggression: Theoretical and empirical reviews*. New York: Academic Press.

Donnerstein, E., Slaby, R. G., & Eron, L. D. (1994). The mass media and youth aggression. In L. D. Eron, J. H. Gentry, & P. Schlegel (Eds.), *Reason to hope: A psychological perspective on violence and youth* (pp. 219–250). Washington, DC: American Psychological Association.

Dorr, A. (1983). No short cuts to judging reality. In J. Bryant & D. R. Anderson (Eds.), *Children's understanding of television: Research on attention and comprehension* (pp. 199–220). New York: Academic Press.

Drabman, R. S., & Thomas, M. H. (1974). Does media violence increase children's toleration of real-life aggression? *Developmental Psychology, 10*, 418–421.

Eagly, A. H., & Crowley, M. (1986). Gender and helping behaviour: A meta-analytic review of the social psychological literature. *Psychological Bulletin, 90*, 1–20.

Eagly, A. H., & Steffen, V. J. (1986). Gender and aggressive behaviour: A meta-analytic review of the social psychological literature. *Psychological Bulletin, 100*(3), 309–330.

Eleey, M. F., Gerbner, G., & Tedesco, N. (1972a). Apples, oranges, and the kitchen sink: An analysis and guide to the comparison of "violence ratings." *Journal of Broadcasting, 17*(1), 21–31.

Elkind, D. (1981). *The hurried child*. Menlo Park, CA: Addison-Wesley.

Ellis, D. P., Wienir, P., & Miller, L. (1971). Does the trigger pull the finger? *Sociometry, 34*, 453–465.

Epstein, E. J. (1973). *News from nowhere*. New York: Random House.

Erickson, E. H. (1977). *Toys and reasons*. New York: Norton.

Ericson, R., Baranek, P., & Chan, J. (1991). *Representing order*. Milton Keynes, UK: Open University Press.

Estep, R., & Macdonald, P. T. (1983). How prime time crime evolved on TV, 1976–1981. *Journalism Quarterly, 60*, 293–300.

Faludi, B. (1992). *Backlash: The undeclared war against women*. London: Chatto.

Fasteau, M. F. (1974). *The male machine*. New York: McGraw-Hill.

Federman, J. (Ed.). (1997). *National television violence study: Vol. 2. Executive summary*. Santa Barbara, CA: The Regents of the University of California.

Feshbach, S. (1972). Reality and fantasy in filmed violence. In J. P. Murray, E. A. Rubinstein, & G. A. Comstock (Eds.), *Television and social behaviour: Vol. 2. Television and social learning* (pp. 318–345). Washington, DC: U.S. Government Printing Office.

Feshbach, S., & Singer, R. D. (1971). *Television and aggression*. San Francisco: Jossey-Bass.

Finn, J. (1986). The relationship between sex role attitudes and attitudes supporting marital violence. *Sex Roles, 14*(5/6), 235–242.

Fisher, R. D., Cook, I. J., & Shirkey, E. C. (1994). Correlates of support for censorship of sexual, sexually violent, and violent media. *Journal of Sex Research, 31*(3), 229–240.

Fiske, J., & Taylor, S. E. (1991). *Social cognition*. New York: McGraw-Hill.

Forgas, J. P., Brown, L. B., & Menyhart, J. (1980). Dimensions of aggression: The perception of aggressive episodes. *British Journal of Social and Clinical Psychology, 19*, 215–227.

Foucault, M. (1975). *Discipline and punish*. London: Allen Lane.

Foucault, M. (1998). *The will to knowledge: The history of sexuality* (Vol. 1). Harmondsworth: Penguin.

Fowler, R. (1991), *Language in the news*. London: Routledge & Kegan Paul.

Freedman, J. L. (1984). Effect of television violence on aggressiveness. *Psychological Bulletin, 99*, 227–246.

French, J., & Pena, S. (1991). Children's hero play of the twentieth century: Changes resulting from television's influence. *Child Study Journal, 21*, 79–94.

French, J., Pena, S., & Homes, R. (1987). The superhero TV dilemma. *The Newsletter of Parenting, 10*(1), 8–9.

Friedman, H. L., & Johnson, R. L. (1972). Mass media use and aggression: A pilot study. In G. A. Comstock & E. A. Rubinstein (Eds.), *Television and social behavior: Vol. 3, Reports and papers* (pp. 336–360). Washington, DC: U.S. Government Printing Office.

Friedrich-Cofer, L., & Huston, A. C. (1986). Television violence and aggression: The debate continues. *Psychological Bulletin, 100*, 364–371.

Frodi, W. D., Macauley, J., & Thome, P. R. (1977). Are woman always less aggressive than men? A review of the experimental literature. *Psychological Bulletin, 84*, 634–660.

Furnham, A., & Gunter, B. (1985). Sex, presentation mode and memory for violent and non-violent news. *Journal of Educational Television, 11*, 99–105.

Galtung, J. (1975). Violence, peace, and peace research. In J. Galtung (Ed.), *Peace, research, education, action, essays in peace research* (Vol. 1, pp. 109–134). Copenhagen: Ejlers.

Galtung, J., & Ruge, M. (1965). The structure of foreign news. *Journal of Peace Research, 2*, 64–91.

Gamson, W. A., & McEvoy, J. (1972). Police violence and its public support. In J. F. Short & M. E. Wolfgang (Eds.), *Collective violence.* Chicago: Aldine.

Gauntlett, D. (1995). *Moving experiences: Understanding television's influences and effects.* London: John Libbey.

Geen, R. G. (1975). The meaning of observed violence: Real vs fictional violence and consequent effects on aggression. *Journal of Research in Personality, 9*, 270–281.

Geen, R. G. (1981). Behavioral and physiological reactions to observed violence: Effects of prior exposure to aggressive stimuli. *Journal of Personality and Social Psychology, 40*(5), 868–875.

Geen, R. G., & Thomas, S. L. (1986). The immediate effects of media violence on behavior. *Journal of Social Issues, 42*(3), 7–27.

Geraghty, C. (1981). The continuous serial: A definition. In P. Marris & S. Thornham (Eds.), *Media studies: A reader* (pp. 362–370). Edinburgh, UK: Edinburgh University Press.

Geraghty, C. (1991). *Women and soap operas.* Cambridge, UK: Polity Press

Gerbner, G. (1972). Violence in television drama: Trends and symbolic functions. In G. A. Comstock & E. A. Rubinstein (Eds.), *Television and social behavior: Vol. 1, Media content and control* (pp. 28–187). Washington, DC: U.S. Government Printing Office.

Gerbner, G. (1988). *Violence and terror in the mass media.* Reports and papers on mass communication, No. 102. Paris: UNESCO

Gerbner, G., & Gross, L. (1976). Living with television: The violence profile. *Journal of Communication, 26*(2), 171–180.

Gerbner, G., Gross, L., Jackson-Beeck, M., Jeffries-Foz, S., & Signorielli, N. (1977). Television violence profile No. 8: The highlights. *Journal of Communication, 27*(2), 171–180.

Gerbner, G., Gross, L., Jackson-Beeck, M., Jeffries-Foz, S., & Signorielli, N. (1978). Cultural indicators: Violence profile No. 9. *Journal of Communication, 28*(3), 176–207.

Gerbner, G., Gross, L., Morgan, M., & Signorielli, N. (1980). The "main-streaming" of America: Violence profile No. 11. *Journal of Communication, 30*(3), 10–29.

Gerbner, G., Gross, L., Morgan, M., & Signorielli, N. (1994). Growing up with television: The cultivation perspective. In J. Bryant & D. Zillmann (Eds.), *Media effects* (pp. 17–41). Hillsdale, NJ: Lawrence Erlbaum Associates.

Gerbner, G., Gross, L., Signorielli, N., Morgan, M., & Jackson-Beeck, M. (1979). The demonstration of power: Violence profile No. 10. *Journal of Communication, 29*(3), 177–196.

Giddens, A. (1984). *The constitution of society.* Berkley: University of California Press.

Gladue, B. A., & Bailey, J. M. (1995). Aggressiveness, competitiveness, and human sexual orientation. *Psychoneuroendocrinology, 20,* 475–485.

Goldstein, J. H. (1998). Immortal Kombat: War toys and violent video games. In J. H. Goldstein (Ed.), *Why we watch: The attraction of violent entertainment* (pp. 53–68). New York: Oxford University Press.

Goranson, R. E. (1970). Media violence and aggressive behavior: A review of the experimental research. In L. Berkowitz (Ed.), *Advances in experimental social psychology* (Vol. 5, pp. 1–31). New York: Academic Press.

Greenberg, B., Edison, N., Korzenny, F., Fernandez-Collado, C., & Atkin, C. K. (1980). In B. S. Greenberg (Ed.), *Life on television: Content analysis of U.S. TV drama* (pp. 99–128). Norwood, NJ: Ablex.

Greenberg, B. S., & Gordon, T. F. (1972a). Children's perception of television violence: A replication. In In G. A. Comstock, E. A. Rubinstein, & J. P. Murray (Eds.), *Television and social behavior: Reports and papers: Vol. 5. Television's effects: Further explorations* (pp. 211–230). Washington, DC: U.S. Government Printing Office.

Greenberg, B. S., & Gordon, T. F. (1972b). Perceptions of violence in television programmes: Critics and the public. In G. A. Comstock & E. A. Rubinstein (Eds.), *Television and social behaviour: Vol. 1, Media content and control,* (pp. 244–258). Rockville, MD: National Institute of Mental Health.

Greenberg, B. S., & Gordon, T. F. (1972c). Social class and racial differences in children's perceptions of television violence. In G. A. Comstock, E. A. Rubinstein, & J. P. Murray (Eds.), *Television and social behavior: Reports and papers: Vol. 5. Television's effects: Further explorations* (pp. 185–210). Washington, DC: U.S. Government Printing Office.

Greenberg, B. S., & Rampoldi-Hnilo, L. (1994). *Who watches daytime soap operas?* Printed Report to the Kaiser Family Foundation, Dept. of Telecommunication, Michigan State University.

Greenblat, C. S. (1983). A hit is a hit is a hit ... or is it? In D. Finkelhor, R. J. Gelles, G. T. Hotaling, & M. A. Straus (Eds.), *The dark side of families: Current family violence research* (pp. 235–260). Beverly Hills, CA: Sage.

Gregory, J., & Lees, S. (1999). *Policing sexual assault.* London: Routledge & Kegan Paul.

Groebel, J., & Gleich, U. (1993). *Gewaltprofil des deutschen Fernsehprogramms. Eine Analyse des Angebots privater und offentlich-rechtlicher Sender.* Opladen: Lleske und Budrich.

Gunter, B. (1981). Measuring television violence: A review and suggestions for a new analytical perspective. *Current Psychological Reviews, 1,* 91–112.

Gunter, B. (1985). *Dimensions of television violence.* Aldershot, UK: Gower.

Gunter, B. (1987). *Poor reception.* Hillsdale, NJ: Lawrence Erlbaum Associates.

Gunter, B. (1994). The question of media violence. In J. Bryant & D. Zillmann (Eds.), *Media effects: Advances in theory and research* (pp. 163–211). Hillsdale, NJ: Lawrence Erlbaum Associates.

Gunter, B. (1997). An audience-based approach to assessing programme quality. In P. Winterhoff-Spurk & T. H. A. van der Voort (Eds.), *New horizons in media psychology* (pp. 11–34). Opladen, Germany: Westdeutscher Vverlag.

Gunter, B. (2000). Avoiding unsavoury television. *The Psychologist, 13*(4), 194–199.

Gunter, B., & Furnham, A. (1983). Personality and the perception of TV violence. *Personality and Individual Differences, 4,* 315–321.

Gunter, B., & Furnham, A. (1984). Perceptions of television violence: Effects of program genre and physical form. *British Journal of Social Psychology, 23,* 155–184.

Gunter, B., Furnham, A., & Gietson, G. (1984). Memory for the news as a function of the channel communication. *Human Learning, 3,* 265–271.

Gunter, B., Furnham, A., & Lineton, Z. (1995). Watching people watching television: What goes on in front of the TV set? *Journal of Educational Television, 21*(3), 165–191.

Gunter, B., & Harrison, J. (1997). Violence in children's programs on British Television. *Children and Society, 11,* 143–156.

Gunter, B., & Harrison, J. (1998). *Violence on television: An analysis of amount, nature, location and origin of violence in British programmes.* London: Routledge & Kegan Paul.

Gunter, B., & McAleer, J. (1997). *Children and television: The one eyed monster?* London: Routledge & Kegan Paul.

Gunter, B., McAleer, J., & Clifford, B. R. (1991). Television police dramas and children's beliefs about the police. *Journal of Educational Television, 17*(2), 81–100.

Gunter, B., & Stipp, H. (1992). Attitudes about sex and violence on television in the United States and in Great Britain: A comparison of research findings. *Media Psychologie, 4*(4), 267–286.

Gunter, B., & Winstone, P. (1992), *TV: The public's view.* London: John Libbey.

Gunter, B., & Wober, M. (1983). Television viewing and public trust. *British Journal of Social Psychology, 22,* 174–176.

Gunter, B., & Wober, M. (1988). *Violence on television: What the viewers think.* London: John Libbey.

Gunther, A. C. (1995). Overrating the X-rating: The third-person perception and support for censorship of pornography. *Journal of Communication, 45*(1), 27–38.

Guttmann, A. (1998). The appeal of violent sports. In J. H. Goldstein (Ed.), *Why we watch: The attractions of violent entertainment* (pp. 1–26). New York: Oxford University Press.

Haines, H. (1983). *Violence on television: A report on the Mental Health Foundation's Media Watch Survey.* Mental Health Foundation of New Zealand, Auckland, New Zealand.

Halderman, B. L., & Jackson, T. T. (1979). Naturalistic study of aggression: Aggressive stimuli and horn honking. *Psychological Reports, 45,* 880–882.

Hall, S. (1973). Encoding/decoding in television discourse. In S. Hall et al. (Eds.), *Culture, media, language* (pp. 128–138). London: Hutchinson.

Hall, S., Critcher, C., Jefferson, T., & Clarke, J. (Eds.). (1978). *Policing the crisis: Mugging, the state, law and order.* London: Macmillan

Halloran, J. D., & Croll, P. (1972). Television programs in Great Britain: Content and control. In G. A. Comstock & E. A. Rubinstein (Eds.), *Television and social behavior: Vol. 1. Media content and control* (pp. 415–492). Washington, DC: U.S. Government Printing Office.

Hamilton, J. T. (1998). *Channeling violence: The economic market for violent television programming.* Princeton, NJ: Princeton University Press.

Hanmer, J., Radford, J., & Stanko, B. (1989). *Women, policing and male violence.* London: Routledge & Kegan Paul.

Hansen, C. H., & Hansen, R. D. (1990). The influence of sex and violence on the appeal of rock music videos. *Communication Research, 21,* 516–546.

Hapkiewicz, W. G., & Stone, R. D. (1974). The effect of realistic versus imaginary aggressive models on children's interpersonal play. *Child Study Journal, 4,* 47–58.

Harris, M. B. (1991). Effects of sex of target, sex of aggressor and relationship on evaluations of physical aggression. *Journal of Interpersonal Violence, 692,* 174–186.

Harris, M. B. (1994). Gender of subject and target as mediators of aggression. *Journal of Applied Social Psychology, 24,* 453–471.

Harris, M. B. (1995). Ethnicity, gender and evaluations of aggression. *Aggressive Behaviour, 21,* 354–357.

Harris, M. B., & Knight-Bohnhoff, K. (1996). Gender and aggression II: Personal aggressiveness. *Sex Roles, 35,* 27–42.

Harris, R. J., & Cook, C. A. (1994). Attributions about spouse abuse: It matters who the batterers and victims are. *Sex Roles, 30*(7/8), 553–565.

Harrison, J. L. (1997). Rescheduling the news: An analysis of ITN's News at Ten. *Political Economy Research Centre (PERC). Policy Paper,* No. 10, November.

Harrison, J. L. (2000). *Terrestrial television news in Britain: The culture of production.* Manchester, UK: Manchester University Press.

Harrison, J. L., & Woods, L. M. (1999). Determining jurisdiction in the digital age. *Journal of European Public Law, 5*(4), 583–600.

Hartley, R., Frank, L., & Goldenson, R. (1952). *Understanding children's play.* London: Routledge & Kegan Paul.

Hartmann, D. P. (1969). Influence of symbolically modelled instrumental aggression and pain cues on aggressive behavior. *Journal of Personality and Social Psychology, 11,* 280–288.

Hawkins, R. P. (1977). The dimensional structure of children's perceptions of television reality. *Communication Research, 4*(3), 299–320.

Head, S. W. (1954). Content analysis of television drama programs. *Quarterly of Film, Radio, and Television, 9,* 175–194.

Heath, L., Bresolin, L. B., & Rinaldi, R. C. (1989). Effects of media violence on children. *Archives of General Psychiatry, 46,* 376–379.

Heidensohn, F. (1986). *Women and crime.* London, UK: Macmillan.

Herman, G., & Leyens, J. P. (1977). Rating films on TV. *Journal of Communication, 27,* 48–53.

Hetherington, A. (1989), *News in the regions.* London: Macmillan.

Hicks, D. J. (1965). Imitation and retention of film-mediated aggressive peer and adult models. *Journal of Personality and Social Psychology, 2,* 97–100.

Himmelweit, H. T., Oppenheim, A. N., & Vince, P. (1958). *Television and the child: An empirical study of the effect of television on the young.* London: Oxford University Press.

Hines, N. J., & Fry, D. P. (1994). Indirect modes of aggression: I. Perceptions of aggression. *Sex Roles, 35,* 1–25.

Hobson, D. (1982). Everything stops for Crossroads: Watching with the audience. In P. Marris & S. Thornham (Eds.), *Media studies: A reader* (pp. 391–398). Edinburgh, UK: Edinburgh University Press.

Hodge, B., & Tripp, D. (1986). *Children and television.* Cambridge, UK: Polity Press.

Hoffner, C. (1998). Framing of the television violence issue in newspaper coverage. In J. T. Hamilton (Ed.), *Television violence and public policy* (pp. 313–333). Ann Arbor, MI: University of Michigan Press.

Hoffner, C., Buchanan, M., Anderson, J. D., Hubbs, L. A., Kamigaki, S. K., Kowalczyk, L., Pastorek, A., Plotkin, R. S., & Silver, K. J. (1999). Support for censorship of television violence: The role of the third-person effect and news exposure. *Communication Research, 26*(6), 726–742.

Hoffner, C., & Cantor, J. (1985). Developmental differences in responses to a television character's appearance and behaviour. *Developmental Psychology, 21,* 1065–1074.

Hollenback, A. A., & Slaby, R. G. (1979). Infant visual responses to television. *Child Development, 50,* 41–54.

Home Office, Research Development and Statistical Directorate. (1999). *Information on the Criminal Justice System in England and Wales: Digest 4.*

Hopkins Burke, R. (2001). *Introduction to criminological theory.* Cullompton, UK: Willan.

Howe, A., Herzberger, S., & Tennen, H. (1988). The influence of personal history of abuse and gender on clinicians' judgments of child abuse. *Journal of Family Violence, 3,* 105–119.

Howitt, D., & Cumberbatch, G. (1974). Audience perceptions of violent television content. *Communication Research, 1*(2), 4–223.

Hoyt, J. L. (1970). The effect of media "justification" on aggression. *Journal of Broadcasting, 6,* 455–464.

Huesmann, L. R. (1986). Psychological processes promoting the relation between exposure to media violence and aggressive behavior by the viewer. *Journal of Social Issues, 42*(3), 125–139.

Huesmann, L. R., & Eron, L. (1986). *Television and the aggressive child: A cross-national comparison.* Hillsdale, NJ: Lawrence Erlbaum Associates.

Huesmann, L. R., Lagerspetz, K., & Eron, L. D. (1984). Intervening variables in the TV-violence-aggression relation: Evidence from two countries. *Developmental Psychology, 20,* 746–775.

Huesmann, L. R., & Miller, L. S. (1994). Long term effects of repeated exposure to media violence in childhood. In L. R. Huesmann (Ed.), *Aggressive behavior: Current perspectives* (pp. 153–186). New York: Plenum.

Hume, E. (1996). The new paradigm for news. In K. Jamieson (Ed.), *The annals of the American Academy of Political and Social Science: The media and politics.* Beverly Hills, CA: Sage.

Huston, A. C., Donnerstein, E., Fairchild, H., Feshbach, N. D., Katz, P. A., Murray, P., Rubinstein, E. A., Wilcox, B. G., & Zuckerman, D. (1992). *Big world, small screen: The role of television in American society.* Lincoln: University of Nebraska Press.

Huston-Stein, A., Fox, S., Greer, D., Watkins, B. A., & Whitaker, J. (1983). The effects of TV action and violence on children's social behavior. *Journal of Genetic Psychology, 138,* 183–191.

Independent Television Commission. (1991). *Programme guidelines.* London: Author.

Independent Television Commission. (1996). *What do children watch and when?* London: Author.

Independent Television Commission. (1999). *Television: The publics' view—1998.* London: Author.

Independent Television Commission. (2000). *Television: The publics' view—1999.* London: Author.

Innes, J. M., & Zeitz, H. (1988). The public's view of the impact of the mass media: A test of the "third-person" effect. *European Journal of Social Psychology, 18*, 457–463.

Iwao, S., de Sola Pool, I., & Hagiwara, S. (1981). Japanese and U.S. media: Some cross-cultural insights into TV violence. *Journal of Communication, 31*(2), 28–36.

Iyengar, S. (1991). *Is anyone responsible? How television frames political issues.* Chicago: University of Chicago Press.

Jennings, C. M., & Gillis-Olion, M. (1980). *The impact of television cartoons on child behavior.* Paper presented at the annual meeting of the National Association for the Education of Young Children. Atlanta, GA: ERIC Document Reproduction Service No. 194–184.

Jones, S. (1998). *Criminology.* London: Butterworths.

Jose, P. E., & Brewer, W. F. (1984). Development of story liking and outcome resolution. *Developmental Psychology, 20*(9), 911–924.

Kane, T., Joseph, J. M., & Tedeschi, J. T. (1976). Personal perception and the Berkowits paradigm for the study of aggression. *Journal of Personality and Social Psychology, 33*, 663–673.

Kaplan, R. M., & Singer, R. D. (1976). Television violence and viewer aggression: A re–examination of the evidence. *Journal of Social Issues, 32*(4), 35–70.

Kaplan, S. L., & Baxter, L. A. (1982). Antisocial and prosocial behavior on prime-time TV. *Journalism Quarterly, 59*, 478–482.

Katzman, N. (1972). Television soap operas: What's been going on anyway. *Public Opinion Quarterly, 36*, 200–212.

Klijn, M. E. (1999, May). *Framing of violence in Dutch and American TV news: Juxtaposing the use of attention and comprehension attributes by public and private broadcasting organizations.* Amsterdam School of Communications Research. Paper presented to ICA, San Francisco.

Kodaira, S. I. (1990). The development of programs for young children in Japan. *Journal of Educational Television, 16*(3), 127–150.

Kodaira, S. I. (1998a). *Children learn from watching TV programs: Experiences in Japan.* NHK Broadcasting Culture Research Institute.

Kodaira, S. I. (1998b). A review of research on media violence in Japan. In U. Carlsson & C. von Feilitzen (Eds.), *Children and media violence, Yearbook from the UNESCO International Clearinghouse on Children and Violence on the Screen.*

Kodaira, S. I. (2000). *Issues on TV for children: An invitation to further discussion.* NHK Broadcasting Culture Research Institute.

Koski, P. R., & Mangold, W. D. (1988). Gender effects in attitudes about family violence. *Journal of Family Violence, 3*, 225–233.

Kostelnik, M. J., Whiren, A. P., & Stein, L. C. (1986). Living with He-Man—Managing superhero fantasy play. *Young Children, 41*(4), 3–9.

Krcmar, M., & Greene, K. (1999). Predicting exposure to and uses of television violence. *Journal of Communication, 49*(3), 24–45.

Kunkel, D. (1997). Why content, not age of viewers, should control what children watch on TV. *The Chronicle of Higher Education, XLIII*(21). B4–B5, January 31.

Kunkel, D., Wilson, B. J., Linz, D., Potter, J., Donnerstein, E., Smith, S. L., Blumenthal, E., & Gray, T. (1995). Violence in television programming overall: University of California, Santa Barbara study. In *National Television Violence Study, Scientific Papers—1994–1995* (pp. 1–172). Los Angeles, CA: Mediascope.

Lagerspetz, K. M. J., Bjorkqvist, K., & Peltonen, T. (1988). Is indirect aggression typical of females? Gender differences in aggressiveness in 11-12-year-old children. *Aggressive Behaviour, 14*, 303–315.

Lagerspetz, K. M., Wahlroos, C., & Wendelin, C. (1978). Facial expression of pre-school children while watching televised violence. *Scandinavian Journal of Psychology, 19,* 213–222.

Larsen, O. N., Gray, L. N., & Fortis, J. G. (1963). Goals and goal achievement in television content: Models for anomia? *Sociological Inquiry, 33,* 180–196.

Lasorsa, D. L. (1989). Real and perceived effects of "Amerika." *Journalism Quarterly, 66,* 373–378, 529.

Lees, S. (1993). *Sugar and spice: Sexuality and adolescent girls.* London: Penguin.

Lees, S. (1995). Media reporting of rape: The British date rape controversy. In D. Kidd-Hewitt & R. Osborne (Eds.), *Crime and the media* (pp. 107–130). London: Pluto.

Levi Strauss, C. (1958). *Structural anthropology.* London, UK: Penguin.

Leyens, J. P., Cisneros, T., & Hossay, J. F. (1976). Decentration as a means for reducing aggression after exposure to violent stimuli. *European Journal of Social Psychology, 6,* 459–473.

Leyens, J. P., & Parke, R. D. (1975). Aggressive slides can induce a weapons effect. *European Journal of Social Psychology, 5,* 229–236.

Leyens, J. P., & Picus, S. (1973). Identification with the winner of a fight and name mediation: Their differential effects upon subsequent aggressive behaviour. *British Journal of Social and Clinical Psychology, 12,* 374–377.

Lichter, S. R., & Amundsen, D. (1992). *A day of television violence.* Washington, DC: Center for Media and Public Affairs.

Liebert, R. M., & Baron, R. A. (1972). Some immediate effects of televised violence on children's behavior. *Developmental Psychology, 6,* 469–475.

Liebes, T., & Katz, E. (1990). *The export of meaning: Cross cultural readings of Dallas.* Oxford, UK: Oxford University Press.

Liebes, T., & Livingstone, S. (1994). The structure of family and romantic ties in the soap opera: An ethnographic approach. *Communication Research, 21*(6), 717–741.

Lincoln, A., & Levinger, G. (1972). Observers' evaluation of the victim and the attacker in an aggressive incident. *Journal of Personality and Social Psychology, 22,* 202–210.

Linz, D. (1985). *Sexual violence in the media: Effects on male viewers and implications for society.* Unpublished doctoral dissertation, University of Wisconsin-Madison.

Linz, D. G., Donnerstein, E., & Penrod, S. (1988). Effects of long-term exposure to violent and sexually degrading depictions of women. *Journal of Personality and Social Psychology, 55,* 759–768.

Linz, S., Donnerstein, E., & Penrod, S. (1984). The effects of multiple exposures to filmed violence against women. *Journal of Communication, 34*(3), 130–147.

Liss, M. B., Reinhardt, L. C., & Fredriksen, S. (1983). TV heroes: The impact of rhetoric and deeds. *Journal of Applied Developmental Psychology, 4,* 175–187.

Livingstone, S. (1996). On the continuing problem of media effects. In J. Curran & M. Gurevitch (Eds.), *Mass media and society* (pp. 305–324). London: Arnold.

Lynn, R., Hampson, S., & Agahi, E. (1989). Television violence and aggression: A genotype-environment, correlation and interaction theory. *Social Behavior and Personality, 17,* 143–164.

Lyons, J. A., & Serbin, L. A. (1986). Observer bias in scoring boys' and girls' aggression. *Sex Roles, 14*(5/6), 301–313.

Macdonald, M. (1995). *Representing women: Myths of femininity in popular culture.* London: Edward Arnold.

Malamuth, N. M. (1981). Rape fantasies as a function of exposure to violent sexual stimuli. *Archives of Sexual Behavior, 10,* 33–47.

Malamuth, N. M., & Check, J. V. P. (1981). The effects of mass media exposure on acceptance of violence against women: A field experiment. *Journal of Research in Personality, 15,* 436–446.

Malamuth, N. M., Haber, S., & Feshbach, S. (1980). Testing hypotheses regarding rape: Exposure to sexual violence, sex differences, and the "normality" of reports. *Journal of Research in Personality, 14,* 121–137.

Marris, P., & Thornham, S. (1996). *Media studies: A reader.* Edinburgh, UK: Edinburgh University Press.

Marshall, W.L. (1988). The use of sexually explicit stimuli by rapists, child molesters and nonoffenders. *Journal of Sex Research, 25,* 267–288.

McCann, T. E., & Sheehan, P. W. (1985). Violence content in Australian television. *Australian Psychologist, 20*(1), 33–42.

McGlynn, R. P., Megas, J. C., & Benson, D. H. (1976). Sex and race as factors affecting the attribution of insanity in a murder trial. *Journal of Psychology, 93,* 93–99.

McNeely, R. L., & Mann, C. R. (1990). Domestic violence is a human issue. *Journal of Interpersonal Violence, 5,* 129–131.

Mees, U. (1990). Constitutive elements of the concept of human aggression. *Aggressive Behavior, 16,* 285–195.

Meyer, T. P. (1972). Effects of viewing justified and unjustified real film violence on aggressive behavior. *Journal of Personality and Social Psychology, 23,* 21–29.

Mitchell, J. (1998). New audio-visual and information services and the protection of children: The European dimension. *Journal of Consumer Policy, 21,* 3–44.

Modleski, T. (1996). The search for tomorrow in today's soap operas. In P. Marris & S. Thornham (Eds.), *Media studies: A reader* (pp. 371–380). Edinburgh, UK: Edinburgh University Press

Morley, D. (1981). The nationwide audience: A critical postscript. *Screen Education,* No. 39.

Moore, D. W., & Saad, L. (1993). Public says: Too much violence on TV. *The Gallup Poll Monthly, 335,* 18–20.

Morkes, J., Chen, H. L., & Roberts, D. F. (1997, May). *Adolescents' responses to movie, television, and computer-game ratings and advisories.* Paper presented at the annual meeting of the International Communication Association, Montreal.

Morrison, D. (1992). *Television and the Gulf war.* London: John Libbey.

Morrison, D. (1993a). The idea of violence. In A. Millwood-Hargrave (Ed.), *Violence in factual television: Broadcasting standards council annual review 1993* (pp. 124–129). London: John Libbey.

Morrison, D. (1993b). *The viewer's view of violence: Attitudes to violence in relation to television guidelines.* Report to the British Broadcasting Corporation. Leeds, UK: University of Leeds.

Morrison, D., & McGregor, R. (1993). *Viewer's response to violence in non-fictional programmes.* London: Broadcasting Standards Commission.

Muncer, S. J., Gorman, B., & Campbell, A. (1986). Sorting out aggression: Dimensional and categorical perceptions of aggressive episodes. *Aggressive Behavior, 12,* 327–336.

Mustonen, A., & Pulkkinen, L. (1993). Aggression in television programs in Finland. *Aggressive Behavior, 19,* 175–183.

Mustonen, A., & Pulkkinen, L. (1997). Television violence: A development of a coding scheme. *Journal of Broadcasting & Electronic Media, 41,* 168–189.

National Television Violence Study (1997). (Vol. 1). Thousand Oaks, CA: Sage.
National Television Violence Study (1998). (Vol. 2). Thousand Oaks, CA: Sage.
National Television Violence Study (1999). (Vol. 3). Thousand Oaks, CA: Sage.
Neale, S. (1983). *Genre.* London: British Film Institute.
Newson, E. (1994). Video violence and the protection of children. *The Psychologist,* June, 272–274.
Noble, G. (1975). *Children in front of the small screen.* London: Constable.
Ogles, R. M., & Hoffner, C. (1987). Film violence and perceptions of crime: The cultivation effect. In M. L. McLaughlin (Ed.), *Communication yearbook 10* (pp. 384–394). Thousand Oaks, CA: Sage.
Oliver, M. B. (1994). Portrayals of crime, race, and aggression in "reality based" police shows: A content analysis. *Journal of Broadcasting & Electronic Media, 38,* 179–192.
Oliver, M. B., & Armstrong, B. (1995). Predictors of viewing and enjoyment of reality-based and fictional crime shows. *Journalism & Mass Communication Quarterly, 72,* 559–570.
Osborn, D. K., & Endsley, R. C. (1971). Emotional reactions of young children to TV violence. *Child Development, 42,* 321–331.
Ostgaard, E. (1965). Factors influencing the flow of news. *Journal of Peace Research, 2,* 39–63.
O'Sullivan T., Dutton, B., & Rayner, P. (1998). *Studying the media.* London: Edward Arnold
Page, M. M., & O' Neal, E. (1977). "Weapons effect" without demand characteristics. *Psychological Reports, 41,* 29–30.
Page, M. M., & Scheidt, R. J. (1971). The elusive weapons effect: Demand awareness, evaluation apprehension and slightly sophisticated subjects. *Journal of Personality and Social Psychology, 20,* 304–318.
Paik, H., & Comstock, G. A. (1994). The effects of television violence on antisocial behavior: A meta-analysis. *Communication Research, 21,* 516–546.
Paley, V. G. (1984). *Boys and girls—Superheroes in the doll corner.* Chicago: University of Chicago Press.
Perloff, R. M. (1996). Perceptions and conceptions of political media impact: The third-person effect and beyond. In A. N. Crigler (Ed.), *The psychology of political communication* (pp. 177–197). Ann Arbor: The University of Michigan Press.
Perry, D. G., & Perry, L. C. (1976). Identification with film characters, covert aggressive verbalization, and reactions to film violence. *Journal of Research in Personality, 10,* 399–409.
Philo, G. (Ed.). (1995). *Glasgow media group reader: Vol. 2. Industry, economy, war and politics.* London: Routledge & Kegan Paul.
Philo, G., & McLaughlin, G. (1995). The British media and the Gulf War. In G. Philo (Ed.), *Glasgow media group reader: Vol. 2. Industry, economy, war and politics* (pp. ???). London: Routledge & Kegan Paul.
Postman, N. (1989), *Amusing ourselves to death.* London: Methuen.
Potter, W. J. (1986). Perceived reality and the cultivation hypothesis. *Journal of Broadcasting & Electronic Media, 30,* 159–174.
Potter, W. J. (1996). Considering policies to protect children from TV violence. *Journal of Communication, 46*(4), 116–138.
Potter, W. J. (1999). *On media violence.* Thousand Oaks, CA: Sage.
Potter, W. J., Linz, D., Wilson, B. J., Kunkel, D., Donnerstein, E., Smith, S, L., Blumenthal, E., & Gray, T. (1996, June). *Content analysis of entertainment television: New methodological developments.* Paper presented at the Duke

University Conference on Media Violence and Public Policy in the Media, Durham, NC.

Potter, W. J., & Smith, S. L. (1999). Consistency in contextual cues across multiple levels of analysis. *Journal of Communication, 49*(4), 121–133.

Potter, W. J., & Vaughan, M. (1997). Aggression in television entertainment: Profiles and trends. *Communication Research Reports, 14*, 116–124.

Potter, W. J., Vaughan, M., Warren, R., Howley, K., Land, A., & Hagemeyer, J. (1995). How real is the portrayal of aggression in television entertainment programming? *Journal of Broadcasting & Electronic Media, 39*, 496–516.

Potter, W. J., & Ware, W. (1987). An analysis of the contexts of antisocial acts on prime-time television. *Communication Research, 14*, 664–686.

Potter, W. J., Warren, R., Vaughan, M., Howley, K., Land, A., & Hagemeyer, J. (1997). Antisocial acts in reality programming on television. *Journal of Broadcasting & Electronic Media, 41*, 69–75.

Potts, R., Huston, A., & Wright, J. C. (1986). The effects of television form and violent content on boys' attention and social behavior. *Journal of Experimental Child Psychology, 41*, 1–17.

Poulos, R. W., Harvey, S. E., & Liebert, R. M. (1976). Saturday morning television: A profile of the 1974–75 children's season. *Psychological Reports, 39*, 1047–1057.

Pribram, D. (1988). *Female spectators: Looking at film and television.* New York: Verso.

Propp, V. (1968). *Morphology of a folk tale* (L. Scott, trans.). Bloomington, IN: Indiana University Press.

Reeves, B. (1978). Perceived TV reality as a predictor of children's social behaviour. *Journalism Quarterly, 55*, 682–689.

Reiner, R. (1992). *The politics of policing.* Brighton, UK: Wheatsheaf.

Remmers, H. H. (1954). *Four years of New York television: 1951–1954.* Urbana, IL: National Association of Educational Broadcasters.

Roberts, D. R. (1998). Media content labelling systems. In R. G. Noll & M. E. Price (Eds.), *A communications cornucopia: Markle Foundation essays on information policy* (pp. 350–375). Washington DC: Brookings Institution Press.

Robinson, J. P., & Bachman, J. G. (1972). Television viewing habits and aggression. In G. A. Comstock & E. A. Rubinstein (Eds.), *Television and social behavior: Reports and papers: Vol. 3. Television and adolescent aggressiveness* (pp. 372–382). Washington, DC: U.S. Government Printing Office.

Robinson, J. P., & Levy, M. R. (1986). *The main source.* Beverly Hills, CA: Sage.

Rogers, E. M., & Dearing, J. W. (1988). Agenda-setting research: Where has it been and where is it going? In J. A. Anderson (Ed.), *Communication yearbook 11* (pp. 555–594). Beverly Hills, CA: Sage.

Rojas, H., Shah, D. V., & Faber, R. J. (1996). For the good of others: Censorship and the third-person effect. *International Journal of Public Opinion Research, 2*, 163–186.

Rosekrans, M. A., & Hartup, W. W. (1967). Imitative influences of consistent and inconsistent response consequences to a model on aggressive behaviour in children. *Journal of Personality and Social Psychology, 7*, 429–434.

Rule, B. G., & Ferguson, T. J. (1986). The effects of media violence on attitudes, emotions, and cognitions. *Journal of Social Issues, 42*(3), 29–50.

Sande, O. (1971). The perception of foreign news. *Journal of Peace Research, 8*, 221–237.

Sander, I. (1997). How violent is TV violence? An empirical investigation of factors influencing viewers' perceptions of TV violence. *European Journal of Communication, 12*(1), 43–98.

Schlesinger, P. (1987). *Putting reality together.* London: Methuen.
Schlesinger, P., Dobash, R., Dobash, R., & Weaver C. (1991). *Women viewing violence.* London: British Film Institute.
Schmidt, G. (1975). Male-female differences in sexual arousal and behavior during and after exposure to sexually explicit stimuli. *Archives of Sexual Behavior, 4,* 353–365.
Schramm, W., Lyle, J., & Parker, E. (1961). *Television in the lives of our children.* Stanford, CA: Stanford University Press.
Segal, L. (1994). *Straight sex: The politics of pleasure.* London, UK: Virago.
Shaw, I., & Newell, D. (1972). *Violence on television: Program content and viewer perception.* London: British Broadcasting Corporation.
Shearer, A. (1991). *Survivors and the media.* Broadcasting Standards Council Research Monograph Series 2. London: John Libbey.
Sheehan, P. W. (1986). Television viewing and its relation to aggression among children in Australia. In L. R. Huesman & L. D. Eron (Eds.), *Television and the aggressive child: A cross national comparison* (pp. ???). Hillsdale, NJ: Lawrence Erlbaum Associates.
Sherman, B. L., & Dominick, J. R. (1986). Violence and sex in music videos: TV and rock 'n' roll. *Journal of Communication, 36*(1), 79–93.
Shoemaker, P., & Reese, S. D. (1996). *Mediating the message.* New York: Longman.
Signorielli, N. (1984). The demography of the television world. In G. Melischek, K. E. Rosengren, & J. Stappers (Eds.), *Cultural indicators: An international symposium.* Vienna, Austria: Austrian Academy of Sciences.
Signorielli, N. (1990). Television's mean and dangerous world: A continuation of the cultural indicators perspective. In N. Signorielli & M. Morgan (Eds.). *Cultivation analysis: New directions in media effects research* (pp. 85–106). Newbury Park, CA: Sage.
Smith, S. (1984). Crime in the news. *British Journal of Criminology, 24,* 289–295.
Smith T.W. (1984). The polls: Gender and attitudes towards violence. *Public Opinion Quarterly, 48,* 384–396.
Smythe, D. W. (1954). Reality as presented by television. *Public Opinion Quarterly, 18,* 143–156.
Soothill, K., & Walby, S. (1991). *Sex crime in the news.* London: Routledge & Kegan Paul.
Sparkes, V. M., & Winter, J. P. (1980). Public interest in foreign news. *Gazette, 20,* 149–170.
Spence, J. T., & Helmreich, R. L. (1978). *Masculinity and femininity: Their psychological dimensions, correlates & antecedents.* Austin: University of Texas Press.
Spitzer, M. L. (1996). *The v chip* (paper prepared for Duke conference on Media Violence and Public Policy). Duke University, Durham, NC, June 28–29.
Stanko, E. (1985). *Intimate intrusions: Women's experience of men's violence.* London: Routledge & Kegan Paul.
Stanko, E. (1990). *Everyday violence.* London: Pandora.
Stark, E., & Flitcraft, A. (1988). Violence among intimates: An epidemiological review. In V. B. Van Hasselt, R. L. Morrison, A. S. Bellack, & M. Hersen (Eds.), *Handbook of family violence.* New York: Plenum.
Stevenson, N. (1997). Media ethics and morality. In J. McGuigan (Ed.), *Cultural methodologies.* London, UK: Sage.
Stipp, H. (1995, May). *Children's viewing of news, reality shows, and other programming.* Paper presented at the annual conference of the International Communication Association, Albuquerque, NM.

Straus, M. A., Gelles, R. J., & Steinmetz, S. K. (1980). *Behind closed doors: Violence in the American family.* Garden City, NY: Anchor.

Sugarman, D. B., & Hotaling, G. T. (1989). Dating violence: Prevalence, context, and risk markers. In M. A. Pirog-Good & J. E. Stets (Eds.), *Violence in dating relationships.* New York: Praeger.

Surbeck, E. (1975). Young children's emotional reactions to TV violence: The effect of children's perceptions of reality. *Dissertation Abstracts International, 35,* 5139-A.

Surbeck, E., & Endsley, R. C. (1979). Children's emotional reactions to TV violence: Effects of film character, reassurance, age and sex. *Journal of Social Psychology, 109,* 269–281.

Swart, C., & Berkowitz, L. (1976). Effects of a stimulus associated with a victim's pain on later aggression. *Journal of Personality and Social Psychology, 33,* 623–631.

Tangney, J. P. (1988). Aspects of the family and children's television viewing content preferences. *Child Development, 59,* 1070–1079.

Tangney, J. P., & Feshbach, S. (1988). Children's television viewing frequency: Individual differences and demographic correlates. *Aggressive Behavior, 14,* 145–158.

Tannenbaum, P.H. (1971). Emotional arousal as a mediator of erotic communication effects. In *Technical Report of the Commission on Obscenity and Pornography* (Vol. 8). Washington, DC: U.S. Government Printing Office.

Thomas, M. H. (1982). Physiological arousal, exposure to a relatively lengthy aggressive film, and aggression behavior. *Journal of Research in Personality, 16,* 72–81.

Thomas, M. H., Horton, R. W., Lippencott, E. C., & Drabman, R. S. (1977). Desensitization to portrayals of real-life aggression as a function of exposure to television violence. *Journal of Personality and Social Psychology, 35,* 450–458.

Thompson, M. E., Chaffee, S. H., & Oshagen, H. H. (1990). Regulating pornography: A public dilemma. *Journal of Communication, 40*(3), 73–83.

Thurber, J. (1948). *The beast in me and other animals.* New York: Harcourt, Brace.

Tolson, A. (1977). *The limits of masculinity.* London: Routledge.

Tracy, M., & Morrison, D. (1979). *Whitehouse.* London: Macmillan.

Tuchman, G. (1978a), *Making news.* New York: The Free Press.

Tuchman, G. (1978b). The symbolic annihilation of women by the mass media. In S. Cohen & J. Young (Eds.), *The manufacture of news: Deviance, social problems and the mass media.* London: Constable.

Tunstall, J. (1971). *Journalists at work.* London: Constable.

Turner, C. W., & Berkowitz, L. (1972). Identification with film aggressor (covert role taking). and reactions to film violence. *Journal of Personality and Social Psychology, 21,* 256–264.

Utting, W. Sir. (1997). *Report of the tribunal of enquiry into failings in residential care in North Wales.* London: Home Office.

Van der Voort, T. H. A. (1986). *Television violence: A child's eye view.* Amsterdam, Holland: Elsevier Science.

Van Eyken, A. (1987). Aggression: Myth or model? *Journal of Applied Philosophy, 4,* 165–170.

Walklate, S. (2001). *Gender, crime and criminal justice.* Cullompton, UK: Willam.

Walters, R. H., & Thomas, E. L. (1963). Enhancement of punitiveness by visual and audiovisual displays. *Canadian Journal of Psychology, 17,* 244–255.

Walters, R. H.,Thomas, E. L., & Acker, C. W. (1962). Enhancement of punitive behavior by audiovisual displays. *Science, 136,* 872–873.

Ward, W. (1973). *The nature of news in three dimensions*. Stillwater: Journalistic Services.

Warner, L., & Henry, W. (1948). The radio daytime serial: A symbolic analysis. *Genetic Psychology Monographs, 38*, 3–71.

Weaver, J. B. (1991). Exploring the links between personality and media preferences. *Personality and Individual Differences, 12*, 1293–1299.

"When violence hits home." (1991). *Time*, April 7.

White, J. W., & Kowalski, R. M. (1994). Deconstructing the myth of the nonaggressive woman. *Psychology of Women Quarterly, 18*, 487–508.

Wicklund, R. A. (1994). *Freedom and reactance*. Hillsdale, NJ: Lawrence Erlbaum Associates.

Williams, T. M., Zabrack, M. L., & Joy, L. A. (1982). The portrayal of aggression on North American television. *Journal of Applied Social Psychology, 12*(5), 360–380.

Wilson, B. J., & Cantor, J. (1985). Developmental difference in empathy with a television protagonist's fear. *Journal of Experimental Child Psychology, 39*, 284–299.

Wilson, B. J., Donnerstein, E., Linz, D., Kunkel, D., Potter, J., Smith, S. L., Blumenthal, E., & Gray, T. (1996, June). *Content analysis of entertainment television: The importance of context*. Paper presented at Duke Conference on Media Violence and Public Policy, Duke University.

Wilson, B. J., Hoffner, C., & Cantor, J. (1987). Children's perceptions of the effectiveness of techniques to reduce fear from mass media. *Journal of Applied Developmental Psychology, 8*, 39–52.

Wilson, B. J., Linz, D., & Randall, B. (1990). Applying social science research to film ratings: A shift from offensiveness to harmful effects. *Journal of Broadcasting and Electronic Media, 34*, 443–468.

Wilson, B. J., & Weiss, A. J. (1993). The effects of sibling co-viewing on preschoolers' reactions to a suspenseful movie scene. *Communication Research, 20*(2), 214–256.

Winn, E. (1977). *The plug in drug*. New York: Viking.

Wober, M. (1982). *The Falklands: Some systematic data on viewing behaviour and attitudes*. London: Independent Broadcasting Authority.

Wober, M. (1997). Violence or other routes to appreciation: TV program makers' options. *Journal of Broadcasting & Electronic Media, 41*, 190–202.

Wober, M., & Fazal, S. (1994). Neighbours at home and away: British viewers' perceptions of Australian soap operas. *Media Information Australia, 71*, 78–87.

Wober, M., & Gunter, B. (1988). *Television and social control*. Aldershot, UK: Gower.

Wober, M., & Gunter, B. (1990). Fearstoppers. *Police Review*, 23 November, 2312–2313.

Wurtzel, A., & Surlin, S. (1978). Viewer attitudes towards television advisory warnings. *Journal of Broadcasting, 22*(1), 19–31.

Wykes, M. (1995). Passion, marriage and murder. In R. Dobash, R. Dobash, & L. Noaks (Eds.), *Gender and crime* (pp. 49–76). Cardiff: University of Wales Press.

Wykes, M. (1998). A family affair: The British press, sex and the Wests. In C. Carter, G. Branston, & S. Allan (Eds.), *News, crime and gender* (pp. 233–247). London: Routledge.

Wykes, M. (2001). *News, crime and culture*. London: Pluto Press.

Young, J. (1982). The myth of drug-takers in the mass media. In S. Cohen & J. Young (Eds.), *The manufacture of news: Deviance, social problems and the mass media*. London: Constable.

Zillmann, D. (1978). Attribution and misattribution of excitatory reactions. In J. H. Harvey, W. Ickes, & R. F. Kidd (Eds.), *New directions in attribution research* (pp. 335–368). Hillsdale, NJ: Lawrence Erlbaum Associates.

Zillman, D. (1979). *Hostility and aggression.* Hillsdale, NJ: Lawrence Erlbaum Associates.

Zillmann, D., Weaver, J. B., Mundorf, N., & Aust, C. F. (1986). Effects of an opposite-gender companion's affect to horror on distress, delight, and attraction. *Journal of Personality and Social Psychology, 51,* 586–594.

Author Index

Page number followed by *n* indicates a footnote.

Subject Index

Page numbers followed by *t* indicate table.
Page numbers followed by *n* indicate footnote.